My Head Held Up High

My Head Held Up High

Avis Noel

To order additional copies of this book, contact:
Xlibris LLC
1-888-795-4274
www.Xlibris.com
Orders@Xlibris.com
551794

Contents

When upon life's billows you are tempest tossed
When you are discouraged, thinking all is lost
Count your many blessings name them one by one
In addition, it will surprise you what the Lord has done

—From "Count Your Blessings"
Johnson Oatman Jr. (1856-1922)

This book is a dedication to the loving memory of my mother, Doris, a woman who never stepped into a classroom for knowledge and education but was blessed with knowledge and intellect to soar high above her own circumstances and care for her nine beautiful children, her extended family, and her community. This is an everlasting dedication to the eternal memory of this beautiful woman, my mother, who exuded love through every pore of her skin and taught us to love each other unconditionally.

Second, this is to the fondest memory of my father, Norman, the son of a South African immigrant. My father, who so believed in education, touched and influenced our lives by educating us. Consequently, we never perceived failure in education and life in general as an option at all. This loving man lived his life with dignity, integrity, enthusiasm, willpower, determination, and honor for us to follow his bright shining star.

I also dedicate this book to the loving and living memory of my three late siblings: Nicholas the, firstborn of my mother; Louis, the sixth; and Plaxedes, the eighth. However, you three died so young, but your legacies live beyond your chronological ages as you continue to touch our lives today in your own special unique ways. Though you are gone you live still in our hearts and will always be loved dearly.

I want to take a special moment to make a special dedication to a loving sister. Unfortunately my eldest sister Melody who had been my pillar of strength and my initial sponsor for my journey to the US passed away after my project was complete but not published. We both married men from Georgetown. We spent our adult lives working in towns closest to each other. In times of hardships I turned to her and she shouldered my burdens. Through the prayers she gave me I was inspired to be a better mother because of the hardships she endured were worse than mine. I now long and miss for the calls she made across the miles as she prayed for me still. I no longer have an older sister to do that for me and the void seems to have been getting bigger and bottomless with each passing day. I long for her advice even from beyond I hope she continues to shine her guiding light on us all and watch over her son.

Dr. Avis, daughter of Doris and Norman, wrote this book.

Prologue

Those of you who are well versed with the African history pretty much know that as Africans, we are not known for handing down our histories in black and white but in oral form, as *Roots* was handed down through generations and later narrated in book form by Alex Hailey. Thus, this is an attempt at breaking virgin ground for our family, trying to coin my own impression in the memories of those present and others to follow that it is something feasible. In the early 1980s, amid the domestic violence, I remember telling my closest friend Samantha, that I would chronicle my domestic abuse one day, but she discouraged me by elaborating that abuses that take place in our married lives, was never done culturally. The long and short of it is that Samantha told me that culturally, we never air our dirty laundry in public. I choose to air the dirty laundry in public because too many women are traumatized forever by the violence of domestic hostility. I feel the trauma needs discussion as it relates not only to the parents but also to the children of the abusive couples equally. The trauma can leave emotional and physical scars that are hard to heal in both parents as well as in their offspring.

I am purposefully breaking away from what tradition dictates, following my own heart, and in the process breaking my best friend Samantha's tender and loving heart. This is something none in my family or clan or relatives have attempted before except for probably my eldest brother, Nicholas, who attempted to write *ngano*s (folktales) in the late 1960s, which were never published. I emulated his example in the 1990s, wrote my own *ngano*s, and gave them to dear friends who were married so that they could have bedtime stories for their children. That was a step further than what my eldest brother had achieved, but to this day, my *ngano*s remain unpublished.

In narrating my own story, I am attempting to find my own niche, the opportunity to let my own oppressed accented voice of an African battered woman to speak. I want my voice to be my microphone and help me find healing for a battered body, mind, and soul. I have always attributed the injuries of trauma from endless domestic violence, the perpetual infidelities, and lack of respect to our marriage, to my own lack of voice back then. Therefore, in this first attempt at writing, I am reclaiming my own voice. This memoir will take a deep introspection of my life as I personally lived and experienced it.

As some of you might know, large numbers of Africans now are known for their scientific contributions; a few are among the noble men and women of Africa who have dared to dream of filling the gigantic political shoes such as those of South Africa's Nelson Mandela and Tanzania's placid socialist Julius Nyerere. On the other hand, some may harbor private dreams of being the reincarnated political versions of villains such as Uganda's Idi Amin and Mobhuto Sese Sekou of Zaire, not to say much of the once-revered-but-now-fallen hero, my own president of Zimbabwe, Robert Gabriel Mugabe. Like the saying goes, "each to his own." I am only fighting for my personal voice as a battered, oppressed, and traumatized woman who survived and excelled beyond what she had ever dreamed possible.

Undeniably, many people among us (the downtrodden and almost invisible section of society) have insurmountable dreams like those of America's Martin Luther King Jr. and achieving world peace like India's Mahatma Gandhi. I can never match their levels, but I am attempting to add my soft and tender voice to the voices of many traumatized women who are used, abused, and have survived. Some of these women rendered voiceless because their culture or traditions dictate otherwise. Culture denies these women their rightful place in the social strata. Through my own voice I am attempting to break away from culture and, in the process, give battered women, almost invisible and ashamed, to share their rightful place.

In the field of literature, there are well-known African authors who include many names such as Chinua Achebe and Ama Ata Aidoo from West Africa; Chinodya and Dangarembga from Zimbabwe, my fellow compatriots; and Ngugi wa Thiong'o from the East Africa. These have made enormous strides in promoting African literature worldwide. These African writers and some political leaders have coined their own histories and rainbows; they have significantly contributed to the world of literacy, and politics in the modern-day society within their own local contexts and internationally have become acclaimed legendary political and literary giants. I so much admire and revere them all, for in their different and silent ways have unknowingly touched and influenced me and urged me to keep on going, even when the going became harder.

According to my culture, we never air our dirty laundry in public. I agree because dirty laundry stinks. It is unpleasant. Culture, therefore, pretends there is no laundry to be aired. My belief is the air takes the stench away, so I ask, why hide the dirt? I want to air the dirty laundry here and now to take the stench away. Domestic violence in my culture is the elephant in the room that everyone tries hard to ignore, yet it is so huge no one could feign ignorance. It is witnessed through the black-and-blue faces women harbor from husbands but are told repeatedly to try and keep peace on the home front. In my culture, peace between couples is negotiated in private with elders; however, no one really knows what happens between the two married people. Negotiated peace with elders is commendable, but more often than not, it ends with the female receiving the short end of the stick. Many times I received that short end of the stick; nonetheless, I feel that my children and their children need to know how I survived this malady that I lived through for so long. I need to let my girls, nieces, and other females know that anything that is done to hurt you personally should not be dictated by how others will negotiate on your behalf nor on how the public will perceive you. You have the right to speak up and act up if necessary.

While I was a traumatized and battered woman, on the other hand, I was a lifelong learner and educator. As such, I feel my narratives might add to the debate and pool of domestic violence and its trauma for those who like to study. I have looked at other people's stories, sorrowfully enjoyed reading their stories, and criticized them for the decisions and actions they chose or their inactions as the case might be. However, academicians are multiple in their various fields. These authors, needless to say, are cited in the worlds of research and add to the pool of empirical studies, drawing different conclusions to different scenarios. I have found their writings thought provoking and very good reading, as I am an avid reader and at times a very analytic reader. However, my voice as a survivor of domestic abuse is not an empirical study. It is my personal story that I have struggled to put down through the years, and I still find it extremely difficult to revisit even on this day.

Prompting me to keep on writing is the fact that I am not content that as an African woman, I have not played a significant role in uplifting the voices of traumatized African women and girls who have been used and abused. I know my voice might be insignificant compared to the vibrant voices of the ever-so-strong Winnie Mandela, the melodious Mirriam Makeba, and the freedom-seeking Mbuya Nehanda, Zimbabwe's first female liberation fighter, yet I know it is unique in its own way. I do not claim international recognition like the humble Mother Teresa, the sterling Lady Diana Spencer, and many other well-renowned female voices that sought peace for women as I have a unique platform. I have the platform of a battered, oppressed, abused, and traumatized African woman because I lived that life. This was my life.

I want to make sure my name is coined forever somewhere as an African woman, learner, educator, and mother who was downtrodden but dared to dream. If in your whole life you grew up in similar circumstances as I did and had ached for tiny recognition, you might make sense of what I am attempting to do and say. I want to add my voice to the voices of abused and battered women. I decided to focus on my life by using the written word hopefully, as the written word is indelible; hence, I will use it to uncover the traditionally covered. I hope this voice will be heard by the younger generations of women, especially those living under adverse conditions as I did. Unbelievably, if you are living with abuse, that is not unique to you only; but many people have been there before you, and sadly many more will be there after you. As such, I invite you to read as we attempt to make sense of why women are battered and continue to live and love their abusers and batterers.

As my people say, *Vatete vachabvepi?*[1] Simply put, families are being dismantled, and there is no longer the coherent family unit or village that I grew up under. As such, my voice might become *vatete*'s voice. My aunt taught me repeatedly about marriage and submission, all that I knew as a supportive wife and mother. I now question myself who

---

[1]   Meaning "where is the aunt now?" Due to industrialization, the aunts, who used to impart traditional values and norms on young girls, are no longer there. The traditional family structure has been dismantled as such literature might as well be called upon to fulfill that role.

will be there for my children, my grandchildren, and my nieces. Who will provide that source of knowledge, that wise aunt with a modern voice of understanding and capability of empathizing with the younger generation? Let my voice be the one and provide an aunt who will tell them not to be submissive, as society socialized me as a young African woman into submitting. I want to be that modern-day aunt's voice that will give them hope and inspiration that if that poor African girl from an unknown village in Zimbabwe could do it, they too can do it.

I deliberately choose my oppressor's language[2] over my own. In a subtle way, I am also acknowledging the oppression of my mother tongue besides the oppression of a black girl in her motherland. I admit at the same time that I love to write in English, the language of my colonizer, because it liberates me. Do you recognize the irony here? English, as a language, gives me the freedom and liberty to say that which culturally I would never attempt, even dare, to mention in my own language and my natural tongue, yet English was also used to oppress me as a worthy human being. Since culture dictated naming my private parts as taboo unmentionable in my mother language and with all the worldly and educational exposure, culture still prevents my tongue from naturally rolling out the words from my mouth as they should. Culture dictates that I should be prim and proper and never mention the unmentionables. Nonetheless, in English, I can get in touch with a wider audience, and I can mention the unmentionables. English affords me freedom and access where I would not have easier access as a person.

Through personal narratives in English, I am able to elaborate on family histories and world-renowned events or anthropologically present this critical and analytical world with its multiple facets and reflections of my personal stories. The written word is never subjected to issues of accents; in that aspect, I feel safe. Many a time living abroad, people have commented on my accent; and in the process, they forget I also hear accents in their voices. Is it a matter of the kettle calling the pot black? Isn't it? So many times I have been relegated to the position of the other.

---

[2]   Zimbabwe was colonized by the British. As such, English became the official language from then on. Our indigenous languages were relegated to second-class status.

I might randomly or chronologically state the events down, that is if memory still saves me right because I never had a journal. Who knew of a journal growing up in my world back then? Times are now different. It was Africa. I was born in Rhodesia in June 1955. Equal rights and provision for equal education in the USA were being fought for. Now can you imagine what was happening in the so-called Dark Continent and Rhodesia back then? I never kept a diary or a journal (as I recall, people doubting James Frey's *A Million Little Pieces*) as not an authentic and true memoir because some of the narration did not hold true under the memoir test.

However, events that happened in my context, as well as nationally and internationally, will aid me. This is an authentic memoir in as much as my memory serves me and as false as I cannot completely recall everything that happened in my life. As mentioned above, world events help shape our history; therefore, the telling of my life story cannot be completely divorced from world events nor be completely married to them, as I do not have complete memories. That being said, I promise to be as forthcoming and as candid as I can be.

I look at my life as puzzle pieces being put together to formulate a whole. Briefly, this means that my life was and still is a jigsaw puzzle, as I have solved what I have lived of it so far, but it is not complete because the last pieces will have to be figured out at some later date. Probably when I am long dead and gone, someone will have the strength to unravel why I did what I did. Some people can piece together pieces of a jigsaw puzzle within a short time, and others can utterly fail to fit the puzzle pieces. I am not sure if I was able to put all the pieces of my battered, abused, and traumatized life together. However, I refused to be muted in the process. Maybe this is a challenge to my children and their children: to solve the story of my life and add other nuances as they find appropriate.

At the same time, I liken my life's journey to a walk in a maze. We do not have manuals to our lives like the washers and dryers. It is more like trial and error, especially in a culture that is closed, as mine was. Walking through the maze might take some people a long time through the twists, turns, and misses, but eventually, some people find their way out, yet others have had to be rescued. Similarly, in life, we might meander; the main objective is not to surrender, but to carry on. I might not have been rescued; one thing is for sure, my life had many meanderings. It totally took me close to three decades to end an eccentric relationship, however, I made it out alive. That is important, to survive and not be killed in the process. It is, therefore, completely up to those who read my memoir to analyze, criticize, unravel, put together, or solve this poor girl's story or walk side by side with her through the maze to share this long arduous journey as a friend or foe alike.

Inside me are a black girl, a child, a teacher, a learner, a mother, a woman, a daughter, a sister, a niece, an aunt, a granddaughter, a daughter-in-law, a grandmother, and a wife used and abused physically, emotionally, and psychologically; an immigrant legal, or illegal; and an academic, struggling or successful. One thing I am sure of: I refuse to be put into one category. I am adamant that each of these facets were responsible for shaping the woman who is writing this today. I inscribe this proudly that one of my greatest successes was as a mother. As a result, I attribute my resilience and determination to being a mother. I truly believe in the eyes of many people I completely failed, but in the eyes of my children, I would never fail; and sure enough, I know I never failed them, not even once, even when the abuses were at their worst.

My children were and will always be the most extraordinary gifts the Lord bestowed on me and my most state-of-the-art achievements in my life. They are an extension of me, for they carry my DNA. As such, they are primary to my success or failure. I know also that the Lord kindly bestows on each one of us these gifts to take care of in the best possible way. I know I would never let my Creator regret having bestowed me with these five special and wonderful gifts of my life. That being said, where you classify me under is completely up to you as there are many facets that compose the entirety of my being, if there ever is such an entity. What I know and strongly believe with all my strength is I eventually found my way out of this confused, troubled, and oppressed world that I lived in. I unraveled the pieces that comprised my life, which I had failed initially to unravel; and like the crossword puzzle, pieces managed to put my physically and emotionally abused life behind me and emerged a completely recovering visionary, new spiritually, refreshed mentally, and a cleansed woman from the maze of my life.

I know my other purpose is to motivate the competitive spirits of people in my family or women and girls who might have grown up under similar circumstances and might have been traumatized by domestic violence as I was. I want them to know that the darkest hour is just before dawn. In my bleakest moment of despair is when I found the strength and courage to kick the man who had abused me, all my adult life to the curb. Marital abuse or not, I now walk in this world with my head held up high like my grandmother Anna; and my mother, Doris, taught me early on in my childhood to always hold my head up high. I had seen domestic abuse, but I had never thought it would be inflicted on my being. As such, do not be ashamed as you are not alone.

I lived my life without fear and without knowingly breaching the laws of neither my nation nor other host nations. I am a true African woman shaped by my upbringing under the guidance of my mother, Doris, and my grandmother Anna. I became an academic, dying to make a difference in the world. I lived and breathed my profession as the most proud mother in the world, as the survivor of all kinds of abuses and traumas who finally came into her own. I am perpetually walking in this life with my head held up high. I refuse that just one of these aspects defines me, but I am a product of them all. This sounds a bit complex; obviously, it is complex because life, by its very nature, is not simple, but very complex.

Chapter One

An introduction to my life

This is a story like the one most women have. A story of being brought up pure and innocent within a loving community of parents, grandparents, and other relatives sheltering you with love. This is the story of my life's journey from childhood to present day. This is a story of a mother living and working to take care of her children. This is a story of being used and abused by the very person who is supposed to love and protect his woman and his wife, the mother of his children. It is a story about how an abused and traumatized woman holds on to a one-sided marriage and hopes that if she piled more love on her abuser and batterer that would take the abuses away.

My story is your story. My struggle is your struggle. My trauma is your trauma. No mother or wife ever wants to admit that the man she married never loved her. No woman or wife ever admits the abuser intentionally inflicted pain on her because he could not stand her. As abused and traumatized women, we are afraid to face the truth because it hurts. As abused and traumatized women, we do not want to admit it because we fear how society would perceive it. However, now years later, I look back, curse, and say to hell with society, to hell with culture, and to hell with what is proper. I tell myself to live my life and be happy before I die. I have one life to live; I might as well, in the end, be happy than never have been happy at all.

In this story, I will tell you of my childhood, my early education, my struggle through secondary and teacher training, my dating time, as well as the first signs of unfaithfulness in my marriage. I will tell you how I hid my bruises and wounds from my family and relatives as Jonathan tried to break my soul and my spirit. I will tell you how I let this man lie to me year after year as he continued to have children and affairs with other women. I will be as candid as I can, and I am doing this as I try to find healing and explain to my three daughters—Teresa, Tiffany, Thelma—and all my nieces that love never hurts. If the man you love or marry beats you or is not there for you all the time, he is not the one for you. Once he hits you, he will hit you again. As soon as he inflicts the first physical pain on you or the first time he lifts his hand to slap you, it is time for you to leave him. As soon as he first cheats on you, it is time for you to leave him. As soon as he tells the first lie, never make excuses for him because he will always lie to you, and you will be subjected to a lifetime of lies, illusions, pretenses, and facades.

It is an account meant to find healing for the writer and motivate other women that if a simple girl who grew up in dismal poverty could rise above her circumstances, how far could those born in a new world with unlimited resources go? It is meant to tell the story through the lens of an abused woman who believed in the sanctity of marriage, the one who held on too long, hoping she could change the man she married. It is a story meant to give hope to those who have almost lost hope. It is a story of being hopelessly in love with love.

I do not claim to be a role model, as role models to me are flawless; personally, I had so many flaws. I only want to tell the story I know is dying to be told. I needed not have remained in that relationship for so long as Jonathan demonstrated right from the onset of our marriage that he was not faithful. My grandmother used to tell me that what you can tell someone to drop is what he or she are holding in their hands, as they can drop them. Not the same can be said about matters of the heart. No matter how hard people fight over loveless relationships, fighting would never bring love. No matter how much one person loves the other, it would never make the other one return their love if they do not feel it in their heart. As a result, never think you can force love from their hearts nor can you mold them into what they are not.

I grew up surrounded by my family, my friends, and many relatives who loved me unconditionally. These people, especially my mother, Doris, as that was her given name, and my paternal grandmother Anna, brought existence to our conversations by using metaphors and proverbs to teach us the philosophical importance of the meaningful journey to life. I grew up to love sayings used by people in different cultures in their everyday lives, for they give intensity to what people are conveying. Some of my most favorite sayings include the following: "Every dog has its own day"; "every dark cloud has a silver lining"; "still waters run deep"; "great big oaks from little acorns grow"; "from a beggar to a king, to live like a king you've got to work like a slave"; and many others that you will most likely read about, if you happen to read further than this page.

These various sayings seem to depict and deliver my innermost outlook and sentiments about my life's struggles and, probably in a way, your life's struggles in general as well. The sayings have become an appropriate and important part of the fabric of my life, for when I reflect on my life, it appears like I was a dog that has had its own day! Could anyone have pictured and guessed that from abject poverty I grew up in, I could have come this far, especially with my education, my travels, my achievements and life experiences including surviving the traumatic effects of matrimonial abuse? I was traumatized in my life at different and unprecedented levels as you will find out as you proceed to read; hopefully you continue reading.

I grew up as a fourth girl child born in a family of nine, from a polygamous father who had fourteen children in total. I was named Avis. I am not sure who named me Avis, but I know my mother must have named me Avis due to the meaning. Being brought up among so many other children, I fought to capture my parents' attention as I grew up, and that probably set precedence: that I had to fight for all I needed in life. Nothing ever came easy. I used to feel as though I would be lost in the sea of faces that were my siblings; as such, I had to leave my unique impressions on my father, Norman, and my mother, Doris. The same was equally true of my primary education, secondary education, and later in teacher training. What I feared the most was to be lost among other students; hence, I worked hard to be recognized. I never wanted to be recognized for notoriety, bad behavior, nor having a child out of wedlock, but I sought recognition for being a good and positive person. Consequently, I tried, by all means, to create and leave the best impression on all people I met in my different walks of life.

I was born in a majority oppressed developing country in the southern part of Africa; it was still named Rhodesia then but became Zimbabwe after independence. My grandmother Anna would tell me of the coming of the colonizers in the late 1800s. She would describe them as the men without knees because of their pants-covered legs. She would tell me the best thing about their coming was access to education and organized religion. I was lucky enough that my father, Anna's only son, Norman, believed in education. As a result, I was an educated and literate woman unlike most girls from my era; they never set foot into a school building.

However, unlike most females, I endured a lot of matrimonial abuse when I later married my husband of more than twenty-five years. It was not merely physical hostility from him. I endured sexual violence; I endured spiritual abuse, persistent emotional hostility, and unrelenting infidelity for close to three decades that I was married to him. I endured all these because first and foremost, I thought and truly believed my love could change him. To a great extent, my upbringing had a lot to do with my endurance to abuse. From as far back as a little girl, I can remember it was indoctrinated in me that my responsibility as a woman was to my husband and my children. Accordingly, I could not fail as a wife and as a mother. As such, I had to persevere, no matter what the circumstances.

This part of my life is still very difficult to recall, as it opens up raw wounds even today. At times, I tell myself to breathe deeply as I hyperventilate simply from recalling the level of abuse and trauma I endured and tolerated in trying to keep my family intact. He beat me when the children were babies. He beat me when we were alone. He beat me when we had visitors, even when his family members were complaining about me. He beat me for refusing him his conjugal rights, and he beat me for "misusing" my own salary. My own salary—can you believe it?—as though it was his for mishandling. I could never know what would bring his wrath on me. I think for the longest time, I was his punching bag for whatever he failed to do as a man in society.

Later in my life, I strived to improve myself academically; despite the odds that were mounted high against me through my marriage, I succeeded. Things were completely different growing up and going through primary school, which was smooth sailing. I only hit a bumpy road after completing an approximate of the tenth grade when my father, Norman, could not afford our tuition. There were no local secondary schools around that time. Though primary schools were plenty, it appeared the oppressor was in no hurry to build as many high schools for the African child. Most high schools were boarding, and they did not come cheap. The burden was heavily burdensome for my father. He had fourteen children altogether; at one point, our educational expenses became too much for him to shoulder. I believe by then there were seven of us in boarding high schools, and the cost became highly prohibitive.

After an approximate of tenth grade, my own education was diverted into teacher training at that early and tender age so that I could help out my father financially. From the time I entered teacher training, I described myself as a conditional teacher because I felt my life circumstances forced me into the teaching field. Though I was the fourth child of my mother, I went for training first because my age and the level I had reached in my own high school education made sense for me to be diverted while my siblings continued on with their education uninterrupted. I did not disappoint neither my parents nor my educators. I worked diligently, and I supported my parents as much as I could from the time I graduated until I got married and started having a family of my own.

The spousal emotional, physical, and mental abuses were released right from the beginning because even as we were dating, Jonathan would double-cross me with other girls. I would visit with him and find other girlfriends in his home, even cooking his meal for the evening or morning. Somehow I thought it would disappear as soon as we were married. Early on, I would turn a blind eye and convince myself that I was much better than the other girls he dated,; as such, I became delusional and convinced myself into believing that he was bound to recognize that I was a better woman and that he would give me the love I deserved. I did not know that, unknowingly on my part, I would be planting the seeds of infidelity, violence, and a propagation of a loveless marriage.

As far as I know, four children were born out of wedlock (there could have been more). A couple were, at one point, imposed on me to care for, and I could not believe the audacity of a cheating husband. First, he cheated on me; and next thing, he wanted me to become the mother to his illegitimate children, whose mothers, in my eyes, had threatened the very essence of my own marriage. However, I would not be humiliated that much as to accepting his children from other women. In that direction, I put down my foot, remained resolute. Every day I live with the reminder of the abuse I put up with for so long. I look at my naked body; I am confronted by numerous scars that are not natural, but the result of his cruelty and brutality. I can even tell the date, time, and year each scar was inflicted on me and what happened afterward. I look at my face; all I could see was the scar of humiliating confrontations. Those scars are the reason I am forever a changed and much stronger and more positive woman.

Having embarked on this journey and struggled to survive; it is apparent I am now reaching for the illusive silver lining. I appear to have risen from being nobody into somebody. Though my life was always tough, poverty stricken, stacked with odds of being born as a black girl from a polygamous family in a colonized country, clamoring for the provision of universal education and health services, I seem to have reached for that unique rainbow. The downbeat odds of my childhood were nothing compared to the spiritual and physical abuses inflicted on me by the person who was supposed to be my lover and protector. His abuses hurt the very core of my being and of my soul. To imagine that I managed to rise above that and completed three degrees while married to such a man is a story worth telling. It is a story that I am a strong woman, and I can use my voice to influence not only my children and their children, but also others in similar circumstances, that they hold the power to change their circumstances in the palms of their own hands.

I know I may not be an important person at the magnitude of being recognized politically, socially, and economically nor can I claim recognition locally, nationally, or otherwise, but I can truly claim recognition within my own family as someone of great stature in my own right. I honestly know I have contributed to the making of my own family's history in unique ways. All my four brothers pioneered in different fields in their own rights. One was a liberation fighter, one was educated in the West, another became a doctor educated in central Africa, Congo Kinshasa to be specific, and the baby of the family was educated in China. As such, education abroad was tested waters for my male family members, and they had claim to that. Locally, my brothers became well-known doctors, engineers, financial administrators, and politicians; so nothing short of me personally becoming a political dynasty, like probably the president of the nation career wise nothing would have been impressive. My four brothers claimed the best of that territory before me.

Thus, where education and surviving marital emotional and physical abuses were concerned, I had to color my own rainbow. I left my own mark as the first woman from my family to venture abroad for my academic achievements and try living and making it in a foreign land with my offspring. This journey of my life would not be easy and would not be undertaken by me alone. I would struggle with my five children. Inexplicably, I would struggle with this man as my dependent, but he would throw my love right back into my face. I acknowledge now for more than half my life I lived with an unfaithful husband who used and abused me as he willed.

So do I guess right that if you have come this far, you are on board? Hence, it is safe to say buckle your emotions and be ready for what I presume to be one of the most uncomfortable rides of the story of my personal life and how I personally survived a lot of traumas.

Chapter Two

Family Background

My name is Avis. I was born in June in the 1955. I had four brothers and four sisters as well as five more brothers and sisters from my father's side. Three of my siblings are late as well as both my parents. I am the fourth born of my mother and the eighth of my father, as he was a polygamous man. I grew up in Rhodesia. The British colonized Rhodesia in the 1800s, and it is now dubbed Zimbabwe. Growing up, I loved history and storytelling. I enjoyed listening to my grandmother Anna, my mother, Doris, and other elderly women tell us these stories. That was how knowledge was handed down to me through the intricacies of history and storytelling.

My life is deeply entrenched in history, that is why I love it. I know that as soon as I have experienced something in my life, it is history. According to my own definition, history is the local, regional, and international people who create it. It is also events that happen locally, nationally, and internationally that accelerate certain historical events more so than others and that enormously change the stories of our lives in general, which ultimately becomes our history. I can remember my grandmother telling us about the coming of the white men, hence the onset of colonization and the change of history on the African continent.

My own family's history stretches only as far as my grandfather Elefi on my father's side. My grandfather came from South Africa. He would migrate to the then Rhodesia in the late 1800s, presumably with the pioneers' column. That was how we were initially told about it, but later, my youngest brother, Levin, did his own research and found out differently. My father's father made several journeys between South Africa and Rhodesia through Mozambique as a trader and eventually settled in Rhodesia, where he later died.

On my mother's side, I know of Cyprian, my mother's father. He was the son of Abel, my mother's grandfather, who lived on the commercial farmlands that surrounded the communal district of Howard, where I grew up. Cyprian was a gentle light-skinned person who was a polygamist himself. I remember him well, as he died in 1970, when I was about fifteen years old. By then I was in high school, and his death would cause a lot of heartache to us three, my sisters Melody, Brenda, and me, as we were in boarding school and as such unable to attend Grandfather Cyprian's funeral.

In my paternal grandfather, Elefi, I found an adventurer, a free spirit, and a man who challenged himself and ultimately spiritually challenged us, his offspring, to explore the unexplored and venture into the unknown, wherever our hearts would lead us. Personally, I think (because I never heard it from the horse's mouth) his life's motto was "live and let live." I suppose my grandfather knew inwardly that he could change his life's circumstances. Therefore, he recognized that "no matter our personal circumstances, whether we are born poor or rich, it is the spirit within each one of us that finally dictates to us whether that sparkle within us would dwindle or whether the sparkle would be kindled to become a burning flame."

Grandfather Elefi later settled in the rural areas of Chiweshe, where he eventually died with his second family in the mid-1960s. Elefi created three wonderful human beings with two different women, and these were my father, Norman, also known as Njanji-Railway Line, as his father Elefi was presumed to have helped construct the railway line between South Africa and Rhodesia then with the pioneers' column. The colonialists' dream was to construct a railway line from Cape Town, South Africa, to Cairo, Egypt. That never came to be. My father, Norman, had fourteen children with three wives. His half-brother Harry had six children of his own, and their one sister and our only aunt, Sophia, was married to a chief and had ten children of their own.

Though Elefi's offspring (his three children) never traveled back to his land of origin, South Africa, his grandchildren, us, would inherit his adventurous spirit. Some of my siblings have been to Asia, others have traveled as far as Europe, while most have been all over neighboring

African countries, and a few ventured far west as the USA. As such, geographically speaking, our worlds were immensely broadened. I know my nieces, nephews, and my own children have been afforded the privileges and opportunities to glimpse into worlds far beyond what they were exposed to by their human eyes. Unlike us, when we grew up, we were limited only to worlds as far as our naked eyes could see. Nonetheless, with educational exposure and travel opportunities, our own children's horizons have broadened beyond our wildest dreams and imaginations, and so have we (my siblings and I) largely.

On my mother, Doris's, side, I know she had four brothers and one elder sister. She also had six brothers and one sister from her father's second wife, who was her mother's sister. My mother was the fifth born out of six of her mother's children and claimed one of her brothers from her father's second wife and her aunt was her twin brother. According to my mother, Doris, she was born in the morning, and her brother Francis was born in the evening on the same day in September of 1928. My mother, Doris, was very close to all her brothers and sisters, but closest to this "twin" brother, Francis.

My grandfather Cyprian had married his wife's younger sister, and they had one daughter and six boys. All in all, Cyprian had thirteen children. With so many uncles and aunts from my mother's side, there was never a shortage of cousins while growing up. Overall, we enjoyed the school holidays we were privileged to spend with them in their village and enjoyed playing with the numerous cousins. Abel Village was about fifteen to twenty miles from my village. Consequently, those two communities initially encompassed my world that early on in my life as I was growing up in Wood. The adults in these two communities were responsible for keeping me on the straight and narrow as I was growing up.

I grew up in the rural area of Howard in Moses District, in my home village. Howard is less than twenty miles out of Harare, our capital city. While growing up, I remember a few bus trips into Harare. In Harare, I would enjoy times spent in the playground on the swings, the slides, the merry-go-round, and the cones of ice cream my parents would buy for us. It was around that time that I was introduced to television from our next-door neighbor. As such, I knew back then that there was another world beyond my world of Howard, but the times in Harare were very limited and do not play a significant role in my growing up and my childhood.

For many years, my life was limited to my local surroundings, and that was my only world. I, however, was able to rise above that and glimpse into another world that I had only heard about in abstract or read about or seen in pictures and or participated in through my strong imagination in the movies and films of my oppressors and never thought one day I could actually attain those acclaimed worlds. As a child, we used to sit round the fire while shelling peanuts or maize and listen to my grandmother's soothing voice or my mother's firm one or other women from the village teach us all about history and geography, ethics and obedience, religion and citizenry. Those lessons meant a lot to us growing up in our communities.

Later, all these lessons would be reinforced in schools, but all the foundation and groundwork had been laid firm into the person that would gradually develop to become the adult that I am today. I was always determined, positive, and comfortable in my own home and my world, which was not huge then because my early childhood had been exposed to neither radio nor television. Therefore, the sayings charity begins at home and that it takes a village to raise a child were realized through these early childhood interactions and are true as to how they relate to my own life and early childhood education. I truly know my own people imparted that love for education in me.

Most of my personal characteristics were first shaped in my home surrounded by my people (mother, father, grandmother, siblings, uncles, aunts, nephews, nieces, and cousins). I loved them the most in the world because they were the only people in my world, and they were my world. That was how big my world was back then. My grandmother would tell us about the Mupfure, Muzvezve, and Munyati and the mountains that I had barely set eyes on because Howard is a plain land with green grass in summer and tall tropical trees that lose their leaves in winter and have red leaves with the coming of spring. There were neither hills nor mountains in Howard. As a result, basically, my eyes could see as far as where the earth rose to meet the sky and where the sky stooped low to meet the earth.

The distances I mostly traveled then was whenever I crossed the river Hunyani into the commercial farming lands north of my home to gather fire wood or when I visited with my grandparents on my mother's side, west of my home. Thus, my world was as large and as limited in scope as far as my own eyes could see within those two existing circumstances. Basically, that was all of my early travel and geography, which comprised my world. However, limited as it was, my life felt so rich and prosperous because I knew nothing else yet. I was happy and reasonably content in it.

My grandmother's stories as well as my mother's and all the other women from the village enabled me to climb the high mountains of Chiweshe to the north of Zimbabwe. To the east, Chimanimani and Nyanga Mountains in my imagination, I climbed those Eastern Mountains. I crossed the crocodile-infested Rivers that separates Zimbabwe from South Africa to the south and enjoyed the wild animals of Zimbabwe in the National Park to the northwest. I could, in my imagination, take the endless picturesque journeys from Harare to Bradley or from Bulawayo to Plumtree. I pictured the lovely Zambezi River that separates Zimbabwe from Zambia to the north whereby lies the beautiful and majestic waterfalls. I could do that because everything was vividly presented to me in story by the adults who brought me up.

I only realized when I was fully grown, when I eventually became a primary school teacher, that those mountains were as real and the rivers were as deep, long, treacherous and as crocodile infested as these women had vividly portrayed them to us in their stories. I was lucky I had my grandmother Anna and my mother, Doris, who influenced me tremendously. I was brought up by these strong women of importance and indomitable characters blessed with intelligence I have not met anywhere else in the world except in my tiny home village. Migration back then was only for workingmen, my father included, who spent their weekdays in towns working for the white men. Every weekend, these men found their way back to their rural villages to be reunited with their loving families.

Growing up, my father, Norman, would come home once a week. He would always bring two boxes of groceries. The entire time one box was larger than the other. The larger box was for my mother and her family; the smaller one for my grandmother and me. I lived with my grandmother Anna from the age of five until the year I started working as a schoolteacher some thirteen years later. Thus, if my memories serve me right, my father had very little influence in my young life except for educating me, that is paying for my tuition. In those days, my father,

Norman, had the final word that kept me disciplined and aware of what not to do. As such, he was the patriarchal disciplinarian.

Way back then, our lives were communal, and my people educated me and handed me down this fathomless well of knowledge. They would take turns in giving me the strong foundation for my education. My aunts (from both my mother's side and my father's side) were responsible for teaching me how to be a good wife. That means submission to the man who would eventually marry me. I attribute my years of submitting to abuse to this socialization early on in my life. I truly believe, though, that I never saw physical abuse inflicted on my mother by my father, but the indoctrination from my aunts had a lot more to do with my tolerance of physical abuse to a great extent later as an adult.

My mother, on the other hand, taught me how to cook and keep a good home as well as become a good mother to my own children. One thing I want to be clear about is that my mother also taught me how to treat my own children, both boys and girls, fairly and equally, something out of the traditional gender roles. My mother never defined our chores at home by traditional gender roles. My brothers were able to grind peanut butter on their knees on the grinding stone just as us girls were. We were taught how to herd cattle just as my brothers were. My mother, Doris, was this way because as a child growing up, she had been made to work on farms, and the money she brought home would be used to send her younger brother to school and not her. I think she never wanted to subject her own girls to this unfair upbringing.

Repeatedly, my mother, Doris, would reiterate to us that no child was ever meant to work for another. As such, she tried to instill that in us and treated us equally. My mother never went to school. She never learned to read and write as a child. Though she worked and made money, the money was invested in her younger brother's education. She learned to read and write later on when Elvin (my son) was going to school. She attended adult literacy classes by the time my son started grade one. I remember one of the happiest days of her life was opening her own banking account. She was really happy to be able to complete that bank slip and sign her name, than put an X for her signature. My mother embraced us all with her love. She had an abundance of love for all her brothers, her two sisters, and all their children that I have never found in anyone else.

My grandmother Anna taught me how to respect elders and people in my community, be a meaningful contributing member of my community, how to love God and Christ through the Anglican songs, prayers, and verses as well as respect of nature. As a woman, she was the only one I ever heard address my mother and other married women by their given names. She was a controversial woman. She gave birth to three children with three different men. I remember my father's youngest sister, Veronica, questioning her *Gogo* (grandmother) multiple times about her own heritage. She never knew who her father was, and many times, she gave *Gogo* a hard time because she wanted to know where she came from. My other Aunt Eileen was the eldest and knew her father's relatives, but up to now, I am not sure that was her real father at all. She too at times would raise hell about the circumstances of her birthright. Most times, sadly, though, *Gogo* did not have real, straightforward answers for both her daughters. I vowed as young as I was then that I would know my children's fathers, no matter what the circumstances of their births.

As for my father, Grandmother Anna, in her wild days, had married my grandfather Elefi, the South African. As soon as she had given birth to my father, Norman, and if I remember well when he was only six months old, my grandmother, *Gogo*, abandoned my father and her husband. Grandfather Elefi had no option but to take my father, Norman, to his own grandmother Ruth, my father's mother's mother. My father's grandmother Ruth was a blind woman, but she was the one who brought up my father. Life was not easy for my father, Norman, as he grew up in his mother's village with an absent mother and an absent father, being brought up by a blind grandmother.

According to my father, Norman, he never had a lot of fun as a child. He was the herd boy of the village cattle while kids of his age went to school. He had no one to speak up for him as his grandmother was blind and depended on the village people to fend for her, including her abandoned grandson. As such, my father suffered a lot in his childhood from his abandonment by his mother, Anna. Retrospectively, I believe that was why he so much wanted us to be educated, and he worked so hard to provide for his family. He knew education would provide us an escape that he was never afforded as a child. He managed to educate his nephews and nieces, all of whom he started to care for before he had turned eighteen years of age himself.

My early education is deeply rooted in these early memories, learning about my people and where they came from, which remains forever colorfully entrenched in the crevices of my mind even today. Home lessons were multiple and varied mostly according to what problems were being addressed currently in our community. In case you are wondering why I have to give you this detailed background, I want you to understand where I came from and what shaped the adult me, Avis, later Mother of Elvin, when I became a married woman. I also write these stories down because I am afraid there would be no one to tell them to my children and my grandchildren, to my nephews and nieces, to my cousins and their children, and to the younger generation of how it was way back then. To tell the younger generation that at some point in our lives we listened and respected our elders, unlike today's children who have a response to everything, in our day; it would have been an unforgettable sign of utter disrespect.

I feel the need to tell my grandchildren who truly is this African woman, who is their grandmother. However, in as much as I have told my own children, I am also afraid the essence of storytelling has been lost; also, we have become so displaced in the world and so separated culturally that I fear no one will narrate these stories to my offspring, as the stories were real. Approximating in my own language, *Vatete vachabvepi,* my voice has to be the much-needed aunt's voice to narrate to my children and their children about how it was way back then, how we were never heard as children, but seen.

As kids, we learned to play all childhood games with my brothers and sisters and the numerous cousins. We played different games especially at night.[3] We played hide-and-seek at night in the maize crops and enjoyed listening to the folktales of *Gogo*. We also enjoyed many wild fruits in the company of our elders as they taught us names of rivers, mountains, and trees. We were also taught of the taboos, things we would never say while in the bush, or we would risk being lost. This was a deep well of knowledge while playing, learning, and growing at the same time, being indoctrinated unknowingly into some roles that, in some of us, would prove detrimental to our self-esteem.

---

[3]   All these games translate to English versions of hopscotch, hide-and-seek, and a diluted version of chess.

As I was growing up, I learned to copy and emulate many things in life. Now as I put together the broken pieces of my life, I find that I have to copy the ways of my colonizer, my oppressor, the one who made me become a fourth-class citizen in my own country. I have to learn to write down my own story in black and white. You question why my oppressor made me a fourth-class citizen? Well, first, it had to be the white male, then the white female, the black male, and finally me—the black female, the place I hated the most, a place where you feel you are below other people. From the early 1890s, when Cecil John Rhodes, Robert Moffat, and the like, who found and discovered landmarks in Africa as though people did not already exist in those lands, history distorted, so I called it. They were responsible for making me a fourth-class citizen in my own country.

Education was used to streamline people into social class; needless to say, therefore, for black females, not many made it beyond the seventh grade or past primary school. I consider myself to have been one of the highly educated and privileged ones to have had access to high school education. Maybe it was then I realized there was perpetuity in the written word. As such, I choose not to hand down my history through the African tradition orally. I choose the tradition of my oppressor, which is undeniably indelible and perpetually strong—the written word. Once put in black and white, who can deny what is written down? Furthermore, who can deny me my place in history, considering I penned everything down personally? I lived this life, so you might as well hear it from the horse's mouth.

I have found sweetness beyond comparison in the written word, strength, intelligence, exposure, realization of oneself, and knowledge for all one can be. In my case, however, I choose to tell this story in the written form, the story that would otherwise remain hidden because our culture is good at keeping things hidden. Yes, I mean hidden, for I have found that Africans have great sciences and scientists. Some can heal some illnesses that modern sciences cannot, but because our science is hidden (it is not shared, published, nor revealed), we cannot claim it (for to claim it, research has to prove it). I have decided to chronicle my story like I learned in school, that this story that I lived and experienced, which I know will touch and influence many lives, has to come out.

I deny remaining hidden all my life, I deny being rendered invisible, and finally, I deny being rendered voiceless because I am a black

African woman as it was back then when I was growing up. I refuse to be ultimately denied my own very existence because of some oversight on my part, I might neglect to tell my offspring who I really was, or as culture dictates, I remain hidden. So I give voice to my right to be heard; I give existence to my being as well as visibility to one of the most invisible atrocities of abuse that occur almost every day in broad daylight—physical abuse in the hands of a loved one.

The abuses inflicted on me were not unique. The abuses and trauma imposed on women still remain invisible because they are not pleasant to talk about. I want to give visibility to spousal abuse and add my accented African voice to the many voices that have spoken before me but have continued to fall on deaf ears. I want people to know that abuse knows no class, that it knows no race and no religion, not limited to geography by neither rivers nor mountains, nor limited to living arrangements. Abuse knows no discrimination of sexuality, cohabitation, marital status, nor prostitution and neither sexual orientation. I am an educated, civilized, well-traveled woman but was traumatized by domestic violence and emotional abuse in my marriage for close to three decades.

I choose to write because undeniably, there is strength in preserving history through the written word, having archival materials (for I now have a few pictures of my life, videocassette, and voice recordings), because written words can cross boundaries without being asked to produce passports or visas. Written words are not limited in time, geography, space, pedagogy, culture, and most important words can even cross language barriers through translations and without being subjected to humiliations of accents of the audible voice.

Due to the fact that the seed and quest for education was implanted in me so early in my life, I aspired to be the best I could be despite my circumstances. I know my life initially gave me lemons, and I was determined to make lemonade out of the hard lessons learned. I wanted to be counted among those who had realized their dreams through education. I might have taken a long and winding route to achieve my ambition, but I finally got there. Yes, as the saying goes, "better late than never." Have you ever heard of the late bloomers? I consider myself to have finally arrived at my destination. As such, I am a late bloomer; and to everything, there is a process, so I followed the process.

All my life, I only learned to read and to write in English. My indigenous or my natural tongue or mother language, as others prefer, was relegated to second-class language! I never used my natural tongue for any other purposes but to speak at home. I used English from the time I started my sub-standard A in 1962 until I graduated as a sub-standard teacher in 1974 (more about my professional qualifications later). I sailed through my primary school education, gained access into secondary school, but failed to make it to the end as the cost of secondary education was too much for my polygamous father, who, by the way, had fourteen children who all became professionals! I took a detour into teaching, which was my career most of my life; I defined myself as a conditional teacher. I did not choose my profession. It chose me, and I strived to improve myself academically, locally and abroad.

All my reading books were English, whereby I read of the snow and never saw a single flake, not even once until I was in my late forties. I enjoyed *Oliver Twist*, *The Count of Monte Cristo*, *Tom Sawyer*, *Lorna Doone*, and *Pride and Prejudice* while in primary school, but no stories of Nehanda, Chaminuka, Musonza, and Kaguvi, some of the African heroes. I read of a white Christmas and never could fully understand what it meant because my Christmases were always wet. Later in college, my theories were derived from Coombs, Darwin, Fullan, and the like, yet none were quite relevant to my environment, scope, and circumstances. Needless to say, when I completed my first degree at the University of Zimbabwe, I wanted to study in America. I had used the American textbooks; they influenced my methods of teaching were the only ones I knew. Their popular culture had become my people's culture. The music was Western, the movies were Western, and Zimbabwe Television (ZTV) was full of lifetime movies. No doubt as soon as I managed to get my student visa to the USA, I was on the first plane crossing the tropical forests and countries of northern Africa. More will be discussed about my education, migration, living, and studying abroad in chapters to come, that is if I have not bored you to death so far. So please get a glass of something to drink and enjoy my first book and the true story of my life! I am now Dr. Avis!

Chapter Three

Childhood with Anna and Doris

I recall that at the tender age of five or six, my father co-opted me to his mother, Anna, so that I could help take care of her or she could take care of me. I am not sure which it was. In my mind as a child then, I did not question because many families in my village had the same living arrangements. I did not even go a hundred yards away to live with my grandmother. It was still in the same village; in fact, my grandmother's hut was just next to my mother's homestead. I remember the first few days my younger sister Brenda was persuaded to come with me until I got used to the idea. I vividly recall my mother, Doris, telling me that she would always have food waiting for me at home; as my greatest fear was they would be having better food than me.

My grandmother Anna's, *Gogo* as we popularly called her, home was made of one round hut and a granary built on top of some rocks, where we stored all our food. Basically, our hut was our cooking, living, and sleeping quarters. No matter how many people were living with my grandmother, depending on the season of the year, we would all sleep in the same hut. Holidays such as Christmas were the most crowded, as other grown-up grandchildren came to visit accompanied by their offspring and husbands.

Boys would lie on the one reed mat, sharing blankets on one side of the hut. Girls would sleep behind Grandmother, and if the married grandchildren happened to be visiting, they too would sleep with their spouses at the front part of the hut, further away from the door, under the same roof in the same hut. Inconceivable, yes, but that was how we were all lovingly brought up. This gave us a sense of togetherness and unity that only we could understand, and people of other cultures would question the morality of it all.

She did other things that made her seem controversial because of her previous flamboyant lifestyle, but definitely, my grandmother was not a child abuser. My grandmother would not have withstood that type of nonsense, as she would have called it, from anyone. In as much as it is unbelievable that I refer to my mother as Doris because our culture demands we refer to our mothers only as *Amai* (mother), yet these were some of the behaviors I inherited from my grandmother. I do not hesitate to call anyone by their first names, a clear indication I am my grandmother's protégé.

Anna, or *Gogo* Anna, never referred to any woman as mother of child, as is the usual indigenous custom, married or not. To her, people had names; therefore, people had to be called by their names. Thus, Anna was a controversial woman for someone from her time and someone who grew up during her era and background, but then my grandmother was no ordinary woman.

Anna would be referred to in these modern times as a woman of the world. Most people her age could not even read the bible nor loved the white men's music nor could boast of the beautiful smile she had (of course they were false teeth bought for her by her only son, my father). She had only three children—two girls and my father—very uncommon in those days so to speak. Most people had more children than three children, but somehow my grandmother managed to limit the number of her offspring to only three.

Up to this day, I remember her impressive smile. She had a beautiful smile because when she lost her natural teeth at an early age, my father, Norman, had her fitted with two complete sets of dentures, and only a few people could boast of that during those days. She had lived her life to the fullest, and unfortunately, though, she had left my father to be brought up by his blind grandmother, Ruth. Norman, sometimes people called him Railway Line (Njanji), as people thought his father, Elefi, had come due to the construction of the railway line, which pioneers intended to construct from Cape to Cairo, never quite forgave his mother for this abandonment at an early age. Norman honestly loved his own mother, the ever-controversial Anna.

As a result of the early abandonment, my father became the cattle boy of the whole village. As such, he did not go far with his education. He, however, backed his intelligence enough during the time; he was schooled because his teachers left him in charge when they were not in the classroom. I guess he used to be the class monitor. I know my father played that role effectively as he was a natural-born leader. I witnessed that side of him all my life. By his very nature, he commanded. People follow without even uttering a word and most times not even raising his voice to demand attention.

In school, my father went as far as fifth grade. My father's embedded memories would one day be reminisced over because of my own eldest son, Elvin. When Elvin was four years old, he did not want me to take him to Georgetown, his father's communal home. Whenever we took Elvin to Georgetown, he was made to herd cattle with boys his age or slightly older. Those boys resented the fact that Elvin had shoes while they did not. They attempted in their own ways to address issues of social class injustices. As a result, they would force Elvin to leave his shoes at home or force him to herd cattle barefooted. My son's soft and tender feet would be subjected to the harsh environment. My son, being brought up in Georgetown, was considered a "softy," and the village boys tried to be boys and subjected Elvin to the hardships they endured every day in order to toughen him up.

One school holiday, when I went to pick up Elvin from Howard, Elvin would not willingly come with me for the holidays. Elvin started to tell my father how the other boys treated him when they went to herd cattle in Georgetown. I had never witnessed my father talk about his difficult childhood. It was my son who made him reminisce over his painful childhood memories. We could clearly tell that his childhood had presented him with hardships more than he had ever opened up to us, his children. He opened up with his grandson that particular night; therefore, a special bond existed between grandparent and grandson, a bond that did not exist between him and us his children. I could feel it in the tenderness and emotion of his voice; there were plenty of childhood memories that he had not revisited in a long time.

Not to lose track of my thoughts, but this gives you a glimpse into the lives of people who brought me up. With this upbringing, my father loved his mother, for he did what no other children had ever done for their parents in those years in the mid1950s. He took care of her like any son who truly loved his mother. He replaced her natural teeth with dentures, which were expensive in those days when she had almost no teeth left. Those false teeth were replaced many times over during Grandmother's lifetime.

Grandmother Anna used to drink, and she would become careless with her dentures and sometimes lost them. She would carelessly drop them. At times, kids would find them and mistook them for toys whereby they would crush those dentures with stones. Occasionally, she fell in her drunken stupor and broke them herself. Each time this occurred, my father had the dentures replaced. I remember the one time he did not have them replaced for close to a year. She complained to her son, my father, Norman, and the gist of his answer was she forgot that he now had a growing family and could not afford replacing expensive broken dentures repeatedly. I clearly remember that was the last time she ever had them replaced because my father had stressed that he was never going to replace them should any mishap befall them again. This was my grandmother Anna.

Each time my father bought us, his children, new clothes we were expected to thank our parents, then we would wear the new clothes and go and kneel and thank Anna too. According to her, it was her son who was doing this for us. As such, she felt entitled to be thanked in the process. There was no way we could get out of it because her home was next to my parents', and such rules were reinforced from both households. As for me, I lived under her roof, and I could not afford otherwise. That was then when children respected their elders and never questioned nor answered back. Even when I could not understand why I had to live with her, my father saw it befitting; as such, I did it to please my father, Norman.

To go back to our living and sleeping arrangements, however, circumstances were specifically difficult with large numbers of people crowded in my grandmother's single little hut during holidays like Christmas. Whenever working husbands came home in those days, the kids would be sent to spend the nights with their grandparents. With huge numbers, sharing sleeping quarters, needless to say, no one would even think of abusing anyone. These were also the sleeping arrangements every week for my sisters when my father Norman came home. My sisters would bring their blankets and spend the night with my grandmother and me.

By the time we were growing up, my parents' homestead comprised of one round hut for cooking and one four-cornered room for my mother and my father's bedroom. When my father was not home, my sisters shared the bedroom with my mother, and my brothers slept in the round hut, where we cooked our food. When my father came home, my sisters slept with my grandmother Anna and me. These were happy, carefree days of growing up. I reminisce over those times and sometimes wish if money could buy youth back, I would sure go back to those carefree days.

With so many people crowded in *Gogo's* hut, stories would be told late into the night; and at times, Grandmother took advantage and gave us work to do. We would shell nuts, corn, and even roast some of the corn or nuts to chew on as we listened to *Gogo*'s stories. Salted peanuts tasted better, and we could never have enough of them while draining buckets of water; and come morning, blankets would be completely drenched, no elaboration needed here. These stories would be filled with moral and ethical lessons of what to do and what not to do. They taught us how to respect our elders, how to live in harmony with our environment, how to respect the wild animals, and how to pay homage to God[4] the creator, who somehow in *Anna's* stories and my culture, was genderless until the white man's religion was introduced.

My early lessons to life took place under these loving orchestrated circumstances. My grandmother was the first one to teach me how to pray and how to read the bible. My living with my grandmother was solely for the purpose of taking care of her as she was getting on in age, which I pretty much knew because it was the thing to do back then. In my culture, we are trained to take care of our aging parents or other relatives. There was no distinguishing between extended and immediate families. It was culturally appropriate that when a family member was in need, the responsibility fell on the younger generation and those around the person to care for them. This responsibility for my grandmother fell on my father as the only son. In that case, my father had to give one of his daughters to his mother, and I happened to be the chosen one. I say this with pride and joy, as it would give me an elevated status in my father's eyes. As his mother's caretaker, he would look upon me as his

---

[4] God somehow in my Gogo's stories was genderless. I later found out gender was introduced because of the Whiteman's Bible.

surrogate mother in a way. No matter what I did, my discipline would be left to my grandmother and not my father. My father was no longer at liberty to discipline me as my parent. As such, I would be spared his firm hand of discipline.

It was now up to my grandmother to spoil me; unfortunately, she would not send me anywhere. My grandmother had to do a good job of raising me, or she would be stuck with a spoiled brat for the rest of her natural life! She taught me the sense of sharing; each time before meals, she expected me to call my siblings and cousins alike so we could partake together. She introduced me early on to some of my passions in life, and those were crocheting and knitting. By the age of nine, I was good at crocheting, knitting like a pro, and learning to sew. These hobbies would become worthy sources of income to supplement my earnings later in my life as an underpaid primary school teacher with five growing children.

The honor of living with my grandmother came with its own sets of responsibilities too. These were fetching us clean drinking water, gathering firewood for cooking and keeping ourselves warm in the cold months, tilling the cornfields with her in the summer, washing our dirty clothes in the river Hunyani, as well as helping her take her baths. Anna would either have her baths in the cornfields camouflaged under the corn plants' green leaves in summer or take the walk to the river, which she did not really like at all. Most times, we hid in the cornfields and enjoyed our warm baths in summer sunshine and occasionally in the river, enjoying the company of other naked village women bathing by the riverside. It was not strange to see naked women as I was growing up. I learned to name the parts of my body from the casual talk of the women by the riverside. Yes, I eavesdropped on adult conversations; and in turn, they carried their adult conversations as though we had no ears. They discussed sexual intimacy by the river in our ears and somehow pretended we did not understand adult language.

The one thing I hated the most would be to provide my grandmother with companionship while she took her many long trips on foot to visit her never-ending relatives almost every weekend. My grandmother had been a well-traveled woman in her younger days, and people had nicknamed her "wondering feet woman," as she seemed to always have the capability to go visiting with her relatives from all the four corners of Howard, our communal district, anytime. Sometimes we would leave home on Friday evenings and would come back on Sunday evenings, in time for me to go to school the following day. Other times we would be gone only for a day and be home by nightfall. She never wanted me to miss school no matter what the circumstances were. No matter how tired, I would be after our traipsing on the country paths; she promoted my education unfailingly.

To me, these trips on foot were unbearable, tiring, never ending, and always a nuisance to endure weekend after weekend. However, I had no choice as my father had talked and instilled it in me, stressing how imperative it was that I followed her wherever she went. I could not be found betraying my father's trust in me. As a result, wherever or whatever my grandmother wanted to do, I would blindly follow like a sheep to the slaughter. Most times, it really felt like I was a real sheep going to the slaughter, as those were no fun activities for a child growing up. I did not enjoy most of these trips as they were undertaken on foot.

In as much as I looked forward to weekends I also began to dread them passionately. If we were not visiting *Gogo*'s many relatives, Sundays were equally bad for me. Early Sunday mornings, I would go with *Gogo* to the Anglican Church three miles away on foot. I would then endure the whole Anglican service on my knees. Though I loved their hymns, kneeling was no fun and never meant for me. The couple of hours in church were pure torture. When I got home, my mother, Doris, would drag me off another mile away to the Salvation Army Church. Between the two women, none would relinquish my religious education to the other. I began to hate Sundays with a passion. Sunday also meant attending the mandatory Sunday school classes; otherwise, Mondays I would be eligible for manual work for not attending lessons, from either my class teacher or the headmaster. That was asking too much of me, I thought, but what could I do as a child? I could not complain. Complaining was one of the most intolerable behaviors from children.

Another chore I hated the most was tilling the fields. The tilling of the fields was a backbreaking chore and one we could never get out of. We would weed the fields from dawn till dusk. We were happy when the rain fell because we would not be expected to work in the rain.[5] These times also bring back memories of the scary things *Gogo* would

---

[5]   The rain was imperative rest as such, for we never worked in the rain. It was always welcome!

make me do especially one incident that traumatized me for life. One day as we were weeding in the cornfields and a chameleon happened to be crossing by, she actually commented that no wonder we had been working slowly that day, it was due to the chameleon's slow pace that had been responsible for impeding our normal pace. Somehow, innocently and like a child, I commented that maybe all chameleons should be killed if they were responsible for such incongruous behavior.

What she made me do next traumatized me for the rest of my life. Up until now, I do not like chameleons because of that childhood incident. I still get goose bumps even from recalling that incident. My grandmother actually forced me to stuff her chewing tobacco[6] into the chameleon's mouth. Her explanation was that wishing death to any animal or any creature was a sin unless I carried out the killing of the innocent little reptile. Moreover, not committing the deed meant death would haunt me the rest of my natural life. In order to cleanse myself of the presumed curse, I had to kill the chameleon. I cried, I pleaded, I persuaded her, and I even tried running away from her, but she would not relent. I had to do her bidding.

Finally, in tears and shaking like a reed in the river, I pressed the back of the chameleon down with a stick that forced its mouth open, enabling me to stuff the chewing tobacco into its mouth. Surely, it did not take more than five minutes for the chameleon to die. I can still visualize that dead chameleon up to this day! Inwardly, I vowed never to be a tobacco chewer. I guessed if chewing tobacco could kill a chameleon in such a short time, what concealed harm would the tobacco do to my beautiful body? I never chewed tobacco because of that incident! Furthermore, it grossed me out the way they (my grandmother and two aunts) spat it out; both my two father's sisters and my grandmother all chewed and sniffed tobacco.

Later that evening when I got home, I could not wait to tell my mother of what had transpired. My mother was livid with anger. After I told her everything, she went to talk to my grandmother. Whatever was discussed between the two women I loved the most in the world, I do not know up to this day. They went behind closed doors and discussed

---

[6]   I grew up with grandmother chewing tobacco and her two daughters sniffed it into their nostrils. I did not like these habits of my grandmother and the tobacco sniffing by her daughters.

the issue, and all I know is from that day onward, my grandmother Anna never made me do anything so cruel ever again. She had taught me to respect animals, yet she was teaching me how to kill. Grandmother Anna was as contrary as ever. At times, I failed to fathom her. Contrary or not, I know I loved her without even having to tell her that I loved her. I also knew she loved me, and that did not have to be put into any words.

It was during these early formative years that I learned to sit up straight, cross-legged, no hunched back, no drooping shoulders, and my chest straight up with my head held up high through my grandmother's guidance. For with my grandmother, good posture and impeccable appearances was everything. Keeping my chest straight up became a problem when I entered puberty; this meant my growing breasts would be showing. To avoid that, I would hunch my shoulders, attempting to hide my maturing womanhood, but Anna would have none of that. She would tell me to hold my shoulders straight and push out my chest.

She taught me to sit on the reed mat with my legs crossed. This was also the birth of my most comfortable sitting position even in yoga. Have you ever tried sitting cross-legged on the floor with your back held straight up? It is quite comfortable. That was my posture sitting on the floor while I had all my meals all my young life and a position I find quite relaxing and comfortable up to this day. That was how early on I learned to hold my head up, look people in their eyes, smile to acknowledge what they were saying, and matured into a beautiful young woman. I point this out because in my culture, when an adult is addressing a young person, to show respect, the young person's head should be bowed down a little, and we were taught never to look adults straight in their eyes, as this was not a sign of respect, especially with girls. My grandmother never taught me that; in fact, she taught me completely the opposite. I learned to look adults in their eyes due to my grandmother's teaching and upbringing. My grandmother would remain controversial until the day she died.

When I was in primary school, I recall how one of my teachers would always be telling other students during assembly that he admired the way I usually held my head up high and smiled to everyone as we walked by and played in the red dusty grounds of Melfort Primary School. Those grounds were as red as I had ever seen any grounds, and it easily made us dirty, but we forged good friendships and had proper guidance from our teachers. The teacher's positive comments left an everlasting impression on my character and personality and forever encouraged me to always have a loving and genuine embracing smile for people I met on the road, in the store, in church, my fellow classmates, my mother, my father, my siblings, and all the numerous cousins I grew up with.

My performance in school was always the best impeccable presentation, and I continuously excelled in my education. I enjoyed reading Charles Dickens's *David Copperfield*, *Oliver Twist*. I read an abridged series of *Pride and Prejudice* while in primary school. Mark Twain's *Huckleberry Finn* and *Tom Sawyer*, as well as *Peyton Place* were some the many books my brother bought me. My eldest brother, Nicholas, could afford to buy for us from his pocket money. Some reading materials were obviously stolen from his literature collection as they were beyond my age. I remember one that I read earlier on that introduced me to sex between a man and a woman. I found the story thrilling, and I somehow experienced a tingling I could not explain nor ask anyone about, but I knew it felt good.

Early on, my world expanded enormously, and I would do book reviews in class, loving every moment presenting my oral book reviews to the class of forty to fifty students with curious faces. One specific memory I have of narrating my book reviews was on *Oliver Twist* when I was in standard four (4), an equivalent of fifth grade. I remember using the words "arrested" and "released" (understand that English is my second language), which made a lasting impression on my class teacher, more so my classmates! Those words were jawbreakers as we referred to any big English words; one had to explain when others did not know the meaning. This tremendously boosted my yen for broadening my English vocabulary through reading and aided my acquisition of self-confidence through my oral book reviews.

My history included the distorted stories of David Livingstone, Cecil John Rhodes, and Robert Moffat, and not Monomotapa, Kaguvi, and Nehanda, a representation of my own people and how I defined myself that I learned through my grandmother at home. Livingstone, Moffat, and Rhodes were some of the individuals who had a lot to do with how my country was colonized and oppressed in a much controversial manner. There were discrepancies presented in the two forms of education—the home and the school. This discrepancy was very clear to my young inquisitive mind even then. The way schoolbooks presented the history somehow differed from the way my grandmother Anna related the same stories to us. I was left to wonder and find out the truth between the two. Years later, as I continued with my education, it would become apparent that from school, I was not learning history that defined my people, but history that defined others whom I had no clue where they belonged. This would always be an intellectual conflict with me all my life.

My eldest brothers, Nicholas and Larry, extended my knowledge and education further to include history, geography, nature,[7] politics, the universe, and flora and fauna. Each school holiday, they would take us into the forests to enjoy the wild fruits, learn the names of trees, and how to harvest honey. These activities kept us from mischief and were well guided by our brothers. These were practical life lessons that remain forever entrenched in the crevices of my memory; unfortunately, some of them were never imparted to my own children. I remember how one day we would be so innocently swimming in the river in our dresses or naked, with our brothers teaching us how to swim. We would feel so happy and so free. Those were the only swimming lessons I ever had in my life but sufficient to give me the skills I needed to survive or save someone from drowning as I later did, saving my very own daughter from drowning during a swimming gala. I am glad I had those lessons with my brothers.

On the other hand, my first international and memorable history lessons were received during these escapades. My brothers told us about the Vietnam War, the war of Biafra, the story of Hitler as it related to the Second World War, but those had little meaning to us, as that world seemed so remote from my world. I felt as though they were wasting their time teaching us about things that were so removed from us. They told us of the first liberation war, the First Liberation War of Zimbabwe as it was known Chimurenga. I felt connected to this at least. I knew about the segregated suburbs of Harare. Some of the suburbs were exclusive to whites only, and the worst looking were exclusively for blacks. Something was definitely wrong with that picture. In my young mind, even then, I could not understand and vocalize it; the discrepancy was clear. My mind was like a sponge absorbing as much knowledge as it could.

---

[7]   In summer, we would go looking for the fruits as *tsvoritsvoto, nhunguru, mazhanje, maroro*. I wonder whether you even know these wild fruits at all! Further still, do they still exist?

Later, I would really live through another liberation war, and my brother Nicholas would be a victim of this Second Liberation War of Zimbabwe. The second liberation war was fought from the late 1960s up until 1979, when it brought about a settlement between the warring factions in the then Rhodesia. These were some of the lessons I would never have received without biases in any classroom setting, especially in history, during that era. Our colonizers prescribed our local history, and they taught us their history instead of ours.

Thus, I always associated my early history lessons in life with my family; especially in as far as our oppression, colonization, and liberation struggles were concerned. The controversies between the ascribed history in school and what I learned from my brothers would stir emotions of my growing up in an unfair world. At times I would even question God in prayer. Why was I born a poor black girl? I felt I should have access to an easier life without having to be classified as below any other human race. I understood the inequalities even back then. They were never fair then, and neither will they ever be.

The most prominent figures in my early education are my grandmother Anna, as you can tell; my brothers Nicholas and Larry; my mother, Doris, and the women from the village who, year after year, featured in my life as much as possible. Way back then, men were mostly disciplinarians; and up to now, I still associate chastity with my father. His usual saying was if his daughters were to ever fall pregnant before marriage, then we would find ourselves living with our maternal grandparents, as that misbehavior would result in him divorcing our mother for not instilling proper moral values in us girls. Talk of fear of sexual intimacy; I would not even consider it until I found a man to marry, not even as a teenager when the hormones were raging, would sex be of any consideration. As such, I kept myself pure for marriage, as I did not want to be the cause of my parent's divorce. Sex was never taught nor was menstrual cycle explained, and at the same time, I matured into a woman without a lot of knowledge about my own anatomy, my sexuality, my sensual feelings, and how they function.

Though the people mentioned above played prominent roles in my education, I do not want to overlook the role my mother and elder sister Melody, a name she gave herself as a teenager. They taught me how to pound peanuts and later ground the crunchy nuts on the grinding stone into smooth peanut butter. These domestic lessons also included how to keep a clean house, fetch water, and all the wifely duties any rural woman performed well in order to be a good wife and mother. The only chore I really hated the most was going to the white men's farms looking for firewood. I was not a lazy person per se, but I hated all the creepy crawly worms that seemed to harbor every possible piece of wood my eyes would fall on. These crawling insects would give me goose bumps and send chills down my spine; as a result, I would scream at the top of my voice, attracting unwanted attention from the farms owners. To prevent me from screaming louder, my mother would simply smother my scream with her hands. I hated going to the commercial farms to fetch firewood. Early on, I wished I was a rich person living in the city and not having to deal with fetching firewood. I do not like any crawly creepy creatures up to this day. As a mother, I would never be able to teach my own children how to love creepy crawly things. In that direction as a mother, I failed dismally.

I have many memories of my education at home and one incident of how to care for our hair stands out in my memory. Most African hair is curly, kinky, and hard to maintain. As such, we would plait it or use hot ironing combs for easier management. As my younger sister Brenda and I were preparing to go to secondary boarding school, I was also entering puberty. My elder sister tried to plait Brenda's hair, but that hurt her scalp so bad she abandoned due to complains. My mother decided to take over, but it was no better. Another woman, Mary, from the village, completed the deed, and when she was finally done, my sister stated she had only kept quiet out of sheer respect for the old woman.

After seeing my younger sister Brenda's torture and she had to go through pain for beauty, I decided not to have my hair plaited at all. Somehow this set precedence to how I would feel about plaiting my hair. I hated the pulling of my scalp as such I never loved the hairstyle at all. Later in boarding school, friends would plait my hair; and in the middle of the night, I would undo due to the pain. I could not stand it. Eventually, none would plait my hair except for my elder sister, as I had developed a reputation of being a whinny and of undoing my hair in the middle of the night. I am glad I never could stand it because some girls developed receding hairlines due to the pulling of the hair follicles. I still have my natural hairline, I am happy to say, to this day.

The following duties were some of the roles we were taught without actually any other choice but simply shut up and do it: pounding, grinding, cleaning house, fetching water, fetching firewood, working all day long in the fields, and so many others hard chores for us growing up. We had to be socialized into doing them well in order to take up the roles as adults. We did the elders' bidding without questioning. My culture believes that children should be seen and not heard. We were never allowed to talk back to our parents. We were not supposed to question their decisions. These lessons also incorporated the socialization into an obedient, submissive wife.

As such, growing up as a child in my village, we had to be seen and not heard. This is one of the reasons why I believe I put up with a lot of the violence later in my marriage because I never learned to question the things adults did on my behalf nor inflicted on my being, for there were none to speak of as I grew. I never developed the skills to negotiate for anything or ague because our life was peaceful and quiet. Some life skills are acquired as we grow, and negotiating was never my forte because it was never part of my life lessons at all.

Consequently, I truly believe that my husband would be like the caring men who surrounded me as I grew. My brothers never beat us, neither did my father, but he threatened many times. Undeniably, he was the disciplinarian and patriarchy of the family. His bark was worse than his bite as such we remained disciplined enough from his barks. As you can see, my life growing up was a time filled with love, joy, and family playing prominent roles. I thought my marriage would emulate my own parents' after these roles learned early on in childhood. Life nonetheless has a funny way of teaching me otherwise.

Instead of the loving faithful man that I looked forward to marrying one day, I got the opposite. Instead of being just a woman to take care of the home and children, life taught me to be independent and strong. I cannot blame things on my then husband but also thank him; otherwise, I would not have lived to my full potential.

Chapter Four

Secondary education and maturing

I was enrolled into primary school in January 1962. I was six and a half years old then. I cruised through primary school without any hiccups at all. The only hiccups were the constant reminders for our building fund from the school administrators. If families were falling behind with these funds, students would be sent home to remind parents. Lucky enough, I had an older sister, and she was the one who would miss classes after being sent home for such reminders, as only the eldest from every family was sent home. I felt sorry for my sister Melody whenever that happened, as that was her responsibility.

Academically, our performances were the best. From sub A until standard five, I knew I was always among the top three in my class. Only in standard four (4) I was not recognize as such. The teacher was a female who had been in love with my eldest brother, and when that affair ended, her way of paying him back was through me, as though I knew anything about love at that tender age. Besides that once, we all went home with awards for good academic performances, and our parents could not have been any prouder of us all each year.

At the end of 1969, I sat my first public examination. These were my standard six examinations. Our education system then was crafted after the British education system. No one would move to the next level of education without passing the examinations set at each level. We sat an examination mostly to test our skills in English, Math, and Content. Passing these initial examinations enabled us to proceed to high school level. If someone did not have passing grades of first or second class (scoring in the eighties and above), chances were little that they would have a place in high school.

I continued religiously with my education uninterrupted until I completed primary education in 1969. In high school, our curriculum then was broader in context to include geography, religious studies, history, chemistry, biology, and physics, with an indigenous language in the mix. Needless to say, minimum efforts were exerted to promote our indigenous languages, but rather, foreign languages were preferred. At the end of 1971, I sat my second major examination (RJC: Rhodesia Junior Certificate Form Two 2). I enjoyed schooling, as I loved reading and absorbing any knowledge teachers were willingly dishing my way. I participated wholeheartedly and would miss neither my assignments nor classes on purpose. However, I found out soon after my RJC examination that I could not go further because my father could not afford to keep me in school.

The imperialists utilized the examination-riddled education system to deprive the indigenous people of education. This lessened competition for their own children and continued to subject natives into the menial positions of employment. As such, while that young, I realized that even though we had access to education in a way, our oppressors were using it to maintain the status quo. I also knew from discussions with my brothers that the prohibitive bottleneck education system kept us on the lower levels of employment.

If anyone happened to make it through this level (RJC), then they would be subjected to another examination after two more years at the O level. The examinations at this level were set and marked by Cambridge or Oxford. Thus, Rhodesian students had the opportunity to compete at a national and an international level. A minimum of five or more subjects with C or better grades were considered admissible to A level. Passing English at the O level was mandatory for advancement. Without such standards, the unfortunate students would automatically be purged out of the educational system. Mostly it was us, the indigenous people.

The bottleneck was forced on us again after two more years, then students would sit the A level examination administered again by both Cambridge and Oxford. The minimum number of subjects at this level was three. At this level, the better the grades, the better one's chances were to be absorbed at the university level. These rigorous examinations were the final testament of intelligence that would eventually set students on their way to the highest institute of education—the university. In a way, they were separating men from boys or girls from women intellectually. We all knew subtly what this implied. By then, it was only one university that could absorb us; as such, we had to study our eyes out. We became real bookworms. We also wanted to be recognized as the elites of society, the ones who attained degrees.

Studying books from cover to cover was easy because we knew our fates depended on us passing those examinations. We had to read and study hard due to those measures put in place to grade our education. Failure was never an option for most black students. Our families counted on us to uplift them from their lives of poverty. We had responsibilities that kept us going. I am proud to say that I was able to meet the standard with flying colors as I knew I could; unfortunately, at the time, I could not proceed beyond RJC.

I had a continuous quest for knowledge that would have carried me through. The years in secondary school were some of the most impressionable, influential, and carefree years of my life yet tumultuous as well due to maturing. These were the years I was growing to be my own person. My education as a whole was preparing a well-rounded person. In secondary school, I met a Canadian female teacher who was also a Salvation Army officer who taught us sciences and exposed us to Canada, her home country, through letter writing. She had us write pen pal letters to different provinces in Canada, and my letter was sent to Quebec. The brochures I received had impressive and memorable images that I vowed there and then that one day I would visit the attractive Canada.

The Canadian teacher was also very good in drama, and I remember in the equivalent grade to tenth grade, we were raising funds to build an old people's home in Chi-town. Mrs. Captain Betty, as that was her name, helped us act a Nigerian play *Odale's Choice*.[8] I was engrossed in this character, Odale, so much that when as Odale, my character, chose death over my own life to avenge my brother Tawiya's death, the audience was shedding real tears. To make matters worse, my elder sister Melody, who acted as one of the village mourners, made people

---

[8]   Though I loved drama and was really good at it, I would never branch into it because acting was not perceived as a career at all. However, if I had a choice, drama would have been my career.

feel as though she was mourning my actual death. I was engrossed in the character that made it so real. The actors found it easy to mourn seeing how torn up my sister was over my character's demise. Had I had a choice back then, acting would have been my career, as I truly loved it.

I was also involved in sporting activities. I could run one hundred meters in under twelve seconds. I was in the youth choir, and I could sing an impressive tenor, as my voice was always deep. I would have trips to other schools for music, for drama, for various church activities, and for sports competitions. I was involved in as many activities as I could make time for. My education in a way was preparing a well-rounded person and befitting a responsible citizen.

Admittedly early on in my life at home, in primary and in secondary school and later in teacher-training college, I continued to excel, and I met extraordinary teachers who nurtured and nourished my insatiable appetite for education. As you can see, my education was not lacking in any shape or form, and just when I was beginning to thrive in this venture and enjoy my emancipation through education, things were about to take a drastic turn. I joyously completed my RJC in 1971. I had no clue that my education was about to come to an unexpected and abrupt end.

As I alluded to earlier, I was born of a polygamous[9] father whose own father had emigrated from South Africa in the late 1800s. The South African, my grandfather Elefi, a Mthembu by tribe, only had three children, and my father was the eldest with a half-sister and half-brother. My father, Norman, initially had three wives, but by the time I was growing up, there was only my mother who was the middle wife.

My father's first wife had two children, Stewart and Sarah. I did not grow up with them, for my memories of my eldest sister and eldest brother (culturally, it is unheard of to call them half siblings; they are my brother and sister and no half nothing) are only of them as adults. My sister Sarah was hard of hearing; as such, she was unable to speak. Back then, we could say she was "deaf and dumb." My father sent her to a school where she learned lip-reading. My sister Sarah had four children of her own—a boy and three girls. My brother Stewart was the eldest child of my father and was born in 1938. I am not sure, but I think he

---

9 My father had six girls and eight boys, and we were all educated beyond primary school. In fact, we were all professionals!

had about fourteen children of his own or somewhere around there, as he divorced about two or more previous women before he married his last wife.

My father and mother had nine of us—four boys and five girls. I was the fourth born. My siblings were Brother Nicholas, who was beheaded during our liberation war, one reason why I do not like to talk about wars. Nicholas was my mother's firstborn; he had one daughter, Doris, named after my mother, and only one to survive him. Next came Larry, who was a medical doctor, and he had seven children—five boys and two girls. He was followed by my elder sister Melody, a grade school teacher, and she had one son. The fourth in line was me, Avis, a grade school teacher and the second doctor in the family. I had five children of my own—three girls and two boys. After me was Brenda; we barely had a year between the two of us. I was born on June 9, one year and Brenda was born on June 2 the following year. Brenda was a high school teacher and had three children—one girl and two boys.

After Brenda was our beloved late brother Louis, whom we grew up with, as our elder brothers were by that time in boarding schools. Louis was an accountant and had three children—two girls and a boy named after his father. Diana was the seventh born, brought up to school-going age by my mother's sister, Aunt Mary. Diana was another accountant and had two girls and a boy. Next was Plaxedes, my adorable sister who died extremely young before she turned thirty. Her two children, one boy and one girl survived her. The last born of our family was my Chinese-educated little brother Levin, an engineer and the father of three children—two girls, and Levin Jr. I am happy to say by the time our parents both died, all our children were all born; and as such, they all know their grandparents. Though some of the grandchildren might have been still too young, but they had the opportunity to meet their grandparents and be held in their grandparents' tender and loving arms.

My other three brothers were Michael, Brian, and Brighton; these were from my father's third wife. Though we did not grow up in the same village, by the time we were all going to secondary school, I remember Brother[10] Michael would come to collect their tuition from our father at beginning of every term. My fondest memory of Brighton

---

[10] We never called our brothers by first name only without using "brother" as a sign of respect and "sister" for any female siblings older than oneself.

was when he asked our father for some pocket money! We all could not believe he had actually said it because we never asked for pocket money as long as we had enough for our school needs and our tuition. Brighton had done it, and he became more of a hero in our young impressionable eyes. In my memory, Michael was the disciplinarian like our father was. Brian was the happy-go-lucky person, easy to get along with but had a terrible temper at times if he felt disrespected. The youngest, Brighton, was the most quiet of us all my father, Norman's, children but had depth to his character, and he always told me one of his daughters reminded him of me all the time. Somehow those observed similarities made me feel closer to him.

I was the fourth born of my mother and the eighth of my father. Of all my siblings, by the time Brenda and I were going to high school, only Stewart and Sarah were married, and the rest of us were of school-going age. With so many young children, it is no surprise our family could not afford some of the things people take for granted now. My father bought me my first pair of shoes when I was fourteen years old and going to high school. This background is essential so that you can understand and appreciate why my father (a hard worker and loving man) could not afford our tuition. As hardworking as he was, he also truly and earnestly believed in education and how education could enable improve our lives for the better and provided for us in the best way he could.

His belief in education was strong. My father believed that education was an instrument that would ensure we develop as a people and as a nation. His motto was to educate us his children beyond his own level of education. Repeatedly, he would tell us that we needed to educate our own children beyond our own educational levels. My father's, Norman's[11], belief was if we kept educating our children then as a people and a nation, we would never retrogress but would be assured of development for our own empowerment. He believed in this till the day he died in 2005.

[11] I do not know really know his actual birthday. His middle name, Njanji (Railway Line), was a depiction of how his father had followed the railway line from South Africa into Rhodesia. It also was very symbolic of the hard life my father lead, as strong as the steel used to make the railway lines, as well as how healthy he was as a man.

With such a huge and young family, no wonder my father could not afford the completion of my sister Brenda's and my education. By then (1972), most of the high schools in the then Rhodesia were provided only through missionaries; and most were boarding schools, which were extremely expensive by our standards. This meant that my younger sister and I had to abandon our quest for education after completing tenth grade. This was one of my greatest disappointments ever in my life. Having been introduced to what our lives could have been with education and glimpsed into a future filled with promise we were devastated by the news that our father could not afford to take us any further educationally.

The first day schools were reopened in January 1972, it was a dark, bleak, and black day, like a day of mourning for Brenda and me of what could have been. Instead of us boarding our local buses heading back to school, we found ourselves herding cattle for the day! The irony of it all would never be lost to both of us for the rest of our natural lives. The events of the day are still crystal clear in my mind except that I cannot recall how we looked after the herd, but I remember that unending tears were shed and prayers were sent heavenward for the heavenly Father's intervention on our behalf. We were grateful by the end of the day that people's crops had not been destroyed as we had a dark cloud hanging over us and cared less for the herd of cattle.

I recall it was two days later that my cousin Michael[12] came home in the evening from Harare and reported that we had been summoned to go back to school. Due to our being well mannered, clever, smart, respectful, polite, and disciplined students that we were, fortunately, that had not gone unnoticed by our school principal and teachers. They wanted us to go back to school as soon as we could. We received the news with tears of joy as well as celebrations. Arrangements for our tuition would be made in due course. Again, we prayed and thanked the Lord for His divine intervention.

---

[12] He was the first albino I had ever met. Of all my aunt's children, he was the one closest to me because we both lived with my grandmother. When he first got employed by Howard District Council, he gave me all of his two pounds he earned a month for safekeeping! After completing form four, he was employed as a garden boy initially until he proved himself and became secretary of that council until his death.

The school officials at Harvard Institute had sent word through my elder sister, Melody (for the three of us were all educated at the same school), that we could go back to school as soon as possible. Immediately, arrangements were implemented for our father to pay our tuition in monthly installments, and that way he could afford to keep us all in school. That was when I learned that the Lord's answers to prayers are immediate,[13] not what I had been made to believe that His answers were slow in coming. I totally believed from then on that He is a merciful, miracle-working God, and He provides answers there and then, and most importantly, when we call upon Him by His name, He answers, and I do not doubt that up to this day. We were the most happy that night with the prospect of going back to school.

We hardly went to sleep that night as we were busy packing our dirty clothes into our school trunks. My mother had recommended we waited for a day to make sure we washed our clothes, but we could not follow her advice. It was as though we were afraid the school authorities would change their minds if we turned up a day later. We hardly had enough money for our bus fare and provisions, my mother managed to scrounge around enough for us to be on our merry way. My sister and I would always remain forever grateful to the Salvation Army and their extended hand of kindness, especially for intervening on our behalf. I know exactly what they mean, "Heart to God and Hand to man." They had extended their hand of kindness to us in our time of need. As a result, we have both remained strong members of the Salvation Army all our lives, and our children have become members too. The Harvard Institute administrators were able to resuscitate my sister's and my dreams. They, at the same time, made us believe in humanity and strengthened our faith.

For the next three years, while in teacher-training, I had to forgo my August holidays. Part of the payment arrangement between my father and the school administrators was that I had to work some school holidays to help defray some of my educational costs. Every August, I would go home for just a week then back to school to help with the interviewing process for the next intake of incoming teacher trainees.

---

[13] In church, I had always been taught we have to wait an awfully long time patiently for the Lord to provide answers to our prayers, but here it looked like he had provided answers immediately.

It was a nice way of my introduction into the work field without the pressure of being supervised like other employees.

I really enjoyed it when prospective students were in the dormitories, for I had company. It was beautiful interacting with high school students and knowing at some point I had been like them. The first time the interviewees were gone, during the first year 1972, that first holiday and the first night was a harsh experience on me. I did not know how I was going to spend the night by myself. I think my supervisors then had forgotten about me being in the dormitories alone.

I prayed all night long as the dormitory became overbearing. I was all alone. I hardly slept a wink. I was scared to death, and I did not turn off the lights. I heard every little noise during that night. The night was too long; I think it was twelve hours longer than usual. I did not cry. I was comforted by telling myself that I was lucky to have the opportunity of having to help establish myself like that. I was grateful to be there, knowing I would remain in school even if it meant me having to go through the fear of spending the night all by myself.

I breathed a sigh of relief when I saw the early signs of dawn for another bright new day beginning. I thought I could go to sleep then. Immediately around six that morning, one of my lecturers pounded loudly on the door. I could not imagine who it was until she called my name and I heard her voice, and realized it was Major Lindberg. I felt all the tension of the night drain away by hearing another human voice. I had never in my life spent a night by myself before that night. When I opened the door to let her in and she realized I was all alone, she literally cried while she held me in her arms. I was shivering like a reed in water with relief that I had made it through the night all alone. She hugged me for the longest time, and she immediately whisked me to her house where she continued to fuss over me like a mother hen for the next hour. She showed me where to shower, and when I was done, she gave me a hearty breakfast. After I had breakfast, she showed me to a bed where I slept until five in the evening. From then on, I knew where to go when the interviewees left. I never experienced another night like that fearful night again all my life.

Though I was never paid, real money for the services rendered went straight to my tuition, boarding, and other related costs. That was how I was introduced to the field of work as an educator in one of the most unconventional ways but very much hands-on. I remain forever grateful to the Harvard Institute administrators and the Salvation Army leadership then for affording me such an opportunity that enabled me to complete my teacher training. I feel as though I was one of the elites, and I always felt a certain resemblance of fulfilling a calling from above for all the years I worked as a primary school teacher.

Despite how I defined myself as a conditional teacher early in my career, I knew where my heart was regarding my profession. I loved my pupils, and I enjoyed seeing how they thrived year after year. As such, my earlier sentiments about my line of work did not really matter as I found absolute fulfillment in what I did for a living. I enjoyed and looked forward to each day that I spent in the school grounds with the students annually.

During the time I worked over the holidays, I missed home terribly as well as being with my family and my friends. I missed especially my grandmother though I no longer had to endure her endless journeys on foot as I did as a child. I knew she was getting on in age, and she had always told me of all the grandchildren she had cared for, I was the most patient one. I loved my grandmother unconditionally. I wanted to make the most of our time together because I did not know how much time she had left. I am happy my grandmother lived to see me graduate as a teacher, and I got to relate with her more as an adult. I also had the joy of doing things for her that other grandchildren had not done for her before she passed on, in April 1977. Anna, the woman who gave life to my father, gave me faith, sense of duty, and responsibility for our own lives and families.

Chapter Five

Tumultuous years in teacher training

As alluded to in the preceding chapters, my enthusiasm for education was nipped in the bud after completion of RJC; but despite the odds, I am happy I was able to go back to school, and I successfully trained to be a primary school teacher. The arrangements between my father and school authorities[14] would affect my first years' experience in teacher training. I was not part of the decision-making process but was simply told what course my education was soon to take. That was the beginning of 1972, and I found myself prematurely enrolled into a teacher-training college and describing myself initially as a conditional teacher. I truly believed that had it not been for the poor circumstances of my background and lack of high schools in my local community, I would have gone further with my education, probably I could have become a lawyer.

That is all water under the bridge, and it is not helpful to cry over spilt milk, and I can safely say I eventually developed a love for my life as a conditional teacher. It was only after I realized the benefits I yielded from my career that I appreciated it. I loved my career because it provided me with a stable source of income to support my children and not be utterly depending on a cheating husband for my livelihood. My career also provided me with an outlet from my troubled home life. It

---

[14] The arrangement was I work during school holidays to help defray my educational costs. On top of that, my father was allowed to make monthly payments toward my sister's education.

also enabled me to realize that I could change the circumstances of my life and not continue living with a batterer eternally.

In as much as the early circumstances of my life forced me into teaching and try as I might to figure what I could have become if not a teacher, I have no idea. Many times I had toyed with the idea of becoming a lawyer. I enjoyed arguing with my siblings and thought maybe that being a lawyer would have been a good career choice. No matter, I went straight from not completing high school to teacher training. Incredible as it was, I embarked onto my teacher-training days as best as I could; but inwardly, I seethed at the hand fate had dealt me.

Now as an adult and reflecting back, somehow I understand that plans and notions are changed due to circumstances fate deals us. Going into teacher training was a major responsibility and a major change for someone who was still dealing with adolescence, let alone having the decision for her life career made for her. All of a sudden, secondary school students who were my friends, colleagues, and classmates the previous year became my protégés the following January. I am not sure where they (administrators and lecturers) thought my maturity would have come from. That first term, I struggled with the word "maturity."

Shocking as that may sound, that was my reality. The previous year, I had been looking forward to furthering my education with my classmates as I looked forward to proceeding to form three (3), and suddenly I was thrown in this position that demanded I become more senior and more mature than they were. My tutors expected me to cordially ease into this position that had been forced upon me and behave more maturely. Their logical reasoning was that I being the elder of the two (between Brenda and I) would be set in a position where I could help my father financially after completing my teacher training. Logically, it all made good sense; but unfortunately, no one had bothered to consult with me or even ask me how I felt. They all assumed that as a child, and especially a girl child, I would be amenable to the idea and take to teaching without any problems.

In this instance, I know my culture was used to oppress me. Our culture endorses the belief that children should be seen and not heard. As such, children are voiceless; the decisions back then were made for us. Let me tell you that I knew back then that I would never do the same with my own children. Well, like they say, easier said than done. In as much as I tried, I did not involve my children in most of the decisions that involved their lives. The difference is they were able to question some of the decisions that I made on their behalf. Sometimes I did not have any answers. Parenthood does not come with handy manuals, but we learn to be better parents as we go. I had my children when I was young, so there was a lot of learning involved as well. Similar to what Oprah always said on her show, "When you know better, you do better."

Moving from high school into teacher training for me was a huge burden and a major responsibility. That transition was the hardest for me to undertake as I was barely sixteen years old. No wonder maturity became the biggest issue between my lecturers and me. I did not even know what they meant by demanding that I started acquainting myself with more mature friends in the teacher-training institute. Teacher-training students were not my age mates; my age mates were still in secondary school. In my mind and my belief, teacher-training students were never going to be my friends. My friends were still in high school. I had no common ground whatsoever with the college students. I felt that had I been a girl from a wealthy background, I would have proceeded with my education uninterrupted. That would have been the proverbial icing on my sweet cake.

My lecturers made my friendships with my former secondary schoolmates appear as misplaced, irresponsible, and absurd. There was completely nothing going on between us to consider inappropriate. Up to this day, I definitely know that my relationships with those high school students, whether boys or girls, were purely on platonic levels. How could they be otherwise? I had been taught of chastity and truly believed that my first intimate relationship with a man would be with my husband. I was also made to believe that any relationship intimate in any sexual form would cause my mother's back to break.

Can you believe it? Talk of imposing the fear of death into the mind of a child. Instead of discussing sex and sexuality in the true sense, we were only scared of getting amorous with the opposite sex. Whoever would want to be the cause of inflicting such a calamity on their mother's health? Obviously, I did not want that person to be me. As such, I avoided boys and sex as though they were the plague. Thus, whether I liked it or not, I was duty-bound to preserve myself for the man whom I eventually married; or put in another way, I waited for my Mr. Right to come along.

Trying to reason with the female and Western-educated lecturers would be of no avail. They were mostly single women Salvation Army officers who somehow believed each relationship between a boy and girl resulted in intimacy. I could not understand why, but now that I have been exposed to the Western culture, I can truly sympathize with them and the mammoth responsibilities they shouldered. Now that I have been exposed to this culture, unbelievably, teenagers as young as thirteen (and sometimes younger) already know of intimacy between men and women. I am not saying it did not and does not happen in my culture, but those were and still are considered extreme cases and were quite rare especially back in those days. On a regular basis, in this Western environment, I hear girls and boys in these young age groups talk of dating and kissing, and I wonder what the world is coming to. As such, my mentors could not understand me. They expected me to relinquish my circle of friends overnight who were still in secondary school just because I was training to be a teacher! It made no logic at all for me.

Definitely, during the first term in teacher training, there was a struggle between my lecturers and me. My dreams had suddenly been disrupted and had been crumbled to nothingness, as I saw them then. Suddenly, my life as I had pictured it (obscure as it was) was totally vanished. I had a vision that was as real as it could be in my young impressionable mind. In a way, I was in mourning for what could have become of my life, and they did not understand it. The struggle made one of my lecturers resort to speaking to me in my indigenous language one day and telling me, "Zororo pasi hauna, zororo riri kudenga," basically stating there was no rest for me here on earth but in the next life. Her words had the desired effect as I started to realize that life at times was unfair, harsh, cruel, unpredictable, and needed tough people to get going. I would recall her words years later, when struggling to make ends meet as a graduate student and single with my five children. Her words of wisdom would help me push myself more, and I believed that when I stopped working hard, I had to be dead.

During that year 1972, Rhodesia was going through an historic era. The Liberation War of Zimbabwe (the Second Liberation Chimurenga War) was an ongoing battle between the Rhodesia Front and the Zimbabwe African National Union -Patriotic Front (ZANU-PF) together with the Zimbabwe African Liberation National Army (ZANLA) who were labeled terrorists, and Africans called them guerilla warriors. I could never quite understand why they were labeled terrorists (or guerillas) because my eldest brother, Nicholas, had joined them. I would never perceive him as a terrorist, and I perceived him as a freedom fighter. Chiweshe (that is where Harvard Institute is located and where I was educated) was one of the major battlefields of Zimbabwe.

Early one morning, we woke up as usual to find the Rhodesian forces had pitched tents in our sports fields, which were directly behind the girls' dormitories. We were all scared and did not know what was going on. We looked at each other not sure how to express our fears. All through that morning, there were no classes. Everything was hanging on the balance, and we had no idea how that would influence our education. Everything seemed to suddenly engage into high gear. The school principal demanded that the Ministry of Education agree to let the whole institute close down for our safety. Harvard Institute was composed of a secondary school, a teacher-training college, a hospital and nursing school, Salvation Army officers training college as well as the Primary Practicing School for teachers in training. This was a huge institute, and this disruption meant grave disruptions to many people's education and, ultimately, their lives. All were to be closed down except for the hospital and the officers' training college.

The administration obviously went into overdrive that morning as by ten o'clock, buses lined up to take us all to our homes. We neither were asked to pay for the fares as this was an emergency nor were we allowed to leave any of our belongings behind within the school buildings as we usually did. These were unpredictable times, full of uncertainty, and no one could foretell how long the institute would remain closed or whether we would be able to ever come back. Many schools had been closing down around the country and not reopening, and we were wondering whether we had become the latest victims of the liberation struggle.

In our minds, it appeared and felt as though that was the end of the road for most of us anyway. It was a traumatic experience to wrap our young minds around. Except for September 11, 2001, I remember this as being the most troubling violent time I had lived through besides the enclosing of people into fences like animals during that liberation war a year later. To see people caged in fences like animals was another trauma that I have always played repeatedly in my mind, and I wish no other people in the world have to ever live like that.

As the second liberation war was raging on in Rhodesia, we knew about it; but somehow as students, we had remained cushioned from the harsh realities of war within the fences of Harvard Institute. The war remained remote from us as a body of students, but individually, we all had been scathed by it as we all had one or more family members that had crossed the borders into Mozambique and other neighboring countries to join the freedom fighters. War was everywhere around us, even in the mountains and villages of Chiweshe. It was in the valleys of Eastern District in Manicaland, and we heard about it on radios. In the south, it was wreaking havoc on the masses. Schools were closing down around us because of the raging battles. In our little corner there at Harvard Institute, somehow we felt safe, but not for long.

Suddenly with the taking over of Harvard Institute as a temporary base for the Rhodesian Front armed forces, we were thrown unaware right into the thick of it. This meant my maturity[15] was not going to be an immediate issue at all, as unexpected ruthless times sometimes force people to mature beyond their chronological ages. However, the closing down of Harvard Institute was a welcome disruption especially for me. This meant a break from the monotony of books, study, and the struggle I was having with my lecturers. This gave me ample time to reassess, reevaluate, and deal with the uncertainty of my settling down into the teaching profession, the profession that chose me.

For six complete unplanned weeks, our school remained closed down. That unplanned interim period forced me into the classroom to interact with primary school students even before being fully prepared as a teacher. My first teaching experience would be at my local community where I grew up and was educated. My teachers from grade one (1) to standard six were Captain Mapondera (sub A), Miss Kunaka (sub b), Mr. Chawuruka, (standard one), Mr. Chiureki (standard two), Mr. Madzivanzira (standard three), and Miss Mundiya (standard four), Mr. Chidamba (standard five), and Mr. Mugwagwa (standard six. I loved them all except my standard four teacher. She had been in love with my eldest brother, Nicholas, and when the affair had soured and was finally over, she vented her anger on me. She was mean toward me. I felt as

---

[15] I could not believe why I was being forced to behave maturely at all. After all, I was only sixteen years old and believed I had a lot more years before it suddenly hit me that I was mature.

though I had been the one responsible for their breaking up. As a result, it was the only grade I never made top three at the end of the year.

During that interim in 1972, when Harvard Institute was closed down, I taught from grade one to grade five. I was with a different mentor[16] every week. What was more fulfilling than being home and teaching my relatives' children, members of my own family, people from my own community where I had grown up? I was working with teachers who had enabled my primary education to become real and the ones who had helped me aspire to be a better person. I was there. Time was there. There was no time for self-pity. There was no time for grieving what could have or might have been. I was granted the opportunity I desperately needed to mature. I had to be responsible. I had been granted the opportunity to realize how lucky I was even training to be a conditional teacher as I labeled myself. I had to demonstrate that I had received a solid foundation and strived daily to be an effective teacher, a significant member of my community, one that my teachers would be proud to point out that I was their product. I did not let them down at all. I worked hard and enjoyed my time there.

Melfort Primary School was now providing me with a nurturing safe haven that I desperately needed in those turbulent times to anchor me down in my profession. Melfort Primary School was affording me the opportunity to realize that I was lucky to be training as a teacher at all! That period made me appreciate the little things I usually took for granted. The temporary closing down of Harvard Institute was like an interlude that had prematurely stopped my life and had suddenly become a comma, which afforded me some fuel to shift full speed ahead. I needed that pause so that I could reassess and appreciate the many blessings of my life that otherwise would have passed unappreciated.

During this time, I learned to appreciate every day as a gift from someone more powerful than me. I knew that gift did not come from Anna, my grandmother, nor did it come from Doris, my mother. From then on and for the rest of my life, I perceived and received my daily life as a present that I did not know how long would be granted. Every

---

[16] Barely two years before, I had been a student there. Realities of what to wear and look like as a teacher were difficult; therefore, I continued to wear my school uniform as I could hardly afford the cost of ordinary clothes.

day was continuously a cherished and treasured gift that the good Lord bestowed on me through His kindness and clemency. I realized then, being a conditional teacher or not, I had the rare opportunity of working with children and an opportunity to be used according to His will.

Teaching suddenly became my obsession and my lifesaver. How could I not fall in love with the children I taught? How could I forget those open, innocent, and trusting faces that I met every morning for those six weeks? Those children were responsible for the huge change and the 180 degrees turn in my attitude toward teaching. I saw myself in their faces just as eager to learn at their ages. I saw myself in their open and trusting faces that teachers knew best. I saw myself in their innocence that I would make it no matter what as long as I continued with my education.

As a result, once again, circumstances made me realize the role and importance of teaching in shaping children's lives. Honestly, teaching was one of my many roles I never took lightly nor for granted. In my life, I had many roles. I had the role as a teacher, a mother, an aunt, a local officer for my church, a best friend, a daughter, an abused wife as well as a willing and able daughter-in-law. In all those roles, I believed in doing everything to the best of my power, ability, and knowledge. In all my life, I never took any of the roles for granted nor lightly no matter how little the role would be.

I loved teaching and truly believed, alleged, and accepted it as my special and personal destiny. I knew I had been predestined to be involved in touching and changing the lives of children. I knew teaching them, being a living example in their lives, or just being available when they needed a shoulder to lean on or provide a friendly listening ear was my most satisfying destiny. I did not claim to be a role model as I felt, and I still feel that role models are supposed to be flawless. As such, as an example, my students would learn from my imperfect life, my experiences, and my many mistakes. I was a person full of flaws. However, every day I strived to improve on being a better person, a better teacher, a better mentor, a better sister, a better daughter, a better mother, a better wife, and a better friend. In all my turmoil, I never lost sight of these multiple roles of my destiny. I now realize how, as human beings, we have become vulnerable to issues that are egotistic, which fade into oblivion. We tend to dwell on the mundane; as such, we tend to lose sight of the more important and meaningful relationships in our lives and life experiences.

All my life lessons of love for family, love of God, love of nature, and love for neighbors alike would be handed down to my school children. It all began in my own community at Melfort Primary School. I recall even today that my own biological children at times felt jealousy of the children I taught. I invested energy into the preparation of my lessons. I managed to be friendly and yet not too friendly that I would lose their respect. I managed to set high expectations and made them all believe in themselves, that there was nothing under the sun they could not achieve. I managed to motivate them that at times it scared me that if they failed and did not encounter teachers or other adults who believed in them, they would fall to pieces. I was glad to go back to school six weeks later, less my negative attitude. I am happy to say I now saw it as a blessing that I even had that opportunity.

In 1974, I completed my three years of the teacher-training course. Before completing my training, I had another traumatic experience in June 1973. The Rhodesian Front government decided to enclose whole villages of people in the Chiweshe Communal lands into fenced communities. These were measures taken to ensure that freedom fighters would starve during the struggle without the villagers' assistance. Talking about it was one thing, seeing the government put their plans into action was another kind of trauma, and I always wondered how we even survived those extremely traumatic years.

The military vehicles were used to transport people from their villages to the enclosed areas. Old people, young people, women, children were all being caged like wild animals. There were no shelters available in those fences. There would be no running water initially. There were no toilets. The atrocities of that era would always give me chills and nightmares all my life. This was right in the middle of our winter months in June. Elderly people, children, able men, and women were subjected to conditions hardly imaginable as possible in my world. I had a lot of compassion and empathy for them, but we were rendered useless because we were still so young.

Missionaries like the Salvation Army officers at Harvard Institute tried to assist, but they were overwhelmed by the enormity of that government exercise. As students, we were requested to assist with the distribution of food and blankets, which only made the trauma even worse on us. We were not just watching from a distance, but we were involved with the worst treatment of human beings ever inflicted on the blacks of Rhodesia by their presumed government. Some of the students at Harvard Institute were from these communities, and come nighttime, all we did was huddle together and comfort each other to sleep.

Domestic animals such as pigs, goats, and donkeys were abandoned. Dogs, chickens, ducks, sheep, and all farm animals were being left to fend for themselves. Someone's own lifetime of hard work was being reduced to nothing just by the click of the prime minister's fingers. All we could do was hold each other at night and cry ourselves to sleep, praying and hoping the morrow would bring something better, but nothing was better with the dawn of a new day. Tomorrow seemed to continuously bring more dismal and depressing news about the struggle. I am not sure how we survived mentally besides turning to our faiths.

During this time, some neighboring schools in Mt. Darwin and Bindura districts were forced to close down, and the students found sanctuary at Harvard Institute. We thought we had endured the worst of the war, but our experiences were nothing compared to theirs, especially students from St. Albert's and Mavhuradonha[17] schools. Their stories were heart-wrenching, graphic, tragic, and nothing anyone would wish on their worst enemy. The hardships brought us closer to our faiths. In church on Sundays, as students, we began to seek greater power than the adults who surrounded, loved, and cared for us. Our songs reflected the inward turmoil we were enduring. We put more effort into our studies and realized we had no option but to just see where the war would either take or leave us, if it ever left us alive.

An excursion of students was occurring overnight. Students were abandoning everything to go and join the freedom fighters. Suddenly, studies that had been of utmost importance, for taking us out of our poverty were not as important. No one could blame us. The war was on our minds, in our lives, obstructing our studies. It was everywhere we turned. Who could blame all the students abandoning everything to join

---

[17] In the mid-1970s, it became common practice that if one school closed due to the struggle, schools still open would absorb the students; but eventually, even the open schools would be so overwhelmed that nothing was happening any more to absorb the unfortunate students.

the good fight? Everyone wanted to be part and parcel of this historical struggle that was taking place right before our eyes.

Amid all the turmoil and confusion, my sister Brenda and I sat down and discussed whether we could afford to abandon our studies and join the noble struggle. We knew the importance of education in uplifting our lives. The importance was drilled in us all our lives. We literally agreed there was no way we were going to abandon our studies and join the good fight. We felt we had paid our dues to the struggle as our oldest brother, Nicholas, had already joined the freedom fighters. He had abandoned his studies at the University of Rhodesia subsequently to become a freedom fighter. In that light, we felt our family was represented in the armed struggle per se. Blood was being shed, and we were not ignorant to the fact. We knew our mother, Doris, could not afford to have another child take off to join the freedom fighters no matter how noble it was.

Growing up, Nicholas had been our role model, our inspiration, and our parents' hope. They had invested in his quality education from the time he was in standard four (4) until he went to the university. His leaving broke our mother's heart, but she always hoped he would come back alive. My mother's health literally nose-dived years later in 1980, when she learned that my brother Nicholas was beheaded during the war. She could not believe that her oldest son had taken off to go and die for the land he so much loved and never came back to say goodbye. As a result, Brenda and I, during our studies, when everyone else around us was leaving to join the good fight, felt obliged to stick it out. We felt the obligation was on us to take our family out of poverty. We made a pact never to quit on our family no matter how hard things became. As a result, the years slowly rolled by as we struggled; but finally, we made it.

Chapter Six

Brothers, sisters, and our education

My oldest brother, Nicholas, was born in December of 1948. He was our mother's firstborn and our father's third born. From our mother, I understood that Nicholas used to cry a lot as a baby; that was why he was also named Crybaby, (Njodzi). Overall, growing up, Nicholas was a healthy, helpful, and obedient son. He started his primary education at Melfort Primary School, our local Salvation Army-sponsored school. By the time he completed standard three (3) at Melfort Primary School, our parents sent Brother Nicholas to boarding school. Back then, Melfort School did not have standards four (4) to six (6). The primary boarding school he went to catered to standards four (4) up to standard six (6). Brother Nicholas spent three years at boarding school completing his primary school education. For his secondary education, forms one (1) to four (4), he went to Mazoe High School. Mazoe High School was administered by Salvationists. Later as an adult, I would meet some of his schoolmates, and they would tell me how sterling he was as a student and a leader. Finally, he completed his high school at Fletcher High School, another boarding school where he completed his form five (5) and six (6).

According to our mother, Nicholas was highly intelligent and a very pragmatic son. Our brother taught our mother how to be a better farmer even though our mother, Doris, did not have many resources at her exposure. Our mother, Doris, claimed that Nicholas would look into the environment and would come up with ideas on how to improve our lives. One such idea I also clearly remember personally was when as kids, we crossed Hunyani River to pick up dry cattle dung from the white farmlands. We would later use the cow dung as manure for our maize crop. We did not have many cattle to provide us the much-needed manure to reap good harvests. As such, Nicholas encouraged us to pick the dry cow dung from the neighboring farmers. We put the cow dung in huge piles and watered it to facilitate the fermentation process so that we could use the cow dung as manure. After the watering, we would pound the dung to crush it into smaller pieces, and we turned the piles over. It was grueling work, but we had a motivator and an inspiration for a big brother in Crybaby.

During school holidays, our brother Nicholas would also bring three of his best friends to help with the plowing and tilling of the maize fields. Our school holidays back then were only three weeks long. The four young teenagers would spend at least one week at our place and the next two in Mhondoro and Chiweshe, where some of our brother's friends came from. In order to work in the fields, the young men would wake us up around half-past four. We would all till and plow the fields until ten or eleven o'clock in the morning, and then we would head home to rest. This would happen religiously every day until school holidays were over or when the tilling or harvesting was completed.

Our brother Nicholas taught us that no work was too hard for us to do. He also taught us no matter how well educated we were, no work was below our standards. Nicholas would not just tell us what to do, but he would be right there with us, teaching and showing us how to do it. He made the manual labor we engaged in seem fun because he would tell us jokes all the time while we worked. Consequently, we would not realize how rapid time passed or how hard the work was. Nicholas distracted us from the tasks by keeping us constantly entertained.

We looked forward to the times he would be home as we were always entertained by his stories and his jokes. As such, when much later in our educational development while at Harvard Institute, when the issue of abandoning our studies came up, for the two of us (Brenda and I), it was no-brainer, as we knew what Nicholas would have told us. I feel at times that we engaged in our studies in order to please our brother Nicholas than to please our parents.

Life for him was like a big happy, enjoyable adventure all the time. For example, when his girlfriend became pregnant, it was like a joke. He jokingly told our mother to prepare the home for visitors who would be coming to join us for life. Our mother would just laugh that off, saying no visitors stayed for life. We only believed him when Mazzie came to stay with us, and she was heavily pregnant with his first child. Mazzie was the mother of his one and only child, Doris, our mother's first granddaughter (our brothers' children were all either named after their grandparents, their fathers, or their aunts except for a couple).

Although my brother loved life, he also was very politically minded. At the end of 1970, our brother Nicholas and his best friends were studying at the University of Rhodesia. I remember one holiday, he had crossed the Rhodesia border into the neighboring Eastern Country to Mozambique to study and observe the freedom fighters' training camps. When he came back home in December 1968, he would tell us the stories of these camps, but to us they were mere stories. We did not really believe they were real. He taught us under the dark of night how to sing some of the liberation war songs (e.g. Ndiwe Ladner Burke ndiwe waunza hondo), and we had fun. For current news on the advancement of the freedom fighting, we listened to Radio Tanzania and another freedom fighters' radio from Lourenco Marques (LM Radio) from Mozambique late at night.

Those were some of our earliest lessons into the African political arena and military leadership for liberation. The African political leaders I recall to present day included Julius Nyerere of Tanzania, Jomo Kenyatta of Kenya, Milton Obote of Uganda, and the assassination of Patrice Lumumba of the Belgian Congo. He talked also of the minorities like Ian Smith of Rhodesia and Hendrik Verwoerd of South Africa. That was the first time I ever heard of the United States of America in combination to the assassination of Patrice Lumumba. My brother Nicholas specified that Patrice Lumumba had been murdered due to the conspiracy between the Belgians protecting their nationals in Belgium Congo and the Americans protecting the national wealth of diamonds (always the capitalist nation). Most of these historical lessons flew above my understanding, as I had no clue where these countries where and who these leaders were. That did not deter my brother's efforts in educating us. It was during that time that I also heard of Kwame Nkuruma of Ghana, Haile Selassie of Ethiopia, Gamal Abdel Nasser of Egypt, the handkerchief-bearing Kenneth Kaunda of Zambia and his very popular slogan "One Zambia, One Nation," and Hasting Kamuzu Banda of Malawi.

By the end of 1970, Brenda and I were enrolled at Harvard Institute for our high school education. By then, my brother was a student at the University of Rhodesia. However, at the end of 1970, as a member of the Harvard Singing Company, we had a trip to Chinhoyi. In Chinhoyi was the last time I saw Brother Nicholas. We had gone there for the weekend church services. One of my friends sprained her ankle. During the lunch break on Saturday, we took her to the clinic. Johanna, the clinical nurse, asked us whether there was anyone with the surname Manning, I was there. As such, I indicated to Johanna I was a Manning. She told me she had something to show me in her backroom. I followed her into the back room, and I saw my eldest brother Nicholas lying smiling on Johanna's bed. Those were strange circumstances for me to see my brother in another woman's bedroom (considering he was already married). Later, I learned that Johanna had been one of his longtime girlfriends, and all people thought at some point that he would marry her. Johanna left my brother and me alone in her bedroom.

I do not completely recall how I reacted, but I was shocked to see him there. I think obviously we greeted, and we exchanged a few pleasantries. I did not sit down, as I could not share the bed with him as a cultural sign of respect to my brother. Moreover, there was no chair in the room. I remained standing. I was not in the room for long, but I still remember his farewell as daylight today. He held my right hand tightly as we bid each other farewell. I could not believe my eyes as tears welled up in his eyes, and he started to cry. I could not fathom why. I was tongue-tied. I wanted to ask him why he was crying, but I could not find the right words. However, it made me sad to see him cry as I had never seen him emotional like that before.

I left that back room with a heavy heart. Later I would tell our mother when we learned at the beginning of 1971 that he had abandoned his studies to join the freedom fighters. We automatically knew I had been the last person to see him alive among family members. Probably my brother Nicholas had cried, knowing what he was about to do. I wished all my life I had asked him one question; I wished I had kept in touch with Johanna. Perhaps she could have shed some light into how our brother Nicholas left Rhodesia and where he went. We never heard any news about his whereabouts until 1979, after the independence talks in London, and the Lancaster House talks, except probably for a troubling dream I had in 1975, the year he was presumably murdered.

By 1975, I was a teacher in Derby. One night in June, I dreamt my brother Nicholas had been held prisoner. In my dream, when I visited him in prison, he was brought to me with his arms tied to his back. He was badly emaciated, and to make matters worse, he was naked. Some people were dragging his body, and he would not say a thing to me. I could not see his face, but instinctively in my dream, I knew it was my brother Nicholas. It was a very disturbing and vivid dream. I was troubled. I never stopped thinking about that strange dream. When I went home the following weekend, I shared my dream with my mother. My mother, Doris, assured me that to dream of someone in ill health meant the person was healthy and living well. She told me it was a good sign that Nicholas was doing well.

Although my mother's interpretation of my dream calmed my spirits, I was always disturbed, and the dream vividly remained with me all these years. It would be after the independence talks in 1979 in London that we would learn about Nicholas's murder. We also learned that Nicholas's execution was sometime in 1975. The 1975 troubling dream would be the basis for my paying particular attention to my dreams. We lost our firstborn and family hero to the liberation war, and his death was revealed to me through dreams. From then on, I became more attentive to my dreams.

After the London and the Lancaster House talks in 1979, there was an agreement for independence for Rhodesia. All the combatants came home. People were reunited with their beloved ones. We waited for our brother to no avail. It was early in 1980, before independence, that we learned about the beheading of my brother from one of his very close friends Enwett, who had survived and came back home. Our beloved brother Nicholas met with his death in a painful way in Plum Tree. According to his friend, Nicholas was betrayed by one of his comrades who was given $25,000 by the Rhodesian Front led by the Rhodesian Front regime circa 1975. The pain inflicted on our family by his loss would always be unbearable, and that part only would most likely take a lot to chronicle here. However, it is part of our family's painful history. As a family, we hope that someday we are going to find out the truth and tell the whole story. We have so far found neither comfort nor closure even with the passage of time.

The story that his friend Enwett told my mother was that her first born son Nicholas was in the High Command of the Zimbabwe African

National Liberation Army (ZANLA), the military wing of Zimbabwe African National Union -Patriotic Front (ZANU-PF), the political wing, which was formed in the 1960s. ZANLA had caches of arms in the south of Wood in Rhodesia. Occasionally, when freedom fighters ran out of arms, they would arrange with some of their comrades within Rhodesia to come and help with digging up of the weapons. In my brother's case, one of his closest friends who was in Rhodesia by the name of Romano sold him out to Rhodesia Front.

My brother had colleagues who remained within the country and they used to meet under the cover of dark at night to unearth their buried weapons. On that particular night in 1975, Nicholas did not know that his friend had become a turncoat. He arrived at the place where they were supposed to retrieve their weapons. As they were exchanging greetings with his friend, there were sudden bright lights that supposedly surprised our brother. Nicholas had simply walked into his death trap conveyed by one of his closest friends, Romano. Our brother Nicholas's execution happened on the spot through a bombardment of gunshot bullets. The turncoat and his fellow evildoers chopped off his head, which they delivered to the Rhodesia Front government. The turncoat received his payment from Rhodesia Front regime. My brothers' comrades in arms later retrieved his headless body and buried his headless body somewhere in a neighboring country south of Rhodesia. That was all we knew about our brother's death. We lost our brother, our family's hero, one of the many unsung heroes of Zimbabwe's liberation.

I know this was not unique to us, but many families endured this loss. I always attribute the downfall of our mother's health to my brother's death. Occasionally, my mother would ask what the Rhodesian Front regime did with his head. No mother should ever have to go through such violent deaths of their children, especially their firstborns.

After Nicholas came Larry. He was born in December of 1950. Larry pretty much followed his older brother's example where his educational pursuits were concerned. He was given a middle name[18] as according to my mother, he enjoyed good health as a baby. I remember Larry did not like physical work like Nicholas, but he kept us laughing. Most times, Larry would try to get out of the plowing and tilling of the fields by

---

[18] Chigwindiri The strong one in our ethnic language, the strong and always jovial one, and it was a befitting name to my second eldest brother.

faking nonexistent illnesses or fights with his younger brother Louis. My mother would always chastise Larry regarding his behavior, but he was extremely smarter than our mother. He would manage to outwit our mother and, most times through, his humor. These are some of my earliest memories of my younger brother. Larry was always jovial, carefree, loving, and laughing. He used to find humor in everything, and some of us would simply laugh along with him, even without getting the joke.

Though he deplored physical labor, Larry was not lacking intellectually. His intelligence challenged the administrators at Mazoe High School, where he was enrolled for forms one (1) to form four (4). He outwitted them so much that at the end of his four years there, they did not give him a good recommendation to complete his high school education. Because of my brother's political exploits, after he completed form four (4) at Mazoe High School, the administrators had endorsed on his school reference letters that he was politically minded. They feared that he would politically influence and pollute other students' minds to follow his political example. During that era, political mindedness meant revolting against the Rhodesia government and the Rhodesian Front Party. Due to that poor recommendation, it appeared as though Larry's education was doomed prematurely terminated at the end of form four (4). However, he would utilize his intelligence and find a way to outwit the Mazoe High School administrators and complete his educational pursuits.

During his struggle to find a school, my Brother Larry's paths crossed with a catholic priest, Father Mangan. The priest was able to integrate my brother into the pool of private students he was mentoring. This Catholic priest was responsible for helping my brother Larry complete his high school education. The same priest was also instrumental in helping get my brother enrolled into a medical school in Congo Kinshasa in 1970. We all celebrated Larry's enrollment into the medical field. This was a first in our family and our community; no one had ever dared become a medical doctor. In 1970, our brother Larry flew away to Congo; it was the same year I was enrolled into secondary school at Harvard Institute for my form one (1).

We used to communicate with our brother through letters and by postcards. As the three sisters at Harvard, we enjoyed receiving his postcards to show off to our school friends. We even tried to hook him up with girls for when he would come home for vacations. I remember one of my own classmates who honestly loved my brother and would wait for days for any form of communication from him. During his holidays when he came home, girls would swarm to him like moths to a candle. As for my friend, she would tell me she did not mind sharing. According to her, as long as she knew when she was with him, she would be the center of his attention that was all she asked for.

From my brother, the doctor-in-training, I learned a lot. I remember that in one of my letters to him, I tried to share my concerns of our grandmother Anna becoming senile. Unfortunately, I had just come across the word "dementia." I described my own diagnosis of her mental status to him. In his response, he educated me that as a nonmedical professional, I never diagnose the disease but give the signs and symptoms. I had no medical qualification to give such a diagnosis, as my diagnosis could have been wrong. I felt as though I had been gently chastised like a child or put in my place. I was not hurt but rather grateful that at least it had been my brother to put me into my proper place.

I remember in August 1975, Larry came home for a much-needed vacation. We really had a good time with him. As he left for the final period before his graduation in Congo Kinshasa, we threw him a going-away party on the balcony of Rhodesia Airport. We all had one too many drinks. It was in the thick of the Second Liberation (Chimurenga) War. Planes were being bombed down. People everywhere were a little paranoid about where the presumed terrorists would turn up. As our brother was boarding to fly away, we all became a little emotional. We began to throw away tables and chairs as we cried. In a short time, we did not observe how the balcony had emptied of all the people who had been waiting to welcome family members and friends. In our drunken demonstrations of emotions, we realized we scared everyone off the balcony with our unbecoming behavior. We were honestly mortified. We felt for a short time we had taken charge of the entire airport. In a silly way, it was exhilarating to us all, except to our down-to-earth mother, Doris. She reprimanded us for drinking beer senselessly.

As such, during our most influential years, our two elder brothers were not home anymore. Nicholas had abandoned his studies at the then University of Rhodesia at the end of 1970. Larry had left for his medical degree in Congo Kinshasa mid-1970. The three sisters, Melody, Brenda, and I, were all in secondary school at Harvard Institute. Whereas Larry came back at the end of 1978, after our Brother Nicholas's murder during the liberation war, we were never the same. Consequently, our elder brothers were not there when we needed them the most. Nonetheless, their influence earlier on in our lives remained with us forever. We had so many good memories and influences from our brothers so much that even during their absence; they continued to influence our decisions. We would always ask ourselves what they would have advised us.

As for Dr. Larry, unfortunately, by the time he came home in 1978, we were all maturing into young women. My sister Melody was married, so I was. By the time he made it back, I was already a mother to my son Elvin. Elvin was barely a year. Before Dr. Larry even knew what was happening, he became the family doctor to the increasing nephews and nieces. Where our children were concerned, there was no baby illness that would go to a private doctor before our brother. We all called him from the four corners of Zimbabwe no matter what time of day or night. One thing I am sure of was that he was glad when those child-rearing years were over, as we kept him busy with our twenty children, not counting his own and Doris, who was a little older than the rest. My brother had seven children of his own with four different women.

We, nonetheless, had younger brothers, Louis and Levin. Though they were much younger, we all have good memories with them too. Louis was born in October of 1960. Louis was very close to Brenda. Most times while young, the two of them would exchange clothes. Many times we would find Brenda in Louis's shorts and vice versa. Initially, people used to reprimand them until they realized how close the two were, and they left them alone. Our mother, Doris, never made an issue of their cross-dressing. For us as kids, we found it funny maybe that was why they continued cross-dressing. We also played all the childhood games with Louis and Levin. Later as adults, Louis appeared closer to us than the rest of our brothers. I truly believe it was because we shared our childhood with him, and that brought him closer to us, and he was closer in age than the other three brothers.

By the time Louis was going to high school, he somehow failed to secure a place anywhere in a conventional school. Our mother took Brother Louis to the Catholic priest who had helped older brother Larry. The priest not only liked Brother Louis, but he also totally fell in love with him. He took my younger brother under his wing. Each time we visited with Louis at the school, he would be running errands for the priest. The

Catholic priest also trusted my young brother with many things. The priest became my brother's mentor right through high school. Walking through the suburbs of Harare with Louis was a revelation. We would not go for long without meeting someone who knew younger brother. His popularity as a young man equaled his popularity as a grown man.

As Louis completed his high school, he found a university in Wales where he went for his first degree. He had his first degree in financial management. We missed having him in our lives during his education abroad as he never took his responsibilities as brother lightly. When he came home, he worked as a government auditor for a short time, and he later transitioned to private banks such as the Zimbabwe Development Bank and the First Merchant Bank. Later in his career, Louis worked for several renowned banks in Zimbabwe. He was financially well informed, and we all as a family continuously sought his advice where money matters were concerned. Louis had three children with three different women. Unfortunately, my brother Louis passed away in July of 2007. He is sincerely missed up to this day.

As for the youngest brother, Levin was on born Easter Day in April of 1968. He was educated at Melfort Primary School. By the time Levin was growing up financially, the family situation was much better. As a result, Levin was educated at Bernard Mzeki High School, one of the most prestigious Anglican High Schools in Zimbabwe. He also enjoyed his final high school years in some of the prestigious secondary schools in elite suburbs of Harare. When it came to his college education, he had a choice between the Eastern and the Western countries. Levin had been offered a place by a Canadian university and a Chinese university. He followed his heart and went to the East. Levin was educated to be an engineer in China.

From late 1988 to early 1993, Levin was studying in China. He was the only one in the family to be educated in the East, and this would later pay him dividends when Zimbabwe underwent sanctions from the West due to Robert Gabriel Mugabe's political ideologies. Chinese businesses started flourishing in Zimbabwe, and my brother never lacked for a well-paying job. As you can tell, all our brothers had ventured elsewhere for their education. It was against such an educational background that personally I ventured against as a sub-standard teacher and longing to fulfill a standing promise to my father in 1974 that I would later strive to improve academically. When I decided to fulfill that promise, I thought of a country that none in the family had ventured to. I wanted to color my own rainbow.

As for my elder sister, Melody, who was born in June 1953, her education was a huge struggle. She completed standard six (6) three years before I did. She could not find a place for form one (1); therefore, the whole of 1967, she was a school dropout. She reenrolled into standard six (6) in 1968 with Nicholas's encouragement and proceeded to secondary school the following year. She went to Harvard Institute, where Brenda and I later joined her in 1970. While in high school, Sister Melody was extremely good in math and science. Math teachers would consult with her for any problems they could not solve. I could never understand how she did it because math was my worst subject. She sailed through high school with ease and trained to be a teacher in 1978. However, she got married before she went for teaching in 1978.

Before she decided to get married in 1974, she taught as a nonprofessional in one of the commercial farmlands of Mazoe. She was there for close to three years. She stayed with one of our younger sisters, Diana, while Diana went to seventh grade there. I enjoyed visiting with her later, as I started working myself. One thing I would always be grateful to her for is sharing her clothes. At the end of 1974, at graduation, I could not afford to buy a graduation dress. Sister Melody lent me two of her own best dresses that I used for all the pre-graduation parties. As for my graduation day dress, I proudly wore my Salvation Army uniform.

My younger sister Brenda and I, because of how Rhodesia readjusted primary school system in 1969, by 1970, we ended up going for form one (1) at the same time. Instead of eight years in primary school, the duration was reduced to seven years. Brenda caught up with me and that was how we ended up going to form one (1) at the same time. Whereas Brenda continued with her secondary education, mine was prematurely nipped and redirected into teacher training. Brenda, after form four (4), spent 1974 involved in a pilot program for students who had completed secondary education at Harvard. Their class taught commercial subjects; unfortunately, the program never really took off the ground. It only lasted for a year. However, at the end, my sister Brenda attended a teacher-training college and became a high school teacher. Educationally, we all excelled, and the three of us became teachers at different levels. I was specialized in infant education, Brenda in secondary education, and my elder sister Melody specialized in upper primary education.

As for our younger sisters, Diana and Plaxedes, they had challenges of their own. These two grew up in a different era than us, the three elder sisters. Diana and Plaxedes were closer to each other and complemented each other very well. While growing up, Diana would be the force behind solving their personal problems. Diana would push Plaxedes to voice concerns. For example, the family pot used to cook our *sadza*[19] in was too small for the growing number of children. One week, when our father came home, Diana pushed Plaxedes to voice that concern. All family members were flabbergasted about how Plaxedes could think of that issue only to learn later that she was voicing Diana's concerns. That was how they were, even as adults when they married. They were closer than thieves, and they were each other's best friend. I felt sorry later for Diana when Plaxedes died prematurely at the age of twenty-nine.

Their education, though much easier than ours because older siblings were in positions to assist financially, examinations remained a deterrent. Diana would have examination fevers, not that she was incapable, but the way of absorbing students into secondary schools was highly questionable. As such, after failing to be absorbed one year, she would approach examinations with a certain apprehension, but she managed to sail through. She was educated at Monte Cassino. Monte Cassino was girls-only high school. She had the influence of the Catholic nuns and, converted to Catholicism.

Diana's education became a victim to the liberation war and the closing down of schools in rural areas. Diana was, thereby, forced to complete her education in surrogate schools in Harare, staying with younger sister Brenda. She later completed her high school education at Moses, which by then was considered one of the most prestigious government schools nationally. Diana later trained to be in finances and worked for different companies including the Department of Taxes. She married in 1984 and had three children.

---

[19] A mash made from corn and could be eaten with different relishes like okra, greens, beans, milk, beef, chicken, pork, etc. *Sadza* is the staple food of Zimbabwe. *Sadza* can be made from maize, rice, *rapokko*, and sorghum. My favorite was rice with beef. I could never have my feel of these.

As for Plaxedes, she went to Nyatsime College. Our father had not anticipated Plaxedes going to secondary school, as she always appeared playful and not serious in nature where her education was concerned. When her grade seven (7) results came, everyone was pleasantly surprised including our father. Unaware of her intelligence, everyone had assumed Plaxedes would spend another year completing her primary education or repeating grade seven. My father scrambled for finances to send her to school. Last minute arrangements were made, and Plaxedes was accepted at Nyatsime College. Nyatsime College was twenty kilometers away from our rural home.

Plaxedes met many challenges in life, and her path to becoming a professional in her career was very difficult. One thing I credit her with was her fighting spirit, Plaxedes was always a fighter. She was involved in politics, and none among us, her siblings, had ever thought she would ever be involved in politics. She was a wonderful secretary for the ruling party to a prominent minister. She had nothing but praises for her boss.

In 1990, Edgar Tekere, and his party Zimbabwe Unity Movement (ZUM) ran against the ruling party ZANU-PF for the presidency. Plaxedes learned that all her siblings had voted for Edgar Tekere. She deservedly gave us a piece of her mind. She would have lost her job if the opposition had won. Honestly, we had not thought that far ahead. We had only wanted to vote for someone who was challenging Robert Gabriel Mugabe. As for Plaxedes, she was genuinely hurt and made her feelings blatantly clear to us all. She never had any problems speaking her mind to us, to her in-laws, our husbands; she was as open as anyone could be yet was filled with compassion and empathy for all friends and relatives.

I remember at the beginning of the 1990s, when people were dying from HIV/AIDS, and I made a careless remark that the people deserved it, as they were promiscuous. Younger sister Plaxedes spoke to me and told me whether I had ever thought that HIV/AIDS was just a disease like any disease. She told me that some people were innocent victims, and it had nothing to do with their promiscuity. Plaxedes truly was blessed with intelligence and foresight well beyond her age. I would be reminded of her words years later when she had long died and as I got to learn more about the illness and how it spread. Unfortunately, Plaxedes left two children, a boy and a girl. Plaxedes passed away in December of 1993.

I give you this educational background so that you can tell I came from a family of rounded, well-educated and united human beings. Though our parents never completed primary education, they provided us with the best they could. As you can see from this background, I was the only one whose education had been terminated after an equivalent of only tenth grade. With this educational background, it was no surprise that I continued to aspire to improve myself academically because I was the least educated in a family of nine. To make matters worse, I earned the least but had the most number of children. As a result, my siblings rallied round me financially because they recognized how much I needed their financial assistance and moral support in my troubled marriage.

Chapter Seven

Signs of infidelity in dating and marriage

I started working at the beginning of 1975. I was barely twenty years old. I was someone suffering from my own traumas of war, but I was also a blossoming young woman. I had to suppress my personal suffering that I endured during training and make a living for myself and help my family anyway possible. I was given a grade one (1) class with more than forty six-year-olds. I was in the rural area of Derby, which was another area where the war was raging. I focused on my faith and on my work. From the day I walked into the first classroom as a teacher, I had love for the students I taught. I continued to teach for the next twenty something years for the Zimbabwe government.

Beginning of each year, I would welcome about forty to fifty new innocent, eager, and trusting young faces into my classes. I bonded with each one of them in unique ways so much that it would hurt. It actually hurt to let them go at the end of the year. Yes, this was such sweet pain because I loved what I did. I enjoyed seeing the changes that came with the children's acquisition of reading skills. I relished the changes that came with their ability to speak English. I looked forward to the sharpness of their being able to compute with ease. The change that came with their individual achievement year after year was affective, and yet to let go of those innocent young children who, throughout the year, had bonded with me trustingly would bring such sweet sorrow. This was my life; I was where I was meant to be, doing what I was meant to be doing. I walked in school each day with pride and joy mixed with a sense of achievement each year, knowing I was making a difference in my students' lives. I knew I was touching their minds, hearts, and souls in ways no other human being had touched, and that gave me unending joy and contentment in my vocation. I loved my God-given job.

During the early years of my career, I taught in many different environments. I was a teacher in rural schools, a teacher in elitist urban multiracial schools, and an acting school principal in a mining community school as well as a senior teacher in a government-administered primary school. As long as there were children, I would not hesitate. I would suit everywhere like a chameleon. It was not pretense at all on my part; it was real. I loved my job. I adored the children I taught. Nothing could take the joy and fulfillment away from my job. I remember January 1990, when schools opened and I had taken a six-month vacation prior. The first day I went back, immediately as I stepped into the school grounds, the first girl who saw me practically ran and threw her body into me. As I was in heels and had not expected such an enthusiastic welcome back, we both landed hard on the ground. I could not have wished for a better welcome than that. Up to now, when I recall such moments, that brings a sense of nostalgia and loss of the relationships I used to have with those children. Year after year, I was someone who molded young people's dreams and visions. I had no other career besides teaching, and I know the nostalgia I have for teaching is authentic and genuine.

I remember during my teacher-training period one of my lectures advising us about the choice of career we had made. Major Jean James told us that teaching was not a career but a calling from God. She told us teaching would never give us noble salaries and luxurious lives, but we were called specially to work with children. Children are the special gifts every being is given by God without favor. As such, parents entrusted their God-given gifts every day into the capable hands of teachers who are supposed to mold their minds and shape the wonderful gifts into wonderful human beings and citizens.

I felt that to work with children was to love them. Every single day, when I left I was never the same person who entered the school gates in the morning. Every day there was bound to be something special. Throughout my career, that something special touched my heart in a special way. I honestly believe the benefits and happiness from my profession somehow trickled to my troubled and loveless marriage.

I clearly recall the day I was introduced to Jonathan by his uncle at Market Square.[20] His uncle was a bus conductor for buses that commuted between Harare and Howard. It was in early November 1976, after a football match between two rival teams. I was heading back to Derby, where I worked as a primary school teacher, after a spending a weekend at home in Howard with my family.

I was munching on an apple while waiting for my bus to arrive. His uncle came to greet me, and he introduced me to his cousin who asked for a bite from my apple. I do not recall giving him the bite. Many times during our friendship, his uncle had alluded to the fact that he wanted to introduce me to one of his nephews. Jonathan was tall, slim, and easy on the eyes. He neither drank nor smoked, and he worked for one of Harare's corporations at the time. Well, at least he had the qualities that I admired in a man. He had a meaningful job. He was easy to look at. Finally yet equally important, he had a good sense of humor. We kept each other company, laughing at sweet nothings until it was time for me to leave.

Before my bus arrived, we exchanged addresses, and letters were exchanged beginning that week. After some time, we became a couple. I would visit with Jonathan in one of Harare high-density suburbs, and he would visit with me at my school in Derby, where I worked. Some weekends we spent at Rufaro Stadium, watching the football games; other weekends we spent loitering in Harare window shopping or going for a meal. I honestly enjoyed his company, and it did not take me long to fall in love with Jonathan.

I did not remain pure for long thereafter. I partook of the forbidden fruit. I distinctly remember the time I found out I was pregnant. Though inwardly I was happy and celebrating the coming of womanhood, embracing the coming of motherhood, gladly looking forward to the birth of my first child, secretly, I was tormented because I had done exactly the opposite of what my parents had instilled in me. Our parents had taught us chastity. Chastity had been grilled into us that well brought up girls should never fell pregnant before marriage. I cannot claim that my pregnancy was a mistake but a conscious decision and a choice I made.

---

[20] Market Square was the hub of activity where long distances buses, from different companies, to and from all the corners of Rhodesia began and ended their long trips.

I was a mature twenty-two-year-old woman. I cannot claim ignorance of what I was doing. I fell pregnant before getting married against my mother's better teaching; as a result, I had to do something to hide my pregnancy from my mother and all my relatives.

The hiding of the pregnancy from my mother began in early May, when I was home for the school holidays. I started by not looking into my own mother's eyes, afraid she would interpret the sadness in mine and read what I had done. I started stooping my head because I was hiding the telltale signs of pregnancy elderly people can dictate in young people's faces. I was hiding signs especially that mothers can easily recognize in their daughters' faces. I was afraid she could tell from my usually pale complexion that something was wrong. One way elder people in my culture can tell when a girl is pregnant is through the change of one's complexion, for it becomes unusually lighter and mine was no exception.

I began to wear loose-fitting clothes. I wanted neither my parents nor my brothers and my sisters to see the shape of my body because they could find out that I was pregnant. Pregnancy before marriage for me spelled D-I-L-E-M-M-A in capital letters for my mother from my father. I did not want to be the cause for breaking her back! Remember earlier on how we were taught to remain virgins because if we indulged in premarital sex, our mother's back would break! I honestly had a genuine fear of that calamity befalling my mother. As naive as that now sounds, back then, I truly believed that would actually happen to my mother's health.

That was only the beginning of how I would not hold my head up high. I was afraid I would lock my eyes with my relatives and friends. I was afraid they could read into my soul and see through to my spirit that something was terribly wrong. Therefore, I stooped my head low. Little did I know back then that this would later develop into a habitual façade, not holding my head up because I would be hiding the emotional wounds of matrimonial abuse? Right from the onset of our relationship, I had to learn some coping mechanisms. As such, the stooping of my head was one, though initially it was to hide my pregnancy. Second, I avoided people's eyes, which I thought would ultimately lead to probing and unpleasant questions. As a result, I started lying to myself that everything was all right.

There was no need for me to stoop my head low as though I had committed a crime. I had never been with any other man. He was my first. Even if my father had learned about my pregnancy, I now know, he would never have harmed neither my mother nor me. However, crying over spilt milk does not bring it back. I am genuinely happy that I have the opportunity now to sit down and write the memoir that most likely will influence some girl somewhere who will find themselves in almost similar predicament.

Falling in love is a natural thing, but love is not completely blind! We romanticize everything. As such, we fail to see or assess things glaring brightly into our open eyes. If ever there is a red flag, stop and take a second and third look before engaging in any relationships that you are uncomfortable with. In a relationship, if there ever is something you are questioning or doubting, it is your gut instinct trying to help you in a way. Our instincts, at best of times, never fail us. Pay attention, for instinct hardly ever is wrong. It is also advisable to never go against all that you were taught because those teachers or elders speak from experience. Unfortunately, like all young people, youth wants to have their cakes and eat them at the same time. Youth always assumes they know better. Later on in life, my gut feeling would be the best source of my most instrumental decisions. I learned to listen to my gut more attentively and believe in myself and in my power to change the difficult circumstances of my life.

I should have known better because I had been working as teacher for almost three years from January 1975 to February 1977, when I fell pregnant. I had the maturity that comes with exposure of someone with a career. I had the common sense to choose what I wanted and what I felt was good for me then, but I did not believe in myself.

I acknowledge I had fallen in and out of love with several men before but I had not experienced love in that sense with any other men. No man had managed to steal my heart the same way my future husband did. I remember, as college students, we had discussed and taught each other the kinds of personalities to look for in good future husbands. At least I had some expectations of what a good husband material should comprise. Among them were faithfulness, loving, caring, kindness, good provider, easygoing, someone who respected me, handsome, with lots of mutual interests, probably same religious beliefs, and family values. Do you realize that faithfulness was right at the top of the qualifications?

At the crucial time, it was easier said than done as I learned to appreciate with the passage of time.

I observed signs of infidelity early on in our dating days, because if anything love is never totally blind unless you choose to be. As a workingwoman, I had also set my own priorities of when I would love to get married and how many children I would love to have. I had a vision of the kind of life I needed to carve for my children, my husband, and myself. Of utmost importance before marriage and an immediate prerequisite was to work and help my parents out.

I had even told one prospective boyfriend that I could not marry him because I felt obligated to help my family before marriage. This was shortly after our short-lived courtship. My suitor wanted to take our relationship to the next level and had asked me to marry him within the first two weeks of dating. When I told this man I still wanted to work for my parents, he was willing and prepared to give me an open checkbook to do all I wanted for my parents.

The sight of that open checkbook could be attractive, but it freaked me out, as I had never come across someone as wealthy as my suitor was. His wealth drove me away. The offer felt as though he was trying to buy his way into my heart. For me, wealth was not an attraction as it was not among my priority list. His chivalrous intentions backfired, and I was left to continue with my search for my Mr. Right. Anyway, an open checkbook would not have brought the same gratification and satisfaction as giving my parents something I had personally worked and sweated for. At least I stuck to this prerequisite. I continued my search.

Not to digress from the reasons of not holding my head up high, I saw the signs of infidelity early on in our relationship. I met Jonathan through his uncle, and we clicked. The first sign of infidelity was when we were still dating back in 1976. Somehow that particular Friday evening I had missed my usual bus from Derby into the city of Harare. When my boyfriend then missed my arrival on the usual evening bus, he must have assumed I would not be coming at all. He went to his home in the suburb. On his way home, he decided to look up one of his girlfriends to cook his dinner that evening and to warm his bed for the night. Maybe in his eyes it was not cheating as we were not yet married nor were we engaged.

Unbeknown to my boyfriend, I managed to get a bus later than usual, and by the time I arrived in his suburb, I found some female was already preparing his dinner. I should have known then that a leopard never changes its spots. As I was making myself comfortable for the evening, the woman simply ran out, afraid a fight was about to erupt. Of course Jonathan was always a sweet talker. He convinced me that it was some joke; he was playing with his cousin Peter, who was visiting with him. Being head over heels in love with him, I totally believed him. He had cast his first bait and being innocent, I was totally reeled in and I was hooked.

In the sweet innocent heart, like any well-meaning and well-brought-up innocent young woman, I naively thought it was one little mistake. As such, I could forgive him. I also truly believed that I could change him, mold him, and teach him how to become a faithful boyfriend, faithful husband, and later loving father to our children. After all, don't people say love conquers all? I honestly believed mine would conquer this first hiccup. I mentioned that was the first sign of infidelity; let me also hasten to mention that was also the first time I unconsciously submitted to an unending lifelong journey of infidelity one affair after another.

If I could turn back the hands of time, I would go back to that first time because it was the time I first subjected myself to an unloving one-sided relationship for close to three decades. Not that I totally regret our relationship, as out of that chaotic bondage came our five precious, astonishing, amazing, generous, caring, kind, dependable, loving, and well-rounded human beings any parent could ever wish for under this sun. I am grateful every day, for they have enriched my life tremendously. I look back and acknowledge to myself that I would not trade any one of my children, even though my relationship with their father was totally dysfunctional.

The second time was when he sent a love letter meant for someone else. He apologized and lied between his teeth that he was trying to let go of this other person gently. Like any green-eyed girl in love, it was not difficult to believe him again. I gave in to this man's treacherous ways for the second time. Unsuspectingly, I personally subjected myself to his initial mundane, deceitful ways and promoted his unfaithful behavior as a boyfriend. Some might perceive them as mundane in comparison, but a sin is a sin, does not matter the degree. I personally enabled, promoted, and abetted his infidel characteristics long before I even became his wife. I gave him the authority to control the strings of my heart and play roughshod with my emotions in ways indescribable.

After giving him control like that later in, life I would say I never saw the signs. I told lies. I lied to my being because I convinced myself that if I loved him enough, he would change. Consequently, I trained myself not to hold my head up during those early days of our union. I became afraid of facing anyone in their eyes, in case they had a secret to tell me about my newly found love. I became perpetually paralyzed and scared of people's faces. On the other hand, I did not want people to recognize the wounds of my emotional abuse so early on in our relationship. I began to hide from people who could possibly question me or tell me we were dating the same man. Meanwhile, I would be pretending that he was the best man for me. I went to the extent of even pretending he had all the qualities I liked in a prospective spouse! I deluded myself and conveniently forgot that marriage was for a lifetime. The second bait was cast. It forced me lie to myself, but the truth was glaring me in the face. I had the love letter meant for someone. How could I ever change that?

The third time was immediately after I found out that I was pregnant. I had gone to spend a weekend with him in town. Jonathan lived in a high-density suburb in Harare. The landlord was literally threatening my fiancé (for by now we had agreed on marriage) that he would chop off his manhood (never mind my not using the "p" word, as this was how I was brought up and do not feel sexually liberated enough to use the word anyway) with an axe or knife as I totally recall. When I questioned my boyfriend, he gave me a lame explanation of his waking up during the night to use the bathroom, somehow along losing his way from the bathroom. He claimed that from the bathroom, he somehow found himself in the kitchen, where the property owner's sister slept. By the way, to get to the kitchen, he had to go outside to the side door that led to kitchen, yet the bathroom was only down the hallway from where our one-room residence was. I again naively chose to believe him, and I lied to myself. What's more, my married caring neighborly women rallied around me and told me that my boyfriend's landlord was jealous of us. Their reasoning was that my boyfriend and I were still young, as such held a promising bright future ahead of us. I was gullible enough to swallow this garbage completely. The third bait from Jonathan was cast, and the plot would only thicken from then on.

In the middle of the night, I would lie awake digesting everything. In my heart of hearts, I knew something was not adding up, but I was a coward. If only back then I had listened to my gut feelings, I would have saved myself all the later heartaches. If only back then I had the courage to tell either my mother or my elder sister, maybe I would not have subjected myself to this lifelong bondage of misery and pain. I would not have subjected myself to the atrociously pounding pain in love I brought upon myself for such a long time; it pains me even to recall. It might be all water under the bridge, but I still feel the pain. The man was ruthless. He wanted to beat my spirit down just like an animal's spirit is bitten down as it is tamed.

I somehow convinced myself that he was telling me the truth and that the landlord was envious of our relationship. In retrospect, I know I failed to realize what the landlord could have been envious about. He had a beautiful home and two wives to boost up his male personality and superiority. To add icing to the cake besides the beautiful sister whom my boyfriend was fooling around with, the man had a company car that came with his good job. In fact, we were the ones who had every reason to be jealous living under his roof, yet at the same time my fiancé had the audacity to cheat on me and, in the process, to manipulate this man's hospitality to his advantage.

I chose to believe Jonathan and my caring neighborly colleagues because I honestly believed in love. I slowly improved on the techniques of lying to myself; I refined my techniques by lying to my friends and polished my skills by lying to my relatives. I would also suffer the consequences eventually. Though as a child I had learned how to look people in their eyes and smile, I had to do a reverse jive. I would never look anyone directly into their eyes from then on where issues of the heart were concerned. I would always deceive myself that everything was rosy between us and as it ought to be.

As such, later in my life, I would require to relearn how to hold my head up and look people straight in their eyes to stop pretending that everything was all right. I had to start facing the truth about the perpetual emotional abuses I deliberately subjected myself to. I thought our marriage foundation was the right one; it was not. Everything was a façade. One thing I can give him credit for is that he never told me to lie. I inflicted that upon myself. I supported him by lying. *Why*, I now ask myself, *why did I do that?*

Due to the landlord incident, at the end of that month, we were compelled to move. Luckily by then, we had become common law husband and wife; we moved to the new growing suburb of Chitungwiza in the late 1970s. It was in September of 1977 that my fiancé paid my bride price *lobola*[21] to my parents. I officially became his common law wife and he my traditional husband.

The previous August, I had paid my first visit to my future in-laws and underwent all the traditional rituals befitting one to become a daughter-in-law. It would be during that time when I learned that my husband had previously brought another woman whom he had promised marriage to. His friends and relatives were all flabbergasted when he took me home as his future wife and not the other woman. This was the man who, unknown to me a few months earlier, had promised undying love to another woman before his relatives and friends. I should have run when I heard that, but I had made my bed.

Somehow the explicit and implicit looks I received from his family and friends left me wondering. Another red flag I chose to purposely ignore. As a result, in the eyes of my future in-laws and his friends, I was the impostor taking over someone else's rightful place. Henceforth, they looked at me apprehensively, wondering where I had come from. Right from the beginning, they had no reason to love and trust me because our relationship in their eyes was based on a shameful arrangement. Do you realize the irony in all this? I was determined to believe I had a good man for a husband, yet in the eyes of his relatives, I was the man snatcher! Right from the beginning, our relationship appeared suspicious, and to make matters worse, I was an educated woman, something alien to their religious beliefs and norms in life. Simply put, we started on the wrong footing; as such, they were all waiting for signs and symptoms of trouble in paradise, which was our marriage.

Such incidents, consequently, from the onset of our marriage, affected both sides of our families. My own relatives unfortunately

---

[21] A parent has the right to name the amount he requires to marry off his daughter, and that is *lobola*. Usually, that is the common law marriage, and the Western wedding would follow after all traditional formalities had been completed.

knew the truth about Jonathan's wandering eye, and they were aware of the troubled signs in our relationship. As such, completely accepting my boyfriend as my husband was difficult for some of them. Regrettably, the part of my husband having promised marriage to another woman was never really explored between us. Occasionally, he would mention how he had hurt the girl, but it would be in jest. His relatives, on the other hand, looked at me as a man snatcher. The irony was from the time I met my boyfriend, he had never told me of having promised marriage to another woman.

At times, I felt as though I deserved the twenty-seven years of emotional abuse in holy matrimony as I felt I should have given him his marching orders when I noticed the first signs of infidelity. The very day he took a woman to his place when I failed to turn up on time at his home in the high-density suburbs should have been the day I walked out of his life. However, I now realize that what you can easily let go is something you are holding in your hands not when it comes to matters of the heart. There and then, I recognized one of my grandmother's wise sayings; unfortunately, I thought things would turn out differently for me one way or another.

Retrospectively, I also realize that I never cheated on him due to my upbringing. I did not deserve the ill-treatment I endured. I had hopes of our life together setting off to unprecedented heights. I fantasized that I would care for our home and children with the love of any young mother and wife in love with her husband. I truly believed if I showered him with lots of love, he would love me back. That was delusional on my part as I learned with the passing of time.

Chapter Eight

Our first home and problems in marriage

It was in Chitungwiza that we invested in our first home. It was a semidetached one-bedroom house with prospects of expansion. Growing up, this had always been the life I had envisioned for myself. I had dreamt of a husband with my own home and children in urban settings. My life was turning out perfectly. I could not have been more proud of our union then. This was the picture perfect life—a husband, a child, and a new home, just like I had imagined as a young girl. Our new home in Chitungwiza was only twenty miles away from our village in Howard, my communal home, where I grew up. Nothing could have made me happier.

Chitungwiza was a budding high-density suburb with the vivacious, relentless promises of growth only a few miles out of the capital city Harare. Young people in the late 1970s were starting their new lives together in Chi-town. My new husband and I with our new baby belonged to this new energetic Chitungwiza generation. I was thrilled to be part and parcel of Chitungwiza, the land of promise; Chi-town, where the initial war of liberation had taken place around the 1890s in the then Rhodesia. It was a time full of promise, a time full of hope, a time full of happiness, and a time that opened my eyes to the lifestyle I had chosen for myself as a married woman.

Let me tell you, little did I know about what marriage entailed before I got married. I had seen my married parents, but most of our lives they lived apart as our father came home once a week and spent two nights before he left. As for other relatives, they followed pretty much the same trend. Husbands spent weekdays in towns working and would only come home for the weekends. The trials and tribulations of married life were hidden from us as kids. Though I knew of the communal fights, polygamous marriages, and drinking problems, our parents had not exposed us to that. As such, I entered married life with my husband with all the optimism of a young bride hoping to make a successful marriage despite the signs of infidelity I had witnessed during our dating days.

It was during our stay in Chitungwiza that our first child was born. As such, it was a time filled with joy, happiness, and celebration. Nothing could overshadow the love of a mother for her newborn child or the love of a father for his firstborn child. We celebrated with my family and, for the first time, with his family. The two families united forever in this holy matrimony, so it seemed to me. New and pleasing relationships were fashioned and distinguished. My people welcomed his brother and mother in our home with warm embraces that they could not find fault as they came with presents for the newborn.

After Elvin's birth, the new in-laws from both sides of the newly united families came together to celebrate customarily with a basket of cornmeal, chicken, plenty of food and drink, and numerous presents for the newborn baby. We were all sharing with my relatives in my own village in Howard. My parents embraced my in-laws, and in turn, my in-laws embraced my parents and friends, and other relatives were embracing each other. They were all praying for blessings on this brand-new family. Little discernment did I have of a lifestyle I knew very little about, and nothing could have prepared me for that lifestyle than just walking that walk, as the saying goes.

I find it essential that you understand that though I had been brought up of a prior polygamous father, I had not actually lived through the life of polygamy unlike Jonathan. His father had five wives, and when his father died, he was in the process of marrying a sixth one. Similarly, his uncles on both sides of the family were polygamous; similarly, his older brothers and male cousins all had multiple wives. This was allowed under their religious beliefs. According to their religion, they do not ascribe to the beliefs of the New Testament but only teachings of the Old Testament. Later I found that they would select certain verses that supported their polygamous beliefs and the oppression of women.

Marrying one wife and being faithful was completely an alien concept from all my husband had learned growing up. I am not trying to make excuses for his unbecoming behavior, but I am trying to enlighten you on how, in my trying to understand his erstwhile behaviors, I also gained insights into his upbringing and consequential behaviors later in our marriage. Usually, people are shaped by their environments and not vice versa. Thus, my husband was not completely removed from this deeply ingrained and intergenerational heritage of having multiple wives as well as a religion where women never spoke up for themselves. My husband was indoctrinated into a system where women were perceived only as appendages of their husbands to use and abuse as they pleased or subjects of either their fathers or brothers. Women were mostly owned as a source of cheap labor to work their husband's cotton fields. As such, in my husband's philosophies, I too was such a possession to be enjoyed when he so desired and discarded when he had another woman as it benefitted his male ego and prestige.

Physical abuse was tolerated in his upbringing. My mother-in-law, my husband's mother, often told me of several beatings inflicted on her by her late husband. She told me that each time those beatings occurred; she pleaded old age in order for the beatings to stop. She would further elude that the reason why modern-day women never got along with their husbands was simply because we refused to submit to our husband's brutality. Intellectually, I could never understand why I had to submit and plead old age when I was barely in my mid-twenties. Socially, I knew that was how women were indoctrinated into submission. Older women were responsible for teaching younger women how to submit to the unending physical torture and emotional abuse under the pretense of not airing dirty laundry.

In my own way, I attempted to understand this upbringing. I knew I had to deal with my husband in a way that allowed him to learn other ways of relating to me as a woman without perpetually abusing me. Though I was a teacher by profession, my strategies were never effective where Jonathan was concerned. I would try to convince him that problems were discussed over, but my husband felt a quicker resolution was to beat me into submission. I tried involving my relatives such as my brothers and uncles into counseling us, but that did not yield the desired results. He would talk to me about how my relatives encouraged him to be gentle and loving with me, but whenever we had a problem, his temper had the better of him. I would also attempt to utilize my aunts, but Jonathan would stubbornly tell me women were never good for anything but taking to bed, rearing children, and keeping the home.

Eventually, I also brought in his relatives to no avail. It took me years to realize that no matter how abusive and unfaithful my husband was, my in-laws failed to counsel us as a couple because of ingrown habits and beliefs. To my in-laws, my husband had no problem; as such, I was perceived as the problematic one. In their eyes, there was nothing wrong when a man had multiple women. His infidelity was considered a public declaration of his intentions to marry another woman. Little did I know that his infidelities were such public declaration that he was a strong man and would never succumb to petticoat government of an overbearing woman? My complaints would, therefore, continue to bounce on deaf ears.

The only person who ever rebuked my husband in my hearing was his younger brother. I remember that he was the only one who ever chastised him for his infidelities and his continued proliferation of children with different women. The younger brother told my husband then that he needed to stop proliferating like a bird and not giving thought to who cared for the children. That was the one and only time anyone would admonish Jonathan within my hearing. For all his efforts, my brother-in-law, on that particular day, was told by my husband that he was way too young to advise his older brother on his behaviors. As it turned out, it was another wasted attempt and opportunity to revisit his philandering ways.

Second, we had different religious faiths. Our religions were not only different but also highly contradictory. I was brought up Christian; I knew all about the enlistment of loyalty and faithfulness in marriage. I ascribed to the essence of one man, one woman, till death do us part, and I intended to do that. I believed in the morals and values that had been bestowed on me, educated in missionary schools by Christian teachers as I was growing up. My teachers and lecturers in high school and teacher-training college were mostly female missionaries; therefore, I strongly believed in what human beings were capable of doing to change their circumstances with proper upbringing and faith.

On the other hand, my husband had been brought up seeing the violence that went on between his parents, the animosity that existed between the co-wives of one husband, and the envious dealings among the half siblings. His religion did not bring him up to believe in Christ but just bits of the Old Testament. Polygamy was permissible according to the Old Testament teaching that he received. That was my husband's upbringing, and he knew nothing else. Their religion reinforces the notion that there is healing power in prayer and that all medication draws you away from the Lord. This was my first time witnessing a church that believed in one segment of the Bible to support their doctrines. It was beyond my own belief that religions selected certain parts of the bible to endorse their own religious practices.

Though that was their belief and ultimately my husband's, on the other hand, I had been brought up believing that with medications combined with the Lord's mercy and the loving blood of Jesus Christ, people could be healed. Growing up, we were taught about the Holy Trinity. When called upon, God the Father, Christ the Son, and the Holy Ghost worked miracles together that enabled healing to take place. This was exemplified by the fact that one of our eldest brothers, Larry, was a medical doctor. The separation between our values (my husband's and mine), religious beliefs, and family values differed like day and night. These should have been the initial red flags I needed to say our union would never function.

Please do not condemn me before you read further. I alluded in the beginning that I thought my love would conquer all and that my Christian upbringing prevented me from considering divorce as an option. Too many aspects of my life worked against me as well. The other aspect was I never learned to speak up for myself. Since entering marriage, odds were high against me. Those odds prevented me from speaking up. The popular thing back then was children were seen and not heard. Remember also what I said earlier that society shapes us to a larger degree; therefore, we are influenced to make decisions according to how society would tolerate or castigate us. Socially, I did not want to be perceived as a failure in my marriage. I knew the repercussions of divorce would be worse than actual death itself. I had moved from being Avis Manning to becoming Avis, wife of Jonathan. I was then the appendage of my husband just as I was of my father before marriage. What would divorce then mean?

Divorce meant going back to my maiden name and going back to living with my parents. Divorce would end my claim to the echelon of married women who are differently perceived in culture. I also feared the exclusion from my social status as a married and privileged woman living in this middle-class society that my husband's economic position afforded my children and me. Consequently and naively, I would continue to pretend and convince myself to believe that our love life was unique and that my love would conquer everything. I had also made my bed; hence, I was determined to lie in it. I knew initially that he cheated on me but had hoped against all hope that he would change for me. I had married my husband for better or worse; I was determined to make it work. I was determined to be a good wife even if it killed me in the process, and kill me it almost did.

Instead, my lack of skills such as female-to-male or husband-wife communication was detrimental. The inability to speak up for myself, the lack of knowledge in sex and sexuality[22] (that I was never actually taught) rendered me vulnerable. My inability to negotiate for safer sex, my gullibility of believing that love would conquer all, and my continued pretenses of keeping facades would bring me to my current situation where I am now. Please understand that I do not blame myself completely. Because as we were celebrating my marriage, no one had ever hinted that when a husband was unfaithful, I had the right to deny him his conjugal rights or to demand that he use protection. Even when my family was united with his family in celebrating our son's birth, no one had ever mentioned that marriage was not a bed of roses. I did not know that thorns on the rose stems would pierce so deeply into my flesh and could cause bleeding that could sap the life out of my body.

My religion too had a lot to do with why I remained steadfast in my troubled marriage. I found strength in other women who opened up about the abuses they suffered in their marriages. I would delude myself and thank God that at least my abuses were not like theirs. Abuse is abuse and should never be compared to others nor tolerated. My church elders and pastors helped perpetuate this continuous abuse and domestic trauma in a way. I clearly remember during one women's church meeting asking my church elders how a woman could turn a

---

[22] All I was taught was how to elongate my labia in preparation for childbirth. I later learned it was for arousal and male sexual pleasure. Every other sexual lesson would be through eavesdropping on my mother and other women at the river as they discussed their intimacy with husbands in our presence as though we were deaf.

husband down when she suspected that he was unfaithful. The female church elder I directed my question to vehemently responded and told me that in church, they never gave lessons on how to deny husbands their conjugal rights. I do not know how many times I have played some of those responses in my head and always wish I had had the courage to challenge them. Unfortunately, I did not, and I will always regret my continued submission to an unfaithful husband and redundant church teachings.

I am an educated woman as you can see, and I failed at times to bring up issues in our marriage that concerned me about my health. I feel I held on to my traditional upbringing too long. By the time I tried to be more vocal, I failed to convince my husband to use protection when we were intimate. This would later lead to a lot of agony and soul-searching on my part. All the wouldas, couldas, and shouldas, but it's a little too late. Again, it was water under the bridge; I had to adjust my own life and carry on living. My only advice is, in as much as some traditions are concerned, some are worth keeping, but never hold on to others that contribute to jeopardize your life. Tradition is not worth that much of a price tag as your own life.

Since I have come this far, I honestly believe my life has a purpose that has yet to be made public. I now strongly trust that the Lord would not have brought me this far to abandon me. He must have a purpose for me to fulfill. I look back to my life as an impoverished daughter from a polygamous father. I am the girl who grew up in colonized Rhodesia, who clamored for her parents' love and attention. I cannot help but wonder why I feel my life was touched and blessed. Maybe an insight into that lifelong journey of the abuses and infidelities would afford you a sneak peek into this misery-filled life that I brought on myself, or was it conveyed on me by someone else? Right now, I completely fail to figure out who brought what on whom. Alternatively, maybe you can be better judges of what really happened. All I know is I was a faithful wife. I did not, for once, step out of our marriage, yet my partner thrived on the affairs. The results of my illness were because I loved him to a fault.

Chapter Nine

Our first child's births and further infidelity

Let me take you back to the beginning of our marriage so that you can comprehend the working of an abused female's mind. It was early on a wet Monday morning at five thirty on November 15, 1977 that our eldest son, Elvin, was born. He was a real blessing as his birth brought the first rains of the summer season that many people had been patiently waiting for. This marked the beginning of summer in Rhodesia. He came into the world weighing 3.35 kilograms; I could not believe I was a mother and responsible for another life. I can never completely describe the warm, unformulated feeling of love, wonderment, and joy inside of me. I knew he was my bundle of joy despite the health issues I had then.

Although physically I was not able to care for my son, I promised in my heart that I would never let him down. To my eyes, he was the most handsome boy ever born. I fell in love with my son at his birth. I could never get over the fact that he was all mine and that I was responsible for creating this wonderful life completely dependent on me for his livelihood! I was happy to have created someone so beautiful in my young life. I cannot say how long he was or anything about his well-being because unfortunately, back then, clinics in Howard did not measure the babies' length nor did they conduct any other general health tests besides their birth weight. All I could tell with my plain loving eye of a brand-new proud mother was that my son was healthy and was a perfect boy in every sense of the word. I could also tell he had a strong pair of lungs as he cried at birth announcing his arrival.

I am sad to say I did not, however, immediately bond with my son after he was born. A couple of months prior to his birth, I was bedridden and incapacitated in many ways. Breast-feeding was a hassle, as physically I could not sit up properly to breast-feed, and I also needed to overcome the inhibitions of any young woman showing her breasts in public to feed her baby for the first time; and besides, both my nipples were sore and tender from suckling. As such, bonding with my son took a couple of days, but I already loved him dearly.

A couple of months before my son's birth, an unidentified insect stung me behind my right knee. The toxins spread so fast that it temporarily incapacitated me from being mobile. My right leg from the knee downward became swollen, and I could hardly put my weight on it. Within a couple of hours after the sting, I could not even carry my own weight. I never identified what insect it was. For the next month, I would be in constant pain, and it would leave all my relatives baffled as to what to do for me. Though I was in excruciating pain most of the time, I felt sorry for my mother, my aunts, my sister, and most relatives as they tried to find instant cures to my poisoned leg.

Unlike the early days of my pregnancy, which were filled with hide-and-seek games, my trying not to show my pregnancy and being sick subsequent to meals, this later phase of my pregnancy was very much open to everyone. Comparably, the bowing down of my head so that my mother would not detect my pregnancy was only minor hiccups; besides that, I was a healthy expectant woman looking forward to what it would be like to be a mother. The morning sickness was something I hid well from my mother, but on the whole, I was healthy in every other aspect.

It was during the seventh month that things absolutely changed and took a 180-degree turn. I had never imagined what it would be like being pregnant and not able to walk. Can you imagine being ill and pregnant, not knowing what was wrong with you? Can you imagine being ill among your family, friends, and relatives who truly love you and the fuss they make irritates you instead of you welcoming it? Can you imagine how frantic they become and want to do everything possible to help you but somehow rendered helpless. My whole family including my father was no exception. Every day they would be looking for quick and magical solutions and cures to heal me from this unwanted and unidentified ailment.

I remember one early morning, my mother, Doris, and Auntie Eileen inflicted pain on my already-sore leg. The two women usually joined forces and would leave home only to bring different potent powders for my healing. For weeks, I was bedridden; I was forced to visit numerous medical doctors, religious prophets, traditional healers, and each had their different solutions to my ailment.

After one of my mother and aunt's early morning escapades in the month of November, the two declared they had found a solution. They came back with some black powder that was supposed to be rubbed into my body after little razor cuts *Nyora*[23] had been made on my leg. No matter how much I tried to fight or put my mother and my aunt off the idea of inflicting further pain on me, the two women were equally determined. With brand-new razor blades, they would make two cuttings up and down my legs and rub the black powder pre-prepared by the witch doctor (*n'anga*)[24] into the cuttings. Their belief was that the powders from the *n'anga* had the influence to cure the toxins in my blood and I would be magically healed or cured. I tried to reason with them because for me there was no logic, but how could I argue with two equally stubborn and elderly women whom I respected totally and loved. In the end, I had to consider their feelings and that they were hurting too on my behalf, so eventually I gave in to their absurd way of treating me.

Two days later, I got really worse so much that when my husband visited us for the weekend, he was overcome by emotion. He openly started crying and all people who were in my mother's round hut left the two of us alone. I remember him telling me that all he could see in my eyes was imminent death, and he even prophesied to smell it looming on my whole body. What the two of us ended up agreeing on was to

---

[23] Nyora little cuts made on one's skin and there is black powder rubbed in, as medications. These cuttings leave permanent scars.

[24] Zimbabwe traditional healers (n'angas) are known to cure ailments that have confounded modern science. The indigenous people have respect for what they do, but sometimes there is no logic in their methods of cure. As such, I was a lot skeptical and did not easily give in to the razor markings my mother and aunt wanted to inflict on my legs.

have me transported to Harare Hospital by ambulance. However, before the ambulance could transport me to Harare, I had one last wish. One of my father's great uncles in his late eighties was there. I still cannot understand nor fathom why I made the weirdest request I did.

I suddenly had a yenning for freshwater fish. I, therefore, requested my father's great uncle to go and catch a freshwater fish for me that I could have before I went to the hospital. Suddenly, everyone in my home started crying. I did not understand it then, but later when I had completely recovered, I would know why. They all thought I wanted to have my last meal before I could die peacefully. My father's great uncle went to Hunyani River and looked for someone who had some freshwater fish, and he quickly bought some that I could enjoy. Sure enough, after days of not eating well, I enjoyed my *sadza* with the fish; but my family was in tears, and I was completely baffled by their emotion. Subsequently, after my plate of *sadza,* the ambulance was called, and it quickly whisked me off to a hospital in Harare.

When I arrived at the hospital, I created a calamity among the doctors, most of whom were black like me, and I could not believe what was strange about the markings on my legs. The doctors clearly could not hide the fact they were flabbergasted because of the *n'anga* marks (as the words "n'anga marks up and down both patient's legs" were clearly written on my health record card). It was like I belonged to the circus. From the moment I arrived, one doctor after the other kept coming and not doing anything much. They would gaze at me and leave speechless and or unbelievably and inconsiderately laughing at the markings, then immediately behind, another doctor would follow. I felt like a circus spectacle or as though I had suddenly developed magical horns. I was deeply mortified due to the marks I had along both my legs and, at the same time, deeply hurt by their total lack of professionalism and consideration for my feelings.

Finally, after the doctors had satisfied their curiosity, they came up with some recommendations for my treatment. Their suggestion was that they were going to induce the birth of my baby, and later they would deal with the issue of my leg. With this communicated to me, I told them I would not have any of it! I would not budge and let them conduct the operation. I was afraid I would lose my child if born prematurely. I also feared for my own life. The doctors made a determination that the illness was not in any way distressing the baby. As such, they recommended that

I would lie in bed with my right leg propped up, probably to neutralize whatever was causing the swelling. I was not admitted; as a result, the Howard Council ambulance drove me back home.

The next couple of weeks were the most unbearable and uncomfortable I had ever endured physically, but I was determined to carry my baby to full term. Every day from then onward, I would be transported to the local clinic for pain medications. As we did not own a car, my form of transportation to the clinic was by wheelbarrow, which everyone took turns to push, with me propped up with lots of blankets to cushion the bumpy ride. Do not ask what the medications were for; up to this day, I have no clue what the nurses were giving me and how the medications were supposed to help. All I know is that it was an uncomfortable fortnight, and I remember most the pain.

November 15, 1977, it was during the early hours around three in the morning that I felt as though I had wet my pants, except my urine felt warm and slimy to my thighs. I woke up my sister Melody and told her. Melody panicked. She went and woke up our parents. My mother came and made her own initial assessment. She concluded that I was in labor; as such, I had to get to the clinic as soon as possible. Without any means of transportation at that time of night in a rural area, the only way they could get me to that clinic was by wheelbarrow again. My aging father, Norman, and Uncle Moses (my mother's brother) took turns to wheel me there again that night. On the way to the clinic, I remember my mother, Doris, telling me to conduct myself as it would not have been proper for me to give birth before my father and uncle. As such, I was able to contain the labor pains on the bumpy wheelbarrow ride as it was not a long distance to the clinic. Somehow there was no pain at all from my right leg all that night. Pain had temporarily disappeared completely, as though the leg pains were taking second stage to the labor pains.

I had labor pains the rest of the night, and my mother kept telling me it was going to be worse. I remember sometime around five thirty, I felt as though I needed to go to the bathroom for bodily functions. I asked my nurse to give me something to use. I knew I could not afford to stand up and walk to the bathroom. My midwife, instead of complying, was putting clean linens on the bed and encouraging me to push. After a few pushes and around five forty-five that morning, my first son entered the world.

As soon as my mother heard my son's first cry, she broke out into song[25] and came in to the delivery room to congratulate the nurse and myself. My father followed right behind her (before I was even fully covered). It was a moment I would never forget. All of a sudden, the labor pains were gone. Immediately, I was overwhelmed by the idea that I was a new mother. My parents, my aunts Eileen and Veronica, and my elder sister as well as my uncle surrounded me at this happy time. I could breathe a sigh of relief. I put down my head to sleep, and I realized that everything was going to be all right. I was happy to be alive and holding my newborn in my arms for the first time. Immediately after giving birth, I felt a different kind of love and respect for my mother. To imagine she had endured the pain of childbirth nine times! I was completely overwhelmed by loving emotions for Doris, my mother.

After delivery, I managed to steal a couple of hours of sleep but woke up from the pain of my leg throbbing again. I could not believe I still had the excruciating pain from my leg! I could not think it had been completely gone while I was in labor but were back a couple of hours later, throbbing more vigorously. At least now you can understand why after so many weeks of lying on my back, it was not easy for me to bond with my firstborn son immediately. At least in my heart I felt I could bear the pain on my own, knowing my son was healthy. I knew I had done my best to carry him full term and thus had ensured he was born healthy.

Jonathan received the news of his son's birth from my father the following day. He left work to come to Howard to meet his son for the first time. My husband then at least demonstrated his love for the child and me for he brought me a congratulations card and a new dress as well as a few baby clothes. Elvin's birth was one of the rare times he ever demonstrated love for me. He amazed me because all he fussed over was the baby's feet. He looked over the baby's feet and his toes. Up to now, I am not sure of what significance the baby's feet were. As our son was born during the week, my husband went back the same evening to Chitungwiza to work until the following weekend, when he came back to spend more time with us.

---

[25] Ndasunungurwa tendai Ishe "The chains of evils that had bound us are broken!" For it really felt like everything that had chained us was let free on that day!

It was a few days after I gave birth that my mother, my sister Melody, and my husband had the courage to prick the swelling behind my right leg and squeeze it. My mother held my hands, my husband held my legs, and my sister was the one squeezing. Whatever had caused the swelling in my leg when squeezed came out as though it was from a faucet, and it shot up at least twelve inches high. I could see the substance in the air when I turned my head. The pain made me scream, but the three people were determined. They squeezed for some time until nothing was oozing out anymore. Talk of relief after the pus and the blood and whatever fluids were squeezed out of my leg. I literally slept like a baby that night. That was my unforgettable introduction to the joys of motherhood for years to come.

A few days went by after my son's birth, I was fully recovered, though still trying to get my balance and be back on my feet, so to speak. At least then, I enjoyed doing what all-new mothers do for their newborn babies. For the first time after a week, I was able to hold Elvin in my arms and breast-feed him properly. I was able to change his diapers and even give him a bath. I was a new mother being taught how to care for my baby by my own mother, Doris. During the second week after his birth, I had the first relaxed opportunity to give my baby a good look over. During that time, I was also able to hold him up properly as I breast-fed him. It was during that week that I knew what baby and mother bonding was all about. It was a good feeling; I was doing all things for my son for the first time. I loved him unconditionally right from the start, and that love never diminished no matter how naughty he was as he grew up.

Elvin was a happy and content baby, easy to care for. After feeding and receiving his bath, my baby would simply go to sleep. It was easy to establish a feeding timetable for him. One thing my mother, Doris, could never understand is why babies had to be fed at certain times only. This marked the changing of times and generations. My mother had been a stay-at-home mom who worked the fields and breast-fed us whenever we needed to be fed. I had to establish a timetable because I intended to go back to work and ensure my son would be all right whenever that eventually happened. Since going on maternity, most of my time had been spent in bed. I had ended my teaching at Derby Primary School in Derby on October 14, 1977, and on October 16, I was supposed to have gone back. I fell sick on the same day and never went back. On

November 15, 1977, I became a mother and my mother's first daughter to make her a grandmother. Therefore, the adjustment to motherhood obviously had challenges to my family and me. My children and I would later call those adjustments "the joys of motherhood."

For some time, the family was deprived of babies to spoil and love for a long time, so to speak. Doris[26], my niece, my brother Nicholas's daughter whom my mother had cared for since she was under a year, was seven years old by then. Doris had been the only baby in the family for the last seven years. By the time Elvin was born, he was the most welcome baby to the family and did not lack for people to care for him at all even before I was fully recovered. As such, we all fought to attend to him. As a mother, I missed holding my baby because everyone wanted to spend time with him.

It was during this time I found that motherhood could be challenging especially at night. Most times, Elvin was a happy, placid child. At night, I would feed him and put him between my mother and me as we slept in our round hut, on the floor. Most times, I would only wake up to change his diaper, and he would continue sleeping. One particular evening, he was crankier than he had ever been. He would not go to sleep until after one in the morning. I was tired. My mother was sleeping peacefully. In my trying to make him sleep, I ended up lying him down behind me and personally falling into a deep sleep, which was disturbed rather rudely. Dogs were barking outside. In my troubled sleep, I was rudely awakened and immediately thought of my baby. After I looked between my mother and me, where my baby usually slept, I failed to locate my baby. I thought the dogs had eaten my newborn baby.

From then on, all hell broke loose. I yelled at the top of my voice that the dogs had eaten the baby. The wail woke my mother and my sisters up. Brenda, unafraid of the night, just opened the kitchen door to go after the dogs. My mother was stunned and could not even stand up, the same as my sister Melody. I kept wailing at the top of my voice for them to get the dogs as they had my baby. Brenda came back inside and claimed she had not seen anything that the dogs were eating. I was inconsolable and kept on screaming at the top of my voice. Somehow

---

[26] My niece was named after my own mother. Doris was my mother's first grandchild from my brother Nicholas her firstborn.

my mother remained still as though she had been turned to stone. After what appeared like a long time, I looked behind me and saw my baby.

I snatched him up and drew him to my chest. I almost snuffed the very life out of him as I rocked him back and forth in my arms. I could not believe my baby was there, and he had not stirred in all the loud commotion and the disturbance. By the time I was telling my mother and sisters that I had found him, we were all in tears. Some tears were from the relief that the baby was safe, and some tears were still from the fear and shock of dogs eating the baby. Up to now, it is one of the best-told and repeated jokes in the family about the joys and challenges of adjusting to motherhood.

Sadly, it was during this time that once again I noticed further signs of infidelity from Jonathan. Culturally, I was supposed to stay with my mother, Doris for three months so that she could teach me how to care for my baby properly. When my husband visited me, we would not sleep together, as he needed treatments with his numerous sexually transmitted diseases (STDs). Little did I know then that I had to protect myself as well even after his treatments? Innocently, I thought as long as he had no physical and outward signs, there would be no need for us to use protection when being intimate. No wonder I would pay dearly for that naivety later on in my life and it would be almost excessively late to do anything by then.

After three months recovering from childbirth, I finally joined my husband in Chitungwiza. Shortly after moving to Chitungwiza, I became hired to teach in one primary school and happily went back to work to provide for my new family. I enjoyed working and loved my job. Every month end, I would give my paycheck to my husband. I had no clue as to what he used it for. I remember one time asking him for some much-needed cash. He literally responded that as the head of the household, he used my paycheck as he saw fit. I did not take well to that because from then on, I kept my paycheck and would use it as I saw fit. I reasoned to myself that if I had worked for it; it was equally befitting that I decided how to spend it. Initially, we fought over my paycheck, but I did not relent. As such, from that time on, we never operated as a united family unit financially. What was his was his, and what was mine was mine with my child.

It was after my son's birth that I transitioned into teaching in urban schools. Urban schools during the mid-and late-1970s era dealt with an influx of students from rural school. The rural schools were closing down rapidly because of the war. Children with relatives in towns were shipped to live with extended families in towns. Because of the liberation war, the urban school created the hot-seating[27] system in order to cope with the influx. Schools endured an influx of children and young adults going back into primary schools and secondary schools. There were shortages of classrooms and teachers, and all resources were in short supply; yet on the other end of the spectrum, the demand for education was high. Most urban schools adapted the double sessions as a means of meeting the educational demands. It was not surprising to find teachers working both sessions (morning and evening) just to keep children in school.

During the times I would be teaching the afternoon session, I would try to surprise my new husband by paying him visits at work. Each time I went to the city to visit my husband at his workplace; I would come back with heartbreak after heartbreak. I cannot recall how many women would also visit him during his lunch breaks as I did. I lost count after the first ten encounters or so; I stopped paying him surprise visits at work. I think to him it appeared as though I had obediently accepted his cheating ways. I know I could not deal with such persistent and continued torture on me with his incessant deceitfulness approach to our marriage. From then on in, inwardly, I knew I was lying to myself that he would ever change.

One thing the encounters taught me, though, was never to pay Jonathan surprise visits at his workplace. I also started looking at all his female workmates with apprehensive eyes and would never warm up to their extended friendships. My attitude and feelings toward our relationship were varied, but I somehow remained optimistic that things would improve with time as we matured together as a married couple.

I regret to say things never really improved in the direction I hoped, except that he matured in his deceiving ways and enhanced his cheating techniques. I now know that right from the beginning; my husband was never faithful to me. I think of the times I would not hear of any affairs;

---

[27] The hot seat involved classes alternating from having morning and afternoon sessions. Every fortnight, the morning session moved to afternoon and vice versa. This continued well after our independence in April 1980.

those times do not reflect his changed ways at all. In fact, those times reflect ignorance on my part of what he was up to and mostly attribute to my not caring attitude and probably complacent attitude towards our marriage. Clearly from the beginning, these numerous affairs should have been the red flags. After I joined my husband in 1978 and started working in Harare, the sexually transmitted diseases (STDs) were part of our clinical regiment, almost on a monthly basis. These treatments were another red flag I boorishly ignored and hoped against hope.

After the affairs so far chronicled, I remember the first one that resulted in the birth of a baby daughter. This was unquestionably an escalation of the emotional abuse to me. This girl's birth was close to my own first daughter's birth, which is my second born, and this was my husband's first child out of wedlock. I learned about the other woman being pregnant while I was teaching at Chitungwiza Primary School. It was 1979, with the promise of a new political dawn in the horizon. I was only two months pregnant, but I do not completely recall the circumstances under which this affair came to my knowledge. As a working professional woman, I thought if I stopped working and let him take care of me and my children, I would be punishing him enough. Depriving us of another source of income meant restrictions on his philandering. My family and friends, even my school principal, questioned the reasoning of my wisdom and sanity when I tendered my resignation letter in November 1979. I would not reveal my reasons to anyone, even family members. I was hurt learning about this affair, and I inwardly justified my actions, but the irony is I was the one who ended up with a valuable and well needed lesson in economics.

The following January 1980, I would not go back to work. Yes, I tendered my resignation; as then before 1982, there were no maternity leave policies for female teachers in Zimbabwe. Back then, as soon as female teachers fell pregnant, we were doomed to have resigned from the teaching profession; therefore, I had to resign from my teaching position according to the ministry's regulations. As a result, from January 1980 until September that year, I was not employed at all. In the process, I was taught enough never to be dependent on my husband neither financially nor economically.

For me, the best economic teacher in life was experience itself. Though one of my cousin sisters had questioned when I got married why I had married so early and so young, I thought her crazy. She had told me marrying young was like racing to have "swollen legs."[28] I did not ask her the wisdom of her saying at the time; with the passage of time, I knew exactly what she meant. I would confess my naivety to her after years of abuse. I hope one day she gets to read this too, as it also became a motto for me to say to other young girls rushing to get married. Where abuse and economic lessons in marriage were concerned, my experiences were my best teachers.

Economically, it made sense for me to continue teaching until the last possible day before handing in my resignation. Emotionally, I was devastated and close to a wreck when I learned about the other expecting woman. I was not happy contributing to our way of life with my husband squandering our hard-earned cash away with other women. I felt justified staying at home and rendering myself exclusively his economic responsibility. I thought he would feel the financial strain then and would appreciate my meager financial contribution subsequently mend his unbecoming behaviors.

Oh! How I wish I had had some prudence into the kind of life I would end up leading for the next nine months until I got a job again. I almost bcame a pauper in my own home. My husband would never give me money for anything during those nine months. He would go to work and come home late into the night or during the wee hours of the morning. To make matters worse, we had an extended family made up of his two sisters, his stepbrother, and his two grown-up cousins. We had a one-bedroom house, and how we managed to accommodate all those people is a real mystery up to this day. The two of us barely had any privacy as a married couple at all. His elder sister would use my cosmetics as though they were hers too. I resented having such a big family under my care. That was the trend in our marriage that I always had his family members living with us all through our marriage.

During the nine months I was miserable, lonely, depressed, broke, and the cheating ways never ceased; instead, the emotional abuse escalated. I could not even afford buying a maternity dress for myself. However, being clever with my hands, I found myself adjusting some of

---

[28] Wamhanyira makumbo kuzvimba- rushing to have swollen legs acts as a metaphor that my cousin used in attempting to explain that in the end, I would have heavier problems to weigh me down in marriage than to continue working as a single mother.

my old dresses to fit my growing and enlarging body. I could not even afford to buy wool to knit some post birth woolens for my daughter. It really saddens me that I put myself through such neglect and continued to love this man. Somehow I managed to live through these dire straits, and I vowed to myself that never again would I subject myself to my husband's financial mercies. I had learned a well-deserved and very difficult economic lesson all through those nine months.

My daughter was one of the firstborn frees of Zimbabwe. She arrived in a world that was completely different from my son's. Zimbabwe was booming politically, economically, and socially; things could not have been better than those initial years of independence. Teresa enjoyed the fruits of being born free in Zimbabwe, and I took that symbolically to represent the freedom bestowed on her as an individual that I also needed to bestow that freedom on myself, but it would be a long treacherous road for me to gain my own freedom.

Teresa, as she became popularly known, was born on May 5, 1980. She was a small and tiny baby, but her life from those early days was as cute as a button and, in her own way, made me very hopeful. She only weighed into the world at 2.5 kilograms and was as dark as I had never known babies to be. Her birth thrilled my son, Elvin, no end. He noticed that his baby sister had two hands, two feet, two eyes, one nose, and one mouth; while laughing, he told everyone "the baby has no teeth." He later reported the same that evening to my parents when he visited them in the company of my elder brother Dr. Larry.

In my daughter's birth, I saw hope, for hope was in everyone and everywhere in the whole country that year. For the first time, we knew what it felt like living in a free country! Soon after delivering our daughter, I thought I heard the nurses ask me for my daughter's name. I thought they wanted the name I was going to give my baby girl, and I automatically answered Hope Teresa. However, she would never be known by this name nor know about this unless she is the one reading the book today. Her birth gave me hope for better things to come.

Hope was everywhere in Zimbabwe in 1980. Hope had been welcomed with the advent of our independence in April of the same year. Hope was in the free health system; hope was in the free education system. It was also in the booming agricultural industry as communal people settled in the former white commercial farms. Hope was in our women's hockey team that won us our first and only gold medal at the Olympics in Moscow later that year. Hope was up and above and surrounding everyone. Hope was in the belief that things were bound to get better for us too in our marriage.

By 1980, school dropouts were going back to school to complete their education; for suddenly, education had become universal. Primary schools were erupting everywhere; high schools were mushrooming in every corner of both rural and urban areas alike. How could I not hope when the world around me was at peace, and everything for once was calm again? Deep in my heart, I was now determined to go back to work and to embrace this hope that I could do everything possible to change my circumstances. I was determined to work for my children and show my husband that I could be an economical dynamite to be reckoned with. My thinking was that if he realized I was a valuable and an industrious wife, then he would stop his philandering and adulterous ways and become a better father and eventually a better husband that I so much desired and longed for.

Somehow going back to work proved to be extremely difficult that year in 1980. Though education was on the expansion, teachers were migrating in their hundreds into urban schools. Who would want to remain in the rural areas where they had suffered such atrocities during the liberation war? We had celebrated our independence in April that year, and some schools in rural areas had closed for years during the struggle for liberation. Most teachers from rural schools were looking for security in urban schools. As a result, it became a real struggle to find a teaching position in urban areas.

Staffing officers in Highfields, one of the suburbs of Harare, were having a hard time dealing with the sudden influx of teachers coupled with meager teaching vacancies in the city as a whole. It became a challenge. Every Thursday, I would religiously take my bus ride from Chitungwiza to Highfields to queue with other prospective teachers looking for employment. Though Jonathan would be headed the same way, he would give excuses for not giving me a ride. My employment efforts did not immediately reap results. I would go for the whole winter season. From May to August, I religiously took that bus ride into Highfields every Thursday, looking for a teaching position. I was almost losing hope by the end of that semester. I was seriously considering relocating to my Melfort Primary School (in Howard, where I grew up) to secure a teaching position there and live with my parents when my efforts were finally rewarded.

Looking for a teaching position had become a mission to ensure employment. It had become that much more necessary because Jonathan's mother was demanding I join them in the rural areas. I was supposed to contribute cheap labor for the communal farm work. I knew in my heart of hearts that I would never subject myself to the life in Georgetown permanently. The religious beliefs and their not visiting the doctor were a clear indication and hindrance that I would never join them on a long-term basis. I would never jeopardize my children's lives that way. As to the mother-in-law's demands, I would remain resolute, that my children would not be subjected to rural life as I was growing up. I felt my own way of life in Chitungwiza was much better, and that is why I turned a deaf ear to her demands. I never considered her demands and they were not worth wasting my time pondering on them. I think at some point and time, I just plugged my ears and stopped caring how much pressure they were exerting on me to go and be part of the free labor in their Georgetown communal lands to work their cotton fields.

Finally, after my efforts paid off at the end of August, I was deployed to go and teach at one of Chitungwiza primary schools. I was assigned to teach a grade three class, and the school head was Mr. Phiri. I celebrated the day I was told the good news. I remember telling my mother that I would never ever intentionally do anything that would situate my children and me under my husband's financial mercies ever again in my life. In this resolution, I would remain stubborn and would work all my life. I also made a promise to myself that no matter how many affairs I learned about, I would never purposefully leave my job. As such, for the next two pregnancies, I never stopped working; I would deliver my babies and immediately go back to work. Imagine after one child delivery, I went back to work after only three days! I needed the paycheck and was not going to give the principal a reason to fire me.

I am not aware of any other love affairs taking place between 1981 and 1983 as my husband was constantly in and out of work. As soon as he settled into one, he would be soon moving into another. Within that short time, he had worked for several companies in light industrial area in Harare, a service station, a refrigeration company, and the Ministry of Lands, Agriculture, and Rural Resettlement in Headlands. He would leave after being accused of misappropriating funds to sheer mismanagement of funds. For me, it all sounded authentic as I knew he had mismanaged funds occasionally.

At one time, when he was working at a service station, he was audited. The owners found that he had thousands of dollars missing. He was told that by morning, they would do a recheck of his books; and if the shortfall was still there, he would be fired. When he came home that evening, he feared the loss of his job. I too feared for him losing his job. I recommended we visited my dad so that my father could bail him out. That evening, we drove to my home in Destination. I told my father about my husband's predicament. My father had a proud sort of what-were-you-thinking kind of laugh that spoke volumes. After that laugh, he gave my husband the amount he needed to have his books balance. He promised to pay back, and my father told him to keep his fingers out of the employer's cash. However, my husband had tasted what it was like to dip his finger into a cash box that was not his. He only lasted three more months at that job, and they fired him for the same reasons. I knew he would never learn. At least I knew he was a leopard, and that would never change its spots in that area.

Later, he worked for the Ministry of Agriculture, Lands, and Rural Resettlement from the beginning of 1981; until the end of the year, we lived separately. He was doing the resettling of people in the rural areas to the east of Zimbabwe, and I remained in Chitungwiza with my two young children. While working for the Ministry of Lands, Agriculture, and Rural Resettlement, one weekend I visited my husband with my two sisters, Diana and Plaxedes. That weekend, an official from the ministry was supposed to come and address a gathering of people who resisted moving from a white man's farm where they were settled illegally. The government official unfortunately never turned up. The gathered people were incensed and threatened Jonathan's life. They did not want to move. They told my husband that the liberation struggle had been wedged so that the majority could have access to land.

The squatters asked my husband who he thought he was to tell them to move from the land that was spilled with their own children's blood. Some of them were wielding axes, some had spears, some had clubs, and others were threatening to knock him out even with their bare fists. I had never seen so many people so insanely passionate about anything before. My sisters and I were genuinely scared. We thought those squatters were capable of killing him or doing him considerable harm. We told my husband not to get off the van and drive us back to Chitungwiza. The following morning, my husband drove into Harare and resigned from his land resettlement position. Again, after only two short months, my husband was out of job. That had been the trend since we were married, and it would continue throughout our married life together.

It was soon after that short and last period of working in rural area that my husband got a more permanent position with a gold mine (one of the multiple Falcon Gold Mines). At least there was a little permanence, for he lasted for eleven years working for Falcon Gold Mines. Initially, I did not want to accompany him. I needed a stable home for my two children. I feared he would not keep his job, and I did not want the embarrassment of his affairs following me. My husband promised me heaven and earth, and that there would be no more affairs. Can you believe it? I was gullible enough to believe he would change overnight. However, I did not forget my vow to my mother of never subjecting myself to his economical leniencies. As a result before we moved, I ensured that I had secured myself a teaching position. Only after I had been assured of an open teaching position did I agree to accompany Jonathan and relocate. I did not want to put my career in jeopardy and compromise my recently acquired economic independence as well as my self-confidence.

We looked for tenants to take over our home in Chitungwiza, as we had to move to one of the Falcon Gold Mines. Soon after the purchase of our home, we had managed to put together materials for expansion. We put the plans on hold. I was still very optimistic that everything between the two of us would work out. However, I had been carving a good career for myself in Chitungwiza; I left my school principal, Mr. Phiri, who really sang praises of me as a virtuous teacher. I had to accompany my husband on this new adventure. Yes, you have guessed right. I would live to regret this move the most of all my troubled married life.

If back then I had the courage not to follow my husband, my life would have been drastically different. Who could blame me? I was still young and in love with the idea of being a married woman. I did not want to give up on my marriage, and by then, it was mostly the cheating, and he had physically abused me once in 1979. I recall that after that initial physical abuse four days later, I would be entertaining his mother and brother in our home. I never let them know what had happened before they came.

The second incidence of physical abuse was at the end of 1980. I did not want to accompany him to his home in Georgetown for Christmas. He was driving there. As I was reluctant to accompany him, he was unwilling to take his sisters and brother with him. His persistence on leaving his siblings with me was an indication he might have been considering taking another woman home with him. As I insisted on him taking his siblings, he got angry and thought he could beat me into submission.

He took some electrical cables, and he beat me so hard I cringe as I recall right now. He beat me all over my body. He left me with two open sores in front of my shoulders that day and multiple bruises on my back. He used his fists to punch, and honestly, he even kicked me once or twice in my ribs. He beat me up with the strength of someone beating an animal into following his training. At some point, I almost thought he saw me as a man who could fight him off; I was only a woman with an eight-month-old baby still breast-feeding. His own baby, for that matter, but he could not spare me his brutality.

As the beatings continued, I started screaming at the top of my voice. At the beginning I had been taking I was absorbing his beatings silently ashamed to scream and let our neighbors know what was going on. Lucky enough, one of my neighbors heard and came to my rescue. Had it not been for my neighbor, I truly believe my husband could have killed me that day. After my neighbor rescued me, my husband got into his car, and he was on his merry way to Georgetown. I am not sure whether he had a merry Christmas; mine definitely was not. Up to this day, I am still grateful to my neighbor for coming to my rescue.

This was just two days before Christmas when he beat me like that. I was still breast-feeding Teresa, and the pain almost prevented me from caring for my daughter in the best way. In my tortured mind and body, I kept telling myself that my husband did not mean to hurt me. Later, I would show those sores to my mother on Christmas day, and all she would tell me was to leave him and save my life while I could. My mother told me I could make it economically on my own with my two children. I did not purposefully ignore my mother's advice, but I feared how society would perceive my early failed marriage. Against my mother's better advice, I decided I needed to persevere.

I persevered, and I went back to take care of his brother and sisters as he had left them behind. His brother and sisters were still too young to care for themselves, and I knew it was not their fault that my husband beat me up. I could not find it in me to hate those children. Though I was hurting, I was able to cook and feed them until he came back after Christmas. He pretended nothing was wrong between us. As I did not wish any more injury inflicted on me, I did not raise the issue of the fight that happened before the Christmas holiday. I focused on my children. I was happy to go back to work at the beginning of the New Year.

Chapter Ten

Adjusting to life in a mining community

After my husband had lost his job with the ministry, he secured another bookkeeping position with Falcon Gold Mines. Nothing had prepared me for life in a mining community. Life in a mining community was completely different from all I was used to growing up in rural Howard. Not even receiving education at Harvard Institute neither living in Derby my first teaching job in a rural area nor my last teaching assignment in the suburb of Chitungwiza had prepared me for a mining community. Mining community or one of the Falcon Gold Mines was a small community made up of mainly foreigners from neighboring Malawi, Zambia, and Mozambique. These foreigners migrated to Zimbabwe looking for employment in Zimbabwe's farming and mining industry in the 1950s and 1960s. I had never interacted at length with these sections of our population in my life. Knowing them and their culture while teaching their children presented challenges I had never faced before in my career. For once, language became a barrier, and I had to learn their language. I, nonetheless, took pride in my ability to socialize with people from all walks of life; as such, I was hopeful that I would be able to fashion new friendships in this new community too.

One thing I had known in Chitungwiza was that my affairs remained my affairs unlike in Falcon Gold Mines; my affairs became everyone's affair. The community was small; everyone knew one another and their business and what was going on in one another's lives. Some of the children I taught knew of the things going on in my private life in more detail than I did personally. I no longer had a private life to speak of, whereas in Chitungwiza, I could be lost among the huge sea of faces. In the new community, most people knew me personally, and they knew my husband with all his behaviors.

Falcon Gold Mines was where I first met Samantha. We taught at the same school when I first moved there. She had grown up in Clinton communal district neighboring Howard. Somehow the fact that we came from neighboring communal lands drew us together, as our upbringings were almost similar. She embraced me wholeheartedly, and the birth of our lasting friendship was immediate. Sharing with Samantha, I expressed my concerns regarding the prying eyes into my private life, especially in connection to my husband's wandering eye. In her wisdom, Samantha told me that everybody had their own crosses to bear. She told me that while other people, especially women, saw my husband carrying on his shenanigans; I too would see their husbands conducting their own shenanigans.

With the passage of time, I learned that Samantha's predictions were true. In the past, I had never witnessed cheating husbands flaunting their extra marital affairs so openly to the public. Certainly at times, I would be riding on the bus from Spring Meadow or to Hartley from Falcon Gold Mines, to our nearest towns for groceries and supplies, sharing seats with my neighbors' husbands surprisingly sharing seats with their current girlfriends. At times, I would join Jonathan at the country club for entertainment, and all his friends would be paired off with their current girlfriends. This opened my eyes to what Jonathan too would be doing when I would be absent from the scene. I did not like what I saw soon after I moved to Falcon Gold Mines. I regretted the move almost soon after moving.

Immediately, I learned to stay at home and not join Jonathan at the country club. That way, I would not witness such blatant infidelity thrown into my face all the time. To have men disrespect me like that was more than I could put up with. However, it appeared as though cheating on wives was fashionable and had become an acceptable social status in that kind of community in the mid-1980s. Almost all married women had a common bond of contention, and that was controlling cheating husbands. In church, married women strengthened each other about cheating husbands. I think I found solace in the numbers. I truly felt a cheating husband was not unique to me alone. I ignored the fact that this did not make cheating acceptable at all. As such, Jonathan had the free will to continue with his infidelity under my very nose and continued to hide in broad daylight.

The mid-1980s were the years of abundance in Zimbabwe soon after our independence. Most people did not lack for anything, and I was on that abundance train, enjoying my life and living my life with my family as it should be. I cared less for what my husband did because economically, I was taking care of my children. Probably then I temporarily ignored his cheating ways because I was content being a mother to my two children. I was enjoying financial stability. Moreover, I loved my job. I also had a neighbor who loved my children as though they were her own. Sometimes when I did not have domestic help, she would care for them while I was at work. Though she was much younger than me, we developed a true friendship. At that time, my neighbor struggled to have a child in her six-year-old marriage. I could understand why she enjoyed spoiling my children. That friend was the first person to teach me one of the foreign languages.[29]

During the first times of moving to one of the Falcon Gold Mines in 1982, I learned about the social lives in small communities. I was learning about how infidelity seemed to be accepted and never condemned. I found myself pregnant again for the third time. No, I was not on any family planning in case you are wondering. Again, it was unplanned. How could I plan a pregnancy in those circumstances? I did not. Planned or not, one thing was certain: It was quite welcome. Honestly, I began to thank the Lord because with each child I had, it was a true gift from Him. Like with any gifts are never planned, the thrill is in the surprise of receiving them. That is how I felt with each of my five children.

I remember one young woman I worked with years later, asking me how I had planned my children. I remember telling her that I had never

---

[29]   Chewa a language from Malawi and was one of the indigenous languages spoken by natives to the west of Zimbabwe. Most parents did not understand my own language; as such, I had to learn theirs for communication purposes. They had migrated to Lucas in the 1950s to work in the farms and mines.

planned any of my children. They just came from the Lord as the blessed presents that they were. In her wise self, the woman had been planning to have a baby. She told me that sounded wonderful. She claimed that she would not plan any more and would let the blessings come, and she would wait to receive whatever the good Lord gave her. Bless her heart, and I hope she enjoyed a better marriage that she was worthy of and that the good Lord gave her the gifts she so naturally deserved.

I honestly thanked the Lord for my third pregnancy and looked forward to the birth of my third child. Talking of a troublesome pregnancy, this was one. Nevertheless, I anxiously looked forward to my daughter's birth. Throughout all my pregnancies, I suffered morning sicknesses. This one was no exception, but my purging during my third pregnancy was not related to morning sickness at all. It went on until it was time to give birth! Each time my husband went out and came home at night, the first thing I would do when he came back at night would be to run to the bathroom and throw up. He would laugh as this appeared funny to him; he would tease, taunt, and ask why I did not throw up before becoming pregnant!

Symbolically, I knew I was throwing up his infidelity and cheating behaviors. Though I had nothing tangible to point out as his infidelity during this period, I knew he could not have changed overnight just like that. I could not stand the idea that I loved someone who did not love me back. It disgusted me to the extent it made me sick so much that the only way I would share his bed was after I symbolically threw him out by my throwing up. This went on for all the nine months I was pregnant with my third child. I could not stand the very sight of my husband and pretend that everything was all right between us. Not everything was all right between us, but by then, I felt I had made my bed. Therefore, I had to lie in it and try to make the best of a bad situation.

There was also a dismal sense of entrapment. I felt trapped in this marriage that was definitely wrong, abnormally unbalanced, and so clearly one sided. I now lived in the small community that seemed to condone all forms of infidelity. The people knew me; they knew how my husband behaved. They were the relatives and friends of the girls he conducted his canoodles with. I felt as though all their eyes were focused on me and how I conducted myself. Suddenly, I wished I had remained in Chitungwiza because the city was enormous, and I would remain lost among the sea of unfamiliar faces. In Chitungwiza, I would have been another faceless woman whose husband did not know any better.

Here in Falcon Gold Mines, the focus was on me; the communities waited to see how I would conduct myself and deal with the problem that threatened our marriage. Among those unfamiliar faces, I felt so lost and so alone. I wanted so much to know the one face of the one woman Jonathan would be cheating on me with, yet I was immobilized by the fear of the pending confrontation that was bound to happen. I cared about how the people whom I met while conducting my errands were related to the last affair I had last heard of. I was full of questions going round and round in my head almost driving me crazy and still equally puzzled by the knowledge. In similar fashion, I continued to stoop my head very low and never held my head high during those tempestuous times in Falcon Gold Mines. Little did I know it would only get worse than anything I had ever known previously?

Unlike Chitungwiza, in this community, I knew the people whose offspring I taught in school every day. I was supposed to be calm and exemplary, and yet they knew the deep hurtful secrets of my life. They all knew what was going on in their compounds regarding my husband's unbecoming behavior and his infidelities under the cover of dark. So what did I do in order to escape reality? I created my own fantasy world. I was living in this never land where nothing would neither touch nor hurt me. I purposely engaged in reading the Mills and Boon[30] romance novels from the Falcon Gold Mines Country Club library.

I began to fantasize about my romantic life and pretended that in the end I would live happily ever after like they did in those novels, only my prince charming was imaginary and had feet of clay. I would read on average two Mills and Boon romance books a day. Every Friday at 4:30 p.m., I would walk the two miles to the country club library to get myself ten romance books and only to take the same journey the following Friday to return them and borrow ten more. It would become a routine for the next five years until I decided to invest my time as

---

[30] Mills and Boon were fictional romance novels I borrowed at the country club every Friday. The heroes in the novels were always tall, dark, and handsome who always rescued their damsels in distress and lived happily ever after, and I fantasized that I had my own love hero.

well as my reading energies into academic books so that I could see the benefits of my hard labor.

In the meantime, as my family grew, so did my children. Sometimes Elvin had questions. I knew he was intelligent, and sometimes I dodged his questions. True to character, a few weeks before my third child was born, Elvin had a question for me regarding reproduction. For some time, I had been preparing them for an additional member to the family. That afternoon, Elvin asked me a question I had not anticipated coming from him. He asked me how the baby got into my belly. Honestly, I had not prepared for that age-appropriate biological lesson. Dismissively, I told him his father's seed and my seed were responsible. I am ashamed to say the following day after school I found my son and his sister swallowing orange pips. When I asked them why, the simple response was they wanted to grow babies of their own. I knew the first lesson had gone terribly wrong.

A week after that terrible biology lesson, Elvin wanted to know how the baby was going to come out. This time, I tried to do a better job. I had magazines and pictures and explained as much as I could to a six-year-old. At the end of it all, I could tell he had no understanding about giving birth. I will always remain grateful to Zimbabwe Television (ZTV) for the valuable childbirth lesson they showed. Within that week ZTV advertised that, they were going to feature actual childbirth. On the day it showed, I sat my two kids in front of the TV. They were both watching. Everything was shown with nothing left to imagination. At the end of the program, I asked Elvin how the child was born. He only laughed and ran away, but I knew he understood. These were times that rock my life, memorable times with my children. I did not know about birds and bees because no one had taught me about birds and bees.

Despite sad moments, beautiful things come along too. On February 18, 1983, our third born, Tiffany, decided it was time to come into our world. I now fully understand what they mean when they say what does not kill you makes you stronger. I started feeling my labor pains around mid-morning. Spring Meadow was twenty miles away from Falcon Gold Mines. At Spring Meadow General Hospital was where I delivered my baby. I went to work as usual, but by nine thirty, it was obvious I could not carry on. After leaving work at ten o'clock that morning, I summoned my husband to come home. After telling him that we were about to have our third baby, we drove all the way to Spring Meadow. I was having heavy labor pains by then.

When we arrived, the nursing sister gave my husband the option to witness the birth of our child, and he turned it down. I could not believe it. I pleaded with him to stay, but he would not hear of it. The main reason I had registered at that particularly expensive maternity home was so that my husband could be part of our child's birth. My husband decided to forego the honors. Whether he was there or not, it did not prevent nature from taking its place. Our daughter Tiffany was born at exactly 1:00 p.m., an hour after my husband left, and she weighed in at 3.32 kilograms.

When Jonathan decided not to stay and participate in Tiffany's birth, to say that I was hurt would be an understatement. I was deeply wounded. I could feel the ache deep in my heart, and I thought I would never recover. His not staying for the birth froze my heart so cold that I thought my heart would never warm up to him ever again. The pain was tangible and acute. The hurt, the disappointment, and the soreness nonetheless did not kill me but made me stronger. I did not die from the hurt and the pain, but something in my heart died a little that time while I was in the maternity home recovering from childbirth.

When I went home three days later, I became calculating; and inwardly, I resolved that divorce was not an option down the immediate road. Initially, I knew that I wanted to have four children, and I decided there and then that no matter how bad our marriage situation was, I would stand it until I had my fourth child. I spent three days in the clinic relaxing, enjoying my newborn, and lavishing every moment of all the luxury offered in that maternity home. After all, I had paid for it, and I intended to make good use of my hard-earned money. As soon as I went home, the luxury was over; there was no more pampering. The reality hit me. My children needed their mother, and I had brought home another new baby. I now had three young lives totally dependent on me for their very livelihood.

I did not have much time to recover. The following Monday, I was back in the classroom. I had to go and teach because at the end of the month, I needed the money. I no longer relied on Jonathan for my children's and my personal financial needs. Had I stayed out of the classroom for longer than three days, the school headmaster would have been compelled to replace me. Even though I was required to be physically fit to go back to work, I had no choice. Physically fit or not, I had to go and earn a living for my children and myself. In the process, I would be supporting my fickle and cheating husband as well. I had learned an important lesson with Teresa's birth, and I was not going to repeat the same mistake twice. I was no longer willing to place my life totally in my husband's hands for his financial mercies.

It was also during this time that I formed another strong friendship with Star.[31] She would also be a pillar of strength when everything else seemed dark and dreary. Star, as I used to call her, belonged to the Jehovah's Witness and a strong woman of faith. Star had a baby son born in 1982 on St. Valentine's Day and appropriately named him Valentine. Exactly a year later, she lost her beloved son, Valentine. It was during her absence that Tiffany was born, and when she came back after her son's funeral, she found I had delivered a baby girl.

Star would tell me that the Lord had sent her another little angel for her to take care of. She found solace and comfort by caring for my daughter. Though most times she would be crying her eyes out with my daughter in her arms, I did not mind. Other people would admonish me for letting Star cry over my baby like that, but that would go in one ear and out the other. As a mother, I knew the pain she was going through. I pictured myself losing one of my three children and knew I could never envision whether I could have managed to have the strength to carry on. She became a dependable friend that I studied the Bible with, but we would never ever touch on the controversial issues of our different faiths. Somehow we managed to find some common ground to comfort each other in our different religions, for we each had our own crosses to bear.

My friend Star was of a different tribe Ndebele. She had fallen in love with a man from my tribe a Shona. In the process, she had fallen pregnant. Her father strongly believed that marriages were never to be across tribes. As such, Star's father would never permit the two to marry. For the longest time even after the baby was born, Star tried to convince her family that she had found the love of her life, but he never relented.

---

[31] This was the second friendship I formed in Falcon Gold Mines and would last all my life. There was a lot of telepathy between Star and myself . . . letters would cross and calls would ring simultaneously from each other we had telepathy.

In the end, she relented and had to let the love of her life go. The worst part was she also lost the baby, whom she loved more than life itself. To this day, Star is one of my all-season friends. No matter how much time passes by before we talk or see each other, we always manage to pick up from where we had left. I also learned an important lesson from Star's love story that love knows no color, religion, nor original barriers. People can be cruel and prevent the marriage, but when it comes to matters of the heart, no one can tell anybody to let go. It brought to mind one of my Grandmother's lessons early in my childhood. I knew exactly what Anna meant. It was exemplified through Star's disastrous love affair.

Chapter Eleven

Decisions consciously made and more children

Honestly, during the period I moved to Falcon Gold Mines until 1986, I used to hear of affairs going on, but it was nothing tangible that I could actually put my fingers on. By then, locally, I had two strong friends at least to share in my joys and misery with. Growing up, my grandmother Anna had taught me that we need all-season friends and seasonal friends in life. Seasonal friends would come and go as befitting the turmoil and needs in our lives. As such, during the course, you will meet some of the all-season and seasonal friends. However, these two became all-season friends, which means through thick and thin the two would be there; likewise, I would always be there for them.

These two became all-season friends because we shared our hurts and joys unconditionally. One of them had gone through personal loss, and that was Star. The other sanctified the Lord for every single day for His grace—Samantha[32], as her parents appropriately named her. Samantha underwent open-heart surgery at the age of ten. That surgery literally turned her heart into a heart of gold. Comparably, my problems were nothing to what these two lady friends had endured. During the hardest times for the period of my marriage, their love, support, friendship, and understanding helped carry me through some of the bleakest moments.

---

[32] Samantha had a middle name in our language Tsitsi—meaning God's Grace.

I had tremendous love for them both and would always miss their closeness especially while studying and working abroad.

It would be toward the end of 1983 and beginning of 1984 that I learned of another affair that would hurt me the most. Luckily, my two friends were there, holding my hands on a daily basis. That was one affair that turned my heart to pieces down to the very core. I cannot deny the hurt from this affair and how it still pains me even now as I write. This affair was with a girl I had hired to help me with the housework and take care of our children while I was at work. I went to the same church with this girl. Her family circumstances were horrendous, and I thought I could hire her, and she would be in a position to help her family out financially. I hired her as my live-in help.

I allowed the girl to go back to school in the evenings so that she could improve herself academically. The reasoning most probably was eventually, she would improve her family's circumstances. Little did I know that Jonathan had his own trappings set for her? I lived with this girl in my own home. She shared the same beds as our children, and we all ate from the same table. I treated this girl as part of my family. She was still under eighteen, and I thought Jonathan would look upon her as one of our own children. I never, for once, imagined Jonathan would disrespect me by having someone sleep with him in our matrimonial bed.

However, with this girl, I had two things to warn me about the affair with my husband. Most summer holidays, I went to Georgetown. I would take the children with me. However, the hired help usually remained behind to take care of the home and cook for Jonathan. All my life for pending doom, I used to have vivid dreams that forewarned me as far as I can remember. In 1985, during the two weeks in my husband's home, I had one such dream. I dreamt my husband being intimate with our domestic help in our home and our bed. I could actually visualize how he held her, how he persuaded her to give in, and how she finally gave in. When I woke up from my dream, I was really sweaty, shaking, and full of goose bumps, and I was bothered. It was no ordinary dream. It was a vision. I could not shake off the feeling of what had been revealed to me in my sleep. It reminded me of the dream when my brother had been murdered back in 1975.

After my vacation, I went home back home to Falcon Gold Mines. I told my husband about my troublesome dream, but he simply dismissed it as only a dream. I, however, was very uneasy because usually my dreams revealed the truth to me. I tried as best as I could to put the dream in the back of my mind. I attempted to dismiss the dream as maybe me still harboring these feelings from past experiences and other preceding infidelities. I failed to obliterate the dream from mind before long I started to hear rumors going round, which was my next warning to this particular infidelity.

The next warning came from school workmates and colleagues. For some time, they had been dropping hints during our tea times in the staff room about men's wandering eyes. Most times, I never bothered to listen. I had become used to putting plugs in my ears and engaged in what I duped discriminatory hearing. I heard and listened to what I chose to hear and listen to. I did the same for seeing what I chose to see and what I wanted to see. That was my public persona, and it would protect me from a lot of heartache in that small community, Falcon Gold Mines.

On this affair, there was a particular person I worked with. She had taken over someone else's husband, and there was no love lost between the two of us. One day, out of the blue, she started questioning me about my domestic help during tea time. The girl by then had long left our household almost five months prior. She was back in the seventh grade via conventional educational system. I took great pride in knowing that I had been instrumental in enabling her to go back to school. When my colleague questioned me, somehow my gut told me it was more than just curiosity, and a red flag went up in my head. She questioned in a subtle manner, as though there was something that I should know yet at the same time something I should not take personally and connect to either me or my husband.

Suddenly, my vision or dream from months before made sense. I decided to go with my gut feeling. Later that evening, I questioned my husband again whether he knew anything about our previous employee being pregnant by a married man. It was non-confrontational, and he would not own up to knowing anything. My colleague's inquiry and my dream kept bothering me. Two weeks later, I decided to take the bull by the horns and approached the girl in question. When I approached my former employee, I could see she was heavily pregnant. All I was able to ask her was whether the rumors were true. She did not say anything but held her head down, and I knew her actions spoke louder than words.

Standing with that girl, I despised my husband in that moment like I had never despised him before.

I had not believed my husband when he did not own up. The girl's actions, however, clearly revealed all I needed to know. After that, I confronted him again, and all he could say was that he was sorry. He acknowledged that after narrating my dream, he knew it was a matter of time before everything was exposed. He further revealed everything had happened exactly as in my dream. He apologized profusely. His apology did not mean a thing. I was deeply hurt. Later, I discussed the problem with my mother, and she advised me again to leave my husband. Somehow I also sought counseling from my pastors at church. They convinced me it was something I could work hard to forgive my husband. Little did they know that this was my husband's second child out of wedlock? Not to blame my pastors wholly as I did not let them into the full circumstances of the first child out of wedlock.

To my own defense, by then, I had started putting my calculated plans into action. What I did not know was how long it would take me to extricate myself from him and how my life would turn out. Inwardly, I believed I had the power to control my own life as well as those of my own children. Though initially I had followed my pastors' advice, gradually, I realized it made no sense. I started disregarding some of my religious teachings and all that had been imparted in me growing up, being a completely submissive and obedient wife.

I started by taking complete control of my finances. I found a bank where I saved almost a quarter of my salary every month. At home I would grudgingly perform the conjugal rights with him, and this started a barrage of beatings almost on a monthly basis. I lost count of the beatings I endured for the same reason. In order to hide the facial bruises, when going to work, I would wear dark glasses to hide the black-and-blue eyes from the public and from my pupils. The more he beat me, the more resolute I became that I would never be intimate with him again nor would I ever give him a single cent from my own salary. I am disappointed in myself that at times, I would not be able to resist his advances because I was too weakened to the natural desires and needs of my own body. I felt that my body betrayed me.

My husband, true to form, had fathered the girl's child and his second child out of wedlock. At that time, it appeared as though each time I had a child, my husband would father another outside our marriage for the next five years or so. My hired help was the first woman I ever confronted. The girl was so innocent in how she responded to me when I approached her that I really felt sorry for her. To imagine that I humiliated myself to that level still bothers me up to this day. I also know what people mean when they say the wife is always the last one to know when her husband is involved in an affair. As frequent and as numerous as my husband's affairs were, you would think I had learned a thing or two, yet I was always the last one to know. It was never less painful, though, with each affair, but the pain of being cheated continued persistently.

By the time I learned of his second child out of wedlock, I had gained a lot of knowledge about mining communities cultures—that nothing would be too sacred to be discussed openly. The infidelity stories in Falcon Gold Mines alone would compose the major part of my memoirs, but I choose merely to permit you a little glimpse into the thinking and reasoning of an abused wife. This many years after my marriage was dissolved; I find there are many issues I am still dealing with on a more personal level. I find that some of the quite intimate and more hurtful issues that were inflicted on me and in my naivety that I endured are still hurtful even to put down on paper today. Those wounds are still as raw today as they were back then. The wounds bleed equally profusely now, and still I do not get what people mean when they say time heals. Time does not seem to do the healing for me.

I can still physically see the faint outlines of the actual scars of my injuries. After years, I thought to myself how could I mend and heal if I do not talk about what it was living my abusive life. Somehow as I relive the life, I seem to find answers. In as much as I tried to hide the abuse from my children, I know the numerous abuses were hurting my children as well. You might be wondering how I could have gone ahead and had two more children when the ones I had were already enduring the scars of their mother's spousal abuse and trauma. Distorted as my thought processing and reasoning were, one thing clearly stood out— that I would only have one man fathering my children was integral. No matter what the other extenuating circumstances were, I was resolute in the constitution that only one man would father my children. I had witnessed my Grandmother Anna's agony of children questioning paternity, and I had made an oath to never do that.

Remember earlier I described the type of community one of the Falcon Gold Mines was. My husband's unfaithfulness caused me a lot of heartache. In my abuse, I decided to enact the popular saying the indigenous people of Chitungwiza love to use: "kana wadya imbwa idya riri gono."[33] Thus, I decided to eat a dog, and I ate a big one. Inwardly, I vowed to never let Jonathan relinquish his responsibilities as a father. I also made up my mind then that when my children were grown up, I would live my life according to what I required and what my heart desired, and this was way back in 1983.

With this mind-set in 1984, I fell pregnant once more. I was hoping for a baby boy. All my baby preparatory clothes were in blue, for I was so sure that I was carrying a boy. On the morning of July 24, 1985, I woke up like any ordinary day. I dressed and went to school as usual. By 10:00 a.m., it became apparent that this was my D-day. The school principal allowed me to go home, and from there, Jonathan picked me up and took me to the local clinic. I no longer had any illusions that he would agree to share the birth of our baby with me. Because of this, I decided I would deliver my baby at our local clinic rather than leave my children alone for an extended period while I recovered from childbirth. I went in to deliver my baby around 11:00 a.m., and the following morning around ten, I was discharged.

Of all the births I experienced, the fourth delivery was the most painful. I talked nonstop until I delivered. By some means, my amniotic membrane did not break. I blame this on the midwife taking care of me as she was not willing to help nature a little. This was nothing new as it had happened previously with my elder girls' births. However, the other midwives had worked with me and had been willing to break the amniotic membranes for me. The amniotic membranes' non-breakage was my first indication that I might have been carrying a baby girl. The midwife wanted nature to take its own course; in the process, she further subjected me to unbearable and unnecessary pain.

By the time I delivered, I had lost my voice, and the people who had seen me at work earlier that morning could not believe how I looked when they visited later to see me and my baby. They thought I had been through a whirlwind, as I looked ashen, disheveled, worn out, exhausted, and voiceless. I felt tired, and to add on, I could not explain

---

[33] When you eat a dog, you might as well eat a big one so that when people laugh at you, it might as well have been for eating a big, juicy, and fleshy dog than a skeletal one.

what had caused the loss of my voice. Maybe my talking to myself to bear the pain, I will never know. I gave birth naturally on a Wednesday afternoon. I was discharged from the clinic on a Thursday morning, and that following Monday, I was back at work, teaching my third graders.

My third daughter took her first breath at 12:45 p.m. on July 24, weighing in at 3.10 kilograms, small but not too small. She looked darker than my other three, but that could not stop my love overflowing to this little life I had created once more. Though I had been looking forward to having a boy, I was not disappointed it was a girl at all. My baby Thelma was perfect, and being a teacher, I had seen too many disabled children not to be grateful to the Creator for this perfect child, my child, while others were struggling to have babies.

However, an incident happened the evening I took my baby home that up to now I still laugh about it. During the two days since her birth, I had not seen my baby urinate. I remember looking between her legs and not seeing her genitalia. Frantic and stricken with fear, I started to prepare to take her back to the clinic for the nursing sister's attention. During that traumatic process, my daughter decided it was time she relieved me of my anxiety, and she urinated straight into my palms! Perfect joy flowed through my body as she urinated. The urine was warm to the touch, and the love I felt for my daughter warmed up my heart. Moments like that brought me the real joys to my motherhood.

My attention had been diverted from observing everything as during the night Thelma was born, she bled from the belly button. Around 8:00 p.m., I drew the midwife's attention to the blood from the belly button. Had I not been alert, my daughter could have easily bled to death that night. Therefore, my concerns that she did not have her female genitalia in place were not without other predominant circumstances.

With my baby healthy, the following Monday, I was happy to be back at work. The children I taught knew I had given birth and wanted to come to my place to see my new bundle of joy. Certainly, a few did come, and I got joy and happiness from my students. I found their unconditional love and acceptance anchoring and affording me the sanity that otherwise eluded me from the entire goings-on in my home and marriage. Children do not judge you like adults sometimes do.

Immediately after the birth of Thelma, I did not learn of another child out of wedlock, but my husband would comment that I should not have any more children. My response to his statement was that he was the one who needed to stop proliferating as he personally had more children than I did. I simply explained further that I was trying to play catch up with his number because I knew secretly I wanted to try for a son if I could make it this time around. I knew that my first born son would have loved a younger brother, so I left my mind open to having another child, or at least try for another boy.

After delivery, it was joyous to be home and taking care of my four children. By the time Thelma was born, Elvin, my eldest son was only eight years old, and I had turned thirty years old that June. Elvin was in third grade. Teresa was in kindergarten. Tiffany was a toddler full of tantrums. All my children were healthy, and that was all I needed. Soon after Thelma's birth, I again made another conscious decision that Elvin would be too lonely without a younger brother to share with as they aged. I observed their father's polygamous background and convinced myself that my son needed a brother to share with in life. I decided once more to fall pregnant as soon as possible. This did not take long as by early March of 1986, I found I was pregnant for the fifth time.

Honestly, you all must be thinking I must have been desolately raving crazy. You are not the only ones, as by then, my siblings, especially Brenda, my younger sister, could not comprehend it too. They were starting to question my sanity and reasons for having one child after the other with such an unfaithful husband. They kept questioning whether the pill was not agreeing with me or whether I could not afford to be on the pill due to the prohibitive costs. I knew what I was doing and what I had vowed to myself that I would not have children with different fathers. Pregnancies also took their toll on my health. I used to have morning sicknesses during my last four pregnancies. That meant I had compromised health from lack of proper nutrition. In this instance, I still wanted to breast-feed Thelma for as long as I could, for she was only seven months when I fell pregnant.

I knew customarily breast-feeding while pregnant was considered taboo. I found myself visiting an obstetrician-gynecologist very early on in my pregnancy. I knew if I got medical attention and reduced on the morning sickness, I would be able to enjoy my pregnancy. The visit was helpful as the doctor prescribed some medications to take care of my morning sickness. Most importantly, he educated me and allayed my fears about breast-feeding my daughter while pregnant. If anything, I had to eat well to nourish the fetus, manufacture milk for my toddler, and have enough to still nourish my own body and be healthy. Fortunately, the medications worked so well. Of all my five pregnancies, the last one was the most enjoyable and healthiest.

I think the fifth pregnancy was the most enjoyable of all as I did not have any morning sicknesses. I was healthy, and my skin was light. My complexion was immaculate. I was eating well. I was happy. My toddler did not have any side effects from my supposedly deteriorated breast milk, and life for me could not have been any better. All up until mid-August, I did not wear any maternity dresses at all. This was another conscious decision so that people would not question. If I had worn a maternity dress while breast-feeding, I know I would have committed the ultimate taboo. Even my own mother, when I went home to deliver by the end of October, could not believe her eyes. I had been home barely a month earlier, and I had still been breast-feeding Thelma. I hid my pregnancy from my own mother, knowing I would be scolded if she had known the truth.

My workmates could not believe it was real pregnancy when schools opened in September, and I was heavy with child. Three weeks prior in August, when schools closed for the second term vacation, I had a normal body, breast-feeding my one-year-old daughter; and three weeks later, I was heavily pregnant wearing a maternity dress. They could not believe their eyes. One friend said the most hilarious thing by suggesting that I needed to have the boil taken care of, as a real child pregnancy could not have grown so fast in my belly. I told her all life is an illusion; people see what the illusionist wanted them to see. I knew I was telling her the truth; after all, I was the queen of illusions as my friends did not know about my physical and emotional abuses. I presented a happy front, and they never saw beyond that.

In a way after that conversation with my workmate, I realized a ring of truth concerning my personal life as a married woman. I had become a real-life illusionist. I never allowed people to see the intensity of abuse I was living under. I deceived myself into believing that my marriage was all a bed of roses. Besides my own family, no one else had an idea that Jonathan was such a wife batterer. Other people knew about his infidelities because he had his affairs openly in the Falcon Gold Mines compound. As to the physical abuses, I tried as much and as hard as I could to conceal everything from neighbors, friends, and colleagues. Though going back to those beatings saddens me, I wish I had sought more counseling than just my church pastors and my mother. I did nothing wrong to deserve the battering and all the cheating that went on.

Chapter Twelve

Memorable times with my mother

Luckily, by 1986, the Ministry of Education and Culture was by then granting maternity leave to all female members of the public sector. We could have forty-five days before birth and forty-five days after birth. As I hoped this would be my last pregnancy, I decided to go on maternity leave and enjoy the ninety days. I desperately wanted to share this last pregnancy with my mother. My first pregnancy had been extremely difficult on my mother and myself, as I had been plagued by health issues. This time, I was healthy, and I wanted to spend some time as an adult with my mother, Doris.

For my mother, Doris, my first pregnancy was her first experience of seeing her own daughter in childbirth. I had been also plagued by illness for some time before giving birth; as such, the memory was not so noble. The night I had my labor pains for my firstborn, I felt sorry for my mother, Doris, because it appeared as though she wanted to spare me the pain of childbearing and bear the baby for me if she could. When I left home around three in the morning, it was as though she had labor pains of her own the whole night. She never left the clinic; she stayed by my side all night long. In the morning, when my son was born around six, she was there by my side. Somehow with my other children, I never went home because I wanted to spare my mother, Doris, going through the pain of childbirth all over again with me. The year 1986, I decided I was healthy. It had been a long time since I had spent quality time with my mother, and I really needed to experience the final birth of my child with her. I looked forward to waiting for the actual birth while spending time with my loving and always very calm mother, Doris.

By mid-October 1986, I left my two elder children, who, by then, were in school, with my husband and went back home to Howard to await the arrival of my last born. I extremely enjoyed the time with my mother. Since getting married, I had not spent more than a week with her, something I had never thought of before marriage, that time with my own mother would be limited due to marriage and be reduced to only sporadic short visits. I looked forward to this time as a break that I desperately needed from my troubled married life. I brought with me Tiffany and Thelma, my youngest two daughters, as well as Emma, my younger sister's daughter who was almost the same age as Tiffany.

This time, my mother had completely relaxed. My three younger sisters had been through four pregnancies of their own; thus, my mother had grown used to having grandchildren and seeing her daughters in childbearing pain. During this time in 1986, sometimes my mother left me alone with my three toddlers. She went to church; she attended women's clubs and even went shopping unlike when I had my first pregnancy with Elvin. This time around, I remember my mother would even let me do some heavy manual work, such as watering the garden. Watering the garden was hard labor due to where the water came from. I drew water from a deep-dug water hole in the garden with a huge five-gallon watering can. That entailed walking down four steps to draw the water and up the four steps, then thirty to forty yards away to water the vegetables,. This became a daily routine, and at times, I wonder why I did not give birth before my due date.

My mother also had a chicken-rearing project, and whenever she was not home, I was responsible for feeding the chickens. Feeding over a hundred chickens was not easy, but I joyously helped her out. I was happy to be home and helping my mother out with such mundane daily chores. I also had three toddlers I was taking care of: Tiffany, Thelma, and my niece Emma. Taking care of three toddlers was a challenge in its own. Giving baths to those toddlers was a backbreaking chore in addition to making sure they were well fed, and one was still being toilet trained. Besides that, Tiffany and Emma fought a lot, but mostly it was the most enjoyable time I had spent home with my mother as an adult.

Every weekend without fail, my husband brought the other kids to spend time with us. He was good in covering up his misdeeds whenever I was home with my parents. He never gave them reason to doubt his love for me. However, even there in my home area, sometimes my husband used to have girlfriends he conducted his miscellaneous activities with. I remember one time when one of my younger sisters complained to me that they had seen him with one of the most promiscuous women in our community. I knew if I asked him, he would give me words that would pierce my heart; as such, I never questioned him. I was hurt. I cannot pretend otherwise, but I did not want any fights to start in my parents' home. Therefore, I knew when to keep my mouth shut.

By Saturday, November 16, 1986, I started dilating, and I knew childbirth was imminent. By the time Jonathan left the following Sunday afternoon, I told him before the night was out, I would be going to the clinic to deliver our last born. The fact that I was dilating before any labor pains gave me hope that my baby was a boy. I never went for any scans or sonograms; each child's birth was a pleasant surprise regarding their gender. I never dilated or broke the amniotic membranes naturally with my three girls. That was different with my eldest son; the amniotic membranes broke naturally. As such, when I started dilating, I became hopeful about the gender of my baby and ecstatic when the membrane broke naturally!

Around eleven that night, I told my mother that I was in labor. Howard District had built a more modern clinic. The clinic was only two miles down the road from our rural home. It was larger with better facilities compared to where Elvin had been born almost a decade earlier. Moreover, the new clinic was along the highway. We could catch rides with people who commuted along the highway but we decided to walk. My mom and uncle Elvis who was visiting carried my baby bag. The two left me without any mishap at the clinic. The walking must have done the trick as around midnight, I was ready to deliver.

As I checked in to clinic, the midwife had told me that I had dilated only five centimeters. She wanted me to dilate naturally to about ten centimeters. Around twelve thirty in the morning, I rang the bell as I felt the urgent need to push. My midwife again told me I had not dilated enough. As the two nurses on night duty left me alone in the labor room, I made up my mind to deliver by myself. The pain was unbearable, and I knew I was ready to deliver my baby. As the midwives were reluctant to be with me, I started to push. Their attitude had shown me they wanted to sleep; as such, I thought I would call them when my baby had finally arrived. I had been through the childbearing process four times before; hence, I knew the pain of childbirth well.

As I was pushing, I could see and touch the head. Immediately, I noticed that the umbilical cord was wound round my son's neck. I stopped pushing and pressed my hand on the bell on the wall next to the bed until the two nurses came running. When they saw that the umbilical cord was wound round my baby's neck, they kept telling me not to push and to breathe in. All I retorted back was that had it not been for the umbilical cord round my baby's neck, I had decided not to call them again until my baby was born. I had only called them because I could not reach over to unwind the umbilical cord. In my heart, I kept praying that my baby was all right. If that had been my first child, I think my son could have died due the cord round his neck.

Elton arrived on November 18, 1986, at 12:45 a.m., just three days after his expected delivery day early on a Monday morning and less than an hour after checking into the clinic. For some time, Elton did not cry because the umbilical cord had been wound three times round his neck. Immediately, after the nurses took care of the cord, my son was born. I held my breath as he did not immediately cry. The nurses were busy suctioning him through the nose, holding him upside down, and slapping him on his back several times before my baby started crying. It was only then after I heard my baby cry that I too could breathe a sigh of relief; I could relax, sleep, and rest. In that moment, I hoped I could rest from childbirth forever in my life. I told myself I had given my eldest son a young brother, whom he would share with the problems of the world, so I thought. Consequently, I could afford to rest from childbirth, and I had achieved my goal of having one man as the father of my five children.

In the morning, my husband called the clinic very early. I told him he was the father of another little boy. I detected the sound of pride and joy in his voice. We had not planned on any baby names. My husband wanted to name him a translation of "we are happy," but I liked Elton. The pregnancy had been a happy interlude, and I felt the name was suitable. After a while, I won the battle of the baby's name. Later, my husband would call all my siblings and spread the news. By the time my mother, Doris, came around ten o'clock that morning, I was ready to go home. My father hired a vehicle to take us home. Moreover, I was in good health, and I could have walked, but he would not hear of that. Elton arrived in style at my parents' home.

I was happy. I was with my mother, my dad, and my toddlers as well as Emma, my niece. The toddlers all enjoyed looking at the baby. They all wanted to look at his fingers, his toes, his eyes, and even change his diaper. I could not stop laughing as they were like little mother hens around their little chick. Thelma, though only sixteen months older than Elton, enjoyed holding him on her lap. It was a fulfilling time. This time, there were no health issues; I was an experienced person at motherhood. I knew how to care for my newborn baby. I was having a break from all the heartache of dealing with a promiscuous husband. My parents loved me. All I wished for was that time would simply stand still so that I could enjoy more time with my parents in peace and calm for a change. It was one of the best times of my adult life that I recall.

Nonetheless, time and tide wait for no man. I had two other children who were driving cross-country every weekend to come and see us. I did not want that to continue anymore. I knew sometimes my husband was a reckless driver, and I feared for my elder children's safety. Difficult as it was, I had to go back to my own troubled home. I remained with my parents until the beginning of December. In the eyes of my parents and relatives, he exhibited himself as a loving and doting husband and father. I could not find fault with his behavior then, and I even looked forward to going home. What was waiting for me at home in Falcon Gold Mines would shock my entire life, and I wished I had remained forever in Howard with my parents.

It was also during these times at home that rumors were surfacing and going around about an illness that was not curable. It was assumed then that people lost a lot of weight, would continuously have diarrhea, and lost most of their hair as well as have poorer skin texture and darker complexion. Some people said it was the slim disease, and others said it was the disease for gay white males. Some said it was the disease of people in the West and others said it was an epidemic for the whole world. The truth was somewhere among the mix, and it would take years before people really knew this disease.

During these initial times I lost one of my uncles to what was assumed to be HIV (Human Immunodeficiency Virus) AIDS (Acquired Immunodeficiency Syndrome). My uncle's relatives and friends were suspecting and were not sure that was the cause of his death. Personally,

I had read several magazines around 1982-83 that had featured stories on HIV and AIDS. Initially, the description for HIV/AIDS was a gay man's disease. Contrary to my uncle, he was a happily married heterosexual man. As such initially, HIV/AIDS was a confusing disease as heterosexual people distanced themselves. Somehow that made it alien to all we knew, and personally, I naively felt safe in my heterosexual world. The initial description made it remote and far removed from main culture and sexual orientation in Zimbabwe.

Though homosexuality is there among my people, it is never talked about openly. It is that big elephant in the room that people pretend they do not see, yet it fills all the room and sucks all the air so no one could be that blind. If homosexuality were not there among my people, then we would not have had an appropriate name in our ethnic language, a word for homosexuality. *Ngochani*[34] (homosexuality), as far as I know among the indigenous, homosexuality had been there since time immemorial; hence, the inclusion of the word in our indigenous vocabulary. My grandmother used to allude to the fact that a male who lived alone and remained single all his life in a village with his family was presumed *Ngochani*, homosexual. According to my grandmother Anna, whether the single male was homosexual or not, the relatives never talked about the sexual orientation openly.

In our communities, people were just beginning to wonder about HIV/AIDS in the mid-1980s. Some alluded to the fact that our independence had brought back the ex-combatants and attributed the disease to them. Some of the liberators had been to the West; therefore, people in Zimbabwe started pointing fingers at the ex-combatants as the culprits because of their exposure to the West. Those times were full of uncertainty, filled with fear of the unknown pandemic that seemed to be spreading like a wildfire. Women and girls were panicking and whispering to each other about the illness yet unsure how to deal with unfaithful husbands and boyfriends.

I was one of those who whispered with friends. We would compare notes of what little knowledge we knew about the pandemic. Some

---

[34]   Ngochani as we had a word for homosexuality and my grandmother had told me it was known that some people could be homosexuals and if we did not have a word for it that meant the concept was foreign to our cultural practices.

rumors were spreading that falling pregnant would exacerbate the deterioration of women's health. Even if I had wanted another baby, I decided I would not have any more, as I was not so sure of what animal HIV/AIDS was. When I was a young girl in secondary school, I used to tell my friends that I would have as many children as I could produce. However, reality was completely different from wishes, and furthermore, children are real and have real needs to meet in real life. As a mother, I was not meeting all of my children's needs. Education was expensive, food was expensive, clothing was a nightmare, and as much as I loved children, I decided my five children were enough. Consequently, I put a halt to my child-rearing days and prayed I would be able to provide for the ones I had. Furthermore, there was a lot of abuse in our marriage; besides, the threat of becoming HIV/AIDS positive was real for me. I did not want to expose myself to that illness. I desperately wanted to see my children mature into adults and probably bear me grandchildren. As a result, I deliberately put a stop to childbearing.

Three years would go by, and my mother would ask me to have another baby. I think it was because we had had a wonderful time together when I had Elton, so much that she wanted me to have a good excuse for me taking another extended stay. When she asked, my mind and plans were no longer in childbearing, but my sights were now set on improving myself academically. I could understand why my mother, Doris, wanted us to be together again because by the time I had Elton, I was more mature; we could discuss some of the issues we could never have discussed with my mother when I was younger. When I had Elton, I could be more of a friend than just a daughter to be guided through life as an adult.

I was also gainfully employed; therefore, I could relieve my mother of the financial burden during that time. My mother was such people that when her daughters were home, she would let us take over the running of her home. We all had no qualms or reservations with that. The only thing she would make a fuss about was making sure that our father had his meals on time and that they were properly cooked. As you can see, the time I had Elton had been filled with joy, laughter, happiness, and getting reacquainted all over again as adults for both my mother and myself.

The joy I felt as I left home that morning on December 2, 1986, would completely evaporate before the week was over, when I got back to Falcon Gold Mines. I was welcomed by other unexpected or expected bombshells of my husband's infidelities during my absence.

Chapter Thirteen

Why do married men batter and cheat?

The bombshells that were waiting for me at Falcon Gold Mines after my fifth and last child's birth in 1986, when I left Howard going back, came from different sources. I learned of several affairs that had been taking place while I was gone giving birth to our child in a span of barely three months. I did not purposely go to my friends soliciting them for information about my husband's behavior during my absence. Most of what I learned was brought to my doorstep by well-meaning friends. Most times, I wondered why I never told them to leave me alone.

For instance, I used to supplement my income through knitting. People loved the designs and patterns for sweaters I came up with. A week after I got back, one woman whose husband was my workmate came to be taught a particular pattern that she really desired. In the process, she was telling me of how Jonathan had befriended one woman in their neighborhood in particular and was rumored to be the father of this woman's child. While the woman was telling me this, I was boiling and seething from the humiliation inside of me. I wished I could tell her to stop because it hurt so much. I kept my mouth shut, and by evening, she went home, and I said nothing to her.

When my husband came home after work that evening, my heart was very cold. I could not believe for the past three months he had continued to receive my salary and had spent it on his womanizing. Following my return to Falcon Gold Mines after Elton's birth, I found out that my husband had been receiving my paycheck, which was before we could have direct deposits for our salaries. The times he had visited me in Howard, my husband had failed to bring me my full paychecks and alluded to the fact that he had not received the checks from the school principal. I did not argue with him, as I did not want to initiate any fights within my parents' home. As a result, he left enough cash for us to get by.

After arriving in Falcon Gold Mines, I inquired after my salary from my school principal. I learned that my husband had collected all three pay checks and my husband had nothing saved from my three months' paid maternity leave. All he had to show me for my three months' salary was a rug that was in one of our children's bedrooms. I was seething inside and dying to find the most opportune time to question him about the assumed affairs and my paychecks. I could not question him in the house, for I knew he would blow off. I did not want the children to be caught in the middle. After the occasion when he had tried to beat one of the children for pleading with him to stop beating me, I never wanted the nastiness of the batteries on me vented while my children witnessed.

The following weekend, the two of us went into Spring Meadow for our monthly groceries. As we were driving back, I questioned him about the rumors that were surfacing as well as my salary. His response was not what I expected. He retorted that he was a man and needed no one to control and monitor his every move and how he spent his time and with whom. I do not know where I got the courage. Immediately, I punched him in the face with my close-fisted right hand. His reaction was immediate. He became exceptionally furious. With the back of his left hand, he struck me back on my face while still driving. I regretted that first punch as soon as it landed on his face, but the force with which he retaliated was not justified. It was brutal. He pulled the car to the side of the road, and the punches continued incessantly. All I did was tried to protect my face, and I kept pleading with him to stop.

He continued to punch my body with his closed fists on any part that was exposed, and his fists inflicted more pain than I had. I cannot even say a real fight ensued as he did all the beating. I think he punched me until he was physically exhausted. I really feared for my life. I could imagine him beating me to death and staging it so that people would think we had been involved in automobile crash. At some point,

I stopped pleading with him and let him work out his wrath and me paying back for whatever unknown sin I had committed in his eyes.

The man was ruthless; he could not even spare me considering I had a newborn baby who was still entirely dependent on his mother for his livelihood. While reflecting on this battery, I am now convinced that was the day it clearly dawned on me that he never loved me, or that if he ever did, he did not know how to show his love and share it properly. By the time we arrived home, I was black and blue on my face and all over my body. As for him, he had nothing to show for my handiwork. I could not even look at my children's innocent faces without crying. That whole month was an ordeal that still gives me chills to this day.

The following Sunday, people from church came to welcome the new baby. Welcoming pastors into my home was a huge challenge physically and emotionally. My face was still black and blue. My body still ached all over. I dabbed some make up on my face to conceal the raw bruises. Whether church colleagues and my pastor noticed anything strange, they did not say. I hosted the party of people from church while biting my bottom lip so as not to break down and cry. When they left after praying with me and my children, I wondered why I had not opened up to the pastor and told them the truth of my abuse.

In that instance, I found peace by comforting and convincing myself to believe that I deserved that beating because I had punched him first. Like all abused women, I realize how I was making excuses for my husband's notorious and his infamous behaviors. I felt as though I had aggravated his anger. As a result, I was responsible for making him angry and ultimately deserved his beating. In my crooked mind, I was convinced I deserved his brutality. No human being deserves brutality at the hands of the one who presumably loves them. If anything, they should be protective. My husband did not protect me. He exposed me to diseases; he abused me physically, mentally, socially, and economically. No wonder my thinking and reasoning was crooked; I endured plenty of psychological traumas each time I found out about his misdeeds and numerous affairs. The bottom line is, a man is not supposed to raise his hands to a woman no matter what the mitigating circumstances are.

I failed to be a good example to my children, but to anyone who cares to listen, please do not let yourself be anyone's piñata. The person battering you is not the last born of the world. The best decision is to run away with your life and sanity. There are plenty better men out there.

For me, I regret every day because I did not have to subject myself to the abuse for so long. Meanwhile, I pretended everything was okay. I continued to care for my children in the best way my battered body and tortured mind could allow me.

In his pure fashion, my husband probably came to his senses or somehow finally realized the magnitude of the pain he had inflicted on me. He could not stop apologizing. One evening, coming from work, he brought me a nice white dress as a token of his heartfelt apology. As the naive, abused, and battered woman that I had become, I accepted the peace offering. Within a short time, I truly forgave him. All I asked him was that at least if he ever cheated on me again, I would rather learn about it from him than from other people.

In my mind, the request made the cheating seem better or made the wrong right. It was a crooked way of thinking, I know. Nevertheless, at that time, I assumed that maybe if he told me himself, I would feel as though I had been forewarned, hence forearmed. As a result, of the knowledge, I would be in a position to respond accordingly by the time other people started soliciting me for information on his infidelities. That was all the thinking of a distorted and disturbed mind as you can tell.

A couple of weeks after this incident, I remember another woman coming to my house to tell me to control my husband and not let him befriend her husband. She told me my husband was not a positive and good influence to her husband. I had never met this woman. I had no idea who her husband was. I could not fathom why she felt it was my responsibility that I tell my husband not to befriend her husband. At that moment, all I managed to retort back was she was the one seeing them together; as such, she had the responsibility of letting my husband and her husband know how she felt. Moreover, if she could keep her husband on a leash, she had to so that her husband would not accompany mine. This time, I did not even bother telling Jonathan of this incident. My body was still recovering from the bruises of the earlier beatings of the previous week; my mind was trying to figure out the best way to pick up the pieces of my battered life. Consequently, I decided to keep my mouth shut. Yes, I had learned; a burnt child dreads fire.

It saddens me and makes me miserable to recall all that even at one point, my husband reduced our marriage to a point where he resorted to befriending husbands of his close and married girlfriends to camouflage his cheating deeds. He would bring them to our matrimonial home as friends. That behavior all began in the early 1980 and we were still in Chitungwiza. Naively, I welcomed both husbands and wives with open arms as friends. Believe me or not, I was totally naive. Back at end of 1980, we could afford buying a car. This meant he was in a position to drive to work. My workplace was our local school; it meant I walked to school every day. My husband would car pool to save on the costs of fuel. This afforded him the opportunity to meet more women whom he could cheat on me with.

I remember meeting a particular woman whom he introduced to me as one of his frequent passengers. She was in the company of her husband. A couple of years later, I learned that she and Jonathan had engaged in an extramarital affair, behind my back and her husband's. I felt sick when I found that out. It destroyed my faith in him as my lover. What I could not understand then and what puzzles me still is how he managed to delude the husbands and befriended them while engaging in extramarital affairs with their wives. I remember this particular woman's husband was really close to my husband. I had entertained them both in my home. Honestly, my husband epitomized the common saying of keeping your friends close and your enemies closer. My husband lived, breathed, and dreamed of how to improve on his deceitful ways of carrying on his inappropriate behaviors during our married life together. All the time, not one single technique was ever the same for all the twenty-seven years of cheating in married bliss.

Most of the domestic violence inflicted on me was when I asked my husband how he spent his salary, why he was late coming home, or when I would request him for money for food. More often than not, those inquiries and those requests ended in my being beaten up. I tried as often as I could to make do with my own income, less than half of what he made. Our family had grown. We had five children, and he earned way more than I did. As such, I could not provide all the school uniforms, school supplies, the food, the clothes, and all the other amenities needed when the children are growing. As a result, the physical violence almost became a regular occurrence. What I did was I tried to keep my mouth shut and never voiced anything that would trigger his vengeance.

I learned to choose my battles. Now looking back on all the notoriety and battery, I realize maybe it was his way of telling me I was a hindrance to his unfaithfulness and freedom. As such, he was not going to stop his philandering. If only back then I had the hindsight to know what I know now. I hope you are still with me when I say chronicling this was all the healing I needed for me and for my children. I hope that my children can finally understand that I was not the terrible partner in this marriage. I never wanted them to grow up exposed to the violence.

My personal intentions were never to alienate my children from their father. Consequently, I tried to hide everything from my children. God forbid, Jonathan is their father, and there is no way I could deny him that right and my children that relationship with their father. In fact, if anything, my children were not fully aware of how terrible things really were between the two of us. If they were, it was not my intention to hurt them (that is what I thought anyway), but it is something I have to live with the rest of my life.

I truly believe that in life, people reap what they have sown; Jonathan sowed seeds of mistrust, doubt, hurt, and disrespect, and that is what he reaped from me. Because I had such mistrust, I had been hurt many times over. My husband had disrespected me and abused the vows of our marriage repeatedly. I, therefore, felt justified to be divorcing him on the grounds of abandonment and mistrust in order to save my own life. Growing up, my grandmother always told me that those who played with knives would die from knife wounds. Those who played with guns would die from gunshot wounds. Those who played in flooded rivers would eventually drown. I ascribe fully to my grandmother's wise sayings and attest the sequential end of our marriage to the things Jonathan loved intensely and I detested the most.

His extramarital relationships with other women, physical abuses, material deprivation, and stubbornness were the eventual downfall of our marriage. I do not wish Jonathan any harm, but I know if he still associates with women and does not stop mistreating them, some women are not as forgiving and patient as I was. He eventually might find himself in trouble with the long arm of the law no matter where he is residing in the world. Karma has a strange way of paying back.

Remember the girl who had mothered my husband's second[35] child out of wedlock while in Falcon Gold Mines? Regrettably she became an ally and at times would alert me to the possibility of other women in

---

[35] The humiliation was she was my domestic paid help. He never, during all our married life, cheated with someone better than me professionally. At

my husband's life. Pathetic as it was that I should befriend his mistress. Once in a while, she told me of several women my husband was dating, and he was none the wiser as to whom was my source of information.

As to the third and fourth children, they were by one woman. The second woman was the one who told me about the third affair to result in children. To him, I presented it as though I had another dream, and he started to call me the dreamer. When he started calling me the dreamer that was when I asked him why married man cheat. He really did not have an answer for me.

The above question why married men cheat has continuously bothered me throughout my life. I know the bias in my statement because sometimes women also cheat on their husbands. However, I am exploring my own abuses, and sometimes I tend to turn a blind eye as to why men are battered by their wives or why people who are same-sex partners are battered or cheated on by their significant others. In the past decade or so, I have come to know of many public figures who have cheated on their wives while married, and I have continuously wondered.

I have known of my own fellow president of Zimbabwe, President Robert Gabriel Mugabe, who fathered two children with Grace, when he was still married to his beautiful wife, Sally his first wife, who has since passed away. I have known of other public figures such as Prince Charles, whose wife was an icon in my eyes, Lady Diana Spencer, and yet he cheated on that beautiful woman. As time passed, I learned and I have heard of many world-famous religious leaders, well-known politicians, government officials, sports icons, and some not-so-well-known individuals who have cheated on their spouses. Whereas all these men had beautiful wives, still they cheated, and I continued to wonder and question why me.

Despite all the concrete evidence of famous people, leaders, politicians, and icons cheating on their spouses, somehow I always thought my own experience should have been different. In a way, I was not wrong in expecting unconditional fidelity from my husband because that was how I was brought up—to believe and expect from my

times, I felt as though it was because I had married below me. But now I know better that men just cheat no matter their positions in life.

husband as my protector, my provider, and my lover. According to that upbringing, there was no way I was ever going to cheat on him.

However, with evidence of people cheating, I knew I was not alone, but that did not make the wrong right. Chastity had been impressed on us girls, so much that we never even thought sexual intimacy outside of marriage was an option at all. When I got married, I held my marriage to a higher and different standard than my husband obviously did. My husband, like me, had been brought up of a polygamous father. That was how far the similarities in our backgrounds went. Whereas he had grown up with it, I had only heard about it.

I had witnessed relatives in polygamous relationships, and I knew they were spiteful. Inwardly, I knew I would never be able to tolerate the dehumanizing effect of polygamy to women. Despite his background, I somehow never expected my husband to be polygamous and unfaithful to me. Nevertheless, now I am more mature; I know I was in complete denial because I had seen the telltale signs even as early as our dating days.

During our dating time, we had discussed these issues, and Jonathan had promised me that he would never be a polygamous husband. He told me of the tensions that always existed between his mother and her co-wives. He told of the strain it put on the children who were half siblings. He also alluded to the fact that he believed the stress of polygamy had caused his father's early death. However, I never discussed the issues of infidelity because I assumed he would automatically know that I would never put up with it at all. Now I come to reflect on the cheatings and all the abuses; I fail to understand why he never kept his word. I think in the back of his mind, my husband might have deplored the behaviors; but despite that, he admired the behaviors in a conflicted sort of way.

I remember early on in my married life, I promised Samantha, my longtime friend, and I that I would write about my marital emotional abuses no matter how long or what it would take. All Samantha would respond was that it would not be appropriate. "Appropriate for whom, Samantha?" I asked her, and she would tell me customarily it would be inappropriate. All I could afford to tell her then was customs had to be changed and should never be static to match modern times.

By the way, Samantha survived an open-heart surgery when she was only ten years old in the then Southern Rhodesia before the Unilateral Declaration of Independence (UDI) by the then prime minister from

1965 till our independence in 1980. However, from 1979 to 1980, there was a brief period when a church bishop was elected prime minister of the short-lived Zimbabwe-Rhodesia government until we finally celebrated our independence in 1980.

Samantha's heart surgery was shortly before UDI. I can safely say Samantha's life was saved just in the nick of time before doctors left Rhodesia for South Africa. No wonder Samantha had such a golden, loving, soft, caring, kind, and compassionate heart. I promised the two of us that no matter when it would be when I would gather enough courage to write, I would write my memoir whether I would still be married to Jonathan or not. I promised my friend this would be a sign of reclaiming my identity and dignity. I also told her I would need to redeem my image and regain my self-respect. My greatest wish is that Samantha will read this memoir, as she played an integral and pivotal role in my taking up my studies. Samantha motivated me to empower myself academically and embark on the ultimate journey to redemption by simply stating if she could do it, so could I.

I have always been true to myself. Therefore, no matter how bad these memories were, I needed to recall each little affair that I could still remember and see if I could find healing. I wanted to show that at times, people do survive under unusually abnormal marital, physical, and emotional abuses and unprecedented traumas, but they go on to even soar to extraordinary heights. This does not mean that I am encouraging women living under abuse and traumatic circumstances not to leave. No, not at all, far be it from me to do that, for in the end I left. Leaving is a process that does not happen overnight. It is like in combat. One has to strategize and plan for battle; otherwise, it is easy to die during the battle if not properly planned.

I left when I was ready to leave on my own terms, and there was nothing my husband could do about it. His famous saying during the time I was pursuing divorce was "I married Avis in Zimbabwe. Therefore, she cannot divorce me while living and studying in the US." Good-naturedly, I would tell him that time and tide waited for no man; similarly, divorce does not wait for the other spouse to be ready. When one partner is no longer invested in the union, no judge can deny you the dissolution of the union, especially where one of the partners' lives is under jeopardy.

When my husband least expected me to divorce him, that is when I decided to make my move. I was ready. He even doubted that I would carry out my "threat," as he called my filing for divorce, to my sister Diana. He told my sister Diana that there had been numerous deserving times I could have divorced him, and I had not. He had beaten me up tens of times. My husband had misappropriated funds meant for our son's tuition several times. He had brought home his mistresses and forced them on me many times. He had fathered children outside our marriage repeatedly, but I had remained by his side.

Sometimes I am ashamed to enumerate the number of times he abused my good-naturedness, my loving heart, my forgiving spirit, my naivety and still continued to assume I would never learn better. True, the man had taken me for granted for close to three decades; therefore, he assumed no matter what he did, I would always love him without any reservations. Understandably, he truly believed he could come and go as he liked because I had tolerated these behaviors for so long. He assumed he could lie around, cheat around, beat me up as he desired, and father as many children as he wished out of wedlock, and I would always welcome him with open arms. Jonathan believed he could have his cake and eat it at the same time. Unfortunately, I had matured and wizened to his character as a husband; thus, I took him by surprise.

I know he never saw my last move coming. Some of you might think, yes, he deserved what I did in the end. Others still might say it was high time I paid him back for his multiple misdeeds. Probably it might have been both because to me it felt so good and liberating. Whether I decide to call it revenge or payback time or decisions consciously or unconsciously made, it does not matter. I had to stop the ill-treatment. All I know is that I made a decision that I am proud of up to today. I got rid of that man before he destroyed my self-worthy beyond redemption.

The idea of leaving my husband had been really given serious consideration later in our marriage, when I started learning and educating myself about Human Immunodeficiency Virus (HIV) and Acquired Immunodeficiency Syndrome (AIDS). The first HIV/AIDS cases were diagnosed in the West in the early 1980s, and therefore, the news started trickling down to my world in Zimbabwe through magazines around at the same time. I used to enjoy the *Personality* magazine, *Vogue*, *Cosmopolitan*, *Readers Digest*, and many others. That is how I learned about this fatal illness initially and an illness that would change my life.

It sunk into me that my life was vulnerable due to the numerous women Jonathan had affairs with.

In the beginning, I read about this illness as a Western gay man's disease, and somehow I felt safe. The Western world was remote from my world. The gay community had nothing that I could identify with. I knew about gays but had never seen one living openly. However, as the years went by and people that were heterosexual became positive, locally, HIV/AIDS was by then affecting people we knew who were not gay, and they quickly succumbed to the illness. Suddenly, HIV/AIDS was there. HIV/AIDS became real faces of real people, faces that we knew. All I knew about HIV/AIDS was it had no cure. It had no known treatment, and then it was described as a long illness. Suddenly, I was really scared for my life.

I was not the only one filled with fear. Most women were filled with fears of HIV/AIDS but had little knowledge of how to control the spread of HIV/AIDS. To make matters worse, HIV/AIDS was not talked about openly and for a long time remained shrouded in blankets of shame and silence. How then could people learn about this deadly disease when it remained taboo? Gratefully, Zimbabwe musicians were putting words to songs that would really affect us in many different ways. I remember Paul, one of Zimbabwe musicians, singing about an illness that had been injected into the water hole that all people drank from. To hear young people sing about it publicly made me realize that no one was safe. I knew back then that my own life was in jeopardy. That was when I realized I needed to be proactive, and I had to take control of my own life.

When I was alerted through strange dreams and through strange friendships with and past girlfriends of Jonathan's fooling around with other women, I knew I had to act. I never went out of my way looking for these other women. Several years would pass before I decided to confront my husband and his mistress then. Though after the initial shock I was angry at how much people knew about our marital problems, I directed my energies elsewhere. I knew I had to improve myself academically and be able to stand on my own financially before I left my husband. When I graduated as a teacher, I had made a promise to my father to improve my academic credentials. The fear of HIV/AIDS made me recall the long-standing promise and act, and the year was1989.

My husband earned way more than I did. He spent his money on his drinking and womanizing. I would stretch my budget to afford to clothe the children, sometimes clothe him in the process and put food on the table. One thing I cannot fault him is he always bought meat for the family. Because my husband loved barbecuing with his friends, we never lacked for meat for all our meals. Schools in Zimbabwe require school uniforms. They were expensive. At one point, I became very good at sewing and knitting; therefore, I supplemented my income by sewing and knitting all the school uniforms and cardigans for my children. At times I sold some of my handiwork not because I loved it, but it was out of necessity. I also sewed and crocheted for profit.

Jonathan, like many of his colleagues, was never faithful; he had never, during all the years of our marriage, used any protection. I was supposedly an educated and enlightened woman, and yet I acknowledge I knew very little about sex and sexuality. During the years of our marriage, I knew my husband had been sexually abusing me through his multiple affairs. Many times, he had forced himself on me without protection and what could I do? I was his wife! I had never used protection and felt that I was vulnerable. In church, I had been told wives never denied their husbands their conjugal rights. The identification of HIV/ AIDS forced me to be a little more open about discussing our sexual and intimate relationship. In my mind, I was a mother primarily, and being a wife was a secondary role. I knew I was not willing to sacrifice my motherhood and my life to this loveless unity only to be snatched from my children before they were mature because of HIV/AIDS. Therefore, the next stance I took would surprise my husband. I felt my life and my motherhood were threatened by his perpetual unfaithfulness.

My personality as a mother and a survivor was about to emerge. I think it was my instinct as a mother that I needed to see my children grow as well as my promise to my father that one day I would improve myself; that helped me gather courage to confront him. Somehow from somewhere within me, I collected enough courage to confront him about his continuously placing our lives at risk by his unrelenting hanky-panky ways. From the first confrontation, I immediately knew I dreaded my demise from HIV/AIDS.

I feared what I had heard and learned that HIV/AIDS could do to one's body. The fear mobilized me into action against my own fears of being beaten up. I did not even know I could peacefully stand up to him without even raising my voice. However, one night, I did after my grocery shopping. While grocery shopping I decided to buy him a pack of condoms. We had occasionally talked about using them, but I had never pressed and pursued the issue. That night, after my evening shower and getting into bed, he put his arms around me. He tried to be intimate with me. I showed him the condoms and told him that I was never going to be intimate with him again that way unless he put one on. He dismissively laughed in my face, and immediately, he turned his back on me.

I did not press the issue; I knew if he really wanted me that way, I had the solution. The following three nights, he did not even attempt to touch me, and I was not bothered. One night, probably after a week, he again made a move; and again, I had the condom ready. This game would go on for some time. Eventually My husband promised me that he would take the condoms and use them with the other woman, and as such, he was in a way protecting me. Honestly, I am not sure what possessed me, but I thought it was better than no protection at all. I was only human, and at some point, I lost my resolve, and I weakened and gave in to him. In a way, my own body's natural needs betrayed me.

Maybe it was due to the fear of the new disease and death. Maybe it was already in me, and I just did not know. After confronting him once, I would incessantly confront him. I also started reading more and more on HIV and AIDS. I insisted he used protection when we were intimate, but it would be a long battle that I would eventually lose. I do not remember how many times I would tell him to protect me, and no matter how much I would scream it at him, I think my screaming would only energize him into being more unfaithful. One year went by, so did the next, then it was the end of the 1980s, and the new decade of the '90s was rolling by.

At one point, I became infected with a Sexually Transmitted Disease (STD) that required me to have a strong injection. The nursing sister told me prior going to the clinic that I had to have a good breakfast before getting my treatment. However, that morning, as I attempted having my breakfast, I felt so dirty. I could not swallow a single morsel of my food. The food all came back up and I gagged. I abandoned the idea of having any breakfast at all. At the clinic, the nursing sister asked whether I had had anything to eat, and I answered in the affirmative. She did not hesitate giving me my double-dosage injection. As soon as we were done, I attempted to walk out, and I could not as I passed out. I woke up to her voice questioning me whether I had had any breakfast, and this time, I told her the truth with tears flowing down my face. I felt so dirty and embarrassed as though I had purposely inflicted the Sexually Transmitted Disease (STD) on myself.

There was nothing as dehumanizing as being repeatedly treated for STDs when all the infidelities were not my responsibility. There were several instances I had been to the clinic for such treatments and had not reacted like I did that day. With the advent of HIV/AIDS, I started to actually question myself whether my marriage was worth more than my own life. The answer was always a definite no; the answer was always that my life was worth preserving than a marriage that was not even worth the paper it was written on. My husband by now had fathered four children out of our marriage that I knew of. I knew the risks to my life were advanced and far greater than previously before HIV/AIDS.

By 1991, I had five children who all ranged in ages five to fourteen. I consciously decided my life and being a mother was worth more than the unhappy marriage. I had five innocent children who were dependent on me for their very livelihood. In the process, I understood what the saying "gehena harina moto," hell hath no fury, like a scorned woman meant. I became so consumed by anger at what I had continuously subjected myself to and risking my life all in pursuit of love and marriage. What I did not know then and would know years later was that even if there was a chance for me at happiness, it would not be possible while I still had my fist clenched on that hopeless marriage. It is only with an open palm one can be free to grab on to something new.

Later, I learned that for me to get the opportunity at happiness, I had to unclench my tight hold on the farce of a marriage. I also learned in church one day that an open heart was likely to receive blessings than a closed one. As such, the chapters that follow are the groundwork that brought about my long personal journey to my liberation. They look at the relinquishing of my hold on a farce of a marriage. They explore the personal quest to end the violence. They are my personal attempt at healing the wounds of the trauma and the long overdue confrontation with me to embark on the self-emancipation and probably another attempt at happiness.

These years have come to be probably what I call the years of self-testing, determination, redemption, self-rediscovery, academic pursuit, and realization of personal dreams long put on hold and eventually realized. They have come to be probably the most successful years of my life with my children as their mother, their role model, provider because of kicking out to the curb the man who used, abused, violated, and traumatized me as he so deserved. They are the years I realized and learned that married men cheat just because they can. It is not that the wife is holding back anything sexual or relationship-wise but that there is a thrill they get from hiding their bad behaviors. It is a way of fulfilling their fantasies in the dark while hiding in broad daylight. It is this period I stopped blaming myself and realized that I can be successful as a human being without marriage to define me. So married men may cheat for the thrill they get, but women do not have to put up with it. Each of us came into the world as individuals. Our destinies were not tied to someone else's or being someone else's wife. As such, women need not be killed nor have their lives jeopardized because they so much desire marriage because their success is individually prescribed. My most successful years were after I became a divorcee. And here is how I went about it then.

Chapter Fourteen

The academic journey and self-empowerment

Amid all the turmoil within my marriage by 1988, I felt I needed to academically empower myself through my career because I had been procrastinating for too long. For more than five years, I had read all the Mills and Boon romance novels on average of ten books a week from Falcon Gold Mines Country Club. My life was so wrapped up in these romance novels, and I know I read them so as to escape the tortured and troubled realities of my marriage. Sometimes with the tall, dark, and handsome guys in the fantasy world, I ended up with my own role, so it was very easy for me to escape into the world of the loving men with a guy of my own making. Unfortunately, fantasy does not become reality; I needed to grow up, to take charge of my life, and to be smart about everything.

At the end of 1988, I was exhausted of being beaten up and always fighting for finances to help care for our children in order to afford them a descent life. I decided to take the bull by the horns and control my own destiny. I made my mind up to invest my reading energies in something positive. I decided it was high time I embarked on my studies. Mills and Boon novels were my escape and coping mechanism with my abuses. I decided it was time I faced my reality that was long overdue; I landed on my own two feet and faced the reality of my world. I had promised my father soon after graduating as a substandard teacher that one day I would work to improve my academic qualifications. I decided there was no better time than the time at hand.

At the beginning of 1989, I enrolled with Cambridge examining board to take my O levels in order to complete my secondary education. During Christmas 1988, my siblings and our spouses were all home in Howard, as we used to alternate our Christmases between our spouses' families and our family. Christmas of 1988 was celebrated in Howard. During that Christmas holiday, in one of our many conversations, I mentioned to my siblings about my intentions to engage in my studies. Brenda interrogated me why it was taking me so long. I had various excuses, but I promised her that before the year 1989 was out, I was going to fulfill my academic dream and sit my O levels. I did not expect anything from my siblings, except for their familial support. In her wisdom, Brenda knew exactly what prevented me from taking my examinations.

By mid-January 1989, I went back to Falcon Gold Mines, and back to work, I received a registered mail. Enclosed in it were $150 and no instructions. It was from Brenda (as we always called her), my younger sister. When I called her later that evening to find out why she had sent me the money, her simple explanation was that as I intended to study and take the O level examinations, the $150 was my registration fees. It was only $30 per subject back then, and for a couple of years, I had intended to register but could never afford an extra $150 from my meager wages as a primary school teacher.

My sister understood my problem without me telling her. She knew I was not content with my economic circumstances nor with my troubled marriage, and here I was deluding myself into believing I was good at putting up façades. Brenda, without any questions and next actions, blew open my facades. She came to my aid when I needed her the most as a sister. I did not have to plead with her for help. She heard in the nuances of my voice and could tell something was not adding up. I would remain forever obliged to my sister for this trust and enablement to realize one of my most cherished dreams.

It meant the entire world to me to improve myself academically. Brenda was by then a secondary school head (principal). She would ask me which subjects I was considering taking so that she could loan me the books from her school. There is a unique and very special bond that exists between sisters and one that I have always cherished in my life. Sisters outmaneuver the saying "as thick as thieves." Personally speaking, my sisters were my best friends, my confidants, my pillars of strength, and losing them meant losing a part of me. There were so many things I did with my sisters that I would not have trusted doing with someone whom I would have bonded with for petty criminal purposes. That is why my sisters have always been in my life, and they are a true extension of me.

My sisters were always my best friends all through my life. No matter how far we were from each other, distance would never separate us. We did many things together, so to say, and we honestly loved each other. I remember one time we even plotted with my younger sisters, Diana and Plaxedes, to have one of my husband's girlfriends beaten up. We knew it was just idle talk because we did not have a drop of bad blood in us, and we never would follow through with it. It was just something to entertain us, and the three of us all somehow knew it. Personally, I knew it was my sisters' own way of showing solidarity with me. They appreciated and sympathized with my anguish as an abused woman. As their sister, I would not hesitate to ask my sisters anything; as long as it was humanly possible and within their capabilities, they would deliver without fail.

I registered to take my O level examination which included English, religious studies, commerce, and human and social biology at the end of 1989. The books were supplied by Brenda. I was excited to be doing this. In the process, however, I allowed my husband and my elder sister's husband to talk me out of registering for all the five required O level subjects. They both convinced me that it was practically impossible to conduct my studies especially taking five subjects at once while working full-time as a school teacher.

Owing to my lack of self-confidence, I was ultimately influenced to register for only four subjects instead of five. When I later told Brenda that I did not want to waste the money, she had entrusted on me as sitting and failing an examination would be just wasting her money. She was not thrilled by my decision. She quizzed me why I did not believe in myself. At the time, I did not tell her why I made that decision. If she had known the reason for that final decision, she would have been extremely disappointed in me.

Whatever the reason was, whether it was lack of confidence or being talked out, finally, I was persuaded to register for only four subjects.

What I forgot to mention was that Samantha, my best friend, remember her, one of my all-season friends, had sat her three O level subjects the previous year, 1988, and had passed them all with flying colors. She would occasionally tell me that she had not invested a lot of time in her studies; therefore, she was confident that if she could make it, there was nothing that would prevent me from succeeding. Samantha became involved in my life just like one of my own elder sisters would. Samantha had witnessed some of my worst heartaches because she lived within the community. We became so emotionally involved in each other's lives, and she would be one of my strongest sources of inspiration.

In 1989, I also bonded with two young uncertified teachers, Nestor and Stephen; they were working under me at Falcon Gold Mines Primary School. I could have labeled them seasonal friends, but our friendships have withstood the test of time so much the friendships have become more of the all-season friends. They and their spouses including their children have earned a lasting spot in my heart. Of the two, one would become my designated English teacher and the other my honorable commerce teacher; and as both were good in religious studies, they would assist me accordingly. Stephen early on recommended I practiced writing English essays, and he would grade my work. I remember my first attempt at writing an English essay, which Stephen ripped apart, and I could not believe it. The gentleman actually gave me a failing grade! I could not believe it. Did he not know that I was a teacher, and that I deserved a good grade? To make matters worse, I was his senior and his acting principal at the time. How could he disrespect me like that? Stephen made no qualms about my poor grade. When I questioned him, Stephen simply told me I had to approach everything seriously if I was to do well at the end of the year. That made me realize I had to change my attitude and approach to my studies more seriously.

The realization really energized me. Every night I would let my children go to bed before perching myself on my desk and study until the early hours of the morning, probably as late as two, and other mornings, until three. I would be up every day around six except for Saturdays and Sundays, when I had the luxury of sleeping in and catching up on my sleep. Every weekday, I woke up early to send my children to school and personally prepare to be on my way to work. I was no longer occupied in fantasy. I was no longer going to the country club for the Mills and Boon romance novels. My life was real, and suddenly, I became busy.

I was determined to make a name for myself. The Mills and Boon romance book club had unfortunately lost one of their biggest fans and were temporarily shelved.

My motto became "if others can do, it so can I." The word "cannot" was no longer in my world and my vocabulary. I was a woman on a mission. A certain force I could not understand pushed me. Suddenly, Jonathan's unfaithfulness no longer occupied my world. I think that gave him the freedom he desperately needed too to carry on with his clandestine affairs without my constant nagging and monitoring. He was no longer my priority anymore. My energies were invested in better things and meaningful aspects of my life. For once, I was doing what I could to change the only person I could change and not someone else, and I realized that person was me.

Right throughout the year, I studied diligently. I had a schedule for my study during the week; I had a schedule for pushing myself to do some mock examinations and to make sure I was comfortable with the syllabus. After I had taken my examinations toward the end of the year 1989, I started having incessant dreams of committing suicide. I could not tell where they were coming from. Not once had I contemplated suicide as an option or as a way out of my distressed life. The methods of my attempts at committing suicide would be different in each dream. One time I would dream poisoning myself, the other I would be hanging myself, at times I would be lying myself on the railway tracks to be run over by a train. This became exceedingly troubling after it continued for a couple of weeks.

The continuous dreams of committing suicide bothered me a lot. I used to tell my sisters that if I should die under some suspicious circumstances, they needed to have my death investigated, as I would never commit suicide. I was not a coward, and I was a believer in the afterlife. First and foremost, I believe people who commit suicide do not go to heaven; and second, I would never intentionally leave my children and, in the process, subject my family to that painful experience.

Suicidal dreams began to worry me until a friend told me she had a dream book. At least the book gave me the relief I needed, for it interpreted that committing suicide meant there would be success beyond belief in the person's life. That suddenly gave me hope. Hope that I had done well in my examinations, and immediately, the suicidal dreams ceased. From November 1989, when I sat my examinations, until February 1990, the wait was long and torturous. I dreaded getting failed results, and I kept wondering what to do should that have been the outcome of my sweat. I dared not even think about the results then.

I will never forget the day I got the results. I was then acting school principal at Falcon Gold Mines Primary School in 1990. The district education officers were desperate after the previous school head had suddenly been promoted, and they needed someone to take her place. I did not have the right credentials, and probably they thought a half-baked potato was better than no potato at all, and I happened to be that half-baked potato. On top of teaching my fourth graders, supervising other teachers, I had a lot of administrative work to do. On days we did not have an office clerk, I was also responsible for all the calls that came in.

I happened to be in the office when the secondary school principal where I sat my examinations that February morning called, and I answered that call. After we had greeted each other politely, he told me that O level results were out. He proceeded to tell me that once they opened the results, he could not contain his excitement. My heart started pounding more rapidly, and it was as though it was in my mouth. He told me that he could not believe what he saw. He told me he could see Bs on my result slip, and when I asked how many Bs, he told me all four. I could not believe my ears too! I had done it! Me, Avis! Unbelievable!

I let out a loud scream that sent all the teachers running to the office, wondering what was going on. I went outside where we used to have our school assembly and screamed at the top of my voice the words "I passed." I was laughing, crying, and shouting at the same time. I realized I was letting go of all the tensions and bonds that held me back for a long time. I felt so liberated. I did not mind disturbing the whole school; I was free, free to do what I wanted with my life. I felt I was in charge of my destiny from then on.

Once I got home, I was on the phone with my father, telling him I had passed. My father was overjoyed on my behalf. I called all my siblings, and I know they already knew, but they all pretended I was the first one to share my success with them. I was ecstatically happy. In fact, I think I became deliriously happy because by that evening, I experienced my first nosebleed in life. I had never in my life had a nosebleed, but that evening marked the first of my many nosebleeds. This would be how I would mark my moments of extreme joy and excessive disappointments, with a nosebleed. I could hardly sleep that night; I felt like sharing with the whole world this success that I was enjoying. My first success back in 1990 totally made me believe I could do anything that I set my mind to. I also realized I could shut my mind out to a lot of things going on in my life and focus on what was important for me at the crucial time. I had shut out the noise in my marriage and believed I could do it, and I did exactly that.

The irony was my husband was not at home but got back the following day. He had taken his first trip to South Africa. He had gone with our eldest daughter Teresa, and soon after I arrived at school, I got word that my husband and my daughter were back. I went home running like a little girl, nervous to share with him my good news. I also wanted to find out what he had brought for me and the kids. I shared my news with him, but I do not recall how he responded. Though I was happy, my husband and daughter were safely home; unfortunately, he brought no presents for me at all including my daughter Tiffany. As a result, I was really disappointed and hurt. My hurt was nothing compared to my daughter's disappointment and hurt. She was inconsolable; she could not understand why her father had not brought her any presents. I could not say anything to console Tiffany that day. She cried so hard. A little part of my heart broke on her behalf. Teresa tried to share some of her own presents with Tiffany, but she neither would be consoled nor would Tiffany accept the presents from Teresa.

However, that afternoon, my sister made Tiffany's day happy for her. As a school, we used to take our children to the library to borrow books in Spring Meadow where my sister worked. When my sister Melody heard of Tiffany's plight and misery, she wanted to be able to console Tiffany. I remember my sister buying Tiffany a pretty dress at Edgar's Dress Shop to console her. My sister too could not understand why her dad had not brought her any presents. There was also a special bond between Tiffany and my sister. When Tiffany was barely three years old, she stayed with my sister for more than a year. During that year, my sister and Tiffany had bonded like mother and daughter. That bond would always be there, even when Tiffany was older and went to boarding high school for her education.

Occasionally, when she was on her way home for school holidays, she would pass through Spring Meadow first to see her "mother" before coming to us. I did not begrudge them that special relationship; I encouraged it. My child is my sister's child and vice versa; so as long as they got along, I did everything I could to encourage it. Such a bond cannot be begrudged between one's sister and their children. In fact, one of my sisters refused to be called aunt whatsoever, and they used to call her *Amai* or Mom T. This went on until my children were adolescents. I am not sure what shifted then, and suddenly, they were calling my younger sister Brenda *mainini*-aunt. In our (the sisters) eyes, there was no difference which sister had given birth to which child.

A few weeks later, after my husband's South African trip, he would ask me to host two men from South Africa. I was not so naive anymore. He did not tell me ahead of time. They simply turned up around eight at night without any notice. I gave them permission to sleep in our home for a night. During the night, I gave my husband an ultimatum. I told him that they needed to make their own arrangements, or I would go to a hotel until they left. His excuse was they had hosted him on his trip to South Africa. I was not the young impressionable and gullible Avis anymore. I could tell there was more to their friendship than simple host-guest relationship.

My gut feeling served me right that time. A couple of years would go by before I learned that the two men were related to his girlfriend, the mother of his two children. He was still into his old ways of bringing his clandestine affairs and people into our home. Only by then, I was older and wiser. He would not fool me into believing that garbage any longer. Like the popular Chinese saying, "fool me once, shame on you. Fool me twice, and shame on me." He was not going to make me believe that their relationship was just what he claimed it to be mere friendship. I was adamant that they would not stay in my home, and as such, I do not have an idea how they spent the rest of their stay in Zimbabwe, and I do not care. They were not under my roof.

I always had a very special and intimate relationship with my siblings, parents, relatives, friends, and God, not in that order necessarily. When I got my results, my brother Louis was in London; when he heard of my success, he wanted to bring me a special present that I would really appreciate. My sister Brenda told him to bring me a hat for my Salvation Army Church uniform. I needed a good hat for my tunic, and somehow I could never afford one. She felt that I probably needed to thank God for the life and success I was enjoying. I know that my faith many times anchored me in all that was positively going on in my life. For faith sees the impossible, believes the incredible, and hears the voiceless whispers.

I was beginning to see the impossible, hear the voiceless whispers, and believe the incredible because of my faith and my success.

Speaking of faith, I know my faith helped me believe I would be strong enough to survive my abuses. During that time in my church, I had served as an auxiliary home league secretary for the Salvation Army Society in Falcon Gold Mines. I had been the society treasurer, songster leader, and multiple other positions; as long as there was a need in my church, I would willingly serve in any position. One of the positions I enjoyed the most was working with teenage girls. I had fun with them while I taught them how to care for themselves and live rich, fulfilling lives.

At times, I wished I had had that type of mentorship when I was a teenager; probably I would have taken time to date around (not being promiscuous) before getting married. These various positions helped me grow in my faith as I guided the girls, balance our checkbooks, or practiced singing with fellow church members or simply worshipping. I am happy to say if the elders of the church eavesdropped on us (the girls and me), they would be shocked. I answered the girls' questions truthfully without sugarcoating the realities of anyone's married life.

It was a time of self-discovery as well as reinforcement of my faith, whenever I interacted with the teenage girls. However, these were the times that HIV and AIDS would come to the forefront in the news, and we would start seeing people with signs of living with HIV/AIDS. Discussing hardships of married life to my protégés also helped question my own safety. On a personal level, I was by then having to make frequent visits to the doctor or to the nursing sister at our local clinic for the treatment of infectious diseases. I genuinely feared for my life. I always went to the clinic as I thought I needed to be safer than sorry. I certainly started being a little more assertive about my sexual decisions.

In the past, I had been to the clinic for treatment of STDs unquestioningly because I started marriage expecting fidelity from my husband, Jonathan. With passing of time, I would tell him he needed to protect me, to be more faithful to me, and to think before he leapt into bed with the next female his male ego took a fancy to. I remember even telling him I would withdraw his conjugal rights if I kept going to the clinic time and time again due to STDs. I know I was not asking for the impossible but normal things that other men think of before they engage in unsafe sexual activities. Most husbands protect their wives; as such, I felt I needed to be reassured that he was doing that for me.

It was not that I was all of a sudden holding him to a higher standard than before, but I was consciously aware of what was happening in my world. I did not have my head buried in the sand. I remember at one time I even requested that if he could not use protection with his other women, at least he would let me protect myself, and we would introduce condoms. That was only the beginning, and at times, I wish I had the strength to stick to my guns. It was difficult because he was a stubborn husband capable of physically abusing me repeatedly. At times, he simply would force himself on me. Those arguments became more frequent; unfortunately. Of course, I would try to fight back, but I was only female, and my physical prowess would not match his as a man. Sometimes I gave in to human nature demands. Nevertheless, I learned to fight smarter.

Chapter Fifteen

The scare of HIV/AIDS and actions taken

Like the saying goes, an idle mind is the devil's workshop. My mind in 1991 was a typical devil's workshop. That year was idle for me; as such, I was prone to observe the mundane things in our relationship that I had let slip when I was busier the previous year. The year nineteen hundred and ninety (1990), I spent working on my Shona, the last of my required five O level subjects. From 1989 to 1990, I was engrossed in my studies. As a result, I cared little what Jonathan did with his time and his money. I was mainly focused on my studies.

However, 1991 marked another change. Some people wonder up this day how I got the scar on my upper lip. In as much as I now hate to look at my face, this scar actually marks a certain era in my marriage that is very difficult to recall, let alone open up to other people about. I know that probably my children were too young to remember as well. It was my last born Elton, who, in 1995, when he was nine years old, asked me the same question of how I got this scar. I would not give him a straightforward answer. I brushed his inquiries aside. Maybe it is time Elton and all the other inquisitive people knew the whole truth.

This scar was due to the second time I decided to confront Jonathan together with his mistress. From 1989 to 1990, I was busy pursuing my O levels, and what my husband did with himself mattered very little to me. During this time, my mind was occupied and focused elsewhere; therefore, his actions meant next to nothing compared to my ultimate goal. By 1991, this third woman who, by then, had two children with Jonathan was basically living as husband and wife under my nose in that little compound of Falcon Gold Mines. I think that is when I had my head buried in the sand like the proverbial ostrich; nonetheless, even with heads buried in the sand, reality has a funny way of imposing itself.

My visits to the clinic for STD treatments became more frequent. Though I hoped that one day my husband would love me as much as I loved him, I realized I had continued to lie to myself. I thought I would give him more love, and he would be all mine. His continuous affairs were an indication that there was a clear threat to my life. That threat was very tangible to me. Consequently, I still remember the circumstances of the worst confrontation we ever had. I had come to the point where I could neither pretend that all was well in paradise nor lie that my love was being reciprocated. I needed us to either separate or have Jonathan give me some direct answers to some direct actions. I was basically tired of the cat-and-mouse games that we were involved in for years. Most importantly, I feared continuously placing my life in jeopardy. By that time, I knew a showdown was eminent.

I can safely say I was becoming tired of being taken for granted. I felt worse than the doormat because I took all the dirt I could from his womanizing and his multiple physical abuses. I almost by then believed and convinced myself that probably I had done something to deserve all the lying, the cheating, and the incessant abuses. I was the woman who was raising his children, the mother of his five beautiful children, and all the gratitude I ever received in return was the continued infidelity coupled with the continuous contamination from all his mistresses. I was the one woman who washed his clothes, who cleaned his home, dressed him properly, and cooked for him. I was the woman who bought him clothes to wear to work, yet he spent his own income on drinking and womanizing, basically being merely an irresponsible father and husband.

Financially, I was the one who was struggling, yet he had one of the best-paying positions at the mine and was considered one of the top echelons of the mining community while I scrounged around to make ends meet. Inwardly, I was furious at him and at myself equally for not demanding better from him. I knew I could not contain the fervor anymore. I felt as though a fire was smoldering inwardly whose fury was worse than the fires of hell. It was as though a volcano was dying to erupt, and if I did not let it out, I was sure it was bound to drown me with its ferocious lava. I really needed to do something to douse the hot flames of that ravenous volcano; otherwise, the fire was bound to consume me as it erupted uncontrollably. In my head, I could picture the ugly scenes either from the volcanic eruption or from the confrontation, neither of which was going to be pleasant at all. I could foresee that it was going to be an unpleasant and an ugly altercation.

On April 7, 1991, I went to an AGAPE women's meeting in Hartley hosted by the Zimbabwe Assemblies of God Church. Jonathan drove me there himself. I remember earnestly praying like I had never prayed for my husband and our marriage as I surrendered everything to Him. Even the leader of that service taught us how to pray unceasingly for the Lord to hear us. One lady there sang-danced the song "I surrender all." I remember women praying for erstwhile husbands. During that meeting, I cried because I could visualize the collapse of my own marriage. I was tired of investing so much energy into this one-sided "holy matrimony" and my partner behaving more and more as though he was still a bachelor. To make matters worse, I was now gripped with the fear of contracting HIV/AIDS and dying an immature death, leaving my children.

That time, I know, from my actions and behavior, I was more like a lioness dying to protect my cubs. Anything that threatened my existence was ultimately bound to threaten my children's lives too. At the same time, I was bound to act to protect my children's security by protecting myself. Though I knew the odds against me were huge, I did not hesitate in carrying out my resolution. Back home that evening from AGAPE, I told Jonathan how the conferences went. He did not seem interested but dismissively left home and went to the club. I was seething inside. My love was not being returned; I had extended an olive branch to him and invited him to go to a couples meeting with me in the hopes we could both benefit, and knowingly, he snubbed my offer.

Later that same month, April 1991, during Easter, the Salvation Army would be celebrating a hundred years of missionary work in Zimbabwe. I went to Harare with members of my congregation, and it was during that Easter weekend celebrations that my concrete decisions to confront my husband were actually concretized in my mind. In as much as I tried to pretend ignorance or convince myself that Jonathan was still in love with me, I could not pretend any longer. I was tired of living a lie, more so lying to myself because his actions were clear to all in the community. I was angrier with myself for letting the marriage continue for as long as it had while I was not being honest with myself, and I felt it was high time I shocked him by doing something unpredictable. I knew I had carried the burden of this farce of a marriage single-handedly long enough while Jonathan continued to have his cake and eating it at the same time.

Before leaving for Harare, I had invited my husband to join us again; he declined my invitation. I was hurt, but I had become good at hiding my emotions. As such, I did not tell him how I really felt inwardly. Honestly, it felt as though he was rejecting me not just once, but over and over. Not only was he rejecting me, I felt as though he was rejecting his children as well. I was riding the bus with his five children when their father could have driven us. All the way to Harare, I was seething with anger and thinking of ways to bring the games to an end.

My husband had told me he would be joining his own family in Georgetown for Easter. I would later learn when I came back that he had taken his girlfriend/mistress to her village. Talk of adding fuel to the fire was all I needed. There I had been the previous Thursday, riding on the bus with all my five children on our way to Harare, yet she (his mistress) had the luxury of enjoying the result of my sweat, my labor, and our family vehicle. The latest knowledge only added actual paraffin to the smoldering fire of my anger. I knew I had to do something or force something to happen. It was time I moved past the pretence and faced reality in the eye.

The Salvation Army centennial celebrations remain a blur in my mind because my mind was not there. I was being consumed up inside by anger and despair. The anger was directed mostly at me and my inactions all through the years of unrelenting abuses. The despair was due to the fact that I was finally letting go of my hold on our marriage; I could literally feel it slip away. I questioned myself why I continued to hold on to this pitiful representation of manhood as my husband. I know in the past I justified my inaction to the fact that economically I would not have been able to support all my children in the same standard of life they had become used to, but in retrospect, I was displaying the battered women syndrome (BWS). I was in this love-hate relationship where I pretended he loved me and that someday I would make him love me. After each abusive incident or discovered infidelity, my husband would apologize. I would feel sorry for him and would forgive him. The cycle was repeated over and over. He knew I was the glue that held our family together despite all the abuses and unfaithfulness he inflicted upon me repeatedly. He knew when he apologized, I would forgive him.

To friends and relatives, I had excuses for everything Jonathan ever did. From then on, I knew these were mere excuses so that the world would not view me as a failure. In the society I grew up in, divorce in marriages was shunned and looked upon as failure. The one held responsible for the failure usually is the woman, as she is expected to keep the home fires burning, clearly depicted through one of our indigenous sayings, "Musha mukadzi."[36] No matter how much I tried to calm myself and attend the celebrations of my church, I failed miserably because I had come to the conclusion I was going to destroy that marriage.

My mother, maybe through her own insights or wisdom, or motherly instincts or ingenuity, she genuinely wanted the children to spend the holidays with her. She requested to have my children for the rest of the holiday. It felt as though manna was falling from heaven where and when I needed it the most. I knew in my heart of hearts that if I took my children back with me to Falcon Gold Mines, they would witness the nastiness that was bound to happen. Little did I know that my children had been privy to a fair share of the abuses already, if not more than I cared to admit, as I later learned to my chagrin? I had finally lost control and feared for my very existence. Thus, my mother's offer was quickly accepted and acted upon without any hesitation at all but gratefulness to her perceptions.

After celebrating Easter and the centennial anniversary in Harare, I took my children home to my mother's because I knew for the first time I was going to engage in a real confrontation with Jonathan together with his presumed mistress. I did not want my children to be around and witness the unpleasantness of it all. As their mother, I wanted to protect them as much as possible from these detestable episodes of our troubled

---

36 *Musha mukadzi* literally is translated to mean "there is no home without a woman." As such, a man cannot claim to have a home for his children without a woman, and no woman can claim to have a home without a man. As such, it is the woman's responsibility to make sure that everything in the home works well in harmony for it to be called home.

life. I thought they did not know that their father engaged in unfaithful relationships, but years later, events would show me otherwise.

On Saturday April 20, 1991, we went to the Falcon Gold Mines Country Club to relax with friends. We spent a pleasant evening with friends shooting darts as usual. My husband proved to be a very loving and attentive partner in public. The husband I had in public places somehow never came home with me to demonstrate the same kind of love I needed in our relationship. I missed the intimacy of just talking with him till the wee hours of the morning, just connecting with him as my partner. He would leave me many a night, wishing he could merely at least wrap his arms around me. As soon as his head touched the pillow, he would be snoring away. I would be left tossing and turning with unfulfilled emotions. At times, I would simply jump out of bed and start my household chores just to exhaust myself physically as a means to deal with the unfulfilled and frustrated physical emotions and sexual needs.

The following day was a Sunday. Jonathan asked me whether I was going to church, and I told him I was. Most times, Jonathan would engage in his shenanigans while I would be in church. Once assured that I was going to church, he left home and told me that he was going to the club. It was a beautiful Sunday. No clouds in the sky; it was a clear blue sky. The birds were chirping harmoniously outside. The hustle and bustle of the children going to school was not there, but loyal churchgoing people were peacefully on their way.

Despite the bright outlook outside, inwardly, my soul was cloudy; I was in turmoil of what I knew was going to happen that day. I convinced myself that church was not a priority that beautiful Sunday. I was going to make my husband's business my business. I was going to push my nose where he never expected to see it. I could feel the rage coming to the surface. In as much as I tried to suppress it, I failed. I cannot claim that I did not know the consequences of my actions that day. I was fully aware of what was bound to happen. I was angry, mad, furious, and the dark clouds inside kept gathering, yet I was scared for my own life as I prepared for the final showdown.

You all know what happens when an elastic band is stretched long and far; it snaps. Many times, I had indicated to him that he had tried my patience and tolerance long enough, that one day I was bound to snap. April 21, 1991, was the day I finally snapped (unfortunately, that is my best friend Samantha's birthday). An hour and a few minutes after he left home, I fervently made a couple of phone calls to make sure my premonition was right. His girlfriend was not at work. My husband was not at the club, and it did not require any rocket scientist's knowledge to place the two of them together somewhere.

I also did not need Miss Maple's investigative skills to conduct this simple feat of investigation. I decided to follow him to where my gut told me, and many times, rumors pointed to me where his mistress lived. Many people in the community had told me a lot of what was going on under my very nose. They were responsible for informing me where the other woman lived and worked as well; what I did with the information was my own decision, especially on that fateful day. I am not sure whether their bringing these unfaithful deeds to me was intentional or unintentional; I know they inflicted a lot of pain to my being. I was tired of Jonathan's public humiliation through his very public extramarital affairs, and moreover, his ill-treatments were putting my very existence in jeopardy. As such, on that fateful day, I decided to act on those rumors in an attempt to put a halt to the transgressions of a married man.

On my way to the other woman's residence, I met one of my workmates. He was a male. He encouraged me to go home because as he said, whatever I was thinking of doing was not worth it. Up to now, I am still puzzled whether he was a mind reader or whether it was the unrelenting determination on my face that gave me away. I responded to him jokingly and continued toward the residence as though a certain spirit had possessed me and kept pushing me ahead. Maybe it was the fact that people knowing my husband carrying on in their neighborhood. Probably it was why it was not difficult for my workmate to guess what my intentions were. Probably my workmate had seen my husband's car parked openly next to the woman's place and had put two and two together.

As I was taking the last corner as if in a frenzy, I met my husband driving from the very place where I had suspected his girlfriend lived. He actually stopped the car and offered to give me a ride. Up to now, I think either he was conveniently stupid, or he too had come to the end of his tether with the entire pretenses of that affair. I peacefully agreed to get in his car and directed him to show me who the other woman was that he was cheating on me with. That was in broad daylight. Honestly, I never, in my wildest dreams, considered he would literally do as I asked.

He neither denied nor reacted to my directive. He simply reversed the car and parked. He left me sitting in the car and went and knocked on a door whereby a woman proceeded to follow him back to the car.

I try to reflect back to that day and recall how I was feeling. It is still clear as the day it happened. I could feel the rage engulfing my physical body. I had a multitude of emotions flooding my body, taking over my thinking, hastening my reasoning and actions. I could not believe Jonathan actually intended to introduce me to his concubine! At the same time, I felt as though my whole body was erupting with fury. I could not restrain myself. I felt as though a power greater than me had complete control over my mind while my body was compelled to do something. I proceeded to get out of the car as though it was an out-of-body experience. The next thing I commit to memory is that we were both on the ground; our bodies were entangled like ferocious cats, clawing, scratching, poking, biting, and rolling around on that dirty ground, each one trying to have an upper hand of the other like two possessed tigresses. We were fighting for our very existences.

I fought like I had never fought anyone before, and that is true; I had never fought in my entire life, so this was completely new to me. I was and still am a peace-loving person. As a child growing up, fights with my siblings were infrequent if we ever had any sibling rivalry. Instead of separating us, Jonathan, from nowhere, was onto both of us kicking, slapping, and whacking us. I surely could not believe that Jonathan was publicly humiliating me like that! I did not actually see what Jonathan was using to beat us. Up to this day, I feel as though I got most of the beating. My body was raw, and I was bleeding; but there and then, I could not figure out where the blood was coming from. I was blinded with rage over my fight and humiliation as well as shocked by how Jonathan reacted to the entire situation.

Luckily, there were people around, and they did not stand by and let him make us a spectacle for a Sunday morning as he continued to do us both some bodily damage. I did not realize that this woman had bitten a chunk off my upper lip. It was only when I saw blood that I realized I had been bitten. I rode home humiliated and hurt but not regretting my actions. Along the way, he remained quiet as though he had turned into a statue. I did not utter a word to him too. In tears, I called the nursing sister to the local clinic to come and attend to me. Unfortunately, I did not have the piece that had been chewed off, and all the nursing sister could do was to apply some antiseptic and a bandage. She also encouraged me to have an anti-tetanus shot.

The nurse told me human bite was worse than a dog's bite. I feared more about contacting tetanus, and immediately, it struck me that I would carry the scar on my upper lip for life. I felt like a marked woman. All because I had given my love to a pathetic, weak, and feeble man in morals and character all these years, and the appreciation I received from him was repeated humiliation day in and day out. I believed I could never hold my head up high ever again in Falcon Gold Mines. Falcon Gold Mines now symbolized and represented my downfall as a female, a wife, and a mother who could not seize her family together, and my worst fear was to be shunned by society. I was a failure; that saddened me beyond the beatings and infidelities I had endured all the time.

There, I have now told you all curious people how I got the scar on my lip, and my dearest Elton, I hope you got your answer at last. I know I never fully responded to your inquisitions at times because somehow those inquisitions required me to confront my worst enemy—myself. The inquisitions also required me to confront my errors in decision making and judgments repeatedly made in my marriage. Now that my sons Elton and Elvin are grown men, I always pray that my sons will never be the cause of any domestic violence on any woman. I pray that they never have to subject any of their wives to the kind of humiliation their mother endured at the hands of their father.

I also pray that my girls Teresa, Tiffany, and Thelma as well as all my nieces and granddaughters to come will never have to be subjected to the same ill-treatments that I put up with in my marriage. I hope that they find husbands who will love them as much as they love themselves. I pray they will have men who will never have to put their hands on them. As to Jonathan, I know I can never revenge by wishing him away. In due course he shall receive his fair judgment. My only prayer is that he is happy because he is my children's father. I used to wish I would outlive him but with the passing of time I know better and it is not like me to seek revenge.

From that day onward, I would never look into the mirror and see me as my mother brought me into the world; I would always see that scar first and what it meant to me. The scar became the rationale I desperately needed to become independent. I definitely know that was the time I entirely and emotionally divorced my ex-husband. What would come later was my attempt to empower myself and leave as a better person than what he had finally reduced me to. I knew in my heart of hearts I had to be able to take care of my children without relying on Jonathan for any financial support. I knew if I left, there would be no way I would leave my children behind with him; and at that particular time, odds were completely against me, as he could provide them a better life.

The courts would have awarded him my children's custody because financially, he made more than I did; furthermore, I had no home to take my children to. Knowing him, I knew that once I left with my children, it would be like I had already divorced his children from him, and he would wash his hands off the responsibility of financially supporting them through school-going years. It felt as though I was between a rock and a hard place. The decision was not easy to make. Therefore, in the end, I endured for a few more years while I found my own steady footing professionally and financially.

On that fateful day, as soon as I got home from the clinic, I called my brothers; and sure enough, they were in Falcon Gold Mines within two hours after the incident. By the time my brothers arrived, my bags were packed, and I was ready to go home. Seeing my brothers there rallying to my support opened the floodgates of my tears. They cried; I cried. They told me to be strong as they were going to beat the daylights out of Jonathan. Like the coward that he was, as soon as Jonathan saw my brothers, he put his tail between his legs and ran to hide at the police station. The police station almost became a battleground with my brothers attempting to revenge the pain my husband had repeatedly inflicted on me. The police officers who were on duty managed to calm and persuade my brothers Louis, Larry, Bonnie, and Levin to seek revenge in the courts of law rather than risk being imprisoned themselves.

I agonizingly left Falcon Gold Mines that same day in the company of my ever-loving and supportive brothers. My mind was made up that I would never set foot ever again in Falcon Gold Mines. Falcon Gold Mines had been my workplace for the last eight years. I had come to Falcon Mine as a starry-eyed mother of two. I was now leaving as a disillusioned, battered, humiliated, and spiritually weakened woman and a mother of five. In the eight years, by hook or by crook, I had grown to love the people of the community. I had a good influential position in my community. I was the acting principal of Falcon Gold

Mines Primary School then, a multiracial single-stream school of grades one through seven. Many people trusted their children to me on a daily basis to provide proper guidance. I felt as though I had not only let myself down that day, but that I had also let down the entire community, especially the trusting parents who entrusted their children to the school daily for good teaching and proper guidance.

I could not imagine ever coming back and commanding the same respects from students and teachers alike, let alone the parents who entrusted their children to me through the school. At that moment and time, I had absolutely fallen out of love with my husband. Try as I might, I could hardly find anything that had attracted me to him in the first place. I no longer cared about how society would perceive or receive me as a divorcee. I only wanted what was good and healthy for me and my children. I was thinking hard on how I could fashion a decent standard of life for us excluding him. I made a promise to whoever had power over my life that I would fight to redeem myself as a mother and a teacher. I knew my grandmother had taught me to walk with my head help up high, and I needed to do something to reclaim that pride and self-respect once more.

Once I got home to my parents, I was enveloped in their unconditional love. I felt sorry for my aging father who was unbelievably and extraordinarily understanding and made me feel at home. All the while, my mother never said a thing. It took a lot to shake her emotionally, but I knew inwardly she was shattered. Even though my mother was quiet, I could feel her eyes penetrating mine and questioning me in silence. Those eyes had disciplined me as a child in silence among people many times, and I knew what each look meant. Her eyes glared at me, staring into nothing but seeing everything clearly. I did not need her words to tell me she was disappointed. As such, she said nothing, but I read the messages in her empty eyes.

Many times my mother had told me that there was no need for me to be abused by a man because I was an economically independent woman. The only time she had exhibited pain on my behalf was when I gave birth to my firstborn way back in November of 1977. I know that April 21 night in 1991; she was feeling the excruciating pain only a mother feels for her abused daughter all over again. Every morning, my mother quietly accompanied me, unquestioningly, not judging me, and in an understanding way to my brother's surgery to be attended to by one of his nurses. She never gave me her opinion then or later. I knew from her silence that she knew not to beat a wounded woman down.

It was a time of healing, but seeing my children was the hardest to bear. I questioned myself over and over again how I could not have chosen a better father for them. The very thought would make me cry more. During the wee hours of the night, when everyone else was sleeping, I agonized over why I allowed myself to be tortured like that. I would reflect on what I could have done to make him love me as I loved him, and each time I could not fault my love for the man I had married. I had left my people to be one with him as the Bible taught me. The Bible teaches us to leave our families and cling to our husbands, which was exactly what I had done. I had never once looked at another man after we became a couple. I had religiously cooked, washed, and cared for him and his children like married women do. I had contributed to the upkeep of our family as a working wife and mother. I had repeatedly asked him to be the man I needed to make our marriage work, but my requests continuously fell on deaf ears.

During those torturous nights while I recuperated in my parents' home, I came to a conscious decision that I was not going to spend my energies in crying over spilt milk. I had already sacrificed more than fourteen years of my life in this marriage. I felt initially it was for my children that I stayed, but I acknowledged to myself now that I had hoped to change him. I admitted to myself that it was impossible to change him; I realized I could possibly die in the process of trying to change him. I realized I did not have to die first before I acknowledged I could not take the abuses anymore. I had put my health at risk through his infidelities multiple times. I had been beaten to a pulp multiple times.

These abuses were taking their toll on me as a person and on my health; at the same time, I was not getting any younger. I vowed to myself lying awake in my parents' home on one of those reckoning mornings that I would never let my husband physically abuse me ever again. If anything, I promised myself he would unknowingly pay me back for all the pain knowingly inflicted on my being, my soul, and my spirit. I hoped somewhere deep inside me I would be able to find the strength and energy to care for my children and myself without ever asking my husband for his financial assistance.

Being home among my family reminded me of one of our popular indigenous sayings that we would throw at each other as children growing up. It also helped give me strength: "Unondishura kufa kwaamai nekwababa kwemurume ndinowana mumwe."[37] I knew there and then that it was a matter of time before I divorced my husband; he was just a man in a pool full of many men. Granted I was still alive, I knew it would be a matter of time before I could find another man who would love me for me. I had made a resolution and promise to myself and would do everything to make it real. It felt good and heartbreaking at the same to be home. It felt good spending time with my parents, which I had not done in a long time, yet at the same time heartbreaking as my parents were aging and could not afford my heartache weighing so heavily on them. My parents, especially my mother, could not understand why I was subjecting myself to this unrelenting emotional and physical abuse because I was an educated and economically independent woman.

It felt so good to be reunited with my children yet heartbreaking because I did not know what to tell them. I used to spend vacations away from my children, but this was the first time I had spent time away from them so that I could have a showdown with their father. Most times, my niece Doris would ask to have the kids for holidays, and I would let them go and enjoy vacations with their cousins. It was heartbreaking because I knew they had questions, but I had no answers to their questions. Years later, Elton would ask me about the scar on my upper lip, and I would not be able to give him a proper answer. How could I tell my son that his father had almost killed me together with his mistress?

Abuse is never easy to talk about especially to one's closest relatives and friends. Now can you understand why I never held my head up high in public except when I was with my students? I loved my job; I loved my schoolchildren. I got satisfaction from what I did, and I knew I did it well. The schoolchildren were nonjudgmental; they did not look at me questioningly. There were no hidden smiles of rejoicing in my pain, and most importantly, they trusted me to do what I was supposed to do, and that was to educate them with all my capabilities. In public, people knew the life I was living. They knew I had subjected myself to perpetual abuse, and that was why I never held my head up high. I was ashamed to look people in their eyes.

---

[37] "What can destroy me is the passing away of my mother or father. As for a husband's death, I can always find another one."

My stay at home while I recovered was really time to ponder and cogitate over my circumstances. Though I had made up my mind never to go back to Falcon Gold Mines, in the end, it was my father and my eldest brother who influenced my ultimate decision. My brother told me that life had to be lived diplomatically. Only years later in life would we all learn that he had endured a lot of unfaithfulness from his wife as well. In a way, I do not blame him; maybe he was also in the marriage for the sake of his three children. Therefore, in his own judicious way, he probably believed I had to endure all the abuses for the sake of my children. I will never know because I never confronted him neither then nor later.

My father told me that I had far too many children not to let their father be a major part of their lives. He pointed out how difficult it would be to provide for them by myself. As I reflect back now, I feel as though he influenced me to sacrifice my happiness and safety for the welfare of my five children. I do not blame him for that. My father, before he even had his own family, had been obligated to care and provide for his nephews and nieces at an early age; as such, family was very important to him. Unfortunate as it may sound, back then, it made sense, and I convinced myself that I would go back but promised myself never to do anything to aggravate my husband's anger on me again. I knew my body could not stand any more physical beatings.

Personally, I believe I went back because I had resolved that I would work harder at improving my position career-wise. I had already taken the initial steps to making that real; all I needed to do was to keep my eyes on the ball and never drop it. I vowed I would never, from that time, confront my husband about his unfaithfulness again. I convinced myself I would strive to work on my studies and be sure I got a better teaching or administrative position that would grant me my financial independence as well as liberate me from the bonds of marriage.

Looking back, I also realize that I had nowhere to go with my five young children. I could not afford to lease a place big enough for all of us. Our home had been sold under my nose, and I regretted never paying more attention to that part of our life together. Ironically, change was imminent, but not in the way that I had anticipated.

Chapter Sixteen

Embarking on a personal journey to redemption

From time immemorial, economically, Zimbabwe depends on its agricultural produce and its natural minerals. When the rainy summers are good the people enjoy good harvests ranging from cotton, tobacco, and corn. Our natural resources such as gold, copper, steel, and platinum have always been monopolized by the Western world companies who took ownership and control of the resources at the petition or colonization of Africa. Nonetheless, the mines provide desirable employment for our locals. In the 1990s, gold sales and all minerals in general were diminishing.

Jonathan was, by that time, employed by Falcon Gold Mines. The Falcon Gold Mines were like all mining industries affected by the downturn in gold prices. The mining administrators started moving employees around and retrenching some of their longtime employees in order to ride the economic downturn of gold. My husband was among those affected in the reassignments and restructuring programs that were implemented. He was reassigned to work at one of the smaller mines known as Venetia Mine but would be accommodated in Spring Meadow, as most employees of his level were there, which was the dormitory town. Venetia was just thirty something miles west of Spring Meadow.

By then, I was acting school principal at Falcon Gold Mines Primary School when the previous head was promoted in January 1990. I was not compelled to live with him in Spring Meadow. I went there only when I felt like, and having that choice made me realize I still could be happy without Jonathan in my life. From May 1990 until August 1992, I continued to enjoy that liberty. However, my freedom was short lived as by August 1992, the school became eligible for a grade three Headmaster. Back then, I did not have the right credentials to qualify for the position. I lost the school head position to a more qualified male applicant in August of 1992. This forced me to rejoin Jonathan and the kids in Spring Meadow on a more permanent basis.

My husband had been transferred in September of 1991. Prior to joining him and the children in Spring Meadow, I had enjoyed the position of acting school principal at Falcon Gold Mines Primary School for close to three years and living independently, not caring much what was going on in his life. That was the time that I earned some of my self-respect and pride back. I would only go to Spring Meadow to check on my children during the day when my husband would be at work. Evenings, I would ride the bus back to Falcon Gold Mines, where I was living in dormitory-like accommodations with my subordinates. I did not drive and had no car, so public transport was my only means of transportation. Subsequently, I knew that I did not have to continuously humiliate myself and pretend I still had any feelings for him. For those years, that ultimately left him as the primary provider for the children. He was by then buying groceries for the children, making sure they woke up in time for school, and fundamentally, he was dealing with their day-to-day welfare. Despite being separated like that, I was happier and started to get acclimatized to how it felt to live separately. For me, it was liberating; while on his part, he soon realized he was no longer having his cake and eating it. The other woman was also becoming more demanding. Maybe it was because she realized our living arrangements were no longer the same therefore she was hopeful she could usurp me and capture my position in his home.

By this time, my husband no longer had access to my income so that he could squander my hard-earned cash on women and booze. The children were his full responsibility. I was not there to provide the matrimonial services I grudgingly provided. We were no longer a couple to be talked about. I was beginning to assert my own independence, and I liked the liberation. The demands on his time and finances most probably forced him to make decisions. He was now the one looking to me for solutions, but I would tell him he had made his bed, and he had to lie in it. That's why my people say "chiri mumoyo chiri muninga chinotoburitswa nemuridzi wacho"—a secret hidden in someone's heart is deeply entrenched as something hidden deep down the deepest cave, and none has access until the secret owner divulges it. He did not know what was in my heart; it was my secret to let him on it or not. I was cunningly planning my independence. It was ironic that he would approach me with suggestions of improving our marital situation, while I was cunningly planning my getaway. Each time he suggested a solution to our marital problems, inwardly, I would be celebrating.

He came up with his first theoretical solution that I could take his two minor children from the other woman so that he would end the affair with their mother. Oh! I could not believe the selfishness and audacity of a cheating man's heart. After all what I had been through, he still truly believed that I could agree to that bizarre arrangement. Honestly, even if I had been crazy in love, that was a nonstarter. I could not conceive any way that I could ever find myself agreeing to his selfish solution. Every morning I looked at my face in the mirror, I saw the scar caused by the other woman. I would not open up about my hurt, and as such, he took my silence for disagreement. Realizing that his first solution would not hoodwink me into acceptance, he sank as low as attempting to con me!

His suggestion was that I give him some cash so that he could pay off the other woman. His assumption was that once she had started cross-border[38] trading between South Africa and Zimbabwe, she would be financially independent. With that eventuality, he thought the other woman would be out of his life and ours for good. Up to this day, I could not believe that the man was even asking me to contribute to paying off his mistress as though I had participated in his cantankerous affairs. What role had I played in conceiving those children so much that I could invest my own meager income in his mistress's business? I acknowledge in our past marriage I had been gullible, but this time he had underestimated me and the wrath of a scorned woman. Nevertheless, I would not reveal my secret to him; it was mine to keep.

---

[38] From 1980, after independence, Zimbabwe women were involved in cross-border trading, and that greatly sustained our economy. Women would go to South Africa and Botswana and sell Zimbabwe goods and buy some southern goods there to sell in Zimbabwe.

From the time my husband came up with his solutions to our marital problems, that was when I realized that I had more intelligence than my husband gave me credit for or that I gave myself credit for. I knew from then on I would outwit him in anything I set myself to do. If anything, I knew in my heart of hearts that I needed to work harder toward getting my own financial and economic independence as well as wean my children's dependence on him for tuition. Our children, as the offspring of a Falcon employee, were entitled to full access to the best schools in the district or any boarding schools in the country. This meant they had good educational resources, 100 percent tuition from the company with access to good teachers. If they were enrolled within the local schools, they would ride on the company bus to and from school. They were picked up and dropped right at our doorstep. My children's welfare as far as education was concerned was secure for as long as their father managed to keep his position with Falcon Gold Mines. As such, I did not wish him ill will where his employment was concerned because it enabled the provision of my own children's education.

Seeing that he was not successful in baiting me with all his lures, he had another suggestion. He suggested I accompany him to beg his mother to take in his children. I used to tell my husband there was no cow that would moo for a calf that was not its own—*"hapana mhou inokumira isiri yayo."* With that in mind, I had no vested interest in his children and would not cry for them as they were not my calves. Sending his illegitimate children to stay with his mother would not be detrimental to my own children in any shape or form consequently; I was not bothered by his suggestion. I knew I had nothing to lose and my children had nothing to lose, so yes, I gladly accompanied him.

I understood from him that his mother had warned him on numerous occasions about his affairs, but he had decided to put sticks in his ears and not listen to her. I am not sure whether that talk had ever happened. On my part, though, I know my mother-in-law several times had mentioned to me personally that she so wished Jonathan could marry another woman who could help her with labor in the cotton fields. Initially, I was hurt by her comments; but as time went on, I learned to respond without holding back. At one point, I told her that as a professional woman, I had kissed goodbye to manual labor the day I received my teaching certificate. As such, I knew I would never be a field laborer, so

I wished her luck with her son, granting her that wish of cheap labor. I know that she did not take it well, but I was beyond caring any longer.

I also supported my husband's suggestion because my reasoning was my mother-in-law was about to reap what she had encouraged her son to sow. She had wished for some cheap labor; as such, she was about to get the children, the results of the cheap labor she so wished for. I had no quandary with the latest arrangement as long as the children were not going to be forced on me, and they were not going to live under my roof. I did not care who else besides me would care for them. I absolutely had nothing to lose. His mother, after throwing imaginary tantrums and feats of indignation, was agreeable to the son's suggestion. What else could she do? She was his mother, and those two children were her grandchildren. Therefore, in my heart of hearts, I was happy she was getting landed with those children. In a way, it was some form of revenge, which I believe is sweet; but in my case, I have never been nauseated by anything as much as having to confront and beg my mother-in-law to take care of her son's children.

After we came back to Spring Meadow, arrangements were under way to have the children transported to their grandmother. That process was an eye-opener to me in another way. I learned that I had not been protecting my children from their father's affairs as I thought. Elton (it was always Elton), he would simply blurt off his little innocent mouth and let me know things I did not even know he knew. The weekend, the two kids were supposed to be taken to Georgetown; Elton mentioned that at least they would get to play with each other more than they were used to. After questioning him, I found that the kids already knew each other. I could not believe my ears! To imagine that the kids knew each other, and here I thought they did not know that their father had other children besides them! I could not believe that his other children had met my children! To add salt to fresh wounds, they had been to the other woman's place many times! Elton so innocently told me how their father would take them riding or out to eat, even shopping together. I was disgusted beyond belief. I regretted burying my head in the sand and pretending my marriage was the best. I was hit in the face by the reality of what I had exposed my children to.

Honestly speaking let me hasten to say I was completely blown away by Elton's confession. I was disgusted and disappointed in myself more than by my husband's actions. As a mother, I was supposed to protect my children from such unpleasant circumstances of our marriage. I really questioned myself where I had really failed or what I had done to deserve the kind of man I got. I would not actually be able to express my feelings. I was dumbfounded and speechless, and I resolved once more that I would divorce him when he least expected it. I wanted him to feel the pain that he had subjected me to all these years. On the other hand, at times I would wonder whether he was still human enough to suffer the kind of pain that he had knowingly inflicted on me. My aim would not be to seek vengeance for what he had done to me because I would never reduce myself to his level and alternatively start cheating on him. I knew I was above that. I vowed he had to feel the pain one way or another. I was determined to do it the smarter way.

The end of that August 1992 school holidays was when I ultimately lost my position as acting school principal at Falcon Gold Mines Primary School. During the August school holidays, I had participated in the 1992 Zimbabwe country census. That meant an extra paycheck. I had managed to start setting aside a little nest egg for myself for the proverbial rainy day. Secretly, I would be saving for when I would desperately need the cash, and it would be able to afford me a new start in life.

The loss of my position forced me to completely move to Spring Meadow to rejoin my husband and the children. I managed to secure a teaching position at one of the best schools in Spring Meadow, Sir Robert Taylor Primary School. I was now back to being a subordinate than a leader, and it would be another experience for me. By now, I no longer referred to myself as the conditional teacher. Teaching was my career. My heart was entirely in my career. I knew I was touching the lives of children and changing them forever. My career also helped me preserve my sanity. In fact, I believe by then I had different personas. Please understand that my life was sustained by the fact that I developed different personalities for my different lives not in an idiosyncratic way. I learned to compartmentalize and prioritize my life. However, more on this subject will come later.

The dawn of 1993 found me still earnestly and desperately still trying to pursue my academic dream. I had not abandoned my dreams of going back to school (I was one of the only two non-degree members in my family besides my elder sister). In fact, my losing the principal position compelled me to resuscitate the dream that I had to acquire the right credentials if ever I was to move up the career ladder in my chosen profession. The move to Spring Meadow was also helpful because I could have access to high schools whereby I could attend night classes. By this time, I had managed to raise sufficient funds to register for my two Cambridge 'A' level examinations, which, by the way, were still inexpensive but somehow remained too expensive for me.

The last weekend of January 1993 was when I pursued the endeavor in full force with my niece Doris (she was named after my mother), who was visiting with my family. Going to the bank and doing all the transactions, Doris would be with me. She also had a pivotal role to play in my marriage unbeknown to her. In 1988, when I had discussed my divorce plans with Doris for my birthday, she gave me a placard with the poem "Don't Quit." As a young student in secondary school in 1971, I had written all the four original verses of this poem on a piece of paper by an unknown poet. Each time things got really rough, I would read that poem as my inspiration not to quit. When Doris sent me that poster, I sent her the treasured, faded, yellow-edged and dog-eared poem on paper so that she would do as she pleased with it.

Though our efforts during that weekend to get me registered were fruitless, as soon as she left, I went ahead and registered to study English literature and our indigenous language at the A level. Doris's "Don't Quit" poster managed to inspire me and bought me at least five more years in my marriage. I never told her that mentally I had already quit many times on my marriage; I was determined, however, on not quitting on my ambitions and dreams of improving myself academically!

Don't Quit—When things go wrong, as they sometimes will,
When the road you're trudging seems all uphill,
When the funds are low and the debts are high,
And you want to smile, but you have to sigh,
When care is pressing you down a bit,
Rest, if you must, but don't you quit.

Life is queer with its twists and turns,
As every one of us sometimes learns,
And many a failure turns about,
When he might have won had he stuck it out;
Don't give up though the pace seems slow—

You may succeed with another blow.

Often the goal is nearer than,
It seems to a faint and faltering man,
Often the struggler has given up,
When he might have captured the victor's cup,
And he learned too late when the night slipped down,
How close he was to the golden crown.

Success is failure turned inside out—
The silver tint of the clouds of doubt,
And you never can tell how close you are,
It may be near when it seems so far,
So stick to the fight when you're hardest hit—
It's when things seem worst that you must not quit.

—Author unknown

I would go to Thompson High for English literature from seven in the evening until nine o'clock on Mondays and on Wednesdays to Morgan High School for indigenous language and, for the first time as an adult, to study with other adult students like me. I enjoyed myself immensely, and my teachers would give me the extra push I needed as I intended to study in one-year courses proposed for two years. There was no lack of effort on my part. I was a highly motivated student, but on a personal level, I was suffering both outwardly and inwardly but would never show it. My youngest sister Plaxedes was diagnosed terminally ill in May 1993, and that year she lost the battle in December. My husband had finally also lost his job in May of the same year. I never thought for one minute that I would be able to sit my examination in November of that year and do well. I was struggling more than I let on.

In May of 1993, my husband had finally been fired from his position with Falcon Gold Mines. This had consequences on our children's education and us as well. We lost the company house; ultimately, that meant my children also lost on the educational benefits that they enjoyed, and I had hoped they would always enjoy. They no longer had access to the elite schools nor were their education free anymore. As a family, we had furniture that filled our five-bedroom, company-owned house.

Suddenly, we had to look for a place to rent that would accommodate us all. Our income was drastically reduced, and this was a very stressful year, but I survived it. I just had to look on my "Don't Quit" Poster. That year made me more resolute to realize my academic ambition than ever. That's when I knew that I was more resilient than I had ever imagined or given myself credit.

Also during that period of study, every weekend, I would take the bus trip to Harare with my elder sister Melody, as we lived in the same town. Plaxedes, my youngest sister, had been terminally ill for some time and had even come to stay for a short time with my elder sister in Spring Meadow. After she went back to Harare every Friday, my sister and I would board the buses to Harare. We managed to spend every weekend with her and our family, and we would be back every Sunday evening. This continued from May until December, when she finally gave in.

Plaxedes's illness did not improve with the passing of time. She got worse. I feared for my sister's life. With each pain Plaxedes went through, I would personally experience the compassionate pains. I never knew compassionate symptoms could be so authentic. For example, one Sunday, we left my sister Plaxedes in pain from a toothache. From the moment I boarded the bus back to Spring Meadow that Sunday evening right through the night and the following day at school, I experienced excruciating pain from one of my wisdom teeth. The pain was persistent the following day in school.

I had to I request my school principal to let me go home early due to the pain. He allowed me to go as I never excused myself unnecessarily. All the way walking home, I was in unbearable pain. As soon as I entered my house, my sister was on the phone, and she was telling me she had experienced a good restful night. She was not in pain anymore. We talked for a few minutes, and honestly, by the time we finished talking, I was wondering what I was doing at home in the middle of the day. The pain was completely gone. I could not believe it, but I stayed home and played hooky for once.

To add on to my having these frequent compassionate pains, I lost a tremendous amount of weight. I remember Diana telling me that her husband had expressed his observation and commented that the family was mainly concerned about Plaxedes's health, yet they were at risk of losing me as well. I had not realized that I had become that wasted and was almost at breaking point. Due to hearing their concerns vocalized, that made it essential that I took better care of myself. Somehow I managed to have the strength to live through these most difficult and trying times I had ever experienced before. Again, I did not quit.

As a person, I strongly believe the saying *what does not kill you only makes you stronger*. I honestly became a stronger woman that year than ever before. I did not lose focus on my studies. My studies became my mainstay. I concentrated on keeping my children in the schools that they were used to. I kept my weekly visits with my terminally ill sister. Let me hasten to say, I know I would not have been able to do that financially without my siblings' support. They all rallied round to supply me with necessary finances so that I would not miss any weekend visits. We all knew we were traveling this final journey with her and needed to make the best of the time we still had together. Unfortunately, my youngest sister Plaxedes lost her battle, and she passed away on December 3, 1993. I had sat my examinations in November that same year, and the results would take a couple of months before they were released, but I remained soundly confident that I had made it.

In the meantime, my husband would remain as stubborn and as unfaithful as ever. I would come back from work and find him writing numerous letters, and I believed he was applying for jobs until one day, I found out otherwise for myself. It was some six weeks after my sister's funeral. I had stayed home in Howard for six weeks to console my mother and my family. I went back home and to work in Spring Meadow toward the end of January 1994. My husband had been home for almost seven months before he thought of going to Harare to look for a job due to my kicking him out for the first time in our entire married life; probably I should have kicked him out sooner.

My husband had lost his job with Falcon Gold Mines in May 1993 and continued to stay home until January 1994, and he enjoyed his life at my expense. That luxury came to an abrupt end one February morning. He left home early that morning. During his absence, the mail was delivered; and I happened to be home, and he was not. There was one letter in particular addressed to him with a South African stamp that I could not resist opening. My eyes basically popped out of their eyeballs as soon as I read the contents. This was no ordinary letter. It was a love letter. It was from the woman who had produced his two illegitimate children, the children he wanted to impose on me at one time. Yes, that very woman, the one I was supposed to bail out financially. I could not believe it. I think for a minute I lost my sanity. The language in that letter was very graphic.

To imagine my husband could abuse my generosity and my patient demeanor by still communicating with his mistress while living under my financial support and under my roof was beyond my understanding. I was horrified! I was beside myself with anger. To make matters worse, in the letter, the subjects for their discussions were my sisters, my brothers, and me. I could not comprehend of what interest my family members and I were to their relationship. I imagine they wanted to be a part of my family, but I would never know. I tried to figure out why we featured so much in their conversations, and for the life of me, it made no sense.

Later that day, when he eventually came home, he asked whether he had received any letters. I threw the opened letter on his lap. He knew the game, and his jig was over. He knew he had been busted, and I desperately needed to know and to hear what he would say. At least he had the decency to have a crestfallen face. I told him if he did not have a convincing reason for communicating with his mistress, he needed to remove his sorry body out of our home that night. That would be the only night he would not spend the night at home because I had basically, single-handedly, and practically threw him. My anger and disgust at his actions gave me the succinctness and forcefulness of voice to convince him I meant it.

In all the years of his infidelity, he had justified his infidelities by telling other people, especially my sisters' husbands, that at least he never slept out. He would always tell them that he would come home no matter how late it was under cover of darkness. He felt that at least he saved me the humility of his being seen by neighbors in the early morning hours coming home to dress and immediately leave off to work. However, this was no justification for his infidelities. His actions always were justified in his eyes only, but this time, he had thrown the last straw, and there was no more mercy to his actions in my eyes.

I honestly felt that I needed to reclaim my dignity. I was worrying myself sick over the impoverished circumstances of our way of life. Jonathan was busy taking advantage of the time I spent at work to communicate with his women. I used to respect him as my children's father and my husband, but that day, I realized he did not deserve my respect at all. I could not believe how he could continuously abuse the extension of my hospitality to him like that. I was stressing myself out on a stringent budget trying to make ends meet. In the meantime, he had the impudence to give my address to his mistress, of all the people in the world! That was the end of my patience with his cheating and lying ways.

Because most times I attributed my inaction to the fact that he was my children's father, therefore, he deserved better treatment. In this particular instance, my actions were attributed to the fact that he had disowned himself from receiving any better treatment from me. I told myself to hell with his position as my children's father. I questioned myself why, if he could not respect me as the mother of his children, I continuously threw my respect away at someone as useless and inconsiderate as he was. From that time onward, in my mind, our divorce date was imminent. It was no longer a probable but a definite, only he was not in the know-how. I was the only one who knew.

In my mind, my reasoning with my husband was beyond my sympathies. I guess I convinced myself I could be a better parent for all my children without him. I was tired of hoping he would change. I had no more room for him in our lives. He had to go, and I felt for once if he remained, I could do him some form of physical harm. That was how incensed I was. Honestly, I know if he had not left, I intended to do something to him at night while he slept. I was planning. The last incident was where I drew the line, and I stuck up for myself without even using violence. His next move was nothing I had imagined because he moved in with my brother-in-law, my own younger sister's husband.

Short of throwing him and his belongings out, he knew he had pushed the envelope too much. I told him after he came home to find someone else to abuse before he found his belongings outside, and by evening, he was gone. There must have been something firm and sincere in my voice, as I never thought he would ever leave without putting up the fight of his life. I felt relieved when he packed his bags and left. Little did I know where he was going, which was another shocker? He went to Harare to pursue his job-hunting there.

After all his continued abuses on me, my husband could not leave and find his own personal friends and relatives who promoted his behavior. Instead, he dumped his useless body and thoughtless mind on my brother-in-law, my younger sister's husband. The man had no foresight. If he had known how his life would shape out without me,

I think he might at least have attempted to treat me with civility. If the connection was not there with me, how could my sister's husband have forged a life for him and all his philandering ways? But our culture is accommodating, and my brother-in-law was kind enough to extend his hospitality to my husband.

I remained in Spring Meadow with my three children. Teresa and Elvin were in secondary boarding schools. They did not witness the hardships the four of us (Tiffany, Thelma, Elton, and I) went through. For months, I would not have enough money to put food on the table. Teresa would write letters and tell me how hard boarding life was for her. In my heart, I would be grateful that at least she was having three genuine meals a day. My daughter never adjusted to boarding life; however, because I was afraid to subject her to male predators like her dad who preyed on young innocent girls, I felt she was safer in boarding schools. The only sad part is I could never share those fears with my daughter, as I would be forced to point out their father's behavior.

On the other hand, I would write letters to my son Elvin and advise him that to live like a king, he had to work like a slave until he started writing it back to me. I knew then the saying had outlived its usefulness. I could tell he was a typical boy. His letters were brief and straight to the point they were almost telegrams. I still vividly remember one such telegram. "More money, more food, I love you mama," my son would write. Once again, I was grateful that he was getting all his three well balanced meals a day. I would not be worried about his welfare. The two of them were having three good meals a day, sleeping in good beds, and their education going on as it was supposed. For such little mercies, I would forever be grateful. I needed to be stronger for my three youngest children who were exposed to our more impoverished and changed living conditions.

It would be my youngest three children who would suffer the most as a result of our changed circumstances. All my working life, I had been used to having domestic help. I remember Elton and Thelma were close in ages, and at one time, I boasted of two girls to help with the domestic work. One was solely responsible for the housework and the other for my children. When my husband lost his job, I had to forgo that luxury. I had to focus on putting food on the table for my children. I needed money for food, for our monthly rent, for my children's school fees, for clothes, and to make matters worse, I had never earned nearly as much as my husband did. Our resources had shrunk more than 75 percent.

Although financially we never operated as a joined family unit, I remember he would buy all the meat as he used to love barbecuing with his friends. My children's education was well taken care of through his benefits at work. Those were major responsibilities that I was now forced to take on single-handedly. To make matters worse, the children were growing, so their education was also becoming more expensive. One of the luxuries we had to get rid of immediately was the domestic help. I discussed with my landlord to let me have someone to co-lease their home. I knew that I had to do something to save our finances without reducing the standard of living my children were used to and without compromising their education. I had to do all I could to preserve my family's livelihood. Somehow we managed to keep our heads above the water.

Toward the end of 1993, I sat my A level examinations while my son Elvin was taking his O level examinations. My results came only two weeks before Elvin's. I celebrated my success; once more, I had one B in Shona and a C in English literature. My mentors made me proud by encouraging me to go to the university as I truly had the qualifications. I did not need any encouragement from anyone at all, as my mind had long been made up. Initially, I had been aiming for Ds in order to qualify to apply to the University of Lucas on mature entry. My B and C were distinctions in my eyes, and I knew when I was ready, the University of Zimbabwe would accept me without any reservations.

Once more, I had proved to myself that I had the intelligence, the resilience, and the determination to focus on the important things when it matters the most. Another trend was also emerging as I celebrated my success. I had my second nosebleed when I got my results that year, February 1994. I was excited and proud of my achievement and myself. The first nosebleed was when I passed my O level examinations in 1989. I was jubilant beyond words could ever describe. I knew then the sky was going to be the limit for me personally. I knew I would have to fight tooth and nail to enroll at the university due to the level of competition, but somehow in my exuberance then, nothing was impossible, and nothing was beyond my capabilities.

Symbolically, in my celebrating, somehow my blood had to be shed; at least that's how I interpreted the meaning of my nosebleeds. I took it as a sign that whatever I had aspired to achieve, I had to shed blood before I could reach for the acclaimed stars. It took me back to the early years of my life as a young girl when I used to fight for my parents and my teachers attention. I knew in my life I would always have to fight for all I needed, but I had to learn to fight smarter. As a result, I had to embark on the journey that would give me skills of exactly what I needed—fighting smartly and intellectually. Jonathan would not be privy to my innermost cunning and planning; as a result, he still thought he was in control of our troubled marriage. Unknown to him, our roles were forever reversed from that moment onward. Only Jonathan would not be aware of that role reversal. He felt that as a man and the head of the family, he was in charge; I knew he by then had lost control of the steering wheel. It was now fully in my control but privately.

Chapter Seventeen

Understanding my optimism and determination

One thing is for sure, I am a very strong, mostly positive, optimistic, and very determined and resilient person. I usually never give up on any project, and failure has never been an option for me personally. I feel there is no mountain too high to climb when I want something. However, in the process of my life, I learned to compartmentalize my own personality. In trying to achieve my life's goals, I developed different personalities. In essence, that helped me to adhere to my priorities.

I became a submissive wife at home, ashamed to lift my head up high in public, afraid to interact with other women in my community and at work in protecting myself from what I did not want to pay attention to, afraid to stand up to my husband's violence yet paralyzed with fear that I would end up HIV/AIDS positive. The identification of HIV/AIDS in the early 1980s was slowly becoming a reality in my community. The illness that was initially meant for gay white males was now being diagnosed in heterosexual couples, people whom we knew.

The second personality was the all-embracing and warm teacher that was my school character. This was the personality that kept me grounded and kept me going through all the years of my emotional abuse in the holy matrimony. I loved and appreciated my school personality as it kept me sane and helped balance my troubled home life. This personality provided me first and foremost with the economic stability that I needed as a mother to take care of my five children. As soon as

I entered the school gates, my school personality overwhelmed me. As soon as I saw my pupils, my heart would do a hundred summersaults a minute in happiness. The moment I saw those trusting faces, everything else melted away like dew into thin air.

I immensely enjoyed being myself within the school grounds and blooming like a new budding flower in early spring sunshine as a person and in my career. Nothing could touch my spirit here within the school grounds; nothing could disturb my soul here. The school and my career were my forte. The important role I played there made me forget the humiliation I suffered constantly in my marriage. Within the school grounds, I would never forget that I was making a huge difference in my students' lives. It is not surprising; therefore, that I continued to teach for the next twenty-two years until 1997, when I decided to go to the university to empower myself academically. That academic journey was a leap of faith and the first huge milestone in my life. It was a leap of faith because I had almost bypassed higher education, something I was constantly reminded of by my father, as he held me to my promise of years earlier when I first started teaching.

The third personality was the mother in me that loved all her children without any reservation. I was the all accepting woman and mother whose children could do no wrong in her eyes and whose children could climb every single mountain in the world and reach the top. I was the type of woman who always thought I could have as many children as I could produce. I later limited my children to five because I realized that potentials at times are not realities. Children come with needs, actual needs, not fantasies. As such, I realized after I had five children that if I could not afford to give them all that they needed; it was no use producing as many as I could. I also realized I risked putting my life in harm's way from HIV/AIDS. However, despite all the turmoil of my marriage, I loved all five of my children. I loved having time to tell them stories. I loved the time I spent reading to them. I had time to play like a child with them, yet they respected me as their mother. I had time to teach them housework, crafts, sports, and hard physical work.

My children and I had our garden in which we grew fruits, flowers, and vegetables. I taught my children firsthand how to nurture plants and knew later in life they would do the same. We also had a booming orchard with all varieties of fruits. Every single fruit tree was a product of our own hard labor. Nonetheless, as a mother, I enjoyed my children's love, and they had mine without any limitations. I had time to watch cartoons like *Casper the Friendly Ghost* with them. I had time to read *Adventures of Tintin*, and *Sweet Valley High*, to name only a few of the literature we read and cartoons I watched with my children as they were growing and learning. I was not wealthy in monetary terms, but I provided them with a wealth of love and knowledge as best as I could. My philosophy was to give my children love and not just material things learned from "Lucky Dube," the South African artist's song we all enjoyed lip syncing to. Together we lavished each other with love, and I truly believe we flourished as a family and grew closer as mother and children.

As you can see, I consciously compartmentalized my life. The three personalities, as you can, tell were not idiosyncratic in any shape or form. The schoolteacher personality, the mother in me, as well as the submissive and abused wife united to keep me going. Even when the situation in my own home was not conducive to any positivity, I continuously persevered. I did my utmost best in my work as a teacher, my role as a mother, and in my submission as a battered wife. As such, I strongly believe survival is possible even under the harshest atmosphere due to the passions we carry in life, and in the process, dreams held can be realized when energies are properly channeled.

As a mother, my personality encouraged me never to quit; even when there were other options, quitting was not an option. I would never quit my role even when the situation was at its bleakest. My five children were dependent on me for love, nurturing, teaching, and provision of stability. I truly and honestly know that the three personalities were interrelated in shaping the person that I was then and who I am now. I proudly say that I did not and still do not possess any idiosyncrasies. I am sure as sane as the next person under the sun is due to the three personalities and the need to be there for my children. Maybe you can find more personalities; please do not let me stop you. Probably these are the personalities that you can analyze and criticize, and I know if you are an academic, you can always find some of my idiosyncrasies I presume.

Since getting married in 1977, I had matured walking with my own head held up high, but that ceased on marriage. Believe you me or not, from the date I found that I was pregnant; my fiancé had been chronically unfaithful. My decisions to marry him were purely out of fear and uncertainty of a future raising a child alone as a single mother, especially for a woman from my era. Growing up, I had aunts who had children, and they had never married. My father had helped raise his nieces and nephews up. As such, when we were growing up, my father had to be sterner with us. Having children out of wedlock was a subject that could neither have been entertained nor tolerated in my family. Consequently, I recognized that I had made my bed, so I had to lie in it.

Let me also hasten to say that my decision to marry after the initial tidbits of infidelity was the total basis of my emotional and physical abuse. It was the initial submission to my perpetual obedience to the traumatic domestic life of living with an unloving and unfaithful husband. The decision to marry him was the birth of my not holding my head up high. I am honest to myself when I say I married for the wrong reasons. I should have just trusted that I would be able to fend for my child by myself. However, my socialization had not been like that at all.

Abuse comes in many shapes and forms, at different levels and varieties. Abuse can be physical, sexual, emotional, and psychological. My abuses were emotional, physical, sexual, and I think a greater level psychological than I had imagined. From the beginning, my fiancé played with my emotions, my innocence in sexuality, and the lack of knowledge thereof. He was physically violent right from the time I fell in love him until the time I decided that enough was enough after twenty-seven years of married bliss. Let me tell you now I know it was twenty-seven years too late.

Probably as young as I was back then, I used to wear my heart on my sleeve; and once my fiancé realized that, I loved him too much to tolerate all his nonsense, he took advantage of me. I also attribute the tolerance to the era I grew up in. We were socialized to be submissive to our husbands. The fact that I put up with his initial emotional abuse is due to the fact that I knew nothing else. His cheating ways multiplied and made him take me for granted continuously. Presumably, he never thought I would one day ever have the willpower to stand up to his abuses and the strength of character to divorce him. I do not think, for once, he ever imagined that one day I would empower myself educationally and realize my dreams and goals and, in the process, relearn to hold my head up high again and talk about this long journey of holy matrimonial emotional abuse. It is a fact that when he least expected it, I threw my husband to the curb. That speaks volumes to my strength of character, my resilience, and my determination while some of you might choose to argue otherwise.

Maybe I need to begin where it all started, this life of an abused woman who grew stronger with each punch and prepared for the journey so much that none in her family could even believe she would make it, out of that bondage alive. I know the abuses I endured for a long time, and I attribute them to making the wrong choices, yet I expected the right results. My marriage was based on the wrong choices, but somehow I expected the right results. I realized this after months of reading and studying other authorities in relationships and abuses. I read Joyce Meyer's book *Beauty for Ashes,* as I was seeking for answers that I needed to understand, whether I could relate my endurance to my emotional abuse to anything anyone had ever experienced. Joyce Meyer takes a Christian perspective in her analysis on the problem of abused and battered women. She assists women who find themselves in similar circumstances as she endured in her first marriage.

I personally realize that religion, also to a certain degree, influenced most of my decisions. My husband then, cunning as a fox, took advantage and encouraged me to always be present in church. Each time he drove me to church on Sundays, I felt loved. My warped reasoning was he was honestly concerned about my not backtracking on my upright and Christian upbringing and faith. Unbeknown to me, as I realized years later, that all the time, his encouragement was out of selfish reasons. The time I would be in church worshipping and feeling blessed would be the windows of opportunities he desperately needed to engage in his notoriety, and he pursued his women. Little did I know my being in church provided him with free time to conduct his shenanigans?

Joyce Meyer further writes about people running away from problems and not facing them. I did exactly that for years. For years, I buried my head in romance novels and my religion. I played a role in all the novels I read. I hoped my God would one day have mercy on me and deliver me from my suffering. I forgot that he can only help those who help themselves. However, I did not run away physically, but emotionally, I tuned out. It took too long for me to get back in tune with my emotions. I certainly did not really need more than twenty years to understand that. Yes, I agree now that emotionally and psychologically, I tuned out

I agree with Joyce Meyer on another aspect that people make the wrong choices and expect to get the right results because I did exactly that. True, I made wrong choices. As Joyce Meyer articulates, people rooted in abuse usually end up with strongholds in their minds and flesh and must be allowed to go through the shadow of death if ever the strongholds are to be pulled down. I completely identify with this observation, as I had to prepare myself not for spiritual uplifting of other people, but for taking up the responsibility to educating my girls, my nieces, and other girls who might think abusive men will ever change. Those men will never change. Maybe from my experiences they might learn other ways of relating with men and not through violence and submission.

Let me tell you one thing from experience—never expect to boil stones and make soup out of them. Listen carefully, it really does not matter how long you boil them or how intensive the heat is; stones will always be stones. Similarly, the tiger never changes its spots. Neither does it matter how long you wash the tiger, you can never remove their spots. If anything, the person anyone is capable of changing is yourself. Listen to me—this is the true story of how I subjected myself to abuse. I thought if I hung in there long enough, he would notice. I went from a proud well-brought-up girl, confident, professional, satisfied career woman into a submissive abused wife.

One good thing was, however, I remained a resolute nurturing mother and strong teacher. Years later, when my abusive husband least expected it, I reclaimed my self-identity. On the other hand, the cost was way too much. I know I have finally found my way; I have relearned some of the things, I had completely forgotten. I have regained myself respect and confidence back. To some extent and at a great cost, I agree that I did not have to endure all I suffered because I know I was a strong human being. As such, I tell you from personal lessons—never underestimate your self-determination, your strength, and your resilience even when you are hardest hit.

As young girls growing up, we fantasize about relationships. Not all relationships are as rosy as in movies or the fairy tales that we are told. Every situation and every relationship is different; as such, learn to deal with the adversity in your own way. Do not ever think your life is totally dependent on another human being to make you happy or to complete you. I know, it sounds as though I am now in total control of my destiny, but it was a process that I had to endure. I almost lost my own life, as you shall learn if you continue to read. So learn from other people's experiences. The man in your life, if he beats and cheats on you, is not worth you losing your life over.

Nowadays, not only can a woman lose their life through violence and trauma in a marriage, but there also is the threat of HIV/AIDS epidemic. People born after 1980 do not know any other world but a world defined by HIV/AIDS. HIV/AIDS, most times, is inflicted on the long-suffering women by men who are supposed to love and protect them. Do you see the irony, the lover and protector, yet he is the abuser at the same time! In trying to keep my family together and trying to please my husband by being the submissive wife, I realized I could lose everything I completely treasured; my life and its preservation was my top priority. Without my life, I would not be available to anchor my children's lives. It took me some time to convince myself that I did not have to endure the humiliation, the traumatic violence as well as the unending infidelities because I was afraid to leave and live my life alone. If I could do it, yes, you too can do it! You have more resilience than you give yourself credit for.

My marriage might have been born out of the wrong reasons, but I honestly and truly loved Jonathan in the beginning. True, we came from different backgrounds, which I acknowledge, but many people with different backgrounds have had successful marriages. I was determined to make it work, but marriage is a two-way relationship. I could not make it work on my own, so you will never make it on your own unless the other person is equally invested in the relationship. I had five children with this man, and I did not come from a background of divorce, and not all we practice has to be endorsed through personal experiences, as we carve the paths that fit us and our situations.

My mother and father had been together from the time my mother was a young teenager of sixteen years, or so she said, until her death shortly before she turned seventy-five years old. That was a long marriage. We had lived through their struggles of trying to fend for their big family not even to mention the extended families from both sides. They were pillars of strength and commitment in our community, and as such, there was no way it was going to be easy for me to throw in the towel on our union, except for the threat to my life and fear of that newly identified terminal illness. On the other hand, my parents never had to deal with the threats of HIV and AIDS; as such, emulating their example was redundant for me. Simply put, what I mean to say is you are the captain of your own life's ship. As you long as you are at the steering wheel, you will be in charge of the controls and can steer that ship in the direction that suits your unique situation.

I was a mother first and foremost; being a wife was a secondary role. As such, I did not have to sacrifice my children's mother for the prestige of being my husband's wife. With that determination and strength of mind, I embarked on the next phase of my life with unmatched reserves of strength, stamina, determination, and consciousness of mind than ever before. I knew I could not continue to suffer in submission. I knew I could not blame the Lord for not helping me; He could only help me if I was willing to help myself. He had blessed me with normal senses and some intellect; as such, I had the basic tools to embark on the next phase of my life. If I could do it, so can you. I know you are way smarter. I have heard Dr. Phil several times on his show say our children will always be more intelligent and better than us. Go for it. The world is filled with oyster shells; go find your oyster and not be subjected to humiliation.

Chapter Eighteen

Success is sweeter than adversity

After completing my O and A levels with flying colors, I had proved not just to myself but to all my cynical friends and workmates that I was made of stunner substance than I or they had ever given me credit for. Admittedly, 1993 was an extremely difficult year financially, emotionally, socially, and even career-wise, but I had persevered. Despite the hurdles of accommodation, my husband losing his job, his unfaithfulness, and the lack of financial support, I excelled. I endured more than his emotional abuse; that year, I suffered my youngest sister's long illness and ultimately losing her at the end of the year. I barely had sufficient funds to feed my children on because he had lost his job. Once more, despite all odds mounted high against me, that year I proved that I could remain resolute, resilient, and determined in realizing my goals and ambitions.

After I received my successful results, I was thrilled to no end; consequently, I started applying to the University of Zimbabwe for a place to engage in my first degree. However, my plans would not be realized then and there as circumstances forced me to put my plans on hold once more. How very typical of women to always have our plans sidetracked because other important matters have priority. Most women the world over are care providers to other people. They are care providers especially to their children, aging parents, or in-laws or grandparents or other such needy family members. As a woman, I found that my goals and needs most times had to be secondary to my five children's needs.

I remember once reading elsewhere that women always have poor health because they always eat last. At the time of reading that article, I dismissed it all as hogwash, but now looking deeply into the circumstances of women worldwide, nothing sounds so true. My needs and plans had to play second fiddle to someone else's because once again, circumstances had changed in my life. My plans to further my education had to be shelved because my children's needs had precedence over my personal needs and desires. As such, when it became apparent that my children needed me, that decision was not difficult to make at all.

By the beginning of 1994, that is when I had enough credits to enroll at the university. During the weeks before my son's results were out, I could tell that I had set a very high precedence for Elvin. By this time, I had completed my A levels as Elvin waited for his O level results. I had initially embarked on my studies to fulfill a long-standing promise to my father and my personal desire that I would eventually improve myself academically as well as, in a small way, to demonstrate to my children, that everything you set your mind to is possible. Though my life circumstances had initially pushed me in one direction, I wanted to demonstrate to my children that with sheer determination and focus, we could always fulfill our lifelong commitments and dreams together.

I almost regretted having decided to go back to school at the same time as my children, as that put some unnecessary pressure on them, especially on my son Elvin. I knew Elvin was still very young and highly impressionable, and anything could have pushed him over the edge. I knew my results could have easily done that if he had not done better himself with his O levels. He had to either beat my standard or match my performance, or he would never have been able to live that down especially from his uncles and my brothers. As loving as his uncles were, they would have teased him no end for not surpassing the standard set by a woman, and for that matter, his mother.

I remember wishing real hard for my son's success. The boy did us all proud, as he did exceptionally well. Elvin went ahead and was enrolled for his A levels. It was at that point I shelved my own plans of pursuing my studies at the university, as by then my husband was no longer employed. By the time Elvin's results were released, my husband had been out of employment for more than nine months. I needed to continue working and providing for my children while keeping them in school. Even though I had to shelve my own plans, I remained resolute that I would have my first degree before my eldest son did. It was all a matter of timing once more and moving the goalpost again.

Though I did not have enough money for Elvin's tuition, my brother Louis and my sister Brenda were responsible for the purchase of his school uniforms and his first term's tuition. I cannot imagine what would have happened to my son had it not been for their generosity and their rallying round to help Elvin and us all. I received all sorts of financial assistance from my family in general during these and other hard and trying times. I remember Diana used to keep chickens for sale. Each time I went to Harare, especially during the time my youngest sister, Plaxedes, was ill, I would come back with four or five chickens for the children's food from Aunt Diana, as we popularly called her. She would also occasionally give me bus fare, so that I would not miss any visits with my terminally ill sister, Plaxedes.

That was my family. It had always been that way, and we always rallied around each other in times of need. One sibling's problem was a problem for all of us. It was never one man for himself and God for us all. Not even once. It was always one for all and all for one. I cannot imagine what my life would have been if I did not have my siblings for my siblings. Surely, life for me would not have turned out the same way. That indicates why I love our popular Shona saying *"Ziva kwawakabva mudzimu weshiri uri mudendere"* (remember where you came from; the bird's spirit is in its nest.)[39] If I should ever forget the blessings I received from my siblings and family, then unknowingly I passed out my heart, thinking it was my feces[40] (another popular Shona saying).

During these trying times at school, my interaction with fellow teachers would also be tried. Some hurtful comments would come to my ears in early January 1994 during break times. We never had a real staff room. Our assembly hall platform was where we all congregated for teatime. Mondays through Fridays, we had tea at ten o'clock. What I heard at school that January morning from some of my colleagues

---

[39] "Ziva kwawakabva mudzimu weshiri uri mudendere!" If you are Shona and have not read this, novel you are missing on one of the well-written Shona novel, that teaches about responsibility.

[40] "Wakamama moyo uchisiya duzvi." In as offensive as this may sound to Shona speakers, forgive me, I had to say it and overcoming my inhibitions in process.

made my skin cringe and me more determined than ever to succeed on my own terms. I walked in on teachers during teatime, and they were talking about how hard it was to go from riches to rags. I was then experiencing hard times as my husband had lost his job. It was not a secret at all.

As soon as I walked in, there was that awkward silence that makes one feel one was the subject of discussion. I had goose bumps all over my body, but there was nothing I could say. They were entitled to their opinions, but they had shown me the kind of fickle and shallow people that they were. I went ahead and had my cup of tea and immediately left the awkward silence that had descended on us. I was happy they were not my friends, for I knew I deserved better. I could not even respect them by labeling them as seasonal friends because they served no purpose at all in my life than to bring me down in order to hinder the accomplishment of my dreams and goals. I did not deserve friends who were as fickle and as shallow as they were; as such, I relegated them to the category colleagues. I knew the difference between workmates, colleagues, and true friends from their actions and the nonverbal language on that day. The tension and silence in that staff room could have been cut with a solid knife.

One thing became very clear to me that day. Most of the women were riding on their husbands' cocktails and not on their own merits of what they had created and achieved for themselves. I knew they saved one purpose, and that was to beat my spirit down, but I refused to listen to such negative comments. I had to trample on them, to prove to them that I was whom I had made myself to be. A friend would tell me years later, when I would be studying in the US, that it was the devil talking and to never allow the devil to dwell in one's mind through such negative comments carelessly passed. She told me, because the devil desires for us to fail, how appropriate to dismiss such negative people and their comments. Failure for me was never an option; as such, the devil had no room in my life and my long-term goals. Thus, I relegated my colleagues to the deserved positions of devil's advocates!

I concentrated on changing myself and struggled with my studies. By the end of the year 1993, I sat my examinations. I waited, and finally, the results were out. In the meantime, my sister had lost her battle in December 1993. The day I collected my A level results in February 1994, I was still teaching at Sir Robert Taylor Primary School. When I saw my results, I was delirious. Once more, I had made it. The fact that I had managed to score seven points (B for Shona, 4 points, and C for English literature, 3 points) left my colleagues ill at ease and somehow all embarrassed. I still remember the looks on some of their faces up to now. Honestly, they were shocked. I still giggle with joy because of how they reacted to my good news and my impressive results. The majority could not make up their minds as to whether to congratulate me or ignore that they had heard my good demonstration of my intellectual prowess once again!

Except for one lady, she was always so open and genuine with me and supportive like a sister. She had encouraged me, and somehow I felt as though I had a younger sister in her. However, in my book of friends, she never earned the all-season friend label too. I used to have the feeling that she pretended to be friendly so that she too would be the source of my colleagues' information behind my back. She congratulated me warmly and gave me a hug.

Although most of my colleagues did not know how to react, my school principal was happy for me. Whereas my colleagues did not know whether to congratulate or pretend they had not heard the demonstration of my intellect prowess once more, my principal was singing my praises to them during assembly as he congratulated me and encouraged students to follow my example. Talk of rubbing it; he did exactly that on my behalf. I had passed again with flying colors for someone living under riches-to-rags circumstances. I wanted to yell it back at them, but I could not afford to be reduced to their level. I learned early on in my life that circumstances do not define us ultimately, but that we can always define circumstances to suit us. I was a living demonstration of how I was changing that definition of being defined by our circumstances.

I had been struggling with my studies and had passed beyond my own imagination! Then and there, I knew I had it within me to succeed in whatever goals I set for myself. That's when I started making plans to go to the university as I had already demonstrated beyond belief to all the critics and cynics that I was in charge of my destiny. To me, whether my colleagues had negative or skeptical attitudes and comments, I had demonstrated that for me, the sky was going to be the limit that would define my own capabilities.

Adversity or not, I knew no one would do it for me. I knew I would paint my own rainbow and make a name for myself, I, Avis, daughter of Norman and Doris; I knew I would not be satisfied with the simple accomplishment of my A levels alone without that college degree. I now wanted more, and the past several years were a clear indication that I had been holding myself down. University education became the limit that I aspired to reach no matter what. I wanted to achieve more and leave my miserable marriage behind so as to excel and become my own success story within my own right. Sure enough, nothing would ever hold me down or ever make me regret the goal I had intentionally or automatically made, for I achieved it not only once, but three times over.

Whether we are born predestined for certain, achievements or not, I almost believed success was never meant for me in the beginning. Let me take you back to the day I had thrown Jonathan out in 1994. He went to stay with my brother-in-law, my younger sister's husband, Drew. After some time of looking for a job, he became a commuter bus conductor. Though this position was very short lived, it obviously was below what he had been all his life. Somehow all the local (Spring Meadow) people who went to Harare from then on all seemed to come across him in his new diminished working position. To add salt to fresh wounds, they all made sure they passed the "good news" to me that they had seen Jonathan in Harare in his new position.

I learned to swallow humble pie, and I would tell them that at least whatever little he was making, it was helping to keep the bacon coming and our children fed. Before he had accepted the position, however, I remember telling him that for him to expect a position like the one he had held prior was really expecting too much. I remember actually encouraging him to humble himself and take up any position so that he could to assist with the home-front expenses. All this had taken part before I threw him out for giving our address to his mistress for their communications. Though financially I was barely keeping my head above water, I would never casually let on to my workmates, neighbors, and other people in my community that our circumstances were really impoverished and that I was struggling financially. I would have died first before letting them into that.

The economic hardships and the abuses were some of the things that I learned early on in my abusive relationship, that no matter how painful they would be, I would never share the hardships of my marriage with anyone except for my family. I had learned that people give sympathy in one's presence, but as soon as their backs were turned and the person would not be within hearing distance, they would celebrate the person's misfortune. I had appropriately coined that the crocodile smile. I thought and coined it like that due to the fact that the crocodile would show its teeth as if smiling at you while inwardly it would be planning and awaiting the first opportunity to swallow you up. As such, I felt their feigned sympathies were a put-up front for me to tell them all my problems, and behind all those feigned sympathies and behind my back, they would be dying to laugh at my misfortunes.

I was never like that at all (give a crocodile smile), and I would never pretend to anyone that I sympathized when I did not. I never could give anyone the crocodile smile. When someone shared their secrets and trusted in me as a friend, that's how far those secrets would go, just my ears, and no one would ever hear about them from me. I would never knowingly betray anyone's trust. Many times my colleagues had shared such secrets with me despite the fact that I would never share mine with them. I did not go soliciting for their trusts, and I was not comfortable sharing after the many comments that had unintentionally come to my ears of the negativity.

As a result of my changed circumstances in 1994, though I had made plans to go to the University of Zimbabwe, I had to shelve those plans for a while. It would be only my sisters who would know of these unfulfilled dreams and personal disappointments. Others would only be surprised when it would be time for me to go to the university. Because of shelving my plans like that, I almost convinced myself that I was never meant to succeed in anything and was doomed to be a failure at everything. These disturbing thoughts I would keep to myself and would never tell even my family.

Chapter Nineteen

Ambivalence and a detour to my dreams

Plans can be made, and until the end of time, plans can fall victim to other more important issues and sub-plans, in our lives as deemed necessary. My plan and intention was to be admitted to the university by early 1995. Before I could put my plans into motion and become admitted at the University of Zimbabwe (UZ), my husband found a job that would take him abroad in April of 1994. He was being sent by the United Nations (UN) to work in Slovenia. He learned about the position sometime at the end of March, and by early April, he was gone.

He was forty, and I was thirty-nine. As simple as that, my husband was gone; and for the first time since getting married, I enjoyed some tranquil in my married life without him. I loved his absence in my life. I loved being alone with my children. I did not have to account to anyone for my comings and goings. I was relaxed mentally, physically, and emotionally. I started to gain a bit of weight. Most of my adult life, I had always been extremely thin; and culturally, that is perceived as a huge sign of trouble in a marriage. I did not care about those perceptions because I had developed a thick skin, and I hid behind my facades. With my husband's absence, I had a taste of freedom once more. I loved the freedom of sharing my bed with my children. Things on the home front could never have been rosier and happier without the tension of our marriage hanging perpetually over my personality.

As for my relationship with my husband, I had ambivalent feelings. My ambivalence was due to the fact that by the time he left, I had kicked him out, and my brother-in-law, Brenda's husband, Drew, had given him sanctuary. By the time he left to go abroad, we pretended everything was mended (we were good at putting up facades again), however, inwardly, I knew what I had promised myself. I needed to improve myself academically. Consequently, from that point, though, my ambition would be shelved temporarily. I knew I could not leave my children alone and pursue my studies at the University of Zimbabwe guilty free. That time was when my children needed my presence the most in their lives because already one parent was not present; hence, I could not perceive myself depriving my children of their mother as well in order to pursue my lifelong dream. I was disappointed, yes, but I remained very hopeful and resolute.

When Jonathan had been gone for almost a month, I received my first letter from him, and I did not know how to respond. It professed his undying love for me. He promised he would be there for all the children and me. Included in the letter was his suggestion that I take over the care of his two children, the ones he had left with his mother in Georgetown (the ones he had with his mistress) again! Immediately, I knew the ulterior motive why he was declaring undying love for me. He wanted to persuade me once more to be the surrogate mother for his two children. Due to that reason, I did not believe his proclamation of undying love because after seventeen years of marriage, I knew the man I had married better than he thought I did.

At least for that first month, he sent us all money. Some of the cash was meant for his siblings, some for his mother, and some for my mother, some for the children, and some for me too. I was pleasantly surprised that I was also included in the monetary benefits. However, I was at a loss as to how to respond to his love letter. I remember telling my sister Diana that I was not sure how to respond to his first letter as it was a love letter, and in my heart, I had no love left for the man at all. By the time he left, I was unsure whether we still had a relationship or not. Honestly speaking, personally, I thought that his leaving to stay in Harare spelt the end of our marriage, and the word "DIVORCE" was written in capital letters on the wall. On the other hand, his trip abroad made me feel as though I was just stuck in one place and not moving anyway due to the fact that I had shelved my own plans.

It took me some time before I responded to his letter. I waited for the next one, and I was taking stock of my own feelings as well. The fact that he declared love for me and requested that I take care of his illegitimate children was a red flag that his love was being proclaimed out of selfish reasons as usual. My husband would call occasionally, and we would talk. I did not have a phone at home, so we basically had no privacy. I would use different offices and different people's homes; as such, our conversations tended to be really watered down depending on who was in the office or home. I remember all the time we talked, I never for once told him that I loved him, and he never said it to me neither.

There was no more cash flow to follow the first bumper after the first month. I had looked forward to him holding up his side of the responsibility as a parent. I had hoped that at least my children would be able to remain in their good schools with his financial support. However, words have to be matched by actions. Later, he would send us fifty-dollars here and there or when one of the children celebrated their birthdays. This was not much at all. In my heart, I concluded he was treating us like his charity cases. That first demonstration to me was a clear indication that he was making good money, and later his not sending any more financial support proved the point that he was still being his usual self-centered person. In my stubborn pride too and attempt to adjust to managing financially and independently, I would never ask him for financial assistance unless it became crucially imperative that I tell him about my own and the children's financial problems or our dire straits.

I was having problems paying our rent on time. I could barely afford anything else after paying our rent. Some days we were forced to skip certain meals because we could not afford them. That was the worst time ever in my life as my children were going hungry. I remember one night I cried on my knees in prayer, asking God for deliverance. I asked God to give me a sign that He had an answer to my financial dilemma. Honestly, I used to think prayers are not answered instantaneously; the answer to my prayer this time was immediate. It was only a couple of days while walking down Spring Meadow that one of the educational district staffing officers would ask me whether I would consider going back to Falcon Gold Mines Primary School to be the acting school head once more. The school was having problems with the appointed school head.

I did not even think twice about it. Straight away, I told him there and then that there was no way I would ever consider that. I had been humiliated in Falcon Gold Mines by my husband's infidelity, and I did not have pleasant memories of that place. Going back to Falcon Gold Mines was not an option I could ever consider at all, I recall telling that education officer. I was sure I had a resolute answer to his query. Conversely, what the heart wants can be in complete contrast to the harsh realities of life. During the wee hours of the night, most people have time to reflect and reassess. I was no different. Later that night, lying in bed surrounded by my children, I reflected on the request to God again. I had especially asked God for some deliverance. Wasn't that His way of providing for my children and me? As a parent I knew the responsible thing to do despite the humiliation I had endured years before. I needed to be able to financially provide for my children. Acknowledging my responsibility made me realize the answer was glaring brightly right into my eyes.

When morning came, I called the staffing officer and told him I had reconsidered and was willing to go back to Falcon Gold Mines. He quickly told me to drop in to the office later that day. I think he was afraid I would renege on my word. As a loving and caring mother, I had to swallow my pride and revisit Falcon Gold Mines again no matter what the circumstances of Falcon Gold Mines had been; I was determined to create a respectable life for my children. My consolation was this time I would be by myself without Jonathan. I felt comforted knowing that I was free to carve a life for my children without his continued humiliation.

The situation at Falcon Gold Mines Primary School was bad, and the administrators desperately needed someone to help correct the mess that had been created in the interim. I swallowed my pride for the sake of my children. I had vowed after the physical abuse and humiliation of 1991 that I would never step my foot on Falcon Gold Mines' red and dirty soil ever again. Little did I know that Falcon Gold Mines' red and dirty soil would be the rock for my financial security as well as the much-needed emotional healing? Accepting the acting position meant I would have free accommodation, free water, and subsidized electricity. On top of that, I would also have a little traveling and subsistence allowance as well

﹐ting allowance once every four months. Nothing exceptionally ﹐orous, not attractive, but in our desperate situation, every little bit of finances helped to improve our dire straits.

My daughter Tiffany was by then in seventh grade. She was the only one I did not want disturbed by our move as she had examinations to sit by the end of the year. Arrangements were made with the mining authorities that she would ride on the company bus to Spring Meadow so that she could remain at Lady Grace until she had taken her end-of-year grade seven examinations. The other two, Thelma and Elton, would transfer to Falcon Gold Mines with me. At least the school had a good reputation. I convinced myself that as their mother, I would personally ensure that I supervised and monitored their education on a daily basis.

Sometime in 2008, my youngest daughter, Thelma, and I would reminisce on their primary education and wonder how they even made it because they were moved from school to school every two years or so. Thelma alone had moved five times in seven years. There was no stability. I was mortified by that realization as a teacher. At the same time, I am grateful every day because the children continued to excel in school despite the disruptions. Elton moved as many times as Thelma, but unlike Thelma, in Elton, I would detect reading problems. I never dedicated enough time to anchor him in his schoolwork as I did with the older children. Elton, as the last born, was given a lot of latitude, and I feel his schoolwork suffered the ramifications.

I was not as strict with Elton as I was with Elvin and the girls. I agree; I always had a weak spot where Elton was concerned. I think if I could at times, I spoiled Elton to the extent I would let him get away with murder. I tried to make up for what lacked in Elton's life; as a result, his schoolwork suffered in the process. I knew Elton missed his father the most; as such, I overcompensated where he was concerned for the lack.

During these trying times, that I tragically neglected Elton's reading; as a result, he never developed reading interests like all my other children. He never had the library trips that his elder siblings enjoyed. His homework was sporadically monitored compared to his elder siblings. I remember one time he faked my signature for his reading assignments. I reprimanded him, but in a much calmer tone than what I would have had been one of his elder siblings. Maybe I had a softer heart because I knew he was my last born. Years later, my eldest son, Elvin would accuse me of playing favoritism with Elton. However, as I perceive it, it was not favoritism. By the time Elton was growing, I had too much on my plate, so I failed to cope but that does not justify my negligence to my son's education. I also continuously and effectively reiterated it to myself that whatever education he received from the school was adequate.

I know I made excuses for my negligence, and at times, I discredit this to the fact that I was maturing as a mother (which is not a valid reason for neglect). Consequently I feel I was learning how to deal better with discipline and ultimately approached their education differently. On the whole, I take my hat off to all my children. They all pursued their studies with diligence, discipline, and responsibility that none had ever claimed from their paternal side of the family. They all matured into responsible adults. They are the first ones on their paternal family to become college graduates. That being the case, I can never be more proud of them and of what together we have achieved and carved as the stories of our lives. I salute the five wonderful beings God gave me.

Moving from place to place or house to house was another thing that I grew weary of during our marriage. We had moved, so much that one of my nephews Harry, at one point, commented that he would never know how we managed to keep track of our home addresses. Most of our moving was when Jonathan was there, and he would gather people to help us move. The move back to Falcon Gold Mines in 1994 was a different situation. I was alone with only my children to help. We moved on a sunny Saturday afternoon. The loading of the truck and trailer and the unloading took their toll on us despite the fact that I paid a couple of people to help us with the loading and unloading. In addition, my husband's two brothers had come to help upload, and appreciated.

I had not underestimated the stress of moving, as we had done it many times over. As much as I could, I had made sure the paid help moved the heavy furniture into the right rooms. Even with that help, my body could not take being overworked. I remember the following Monday morning, as I was getting ready for my first day at Falcon Gold Mines School, after taking my bath in the morning while getting dressed, I just collapsed on to the floor from fatigue. My children did not know what to do. I was out for some time, and I am not sure for how long. All I could hear were their voices; they seemed to be coming from somewhere very far away calling me "Mama, Mama, Mama" repeatedly. I am not sure what could have happened if they had not kept

ie. I kept listening for those voices until I could make out their
At first, somehow I saw all their faces blurred and crooked. When
ally regained full consciousness, I was scared. I somehow managed
to go to work that day, but my experience had scared the daylights out of
me. It was a clear indication that I needed to take better care of myself.
I know at times I neglected my own health and focused more on my
children. I had to reassess my priorities because my health was an equal
part of my children's livelihood.

From that day onward, I never slept in separate rooms from my
children. I wanted us to be close together. I realized my life could be
taken away in the blink of an eye. I learned to appreciate each day and
look on it as a blessing and an opportunity for me to praise my Maker
and use the opportunity to show my children how much I loved them. I
think we were all scared that something would devastate us if we were
separated during the night. This was a period I bonded the most with my
last three children.

That year, we became bonded as mother and children in our attempts
to settle and be secure. During those trying days, Elton demonstrated
that he was a young man; he was only a little over eight years old. All
the electrical gadgets that his sisters and I could not assemble would be
left for Elton to take care of. His comments would be "a man is a man
no matter how young, Mama." He eventually had all electrical gadgets
up and running. Everything was finally safely connected, and we were
home safe and secure, mother and children. Hopefully, we were home to
stay for longer without moving for some foreseeable time.

For the next three years, my academic plans were temporarily
shelved. I could not go to the university, leaving my children by
themselves. They needed me. They needed my love and support. I
needed the financial stability of my job to care for my children and keep
them in school and their lives secured. I continued to work as hard as
I could. I focused on the important issues and tried to make it one step
at a time. After all, I was still trying to recover from my wounds as a
battered woman. Women in the community never failed to tell me how
much they admired my progressive thinking and my tenacity.

As for my career, I planned for fundraisers, I planned for the
expansion of classrooms, I planned for the enrollment of more children
to our school and for more teachers to be allocated to our school. The
demands were too much as I was a full-time teaching school head. I had

a class of twenty-five students besides the administrative duties. I w
overworked, but I did the best under the circumstances. The school hau
not improved much during the time I had left. It was still a single-stream
school with an average of twenty children per class. Some of the classes
were combined under one teacher like grades three and four as well as
grades five and six.

We needed more children, but the cost of tuition, meager as it was,
prevented more parents from sending their children to our school.
Instead, the children from our side of the compound went across the
river to the sister schools, Falconer 1 and Falconer 11, where tuition was
very minimal. Thus, from August 1994 till December 1996, I remained
in Falcon Gold Mines Primary School. I know I was an effective leader.
By the end of three years we had seven teachers, classes were no longer
combined. I butted heads with some of my subordinates. That was to be
expected, as some of them had envied the same position. Furthermore,
in any leadership if things are changing conflicts are bound to happen
and I took our conflicts as part of implementing change.

I also met with resistance from the School Development Association
(SDA), especially the treasurer, and I knew it was because I was a woman.
Men in a patriarchal society like Zimbabwe do not take kindly to being
directed by women. I would look for friendlier males; I would get their
empathy and utilize them to the optimum. Nevertheless, the chairperson
of the SDA was a very respectful man; as a result, I enjoyed a lot of
support and cooperation from him. Had it not been for his support, the
school would not have grown at all.

Our main goal that year was to have a single-stream school, grades
one to seven, with no classes combined at all. Our hard work was
rewarded; by the end of the year, we achieved our major goal. We had
seven classes, each with its own teacher from grade one to seven. That
was no mean feat. It took a lot of persuading, negotiating, and convincing
for us to have the school we needed for our students. Our school results
bore testimony in convincing parents we were doing a sterling job. Our
Grade Seven results were top in the district for two tears in a row. I also
was grateful to the school heads of the sister schools as they constantly
encouraged more parents to send their children our way. I was happy
because I was making my mark as an educational leader. I was no longer
overshadowed by the abusiveness of my husband. Eventually, I found
my own leadership voice, and I used it effectively during that time.

my time at Falcon Gold Mines Primary School, I bonded ith one young lady who became our school secretary as well grade two teacher, Cherry. In case you are wondering what ιdship category she belonged to, she became an all-season friend. we were sharing my accommodation; we were sharing our meager financial resources. She was more helpful to me than I was to her. In many ways, she became a surrogate mother for my children especially when I was not home, attending numerous meetings.

It was also during this second stay in Falcon Gold Mines Primary School that I finally learned to drive. All my life, I had lived under the shadow of my husband, but his going away also liberated me in other ways I had never imagined. I managed to buy myself a car, and trips with family were easier. We were not completely financially comfortable, but we could afford a few luxuries by then fairly well. A car meant I could afford to drive my children to various places for vacations. At times, we used the car to generate much-needed income as we would give rides to people commuting back and forth between Hartley and Falcon Gold Mines. I was happy because I realized I did not need my husband to be there beating the crap out of me to be the person I was meant to be. I was free to spread my wings and literally soar.

It was toward the end of 1996 that Falcon Gold Mines Primary School once again was advertisement for a substantive grade three school head. This time around, I expected to win the position because by then, I had completed my Cambridge 'O' levels and 'A' levels and felt more confident. Somehow I did not get the anticipated promotion because once more, I did not have the much-required experience and proper credentials to be a school administrator. What I had academically had not been matched or cemented by experience and certification to be the school head.

I got that fact, but I was still disappointed. I had worked hard to bring that school from the brink of collapse, yet my efforts were not being acknowledged once again. I would deliver my end-of-year speech with the appointed school head among the audience. It was not a daunting experience like I had imagined. This time around, I was not bitter because I did not lose the school to a man but to another woman. Somehow it appeared as though the patriarchal leadership had not connived to boot me out. I also had better prospects for myself as I had started my application process with the University of Zimbabwe. I had

even attended one of their interviews in October; as such, I h
hopes of a better future. I readily relinquished the administrative
to the new head and sailed quietly on into the horizon once again.

In October 1996, the UZ had invited me for a written interview.
had never been to the institute of higher learning in my country in all
my forty-one years. By then, my eldest son, Elvin, was nineteen, and he
drove me to the interview. By mid-1996, my husband's contract with the
UN had run out. He had come home, and this time he would be living
under my roof and under my financial support again. By the end of the
year, he had secured employment with Broken Hills Properties (BHP).
I had not mentioned the interview to Jonathan prior because I knew he
would prevent me from taking the family car. Between the two of us,
my son and I connived and created a story of the telegram having been
delivered that morning and as such had no choice but to take his car and
go! By the time we drove into Harare, my husband had already left for
work (as he was picked up by the company bus around 6:00 a.m., and
by 6:15 a.m., my son and I were on our way). As to my secret with my
son, my husband would never be any the wiser. Yes, he swallowed the
lies we told him hook, line and sinker.

All through the years of our marriage, I had learned that my husband
never questioned a lot of things; therefore, at times I simply took
advantage of his being naive. That was one of the many times I realized
that I was way smarter than him in aspects that mattered the most in my
life. Where he physically beat me up, intellectually, I knew I was heads
and shoulders above him without question. As a result, I learned to use
my intellectual skills more and more where decisions of carving my
life ahead without giving him too much information. Maybe I learned
like my sister Diana would mention years later, I learned to shift the
goalpost, and I believe that is a very strong strategy especially in battle.
For me I was involved in a lifetime battle of survival, and yes, I moved
the goalpost when necessary and when it suited my purpose.

Smart or not, when I walked on campus that day, I felt so intimidated.
I was shaking inside. There were many prospective students waiting in
the foyer and in the hallways to be called in for their interviews. I was not
even sure where to go. The only thing that gave me confidence was my
attire. As a professional, I knew how to dress and make an impression;
as such, I drew strength from my appearance. I had also learned how
to walk as though I owned the world; with a lot of confidence, there

apologetic about my gait. Though inwardly I was petrified, I exuded confidence and walked as though I knew many w̖ campus. Later, some of my classmates would reveal that they ᴵI was one of the seasoned professors only to be surprised when ᴄre taking our interviews together.

The questions for our written interviews were on policy and what ᴣ hoped to change as school administrators. I remember writing ᴀy personal story and how I would help to formulate and influence friendlier policies directed at girl child education. After the interview, I realized there were a couple of people I had been to school with. As we were chatting and catching up on our lives, the conversation then moved to the written interview, and some of them were already administrators. They explained which educational policies they had analyzed. I felt so low and did not volunteer how I had approached mine. I felt as though I was the only one who had answered out of topic, but I was grateful I had even been invited at all. To me the invitation alone was a success story. I went home to await the results of the interview.

As alluded to above, my husband had lost his contract with the UN in July of 1996 and had come back home. Once more, We appeared reunited as a loving family to the outside world, but I knew how much I wanted to pursue my studies and free myself from the many years of bondage from an unfaithful man. Even when he was abroad, he continued with his cheating ways. For example, while he worked abroad, each time he came home for vacations, I noticed he would bring presents from assumed female friends for all his children. Those friends never once sent me anything. I knew from their inactions without asking him that those were his presumed current girlfriends, hence their lack of acknowledging me. I did not need him neither denying nor confirming my sentiments. If they had been platonic friends, I knew the least they could have done was acknowledge my presence in his life; their lack of acknowledgement confirmed my suspicions. I knew he was cheating, and how could I fool myself into believing otherwise?

Financially, I cannot say he came back with any form of financial capital and financial relief for all his years working abroad and earning the coveted US dollar. We managed, however, to secure a loan from the bank to finance our second home together, but the sale fell through, as there were other perceptive buyers who coveted the same home and influenced the owner to sell it behind our backs at a higher price.

However, by the end of 1997, we managed to secure a beautiful home in Hartley. As I was the one who always had a stable job, we managed to secure a mortgage from one of the building societies in Zimbabwe, and the government provided me with the collateral to our second home.

In December of 1996, at the end of the school year, we moved to Spring Meadow, as I had lost the school again to another head. In January 1997, I went back to teach at Sir Robert Taylor Primary School to be a classroom teacher once more. From the time I had taken my interview in October 1996 until the end February 1997, all the people I had met at the UZ during our interview had in one way or another been contacted, and they all knew that they had either been turned down or accepted. Three months into the new academic year I had not received nor heard anything from the university. In my heart, I knew I was a little disappointed and had almost given up on receiving any communication from them at all. To my friends, I concealed the disappointment by telling them that to me, just being invited for that interview was an accomplishment in its own. I never thought among the hundreds of people I had met that day I had managed to stand out, let alone had a fighting chance of being admitted.

Later, I was to learn never to underestimate the goals I set for myself, for they build bridges where I never thought bridges would be constructed at all. My acceptance letter was an absolute surprise. Late February 1997, I received a letter from the university. I had been offered a place to study for two years as a full-time student from March 1997 to November 1998! I could not believe it; I was finally about to fulfill my destiny. This was exactly twenty-four years after graduating as a sub-standard teacher at Harvard Institute. I had almost given up on ever having a university degree, and now I had the best opportunity. I was purely ecstatic. I had never experienced what it felt like to be on cloud nine, but that day, I knew the sensation. In my mind, I could simply picture doors literally opening up for me in a way I had never imagined. Later that night, I had another nosebleed from the excitement and joy the acceptance letter brought.

The very day I got my acceptance letter, I hastily told my school principal that I was going on study leave immediately. I told my students that I was leaving and going to the university; they were happy for me. I also told my husband who had no response to my good news. I told my brothers and sisters over the phone, and they had never been happier nor more proud of me than then. The following weekend, I went home to share with my father. I told my father, and his face just lit up for me. My mother just ululated[41] to express her happiness on my behalf. I knew I was going to have the time of my life despite being an elder student at the institute of higher learning. My ecstasy was rooted in the notion that after all, having a degree had not completely eluded me as I had imagined. I could at least start to believe that I was not doomed to fail. I felt as though I had broken the chains that had tied me down for so long! In my mind, I could see all the possible things I would do with my first university degree.

I started the process of acquiring my study leave with the Ministry of Education, Youth, Sports, and Culture, but they turned my application down. Their reason was that my field of study and my degree was not going to be relevant to my career. I did not understand what else I needed to study in order to have the right credentials to fulfill my career goal of being a school principal. I knew I had to take other measures to fulfill my goal. Before the end of the month, I was in the regional office of Mashonaland West presenting my case to my regional educational director. I was desperately trying to influence her to rescind the ministry's decision.

In the process of pleading my case, I was most disappointed with her than any other educational leader had ever disappointed me in my whole career. She told me that I could not go to the university because the ministry's policy was clearly stated. The policy stated for one to be granted study leave, one had to pursue a degree in line with one's career. I could not fathom what was not in line with a classroom teacher aspiring to be a school principal and going to study educational administration. To me, it appeared the oppressive policies drafted by men were being used to oppress my career goals as a woman. That was as clear as daylight for me. There and then, I felt as though I would never escape a world whose rules and policies were written to be friendly to men and dictated by men while oppressing women.

The other disappointment was also from the fact that my regional educational director then was a woman. I felt as though she was being

---

[41] We ululate in times of joy. That's one sound I would always miss when living and studying abroad. The village women made everything sound so beautiful with their voices, and I miss that more than I ever let on.

used as a stooge to implement polices formulated to promote the males' interests. I had hoped that she would be more sympathetic to the cause of fellow women, but surprisingly, she was actually endorsing the regulations of the patriarchal society by endorsing their oppressive policies on a fellow woman. I took everything personally, forgetting there were hundreds others in the same boat as I was. I also clearly remember that day was the fourth time I had a nosebleed. I could not believe my ears; I thought I heard wrong. I so much wanted to go to the university to fulfill one of my life's academic dreams. I started crying. The crying triggered some nosebleed, which was so bad that I had to excuse myself to use the bathroom. I could not believe my dreams and goals were being dashed away before they became reality and even before they had a fighting chance to sprout into anything.

I think my breaking down appeared real and genuine in my regional director's eyes. When I went back from crying in the bathroom, my director sort of had a softer tone of voice. She sounded more encouraging and mentioned that in life we had to fight for what we really believed in. She told me tears had to flow, sweat had to be wiped, and blood drawn for all we truly believed in. Not in the same exact words, but I held on to the fact she was attempting to address basically that I had to fight for what I truly believe in. To me, those were the best words of encouragement, and I clung to them with my very life. As a result, before I left her office, I had resolved in my heart of hearts that whatever the consequences would be, I was going to abandon my teaching assignment and fulfill my dream. After all, I believed the old proverb "fortune comes but once in a lifetime," and this was my fortune, and I was not going to let it slip through my very fingertips. I was going to dig my nails right in.

While I make it sound like it was easy to come to my decision, it was not an easy decision at all. I knew the goal I was pursuing was enormous, but I was so poorly prepared for achieving the goal ultimately because I had lots of hurdles to overcome. Despite it not being easy, I was equally determined to find that needle in the haystack. The first hurdle was I had not saved financially for this academic journey and not having my sabbatical approved meant I would not be receiving a salary at all for the next two years. What I had not anticipated was that the bureaucratic machinery would be on fast track, and my salary would be ceased there and then. I started at the university beginning of March, and by end of March 1997, I did not have an income. I almost panicked but decided to

Avis Noel

fight for what I truly believed I was entitled to as my right and ultimate fulfillment of my own destiny.

On the home front, I also had another battle to fight. Remember I had also told my husband about being accepted at the UZ and having no response from him? I decided to take the bull by the horns. One evening during dinner, I tackled the issue at the dining table. I mentioned casually to the kids that their father had not given me a response about my pursuing my studies at the UZ. Elton answered for them all. He simply mentioned that I had to go, and when I asked him why, his simple answer was, "Mom, Dad was away for two years, and you took care of us. You can go, and it's Dad's turn to take care of us." My husband just took it in his stride and asked Elton whether he was now making decisions for the family. Elton, in pure Elton fashion, retorted back and said, "Fair is fair, baba-dad." Whatever else that meant, nothing was said after that.

That was the end of that conversation. My husband never gave me his word neither to go nor to deny. Even if he had attempted to deny, it was one battle he was bound to lose anyway. My mind had been made up years earlier without his input. With this status quo, I prepared for life as a university student. I was really enthusiastic and looking forward to the next two tears. This was something that had almost eluded me but now was almost within my reach! Here I was thinking I was going to be the oldest student in my class until I arrived for my course work.

There were fellow students in my class who were decades older than I was, and on the other hand, there were students in my cohort who were also decades younger than I was. Ultimately, I realized the saying learning does not end true meaning. I was happy to be part and parcel of this cohort. I was happy despite the financial uphill battle I knew awaited me. I was living in the moment, and nothing could take my happiness away. I enjoyed relishing in every little bit of my study, and I never regretted those two years. Those two years were the epitome of joy and the happiest years I had ever experienced as an adult, especially since getting married. I glowed in every sense of the word for those two years at the University of Zimbabwe.

Chapter Twenty

A life's journey and dreams fulfilled

I was enrolled at the University of Zimbabwe in March 1997. At the beginning of my study, life as a university student was exciting. I actually moved myself onto campus and was just like any freshmen in any university setting. I shared a two-bed, one-room dormitory with another mature female education student. I used the dining room for all my meals every day. In the evenings, after meals, I would take walks with my fellow classmates and reminisce over what we had almost missed in our lives. Most nights, my roommate and I would study until the wee hours of the morning. Those were the only other carefree days I had; I had last enjoyed carefree days when I was a student in high school or college training to be a teacher. However, those had been marred by the memories and experiences of war. As a more mature student, I could not imagine that I could have almost missed out on this experience, my best and ultimate accomplishment.

Not having children to come home to in the evening was something I was beginning to enjoy as a mature student at the varsity. The added bonus was not having Jonathan, him demanding his conjugal rights every night, which I grudgingly rendered because I knew what, would happen if I withheld my services. Despite having five children, not all was rosy within our married life, as I alluded to many times in this memoir. Sometimes my husband forced himself on me, and certain times I would just lie there like a log, looking up the ceiling, willing him to get off me as soon as possible. Other times, of course, we were like any loving couple. As such, you can believe me when I say the first days at the university were full of relaxation and peaceful undisturbed sleep. I felt really free that I could have that much needed break away from my husband and children and invest time and knowledge in myself. I did not have anyone's unwelcome hands crawling and creeping round my waist in the middle of the night, demanding attention. I had enjoyed very little sleep since his coming back from Slovenia in 1996. I started thinking that probably I needed to divorce him then, but in the eyes of society, I would have been the one to be condemned. He was home, doing his fatherly duties, and I was pursuing elusive dreams of self-actualization. None of my friends understood why I needed time away from home and my husband. How could they when they had dependable strong men who treated them like their African queens? I felt the deepest and most urgent need to carve some accomplishment of my own.

I know the desire was born out of having been brought up by a mother who believed I could stand up on my two feet without leaning on any man for financial stability, let alone a man who battered and abused me like my husband did. I felt as though my mission had been accomplished just by enrolling at the university. I also felt what better way than just take off and educate myself like it should have been if I had undertaken my studies before marriage. No one would understand that need except probably my mother and sisters. It was not as though I was neglecting my children and my husband. I was not doing that. I knew my responsibilities as a mother and a wife, but I could not help feel liberated and happy.

Every weekend, that is Friday evening after all my classes, I went home to Spring Meadow to my husband and my children. Monday mornings, without fail, I boarded the bus on my way back to Harare, Mt. Pleasant, where the UZ is located. I rode those buses back and forth Spring Meadow to my children and husband religiously without fail. I remember one weekend Elton telling me to remain in Harare. When I asked him why, Elton told me that their father bought them nice food during my absence. It hurt my feelings a little, of course, that Jonathan could afford to buy them food during my absence as though he was trying to buy their love. After thinking about it some more, I realized I was relieved that he was taking extra good care of his children and probably was overcompensating for my absence.

In a way, it helped to know that at least they were not going hungry neither for food nor for his attention. As such, I did not need not to worry my pretty head over their welfare. Once again, thanks to Elton for blurting out his mouth. I let go of my own guilty feelings for enjoying myself while my children lacked my attention. I knew my children were well fed without me being the primary provider for a change! I liked that for once, that their father was building a relationship with his children with me absent in the picture to influence their decisions on a daily basis. I was not in control and felt they could do what pleased them.

On another sad note, strange as it may sound, I could not afford my bus fare back and forth for my studies at the UZ. As soon as I enrolled with the UZ, my salary was ceased immediately thereafter. I was not the only one in this predicament; most of my classmates were in the same boat with me, embroiled in the struggle for what we felt the ministry owed us. I, however, pursued the issue with the Ministry of Education, Youth, Sports, and Culture, and nothing ever materialized for close to a year. My siblings rallied round me once more, giving me the much-needed financial assistance to buy books, food, and use for bus fares to enable me to take my weekly trips.

I reached out to fellow students with similar financial problems of not being granted sabbatical as we were all in a similar quagmire. In my discussions with fellow students, someone suggested I should arrange a meeting with the ombudsman. I went to the ombudsman's office to find out what he could do for me. I had worked for the government loyally for more than twenty years, and to simply imagine the ministry would not allow me to go on a sabbatical for just two years was beyond my imagination. I knew I was not going to abandon my career but only seeking to advance myself. As such, I could not comprehend why the ministry had turned me down. I felt that the ministry owed me at least a minimum of two years of sabbatical for all the years of loyal service I had given them; as such, they had to hold up their end.

I made my appointment with the ombudsman's office and was granted one three months into my studies. When I went to meet with him, I broke down and cried hysterically as I was telling him my story. As soon as I broke down, he spoke to me in a tough firm voice as though he was admonishing a little child. Somehow that caught my attention, and I wiped my eyes dry. He proceeded to tell me that crying was a sign of weakness and that men always recognized it as such, and they would always take advantage of the perceived weaknesses. The ombudsman told me that men jam-packed the top leadership positions. Some of them had been in the same positions, sitting idle for decades without doing anything to advance their careers. According to him, the discriminatory policies were meant to safeguard men's positions; as such, women had to fight for what they felt were their professional and rightful places as well.

The ombudsman further went on to explain that most men were doing nothing to advance themselves academically; hence, they felt threatened by those who sought improvement. As such, seeking further studies was a clear indication that I was aspiring to be in one of those leadership positions. According to him, all roadblocks would be raised to ensure the idle leaders remained safe and secure. I know I heard him clearly when he stated that men protected their turf. He elaborated that policy makers put into place policies that would impede other people (to my mind, it was women and not just other people) from advancing.

I left his office with a smoldering determination in me to make sure I never gave in and was resolute to fight for what I believed was rightfully mine. In the end, the ombudsman also promised to investigate the issue further on my behalf. Before meeting with the ombudsman, I used to be a terrible crybaby. One of my brothers-in-law, at some point, had indicated that crying obscured my thinking through problems. Undeniably, after crying, I would feel some relief, but I would forget the problem still existed anyway. I recognized that I had two professional men who were sympathetic to my cause; as such, I paid attention to their words of wisdom. From that day onward, I learned to be stronger, to think through issues, and to argue my point to a certain degree without breaking down in tears. I started analyzing problems than just crying over problems. This would be a powerful tool in my personal life as well. I learned to assess better my miserable situation without simply crying over the situation.

The ombudsman's investigations in the end reaped good results on my behalf as I was paid for my sabbatical in retrospect after a year. I managed to have a little nest egg put aside for me. When some of my classmates learned that I had been reimbursed my salary, they followed suit. Most of them were told that I had been making a lot of noise, and they were all grateful to me, as we all ended up getting paid for our study time. That reimbursement of my salary taught me never to simply give up but explore all avenues before I could surrender.

I continued to concentrate and excel at my studies. I did well every semester. Initially, I did not believe I could do well, but after the first semester's results were posted on the notice board, and I found myself with distinctions. I knew I was going to make it. I was studying with the best of the cream of Lucas academia. It was not easy to be accepted at UL. Academically, the standards were very high. To imagine I managed to cope with the best of them resurrected the mental prowess and confidence I had as a youth in secondary school. Of all my classmates, some of them were seasoned school administrators, young teachers, some fresh from college, and I had very little experience in administration. Initially, I looked at them and convinced myself that there was no way I was going to cope with such intelligence, but my results proved something—that I had underestimated my own smartness.

Once again, I had taken myself for granted and underestimated my own capabilities, but after that first semester, I started to regain my confidence. I started to immensely enjoy my class presentations, doing my assignments way ahead of time, and generally participating actively in classroom discussions and debates, something that I had given up on long ago. I used to keep my mouth shut in case I said or asked something stupid until I learned there is never a stupid question. Initially, my lecturers had to draw the arguments out of me in order to enable me to participate more in the classroom arguments. They helped me come out of my shell. Somehow my mind, as I write now, connects the self-doubt and lack of self-confidence to the abuses that I endured. I never thought I was good for anything anymore.

I had been trodden on for so long that I almost believed that by myself I could never operate fully. I had forgotten that I had worked as a school principal, a student teacher, and all I ever saw most times was this battered woman who never lifted a finger to challenge her husband. I had forgotten I was my children's example, and all I saw was this emotionally controlled woman who had no voice. With my success in school, I realized I was coming into my own as a confident woman with a sense of accomplishment. I started to flourish as a woman, a student, and a mother who believed everything was possible and within reach.

If someone had asked me at that point and time whether I needed the role as a wife, my response would have been a resounding no. By then, I had the image of the sky being the limit to my aspirations and hopes with no husband to bring me down. Despite the turmoil I had put up with most of my married life, most of my classmates thought I was happily married. I once again presented the facade of someone who was happy to go home at the end of the week to be with her children and loving husband. Inwardly, I would be seething from being duty bound to grudgingly perform my wifely duties while at the same time lovingly conducting my motherly responsibilities. I looked forward to those moments with my children as I loved them unconditionally. As for the other role, I knew I was bidding the rightful and most opportune time to carry out my anticipated deed. The resentment to the wifely duties would enable to keep me focused on my academic goals. Every day in front of the mirror, my reflection reminded me the degree of abuse and trauma.

Earlier in 1989, when I had embarked on my O levels, my sister Brenda had been instrumental in my accomplishments because she had believed in me more than I believed in myself. She had given me the finances that set me on the way to realizing my accomplishment. This phase was no different. I depended solely on my siblings. On this journey to the university, I had Brenda's support again; Diana, my younger sister, and my younger brother, Louis, helped to boost me up financially and morally. Not that my other siblings, Levin, Dr. Larry, and my sister Melody did not play any prominent roles. Once in a while, they too would provide me with rides, food, and clothes for the children especially over school holidays. My husband never once assisted me financially where my studies were concerned. As such, I continued in my determination to strategize about our divorce; only Jonathan was in the dark all the time.

I remember early on in May 1997 some of the books on our reading lists were not readily available in Zimbabwe bookstores or where too expensive for my shallow pockets. My brother Louis was taking a business trip to South Africa. He requested that I give him a list of all the books that were not readily available. By the end of the week when he came back, he had every single one of those books on my reading list. Besides me, who else was lucky to be born into the family they were born into? I knew what it meant to have my siblings' unconditional support. I knew that through thick and thin, in good and in bad times, I could always count on my brothers and sisters for their unfailing and unwavering familial support.

On another level, though my husband did not support my personal endeavors, my husband and I still operated as a married couple. Early on in our marriage, we had secured a home, and he had sold it in 1984 while we were in Falcon Gold Mines. I hated the idea of paying rent. I always thought it made sense to pay my own mortgage in the hopes of owning something I could eventually hand down to my children. Economically, it made sense that I invested in something of my own than paying other people. By the end of 1997 and in early 1998, my husband and I were finally able to secure a government loan for our second home together.

The first home we had bought as newlyweds had been sold for very little when we moved to Falcon Gold Mines. The deal fell through with the other home we had attempted to buy in 1996. Between 1994 and 1995, we had secured a piece of land, but we agreed to sell it. The problem was I could never see myself overseeing a construction project. Construction for me was too demanding on time, energy, and resources. We both agreed that buying a completed home was less of a hassle than building one. We purchased one at the end of 1997 in Hartley. Hartley is a few miles nearer to Harare than Spring Meadow. With the purchase of the new home, I decided to commute on a daily basis from Hartley to the UZ.

The onset of the 1998 academic year found me commuting from our home in Hartley to the university in Harare. At least I was certain that I could cope with the pressure of my studies. I had spent a year living on campus and passing with flying colors. I felt more comfortable going home and commuting every day as I did not spend a lot of time on the road. Moreover, Thelma and Elton were now both in boarding schools. Commuting between Hartley and UZ would not pose a threat to my studies nor disturb me otherwise. The least expected disturbance in my home was the one that affected me more than I had ever thought.

I never thought the quietness of not having my children would adversely affect me. The lack of human noise, especially my children, affected me. From the time I had my children, they were rowdy, active, rambunctious, and pretty loud at best times. At times while studying at home, my children never learned to walk on eggshells in case they disturbed me. I had queer study habits. I loved to hear their noises in the background; that way I knew they were all right. They would scream and shout, and I would never tell them to be quiet because they disturbed my studying. The only times I told them that was when my own mind was wondering and not concentrated on my studying.

When I decided to commute from home, the quietness devoured my heartstrings every evening. Jonathan would go to the pub after work. I would be by myself. The TV would not cover up for my loneliness. As it became too much for me, one evening, on my way home, I stopped by an aviary and bought myself five canaries and named them all after my children. Those five birds woke me up at the crack of dawn with their sweet music, and I had something to distract me from too much study, quietness, mounted boredom, and loneliness of my own home. I had never heard anyone say they were ever lonely in their own home, and I thought that was really strange, but funny enough, it highlighted how Jonathan and I were no longer close as a couple.

When Elton came home for the first weekend, he was flabbergasted at how I could send all my children to boarding schools and resort to buying birds to be my children. Well, at least where my children's education was concerned, I always believed I had to give them the best that I could afford. I would continue to sacrifice for my children right through their college years to be as supportive of a mother as I could be. I provided them with counseling, financial support, moral support, residential support, and any other problems, social or otherwise. My children knew they would always count on their mother's unfailing and unwavering support and advice any time of day or night. My children became the epicenter of my troubled world; that way, in most difficult times, my love for them kept me grounded and helped me keep focused and going. Before going abroad and after embarking on my studies living in the USA, I focused mainly on their stability to keep going.

Chapter Twenty-One

What does a person do in the face of adversity?

The two years at the UZ were not all rosy nor were they as smooth sailing as I would have wanted. Besides my ever-troubled marriage, finance was my biggest hurdle. I was lucky to be born with the brothers and sisters I had. They helped me financially in every way possible. On top of my dire straits, there was a constant thorn in my flesh and well-being. The constant cause of pain was my husband's children with the other women and one woman in particular. In 1998, there was an argument for where he could keep one of his children. The care of that boy was another added issue on our already-troubled marriage. The children were the constant reminder of my husband's infidelity.

In this particular instance, I remember coming home from the UZ one evening and finding this heavyset child around ten years of age in my living room. I could not recognize the boy as he had put on so much weight. My husband and his girlfriend were having problems. My husband felt he had no option but to bring his son to our matrimonial home. He did that without even consulting with me. On realizing who the child was, I became incensed. I could not believe the boldness of a lying and cheating husband; I was shocked. To say I freaked out is putting it mildly. I literally lost my mind with rage.

I could not stand the sight of a child of infidelity between my husband and his other woman. In my analysis, my husband's child's mother had in various ways been one of the causes for my failed marriage and my definitive unhappiness in wedlock. Each time I looked at that child, I saw the two people I resented the most—the father and the mother in bed together. To me it was like a slap in my face, and for what misdeed on my part, I did not know. My husband demonstrated that he cared little about my feelings and utterly disregarded me as his wife and partner. What I could not understand was why he disregarded me like that.

During our marriage, I had never strayed from our marriage not even once, not even when we were still dating. All I knew was I deserved better treatment from my husband. I treated him with utter respect and love due to the fact that he was the father of my five children and the man I had married because I loved him. All I ever received from him in return was relentless, inexorable, unremitting, ceaseless physical abuses, and constant reminders of his cheating ways and unending emotional abuses that traumatized me permanently. I recalled that for the third time my husband was trying to force one of his bastards (I am sorry for the unfortunate word, but that was how I felt exactly) down my throat. I would question myself frequently what I had done to deserve the worst treatment from the man I had honestly and truly loved with all my heart.

We had a fight like we had never fought before over any of his children that night. I did not want that child to sleep with my son Elton that night. In my eyes, my husband had disrespected me because he brought his child without even negotiating with me. Though he might deservedly as the 'husband' and supposedly head of our household, the least he could have done was an attempt to convince me of his son's dire straits. For the longest time, my husband had taken me for granted. He had lied to me many times over. He had fathered children over and over. He had beaten me to a pulp many times over. From those abuses, I had learned my lessons well, never to question in case he would beat me up again. This time, he had underestimated my strength. I was slowly regaining my identity, finding my own voice, and I would not relent.

By 1997, I was no longer the young impressionable Avis he had married. I was no longer willing to be the submissive wife that I had been socialized to be as a child. I was no longer lying to myself that everything was in good form in my marriage; I was a different woman with a mission. The mission was to set myself free. I was determined to liberate myself from the bonds of matrimony as a means to escape the abuse by any way possible and accessible to me. I was determined to regain my own identity. I was mentally adamant; as such, I had to assert myself in the current issue. There was no way I was going to back down, not that night and not ever again. I had backed down many times over, but this was not going to be one of those times.

The whole evening, we were engaged in a furious vocal fight. I knew it was bound to end in him beating me up; as such, I decided to escape to nearest police camp as I feared his physical wrath on my body. Jonathan followed me there. At the police station, we talked to the officer on duty. Surprisingly, he was an understanding mature man. He told my husband that he did not have to force his child down my throat and to actually reason with me to be a surrogate mother to his bastard. The police officer was actually the only police officer who ever made a lasting impression on me where issues of domestic violence were concerned in my town. He spoke respectfully of the marital union. He obviously respected marriage as an institution, as I perceived from our conversation. Due to that fact, for the time we were interacting, I listened to the officer. Consequently, he was able to convince me to keep the innocent child overnight.

The following day was a Tuesday, and I remember very well. The police officer came to check on us early in the morning. By the time the officer came, Jonathan had already left for work as always, and he had left me with his son whom I was having a hard time feeding. The police officer once again counseled me and advised me to have sympathy on the innocent child and extend my motherly love to him. No matter what the police officer said, it went in one ear and out the other. Even though I was a Christian woman, I could not find any place in my Christian heart to love and accommodate the child of two cheating and adulterous parents. Even if that meant there would be no paradise for my soul in heaven, I was willing to risk that. The police officer and I spoke at length with each other. He completely failed to convince me. When he left, I knew in my heart I was never going to sleep another night in the same house as Jonathan and his son. The fight continued that evening when he came home. For the first time in all our troubled marriage I slept on the couch. I had never left my bed ever but in this I did not relent.

To cut a long story short, Jonathan managed to secure his son a boarding place at a neighboring primary boarding school. At least the boy was not in my face all the time. I cared less for the resources that would be used to keep the boy in an expensive boarding school. The boy was my husband's child; hence, my husband owed his son the best education he could afford. I did not begrudge the child getting a good education he deserved from his father. It was the boy's right for his father to be responsible anyway and not me. I had not come between the boy's mother and his father. I had never gone after another woman's husband. The boy's parents had crossed that line and not me. Consequently, I did not owe the child anything; his mother and his father owed him his upkeep, so I tried to justify everything in my mind.

By then, my girls were teenagers, and I felt that it was high time I showed my own girls that they did not have to put up with disrespect, infidelity, and males' cheating ways especially in the time and era of HIV/AIDS. My girls were growing and maturing. I felt it was up to me as their mother to become a better example and mother; as such, I had to show them they did not have to submit to abuse. I knew most children live what they grew up with, and I felt it was time I showed Jonathan that it was time he recognized that and stopped behaving as though he was still in his twenties. By 1998, when all this was happening, our eldest son Elvin was twenty-one. I felt sad that my children were being subjected to the disrespectful side of our union.

I know and I knew back then the child had nothing to do with the circumstances of his birth, but I was not ready to care for their child in my home. At least the boy, by the time another custodial battle erupted, was eleven years old. He spent his school holidays with his grandmother. During that time, he told his grandmother that he would never agree to come and live with us ever again. From then, I clearly understood why stepmothers had a bad smack or name for abusing stepchildren. Usually, circumstances similar to mine would force a woman to just snap and lose it when confronted with such monstrosity in her life. I did not want to be that woman. I could see it was easy to confuse the child from the adulterous affair with the adulterous adults and inflict pain on the innocent child. Honestly, I could not look and see the child; I could see his mother in him and my husband's infidelity written all over his face every time. I am delighted that I stood my ground; otherwise, I would have ended up behind bars for inflicting harm on an innocent child and added to the statistics of the proverbially evil stepmother.

At the university, I continued to do well despite all these other extenuating problems in my private life at home. I know I was very good at compartmentalizing issues in my life and never confused the different issues. Earlier on in my troubled marriage, I had developed my three personalities to survive. This time, I knew that I needed the strength and determination of a warrior to accomplish my goal. I needed the fighting spirit in me to help me think past my domestic problems and focus on my studies. I continued to draw inner strength from my children, my faith, and my motivation from the desire to change my personal circumstances. As such, I continued to do well in my studies, and by the end of 1998, I was looking forward to sitting my final examination on Monday, November 9.

During the last semester of 1998 from October to November, my husband's mother and his youngest sister had been staying with us as well as Auntie Antoinette. His youngest sister needed a safe place to be able to deliver her first baby after several failed pregnancies. I was happy to provide them with that sanctuary in my home. My husband's sister had a normal delivery to a baby girl in October. The new baby, the new mother, and grandmother remained with us. From October 20, when the baby was born, until Friday, November 6, 1998, they were with us in Hartley. By then, his mother and younger sister intended to go back home to Georgetown. We had previously agreed that November 6, 1998, was when the extended family would be driven home with their bundle of joy. I did not have problems with that as we intended to drop them and be back home in Hartley that night.

Naturally, I am not a highly superstitious person, but the happenings of that weekend made me think that I should have paid more attention to the happenings than usual. Maybe our cars like our pets and our bodies can tell us of things to come before they actually happen. As we drove the extended family to Georgetown that evening, after a distance of fifty miles, our BMW just stalled and died in the middle of the road around eight at night at Golden Valley Mine. We could not get it to start; as such, we hitchhiked in the middle of the night and went home to Hartley.

In the morning, my husband and Elton went to collect the car, and funny enough, Jonathan later told us there had been nothing wrong with the car. As Jonathan was a staunch Dynamos supporter, that very Saturday afternoon Dynamos had a match with Caps in Harare. Elton and his father went to the football match, and I remained home with his mother and his sisters with the new baby. I had so much ground to cover in preparation before my examinations the following Monday. Likewise I was ready to study and had my books piled on my desk. The study task proved to be a challenge as Auntie Antoinette kept disturbing me. She came and sat next to me and distracted me. Usually, she was never like that; but that day, Auntie Antoinette had intentionally turned deaf to my pleas for solitude and need for studying by myself.

In as much as I wanted to cram for the pending examinations, I kept getting disturbed. Auntie Antoinette was Jonathan's sister, who had been brought up by Jonathan's mother after Auntie Antoinette's own mother died during her birth. Auntie Antoinette had, during the course of our marriage, been a constant visitor and occasionally lived with us on extended periods of time. During this period, she had been with us for more than six months. On that particular Saturday, as I tried hard to study, she decided it was the best day to tell me the story of her life. In as much as I tried to tell her that I needed to prepare for my examination the following Monday, somehow Auntie Antoinette would not listen and would not leave me alone. I know Auntie Antoinette was my biggest fan; she would often tell me that she would buy me the cap of knowledge for my graduation attire from her own pocket. Though she did not work, I knew somehow she would do it for me.

Also for the first time ever in her life, that particular Saturday, she did something she had never done for me. I was the one who bought her things, but she never returned the favor, not that I expected anything in return. That day, for the first time, she bought me two bottles of Coca-Cola. Since I got married to her brother she had never done anything like that for me; as such, I was pleasantly surprised. I was used to giving and buying her things and never expected anything in return. I tried to give one of the Coca-Cola bottles to her younger sister, but she would not hear of it. Her actual comment was all I ever did was give, yet I never received anything from anyone. I told her I did not give because I expected anything back, but that was how I had been brought up. Furthermore, I told her I could afford it. I went on to explain to her that it also gave me great pleasure to give.

In a playful and jocular manner, she declared that she was about to give me something that would shock me. The comment did not strike me as strange at the time, but later I would always remember her by that comment that I regrettably wish had asked what she meant. At the time, I could never, for the life of me, figure out what the shock would be. This has always haunted me, that I should have paid more attention to her words. Subsequently, I now pay more attention to what people are saying than just passing them off as mere words during conversations.

I could see that studying for me that day was a lost cause and a foregone conclusion. I ended up abandoning my studying, and Auntie Antoinette spent the whole day telling me about her life, growing up as an orphan, her failed marriage, and the kind of funeral she would expect should she die before me. She even went to the extent of telling me that if I could not afford her funeral expenses, I had to go to her rural home and sell one of her two cows to raise sufficient funds to give her a decent burial. She even elaborated on the brand of casket she wanted to be buried in and the place where she wanted to be buried (beside her own father's grave). The whole day, it appears (now I reflect back), was weird that she prayed for a fast and painless death. I questioned her why. She told me because she had no children of her own, and she felt duty bound to let someone know of her dying wishes. Little did I know that her death would be sooner than I expected. To her, I was that someone she trusted like a daughter to carry out her wishes. Even after she said that, did the statement raise any red flags at all in my examination-preoccupied mind?

Up to this day, I believe that whether we are Christians or not, the Lord grants us our final dying wishes when we earnestly ask Him. This was not the first time Auntie Antoinette had told me that she always prayed for an instant death. She had married once and had divorced many years before I even married her brother and was perpetually scared she would succumb to HIV/ AIDS. According to her, she had enjoyed a flamboyant life with lots of men. As such, her fears of HIV/AIDS were real. Occasionally, she told me that if she should ever succumb to the long illness, she would commit suicide. Other times she would persuade me to promise to speed up her death if she should ever become an HIV/ AIDS victim. I never gave her my word. I do not believe in mercy killings. I do not think I would have aided in speeding up her death.

There were strange things that were continuously happening that weekend, especially that Sunday, November 8, 1998. Up to this day, I have no explanation for the occurrences. I did not think much about the occurrence then. Such incidences as our deep freezer, which we had bought and was not behind in payments, was almost recollected for no apparent reason. For unknown reasons that morning, the new baby could not stop crying. No matter what we did, the baby would not suckle from its mother. On top of all that, I had my own obsessions with my examinations, and my determination to have my hair done was beyond anything I had ever done. Maybe going to the salon was meant to be the escape route for me from the accident. If only I had paid more attention and not accompanied my husband to Georgetown on that fateful day.

I was so preoccupied with my examinations that I did not think much about anything. In the morning, on Sunday, November 8, my husband went to work as he claimed he had some backlog he needed to attend to. Around midday, I was walking to the salon to have a shampoo and a set when I met him driving back. He picked me up on his way back from BHP, the company he worked for, on my way to the salon. We argued there by the road as I told him I was not going to accompany him and his family to Georgetown. I needed to get ready for my busy week at the varsity, as such, needed to have my hair shampooed. My husband was equally adamant and told me we were going to Georgetown to drop off his mother and sister. It was rather unladylike for me to continue arguing with my husband by the side of the road. I found myself getting into the car going back home. Though every fiber of my body told me it was a bad idea to join him for the trip, I surmised we were drawing unnecessary attention. As such, I climbed into the car, and we went home. My gut was telling me not to go, but after my argument with Jonathan by the roadside, I did not pay attention to my gut also.

Because I failed to convince my husband that I needed to prepare my hair for the busy week of my examinations, I accompanied him to Georgetown. Elton, my youngest son, wanted to come with us, but somehow I did not have a good feeling about the trip. Call it premonition or whatever, I did not concede to Elton's persuasions. In the process of getting ready, Auntie Antoinette had a strange request. She asked for one of my black belts. I jokingly questioned her why she needed a belt for a dress that she had worn numerous times and for years without a belt. As Auntie Antoinette insisted in the end, I gave in and handed her my favorite belt. I had no backbone that day as I was giving in to everything. I gave in to Auntie Antoinette many times before because I honestly and truly loved her, but it somehow felt strange handing her my belt.

To say I participated in the conversation on our way to Georgetown would be a lie. All I did was revise on my notes as I tried to prepare for the following Monday. Jonathan and his sister Auntie Antoinette were drinking beer all the way to Georgetown, and he was driving. I never touched any intoxicating beverages; as such, I was having soft drinks, which I shared with his younger sister and mother. By then, the baby was quiet and sleeping peacefully. Our ride to Georgetown was uneventful this time. I could tell everyone was having a good time from the conversations around me, and I concentrated on my revising. Unlike the previous Friday, there were no breakdowns. We arrived home safely, but by then, Jonathan was drunk.

Around two in the afternoon, we arrived at their village. Somehow Aunt Antoinette was quite jovial, giving everyone hugs, something she rarely demonstrated in all our previous visits. In my own way, I could not explain why I was literally cold, and my body was shivering and shaking inexplicably all the time we were there. This was in the middle of summer, and it was as hot as it ever gets in the midlands in Zimbabwe during that time of the year. I hardly took part in the conversations. My in-laws kept asking me whether there was anything wrong. I could not explain the sensation or premonition or the feeling of pending doom as I could not put the feeling into words.

We stayed home for more than four hours. Aunt Antoinette was extraordinarily warm toward everyone within that short time, and I was the cold one. It was as though our roles in life had been reversed. Usually, I was the warm one, and Auntie Antoinette used to have a hard time welcoming people. I relate well to people, which is one of my strengths, but that day was different. The more I think about everything in retrospect, the more everything becomes more foreign all the time. Everything felt as though there was a cloud of doom hanging over us.

As we left my husband's rural home, he started drinking again. I asked him to let me drive. My husband would not let me drive. As we were passing the development center of Agricultural and Rural Development Association (ARDA) in St. Albert's, my husband bought more beers for him and his sister, and he bought Cokes for his nephew and me. At that point, I told him again that I could drive. My husband was obstinate and insisted that he could still drive safely. Henceforth, we started again on our way. In the background, I heard them discuss plans for Christmas. Auntie Antoinette wanted us to spend Christmas with her and her relatives in her own father's village in Dearbone. At one point, I was asked to give my opinion, and I agreed that it made sense. I went back to my obsession—my study. We passed one sharp corner whereby Jonathan erratically swerved, and this time, Auntie Antoinette requested my husband to let me drive. Once more, he remained immovable.

We continued on our way, and in the back of my mind, I was a little concerned. However, I convinced myself that I needed to pay attention to my studying. It was like nothing else really mattered besides my examinations as though it was my first examination ever.

I think my obsession with study that day was a way of distracting myself from my husband's reckless driving. We usually argued about that most times on our road trips. Sometimes we avoided taking our children because I never felt safe due to his drinking and driving habits. This particular Sunday evening was no different, only I was engrossed in my books, so I did not argue with him about his driving. Besides being drunk, I knew my husband drove fast. I knew all the risks of riding with him when drunk and I tried to avoid it as much as possible. Most times he would never relent to me driving because he hated my slow speed, and I would always tell him to be better safe than sorry. Somehow that day, I did not have the energy to keep on arguing with him to let me drive.

The next time, probably after an hour and some minutes or more, after Auntie Antoinette's last plea for me to drive, I realized that my husband had totally lost control of the car. Up till then, I heard people say in times of emergency, our whole lives flash right before our eyes, and I had never believed nor paid attention to them. My life—I mean my whole entire life—flashed before me. All I remember was saying a prayer to the merciful God to the effect that I did not want to die and leave my children as they were young. I even pleaded with God and told Him that I would be so disappointed, and I would never believe in Him again if I left my children then and there. I pleaded that I needed to finish my examination just this once. I know it does not make sense. How could I have said all this? The time was short, but I know I said a lot within that short time. It was like my whole life really flashed before my eyes. All I could think about were my children and the imminent examinations! It was very prominent in my mind; even if I had died, those would have been my final thoughts.

I had my seat belt on; somehow I thankfully managed to roll my whole body into the fetal position. I felt the car rolling and cruising on its roof, grinding and crushing onto the huge tropical *musasa* and *munondo* trees for the longest time before coming to a halt on its roof. I could only hear and not see, as I closed my eyes, as I did not want to look death in the eye as it took me away. That was the longest time I ever held my breath. The car seemed to be crashing against trees and plowing into the grass. As the car came to a sudden halt, it appeared as though the world continued to whirl and spin in my head. It was as though nothing would ever stop spinning, and I kept myself in the fetal position while praying for my life to be spared. Retrospectively, I feel as though the car rolled three times; and when it finally came to a standstill, we were about a hundred yards on the right side of the road. When it finally stopped, I realized that my life had been spared, and for what reason I could not tell there and then; but years later, it would be revealed why I feel even now, as though my life was purposefully spared for a reason.

I could distinguish that the car was upside down. I could see Jonathan was no longer beside me. I called my husband's name, and he did not answer; then I called Auntie Antoinette, and there was no response. Lastly, I called his nephew. He responded. That's when I proceeded to tell him we needed to get out, or the car would explode on us. We crawled out of the side windows. We did not even think about opening doors; I think my cuts and bruises and one laceration on my shin were from the broken glass. I had no serious injuries and was grateful that I was alive. I knew immediately that I could live to see my children again as well as sit my unconquerable examinations. It was almost an obsession to think of examinations at that critical and shocking time, but that's what came to my mind, immediately coupled with my children's welfare.

As soon as we were out of the wreckage, I spotted Jonathan about ten feet away from the car. I crawled over to him all the time, crying to his nephew to look for Auntie Antoinette. I touched his entire body, which felt wet to my fingers. It appeared as though buckets of water had been poured on him. I tried calling him. He did not answer me back, but I was thankful he was breathing. As I was trying to locate his sister, there was a bus passing by on the country road that we had been cruising on a couple of minutes prior. By then, it was early evening, getting slightly dark. I shouted to my husband's nephew to go seek help. Andrew ran to flag the bus down. It stopped. The passengers ran over to see how they could render assistance. I cried to them that I couldn't locate my aunt. They made me sit down. I realized I only had minor cuts and bruises on my hands and legs and no major injuries, but I was in total shock.

The people from the bus were able to locate Auntie Antoinette as well as my husband. They gently broke the news to me that Auntie Antoinette had died on the spot. I could not believe it. I wanted to go to her body to see for myself, but they would not let me. Some of them kept me pinned to the ground. I was making deep noises like an injured animal, yet I was not crying. I was too shocked to cry. The reality had not really hit me yet that Auntie Antoinette was actually dead. In the car, I had a white drying towel that I had wrapped round my legs, and I told the people to cover Auntie Antoinette's body with it. I could not believe it. Five minutes earlier, we were all alive and discussing about Christmas, and now one of us was no more.

That made me realize how most times we take life for granted, how we spend time being bitter instead of demonstrating love and care to each other. I realized there and then how time is too short and too precious to spend harboring ill feelings and hurting each other and not loving one another and demonstrating love to one another. The driver of the bus indicated they had to go, and they all left. I felt desolate in the middle of nowhere, and it was fast becoming dark. I realized night was fast approaching. I was afraid of the nocturnal animals that lurched in the dark. I had no clue how we were going to get home.

As I was torturing myself on the tragedy and what to do next, a truck on its way to Harare stopped to offer us help. The driver was willing to carry my husband and his nephew to Spring Meadow. I wanted to remain behind to watch over Auntie Antoinette's body. However, it was getting darker; and in the middle of nowhere, the driver convinced me there was no need for me to remain behind because Auntie Antoinette could not feel anything anymore. She was just a body. Hearing him put Auntie Antoinette's death into words just brought the fact home to me that she would never experience any more Christmases with us. That was when I started crying. I could not stop crying until we arrived in Spring Meadow. I was in the back of the Good Samaritan's van whom I did not even ask for his name. Up to this day, I remain grateful to that Good Samaritan, but somehow I never could express my sincere gratitude to him. He was very thoughtful and kind in how he rendered help to us when we were in need. I am always indebted to this unknown Good Samaritan's kindness even though I do not know him by name up to now.

As I was crying, I could not think of anything else besides how we had spent the previous Saturday. I went over how Auntie Antoinette had disrupted my study, and my husband had gone to Harare for the football game. I revisited Friday evening and felt it had been a warning of some pending disaster, but we were all preoccupied by other things and had not paid attention. The events of that morning before leaving Hartley repeated themselves in my mind, and I regretted ignoring everything I had ever learned about paying attention to my gut feeling.

As I was torturing myself mentally all the way to Spring Meadow, my husband was in pain. He kept moving his body from side to side. He kept trying to jump out of the moving truck, and I had to use all my strength to restrain him. It was not easy as he was a huge man. I tried to calm him down by talking to him. Somehow his mind had gone back in time. He kept telling me about the match he had gone to watch in Harare the previous day. I almost thought he had lost his mind. I prayed for him to have suffered other physical injuries than to have lost his mind, as I thought I could not deal with a man who was totally dependent on me for his livelihood. However, I could not see any bleeding outwardly; I recalled that he had been drinking and attributed his loss of memory temporarily due to the shock and the drunken stupor that he was in before the accident. That journey honestly trebled in length because as much as I willed us to arrive, it appeared as though we kept going on and on. I had traveled that stretch of the road hundreds of times over and had never realized it was that far away from Spring Meadow. I guess it was the anxiety that added to the stress of the unforgettable journey.

I was extremely relieved when we finally arrived at Spring Meadow Hospital. At least Jonathan and his nephew had made it alive, and I could surrender the responsibility of their care to capable hands of health professionals. The night nurses were very professional, and one of my best friend's neighbors recognized me. She asked me whom I wanted to be contacted. I gave her numbers to call my sister and my close friends in Spring Meadow. Fifteen minutes later, she came back, as none of the numbers were working. I looked at the numbers I had given her, and I could not recognize any of them. Luckily, they had a telephone directory. I could not recall my own sister's telephone number that I had dialed millions of times prior. It must have been the shock. Finally, she had the correct numbers and was able to get hold of my elder sister.

Within a short time, my sister Melody and her husband were there. I broke down, and I cried uncontrollably in her arms. I could not believe I had lived through that accident. I knew something or someone had spared my life. I was too angry to acknowledge God because of Auntie Antoinette's demise. She was my friend and companion, especially when going through tough times in my marriage with her brother. Though she was a pest most times, I honestly loved her unconditionally. Her drinking and smoking habits stretched me to the limits sometimes, especially when the funds were low. At her best, she relieved me of the housework, and I confided in her some of the hidden aspects of my troubled marriage. She had also lived with an abusive husband once. Occasionally, she and I would share. We drew strength from one another. She used to tell me to be strong on her behalf too. I used to tell her that if ever I should ever divorce her brother, she would come and live with me. I meant that wholeheartedly as we had connected like sisters, and my children loved her dearly.

Sometime after eleven that night, the police were on their way to recover her body. My sister took me to her place, and I left Jonathan and his nephew in hospital. At my sister's place, I took a shower so that I could wear clean clothes. My own clothes had been soaked with blood and dirt. I needed to wash away the immediate scars of the accident. All the while, I was mourning Auntie Antoinette's death. The police called me when they arrived at the scene of the accident, they told me they could not find the body. I ended up telling them she had been thrown almost fifty yards away from the wreckage, and at the same time, I was wondering whether I had left her while still alive, thinking she had expired. I thought maybe she had revived and walked off.

I began to imagine what could have happened, and I tortured myself in the meantime. My sister told me to calm down and try to eat something. I could not swallow any food; it tasted as though a lot of sand had been put in it. It was strange. Though I was hungry, I had lost all appetite forever, so it seemed. However, after five minutes, the police called back and assured me they had located the body. I felt desolately alone. Auntie Antoinette and I had bonded during the years of my troubled marriage. We had managed to develop a really good and respectful relationship despite my abuses at the hands of her brother. I wondered what I would do without her as I had grown to love her as a person and an aunt for my children. Despite being put through hell by her brother, she listened to me, and we were helping each other cope with the perceived unfairness life had dealt us both.

In the hurry and shock of leaving the car, I never thought of carrying my handbag, my books, nor any other valuables we had in the car. We never recovered any of them at all. I lost my books, my identification cards, and my driver's license. Most likely, passersby just looted the car; hence, we never recovered Auntie Antoinette's identity card as well. That would prove a point to me before her funeral was conducted, for I am now convinced she had a feeling of some impending doom and in her own way had prepared me for the ultimate.

As I tried later to go home to Hartley that evening, my sister managed to get her husband's uncle to drive me. As though one mishap a night was not enough, we ended up with a burst tire just three miles down Harare-Mhondoro main highway. I know I was pretty shaken by then, but I still wanted to make it home that night. Nothing would shake me from my resolution of going to sit my examination the following day, not even Auntie Antoinette's passing away. I hitchhiked from there, a distance of forty miles from Spring Meadow to Hartley, and made it home around two in the morning of November 9, the day I was to sit some of my finals. The ride home was uneventful. I hired a cab from the bus stop to take me home as I could not walk by myself that time of the night.

My home's gate was about a hundred yards from the house. The taxi driver blew the horn, but my domestic helper was a heavy sleeper, and she did not hear the horn. He kept blowing until eventually it was Elton who heard us. Elton came to unlock the gate for me. Immediately realizing I was alone, he wanted to know what had happened to his father and aunt, and I told him. Inside the house, Elton came to bed with me. My baby son held me in his arms the whole night, and we did not sleep a wink. He would not let me go of me, and I knew my son loved me. He was still young, but when I needed his strength the most that night, Elton was there for his mother. We talked the night away, and by daylight, I was afraid to find out what had happened to Jonathan during the night.

In my mind, I was convinced my husband had passed away during the night, as he had moaned all the way from the scene of the accident until we arrived at Spring Meadow Hospital. Though the nurses had conducted their initial assessment, I was not convinced my husband had not suffered some internal injuries at all. The police had tried to conduct a breath examination, but the nurses had protected him. Though the nurses could tell my husband was drunk, they told the police his life was hanging by the thread; as such, they needed doctors to work with him as soon as possible. Those ladies were wonderful. I do not know what the charges would have been if that investigation had been conducted that night. All I know from that incident is the realization of the saying "a friend in need is a friend in deed." I never got to thank them personally, but I said many prayers on their behalf.

In the morning, I called the hospital; and when someone answered, I thought to myself if they told me something had happened to my husband during the night, I questioned myself, whether I would be strong enough to receive the news. As soon as I got connected, I hung up. I told Elton to get ready to go to school with the then domestic helper. I was on my way to sit the first of my examinations at the University of Zimbabwe. My examinations had to go on no matter what stood in the way. I was not willing to let go of my lifelong dream. As long as I was still breathing, I knew I would go and sit that examination. I got a ride into Harare from a driver who was carelessly weaving in and out of the busy Monday early morning traffic.

After about twenty miles of his erratic driving, I told him to pull over and drop me as I could not afford another accident that morning. He was sympathetic after my explanation and became more careful. He even took it upon himself to drop me off at the UZ, and he never charged me for that ride. I thanked him and made my way to the hall where we set all our examinations from. I was ready for that first test of the last semester as a bachelor's degree student. I was not going to let anything stop me. I was determined to write even when friends advised me not to. I saw it as paying homage to Auntie Antoinette if I passed my test under those most difficult circumstances.

I am not sure how I made it, but several times during that three-hour long examination, I would realize that my answer sheets would be wet, and I would start all over again. I was crumpling the answer sheets over and over, and at one point, I almost approached the invigilator to let them know that I was in no frame of mind to sit that test. I prayed, but I do not know to whom I prayed to because at that critical time, I know it was not God, for I was still mad at Him for taking away Auntie Antoinette. Whoever I prayed to must have heard my prayer. I had close to two hours to write the four prose answers to the questions in longhand. I managed to complete on time but could not revise or go over what I had written. Inwardly, I felt calm that I had managed to complete my first examination. It was time for me to go home and face the harsh realities of the previous night.

At the end of the day, I went straight to Spring Meadow. It was a good thing that on Tuesday I did not have to sit any examinations. When I arrived in Spring Meadow, Auntie Antoinette's relatives were all mad at me. They could not imagine how I could go and take my examination while Auntie Antoinette was in the mortuary. Luckily, when I went there, my elder sister Melody had accompanied me. She told me we did not have to answer them, and we immediately left. Try as they might to goad me into responding to their anger, I felt it was misdirected. I too could have easily lost my life in that accident. All they could think of was to criticize my decisions. What I did with my life was none of their business; as such, I left their home with my dignity intact. I went to Spring Meadow Hospital, where another shock of the day awaited me.

When I saw my husband, I was convinced he had completely lost his mind. He did not recall driving to Georgetown the precious day. He could not remember anything about the accident at all. All he was still bragging about was the Dynamos win over Caps on Saturday. I was shocked. The whites of his eyes were extremely white, and his eyes were almost popping out of their sockets. Each time he tried to move, he would grunt and scream in pain. I inquired whether he had X-rays taken and was told that he had and that no bones were broken. I could not believe it, but I had to take care of immediate business. At least in my mind, Jonathan was in hospital; and whether I believed the doctors' diagnosis or not, I had immediate business to take care of, and that business was to arrange for his sister's funeral.

I knew I had to be strong to make necessary arrangements for Auntie Antoinette's body, which needed to be buried. I had to file for her death and get the death certificate. By the end of day on Monday, most of Jonathan's family from Georgetown had arrived. In the morning on Tuesday, two of Jonathan's brothers would accompany me everywhere. It was in the registrar's office that we realized we did not have Auntie Antoinette's identification cards. Between the two of them (my husband's brothers), none knew Auntie Antoinette's birthday. Neither did they know her place of birth, the name of the village she came from, her local chief, nor any of the details needed to complete the documentation.

These were details she had told me only two days prior. It hit me that it was as though she had a premonition that I would need that information for her death certificate. The registrar even questioned my in-laws why they did not know their own sister's birthday. All they could come up with was because she lived with me most times, to which he responded what happened to growing up together as siblings. I did not need this exchange to know that Auntie Antoinette had somehow had a premonition about her death. Suddenly it felt as though my eyes had been opened to something I had not dared to face. I truly believe from her passing that we all know when the inevitable is about to happen; only we are not at liberty to reveal to our loved ones.

At the funeral home, I got her the casket she had described to me the previous Saturday. Unbelievable! It was as though she had foreseen her own death and in her own way had prepared me to be ready for it. The casket was an expensive one. My two brothers-in-law almost convinced me to get her a cheaper casket, but I would not be swayed. I managed to do everything between Monday evening and Tuesday, as I did not have to commute to the university on Tuesday. That night, I slept at home. I needed time to rest my bruised and battered body as well as afford my mind time to rethink and accept the death of Auntie Antoinette. From the time the accident had happened, I had been operating on adrenalin, and my body desired some emotional and physical rest.

On Tuesday morning, I went to the funeral home to find the hearse that would transport Auntie Antoinette's body home to Dearbone. Everything went on smoothly until some of Auntie Antoinette's relatives started demanding that I foot their traveling expenses to the village. I had reason to draw a line somewhere that no matter what the circumstances of Auntie Antoinette's death were, people had to find their way to her funeral. As such, I sponsored only the transportation of the body to the rural home. I told Jonathan's mother she would be riding with her daughter's body together with her younger sister. As for the rest of the relatives, if they were looking at me to sponsor their way, they were in for shocks. I kept my mouth shut and did what I felt was my responsibility. I could not accompany the body that Tuesday as I had another final examination on Wednesday, when the body was due for burial.

That Tuesday, I had to break the news of his sister's death to Jonathan. No one had done it as they felt he was not in a state of mind to accept the news. I left it as late as possible as I did not want to leave him in the dark while his sister's body was being transported home. He was tortured, but I could see he was also in physical pain, and his doctors kept telling me he had no broken bones. Contrary to their diagnosis, each time he tried to sit or stand, he would scream in pain. I could not believe that he did not have any broken bones or internal injuries. I convinced myself that as long as he was in hospital, I would leave him there and go to the funeral the following day after sitting my next examination in the morning. I had to take one step at a time to be able to make it; otherwise, I could not afford the luxury of personally breaking down mentally or physically.

My husband, his family, and I went to the mortuary to have the body transported to her rural home for the burial. Auntie Antoinette looked at peace. I saw a big gush on her forehead, and I knew that the big gush was the one that had snuffed out her life. It was then that my husband clearly realized what had happened. He started to mourn for his sister. After the body was on its way to its resting place and my husband back on his hospital bed, I felt drained of all energy. After all the events of the day, I was mentally and physically exhausted. I needed to go home to rest my weary body and mind.

I went home that night, and due to exhaustion, I slept all through the night. In the morning, I got a ride to Mount Pleasant, the suburb where UZ is located. I sat the second of my final examinations. This time, I knew that there was nothing I could do to bring Auntie Antoinette back. When my examination ordeal was over, my youngest brother, Levin, was waiting for me. Levin drove me to Avondale, where my brother Louis and his wife, Beverley, were waiting to take me to the funeral. None among us had ever been to Dearbone, but we managed to find our way because Auntie Antoinette had given me the directions the previous Saturday. It was unbelievable how everything kept falling into place. It was as though she had charted everything for me so that her burial would be exactly as she wanted it to be.

Even though we arrived too late for the burial, I was able to go and place flowers on her newly filled grave beside her father, one of her dying wishes. It was only months later that one of her sisters would reveal to me that Auntie Antoinette had received the best funeral anyone in their family and village had ever been afforded. I paid my respects to the elders of the village, and they were very gracious. They thanked me for shouldering the burden of the funeral expenses. Though I knew there were some rumblings about her death, I purposefully ignored them.

My sister, my brother, and I as well as a friend from the university went back on our way. It was then I noticed that every couple of hours, my brother would stop the car for frequent bathroom breaks. He would not go far, and we would put our heads down. I could tell something was happening with his health. One thing that I was not ready to face was the reality that possibly my brother was not physically well. It appeared from then on his health would continue to deteriorate.

On our way back from the funeral on that Wednesday, I passed through the hospital, and Jonathan was inconsolable. Finally, it was sinking in that his sister was gone forever. He wished he had been able to attend the funeral. I went home and came back to the hospital in the morning. I had my husband released and took him home to Hartley to another doctor so that I would reduce on the trips to and from Spring Meadow as well as on the expenses of all the bus rides. A friend who was a doctor personally admitted him into Hartley Hospital. My last examination was on Friday; I went and sat the last of my examinations. The end of my examinations afforded me the ability to invest all my energies on my husband's health. Though the second doctor I took him to could not find anything wrong, I told him of my concerns. My husband was an inpatient at Hartley Hospital, yet he still complained of pain in his back. The admitting doctor gave me referral letters to take him to a specialist in Harare. That was more than a week after the accident.

In Harare, we met with the specialist. He ordered X-rays of his back and chest. When the X-rays came back, they could not believe why the two hospitals had missed that my husband Jonathan had five broken ribs. The specialist ended up referring my husband to another bone specialist. Due to the passage of time between his injuries and the time we found out about the broken ribs, the bone specialist could only educate my husband on how to manage the pain. The bone specialist told him he was lucky because he was a big man. If my husband had been a smaller person, he could also have died on the spot just like his sister. He was not going to interfere as the healing process had already started.

Though there was nothing he could do at that time, at least the knowledge of broken ribs was a relief. Finally, I knew something was wrong, and we had to learn to manage his pain. We went home, and my husband would start his healing process. He was not an easy patient to take care of at home. Giving him baths were the most challenging, but somehow we managed to muddle through those baths. In the meantime, I would wait anxiously for my examination results. In that midst, his illegitimate son, when schools closed, became homeless. The son's grandmother had a falling out with her own mother. While my husband was under my care like that, my husband wanted me to care for his son. I simply told him if he could not persuade me when he was healthy, there was no way he could when he was an invalid. I am not sure who he contacted, but before the end of the day, the son was gone. The care of those children was always a constant thorn in the flesh and a reminder of all the garbage I had put up with.

The wait for my results was not long. Luckily, soon after New Year's Eve, the results were out. I found out that once again I had managed to shut out of my mind all the turmoil going on in my life and passed all my examinations as though I had not had any turbulence at all. This time, there was no nosebleed. I will always look at that phase in my life and tell myself that no matter what life threw at me, I knew I would always have reservations of strength from somewhere within me that I needed to focus on the bigger picture. I was a resilient woman, or so I told myself. I began to describe myself as a survivor, and little did I know that one day I would be a real survivor. I think all these trials and tribulations were occurring in order to prepare me for the worst challenge of my life. In that moment and time, it appeared as nothing worse would ever happen to me at all, but I was wrong, as I would learn years later.

It might have been sheer shock or adrenalin or my strong body constitution or strength of character; all I know is something pushed me through those tough times. I had managed to care for my husband, take care of the details of Auntie Antoinette's funeral, and sit my examinations and pass what more would I need. I thanked the Lord for sparing my life (as by then my faith was still being tested), for by then I knew it had to be Him who had sent his angels to protect me, and I was grateful to Him for granting me the second gift of life.

In review of all the facts regarding my survival, I no longer take life for granted. I know each day is a gift bestowed on us through His kindness and mercy. At the dawn of each day and at the end or every day, I thank Him and ask Him to guide me through everything as He deems necessary. I am always grateful for everything no matter how big or small, good or bad. I look on Him as the giver of life and sincerely thank Him with all my heart for each day that I live on His earth.

As I reminisce over my childhood with my mother and grandmother, I realize there was no way they could have prepared me for everything in life. In as much as they taught me most of what I knew I wish they had taught me about surviving domestic violence, economical and emotional abuse and dealing with life's traumas. I survived domestic violence, I survived a fatal road accident, and I survived the ravages of war early on as a teenager. Each time I sat my life-changing examinations, there would be something upsetting going on in my personal life that could have prevented success, but each time, I triumphed. Hey, I do sit down many times and reflect and say even though I had fought and competed with my siblings for the love and attention of my parents, these real life's turbulences and traumas taught me to fight harder and smarter.

I became more resilient. I understood what the word "determination" means. I found out that life does not come with a manual. We create our manuals as we go along, and another person would never duplicate someone's life experiences completely. Thus, according to my own philosophy, life's manuals are as multiple as we are, and what works for someone would never completely work for another. We would never completely learn from other people's experiences but would use their experiences to gain insight into what life could be all about. Thus, in my life as a mother, a teacher, a wife, a daughter, my experiences made me aspire to be better and want to live another day to improve other people's lives.

Chapter Twenty-Two

Disappointments and disillusionments

After working hard in the last two years, 1997 and 1998, at the UZ, after enduring all I had endured, long study hours, papers written and presented, and financial dire straits, I really looked forward to going back to work in January of 1999. I looked forward to possibly being generously rewarded for earning my first college degree. On a personal level, I looked forward to being allocated a higher grade to teach. My school principal did not execute that. He found it appropriate instead to allocate me a grade three (3) class again.

Initially, I was angry and thought he needed to demonstrate to me that he was the boss and somehow required to spite me. I had bragged a lot before leaving for my sabbatical, so I thought I was being made to pay for my sins. I almost did not prepare any transitional work for my class. I honestly felt ready for more challenging work, but I was disillusioned with the little or lack of acknowledgment of my recently acquired credentials. It was as though I had not done anything to develop myself professionally. The last straw was when I received my January paycheck. There was no increment salary-wise, and then I knew I was bitterly disillusioned with the educational system in Zimbabwe as a whole.

Though I had initially described myself as a conditional teacher, by the time I had my first class, that first year teaching in 1975, I totally loved my job. Likewise, in 1999, I realized these children were no different from all the endearing children, I had taught right through my career. By the end of the first two weeks, I convinced myself the kids were innocent; they had done nothing to deserve my complacence. I knew instead they depended on me to give them the best education. Hence, from then on, which was end of January 1999, I threw myself wholeheartedly into my work as usual. I would have our daily reading lessons, assign homework as usual, and ensured we covered the entire curriculum on the school timetable on a daily basis. I can, however, truthfully own up that I no longer felt obliged to go that extra mile like I used to. At 12:30 p.m. on the dot, I dismissed my class. My heart was no longer in every respect into my job.

To add on to my negative attitude, I also started having problems with discipline in my class. My pupils started getting out of hand, and I seemed not to care at all. I became more like a doting grandmother than a teacher and really felt disappointed with myself and my poor execution of my responsibilities. To make matters worse, I had to mentor a student teacher who was still in college. Whatever I suggested, she thought she knew better. Honestly, I had no time for her patronizing attitude and neither did I care anymore. As a result, two months into the term, when her tutors visited her, they found that she had no lesson plans for more than two weeks. I felt embarrassed as her mentor but could have cared less for her messing up her own career. It was her life she was screwing, and I did not care at all. People talked of my irresponsible behavior, and I did not give a hoot. The conscientious teacher and mentor in me seemed to have somehow completely deserted me, and I did not like who I was becoming professionally. I felt disillusioned after completing my studies at the UZ beginning of 1999 for the first time in my career.

Another problem affected me more than I realized then was the children's illnesses. I think that year I had three or four seriously ill children who missed school on a regular basis. I attempted to find out from their parents what ailed these children, but I never got any real or straightforward answers. I approached my principal with my concerns; all he told me was to simply listen to what the parents told me. Basically, he told me not to be too involved with mundane issues. My jaw dropped, as I could not fathom how students' health could be considered mundane issues to their education. Their ill health adversely affected their performance. As any caring teacher, I felt duty bound to know how to assist my pupils.

What my principal and probably some of the parents overlooked, however, was the degree of how the illnesses affected the pupils. Some of those children would be sleeping in the classroom or coughing so bad it would be difficult for them to breathe. Other children would become seriously nauseated in the classroom and would even throw up. This affected not only me but also their classmates. I barely had the relevant skills on how to help the students in my class; neither did I have the endurance anymore to deal with all the illnesses. Most parents pretended there was nothing wrong with their children's health. I could not fathom their denials or lack of the health problem acknowledgment.

This was my twenty-second year teaching primary school children, and no one stays that long in the teaching field without a real passion, real love, and utter commitment to the children and their job. Whereas I lacked for neither capability nor passion for my job, this time around, I knew I had to do something to be proactive; otherwise, all these negative forces were going to draw me down. That first school term back at work was really challenging, as I also noticed another trend that year with my pupils. Almost a quarter of the children's parents were no longer in the country, especially those children whose parents were nurses and those in the health sector. Nurses were departing and going abroad in huge numbers to seek greener pastures. Some parents were leaving young kids with extended families, and others were dumping their children into boarding schools like ours. My class had many students in this category whose parents had left the country. I felt sorry for those children as they felt abandoned. I was not just a teacher but was also providing parental love and guidance to some of my pupils.

Toward the end of the 1990s, the Zimbabwe economy was fast deteriorating. In such instances, Zimbabwe women have been very enterprising, resilient, economically adventurous, and not afraid to work hard for their families. As such, the women were once more rising to the occasion and were taking care of business like before. The women of Lucas pulled up their socks once more; the economy forced them to take good care of their families in the most unconventional ways. In the early 1980 and early 1990s, Zimbabwe women had been involved in cross-border trading with South Africa and Botswana, later with, Namibia and Zambia. I know the Zimbabwe women helped rally the economy around then in ways beyond imagination. Comparably in the 1980s, the country's currency was still stronger in relation to the neighboring countries, but as the troubled 1990s ended, the country's currency was fast losing its trading value.

Personally, I attribute the failure of the country's currency to two events. I honestly believe this was due to the demobilization of the country's liberation war veterans and Zimbabwe's involvement in the Democratic of Republic of Zaire war with the rebels of 1997. The Zimbabwe Liberation War veterans were demanding some compensation for having participated in the liberation struggle. The country president made an executive decision overnight and gave them all some unbudgeted fifty thousand Zimbabwe dollars at the drop of a hat. Some of the ex-combatants made good use of the money. Others felt the need to be wasteful, and of course, they wasted it too. Political leaders were not left unscathed in all this scandal, as some of them claimed what was not rightfully theirs, and they got away with it, yet others still succumbed to the scandal as well, and that caused the downfall of their political careers.

During the same time, the president of the Democratic Republic of Zaire was experiencing some pressure from the dissidents in his country. Zimbabwe President Robert Gabriel Mugabe did not hesitate rendering him the necessary military assistance. Overnight, some of our forces were shipped to the Democratic Republic of Zaire to help stabilize the government. The members of the Zimbabwe forces were excited because for the duration they were deployed to the Democratic Republic of Zaire, they would be paid in the most coveted currency—the US dollar. They were flashing the USA currency as though there was no tomorrow. That also brought with it a lot of health hazards from that African country. Some young men were coming home with undetermined illnesses with Ebola-like symptoms. I know so because I lost several of my own relatives to this mysterious illness. As the armed forces personnel were paid in the foreign currency, Zimbabwe's economy was taken to the gutter. This was also exacerbated by the double whammy of the military losing young vibrant men to the unidentified illness. The above reasons caused many people to question their own economical survival, hence a brain drain to the West and other countries that could help the country of Zimbabwe stabilize their lives financially.

More pressure on our economy was due to the Economic Structural Adjustment Programs (ESAP) of 1995 imposed on Lucas through the International Monetary Fund (IMF) and the World Bank. We had enjoyed ten years of independence and with most Western countries and governments investing as well as donating aid to our young nation.

With the ending of the Lancaster House agreement, some of the Western nations and banks were rather lethargic with the way of governance. The first ten years after independence were record years of abundance and rejoicing in the newfound political independence. Definitely, in the mid-1990s, things started taking a downward spiral in Zimbabwe economically due to some of the reasons elaborated above.

In 1999, as a teacher, a mother, and an emotionally abused woman and wife, I continued to do what I did best. I threw my heart into my work, telling myself I would be more motivated once I saw my raise. I awaited that raise with abated breath. I was expectant because the Ministry of Education, Youth, Sports, and Culture used to promise incentives to those who embarked on self-development programs. I felt I had paid my dues. After three months, the raise reflected on my pay stub. I was really humbled and disappointed by how little it was. It did not even come to fifty dollars more than what I had been earning prior to receiving my degree. I could not believe it was a pittance in comparison to what I had expected. I had worked hard, struggled for two years, telling myself things would improve once the ministry recognized that I had improved my academic credentials. I almost walked out on my job that day but knew I needed that income. I knew I could not afford the luxury of walking out on my job no matter how little I was paid. I had five reasons not to do that. My children were and would be dependent on me financially for a long time.

On the home front, things had taken a turn for the worse. The Broken Hill Properties (BHP) that Jonathan had been working for the past two years had also closed down. Our son Elvin, who also worked for the same company, no longer had a job as well. That meant I was the only adult in our household with a reliable source of income. Trying to make ends meet on the humble salary of a teacher was like trying to cage a lion into a matchbox! We had a mortgage that was only two years old. All our younger children were in boarding secondary schools, which happen to be a little bit more expensive than public schools. I spent many sleepless nights wondering how we would manage to continue to care for our children and provide for all their needs especially where their education was concerned. I also worried about the mortgage. As they say, for every gray cloud, there is a silver lining. That silver lining came in the most unexpected shape and form but was completely welcome.

It was at this that time that Old Mutual decided to demutualize and share its profits with all people who had insurances with it. I had been a client of Old Mutual since I started teaching in 1975. The demutualization process had two options: either be paid a lump sum or reinvest in the company. I decided to go with the former. I had decided to invest all of my funds in my eldest son, Elvin. Our son, in 1995, had applied to a college in Florida in the US and had been accepted. As we could not afford the tuition then, he resorted to being a laborer in a mine. I was not pleased with that. I wanted him to have some professional training of some sort. As a result, the demutualization was truly a divine intervention. I could tell that the economy was not getting any better. By then I was struggling to keep my children in the good boarding schools. I was being forced to bring them back to be day scholars in our local community. In comparison, my father had invested well in my education; and as such, I felt as though I was failing as I could not afford my children quality education. I could hardly sleep at night. My mind was tortured. I had to do something to improve our circumstances.

I decided to invest my twenty thousand dollars from the demutualization by Old Mutual in helping Elvin pursue his education abroad. It was no hard task to decide as I felt that most people were migrating to the West. My demutualization came at the right time for the right purpose to enable my son's transition. From the time he was accepted by the Floridian university, I tried to put funds together in preparation for the pending trip, but it appeared that whatever bank I was putting the money into had more coming out than going in. We were barely able to purchase his flight tickets. As such, the demutualization was really godsend.

On the day of Elvin's departure, my brother Dr. Larry spoke powerfully to my husband and me. He stressed that we needed to give Elvin a little more financial aid so that he would be able to sustain himself while he looked for employment. In fact, it was an ultimatum— either we increased the funds or Elvin would not go anywhere. I had never been abroad neither to visit nor to live. I, therefore, had a genuine excuse to my ignorance. I thought simply giving a hundred dollars to my son was enough? My husband had worked in the West and at least should have anticipated the hardships of transitioning in a foreign country. My brother had been a student abroad and as such had some clue as to how life could be challenging to foreigners trying to make it.

I was in a complete crisis. We needed to raise money as fast as possible, but I had no idea where from. The demutualization had raised enough for his flights and couple hundred dollars extra.

With the threat of the ultimatum from my brother conveyed to all my siblings hanging over us, that unless we could all come up with at least a thousand USA dollars, Elvin's trip would be canceled. Everyone rose to the occasion, and within hours, we had collected enough once more. Thanks to my siblings and my niece Doris, we managed to let Elvin embark on his first trip abroad alone as a young man! We let him go with a lot of heartache. My son was burdened by the expectation of his whole tribe; as such, he had a lot weighing his young shoulders down than just his baggage when he boarded that plane.

My son was exactly twenty-two years old when he came to the States. He had never been exposed to any other world besides our homes. As a family, we knew no one else in the US, neither as family nor as friends. The previous year, Elvin had plans to spend his twenty-first birthday in Mozambique, but his plans were waylaid due to our accident. I am sure Elvin had never ventured outside the Zimbabwe borders. Putting that into consideration, he displayed courage and strength of character that I admired tremendously even as a mother. I had never seen his strength of character tested to that extent before.

By November that year (1999), Elvin undertook his trip to the United States alone, a young man with not only his hopes and ambitions, but also weighed down by those of his parents, his siblings, his grandparents, and the whole enchilada of the extended family. From the moment he took off from the Harare International airport, I did not hear from my eldest son for three whole days. I was extremely anxious. I hardly slept, wondering whether I had sent my son to the proverbial wolves of the West. This was my eldest son, and I had influenced him to go abroad and see if the land of opportunity would smile brightly on him. I had mixed feelings over many things. I knew we had not done right, but it was no use crying over spilt milk. He was gone, and all I could do was keep my fingers crossed and hope for the best.

For three days, I walked around like a zombie. I was not sure I had made the right decision for my eldest son. Before Elvin left and while preparing for departure, everything was exciting as well as talking about the pending journey; however, when it eventually happened, I was tortured. I went to work and back as though I carried the weight of the world on my shoulders. I worried night and day about my firstborn son. I could not believe almost three days had gone by without hearing his voice. I was going insane with worry. I wished I could have my son back.

On the day he finally called, I was walking to the bus terminus after school when I heard his voice on my cell phone. I breathed a sigh of relief. From the time he had left until then, I could hardly sleep nor eat. I heard my son's voice as though he was next to me. I was highly impressed by technology then and loved it there and then. My son from thousands of miles away, distance I had never imagined in my wildest dreams, I could hear his voice as though he was only standing there right next to me. It was amazing and emotional for me to speak to him then. I had been worried and was almost regretting sending him abroad. After that one call, when I got home, I realized I was famished and exhausted. All I wanted to do was eat and go to bed. Surely that night, I slept like a baby; my son was safe. Thank you, Lord, as I said a little prayer of gratefulness. After sharing with his father, he too revealed to me that he had been worried but had hidden his emotions well from me.

Chapter Twenty-Three

Reasons for migrating

As an educator, I valued my own children's education more than I could ever convince Jonathan. I pretty much understood my husband and his background and how, through their religion, education was the least promoted commodity. Encouraging education is perceived as endorsing an independent reckoning tool especially among young girls and women. According to their religion, women and girls are perpetual appendages of men; as such, for them, education is never really encouraged. Education enables the females to acquire skills to negotiate for better statuses in life, hence rebel against their own oppression imposed on them by the patriarchy in the family. With this background, my husband never valued our children's education as much as I did.

Growing up for me as my father's daughter, I knew my father had instilled in us the value for education. Despite everything else, I knew my father did his best to educate us all to become professionals. My father, Norman, had educated his nephews and nieces and gave them the best education he could in that period. Consequently, before I had children of my own, I knew and appreciated the difference education makes in people's lives. I never underestimated what my parents had done for me; therefore, I strived to do the best for my own children. When I look back, I realize at times I made risky decisions; though they might appear as risky decisions now, at that time, I believed they were the best with the knowledge I had then. In many ways, I could have almost failed to provide my children with the best education.

In late 1999 and early 2000, I decided I needed to explore greener pastures. It is not easy to completely uproot oneself from all that is familiar and comfortable to something completely new, foreign, unknown, and unfamiliar, sometimes scary to venture into unchartered waters. I spent a lot of sleepless nights weighing the odds for and against migration. For me then, the Lucas economy was no longer working to promote the interests of my family. Though we were living together, my husband did not have an income. My children were fast approaching college going ages, and I needed to do something drastic. When the situation in Zimbabwe was no longer working for me and my family, I looked beyond my boundaries, and I was not the only one, professionally or otherwise.

Whereas Zimbabwe people (especially women) had been engaging in cross-border trading in the 1980s, by the end of the 1990s, I began to see another trend. By the end of the 1990s, more and more professionals from the country were migrating to look for better lives than what cross-border trading afforded them. Most of these people were professionals like me. Those people had their reasons for migrating, and I knew I had mine too. I had five good tangible breathing reasons why the unknown felt more attractive than what I was familiar with. My five reasons were my five children—Elvin, Teresa, Tiffany, Thelma, and Elton. I had to provide them with the best education and support these five God-given precious gifts of mine.

Since my husband was by then no longer employed, things were extremely difficult financially on the home front. Attempting to support our four children and staying in Zimbabwe proved to be a daily challenge unlike any I had ever confronted. Teresa had completed her 'A' levels in 1997. She had not been able to be absorbed by any of the country's universities. Teresa stayed with my brother Louis in Harare, trying to supplement on her 'A' level subjects during the year of 1998. By the beginning of 1999, she ventured into Hotel and Tourism. This venture meant she was again uprooted to go and stay with my younger sister Brenda in Marondera, where the college she attended was located. It appears among my five children, Teresa was the one who stayed with all my siblings yet was the one who missed home the most. While studying in boarding school, Teresa would always tell me boarding life was hard and that she missed home. During all these struggles, she was ferried between my parents, my siblings, and our home in pursuant to a stable education for her. I hope she understood and now understands better the reasons for all this. I was always torn in the prospect that I could not provide them with everything and forever grateful that I had siblings and parents who were helpful like that.

However, by the year 2000, it was apparent I could not afford to keep Teresa in school. Teresa had to abandon her dreams of making it in hotel and tourism; she had to come home. At the beginning of 2000, she had to look for a temporary position in teaching. My sister Brenda was by then a staffing education officer. She managed to pull strings, and Teresa found a teaching position in rural Bethany. Except for visiting with their grandparents during school vacations, my children had never lived in rural Zimbabwe. My daughter's going to Bethany was a clear indication that times were becoming extremely difficult for our family. Teresa went to a rural primary school in Bethany, and my son Elton accompanied her on the first trip.

Later, when Elton came home, he told me how difficult it had been for him to leave his sister behind in rural Bethany. The following weekend, Jonathan and I traveled to Bethany to bring her a bed, which at least would make her life a little bearable. That was the only time I ever saw Jonathan become emotional when it came to our children. By the time we were leaving, he was crying, Teresa was crying, and I was having a hard time keeping it together. I knew we had to let her grow up and start making a living as an adult and on her own. By then, we desperately needed everyone to help out financially.

On the other hand, by 1999, Tiffany was sitting her O levels at Freedom High School. To say she was an A student would be to overrate her. She really gave me the most cause for concern, as she was an average student. At best times, she tended not to apply her abilities fully. She used to have the laid-back attitude toward schoolwork all her life. However, one of her strongest personalities is her fighting spirit. Though she did not do well during her midyear examinations, I believe my first university graduation shook her into facing reality. I had almost given up on her because I had underestimated her fighting spirit. Of all my children, I now know Tiffany is a fighter. She does not give up easily.

I needed to do something to help Tiffany improve her grades. Even with tighter finances, I managed to come up with enough additional cash for her to go for the extra coaching she needed during the August holidays. She must have worked really hard during that term for when she came back home in November of that year, my daughter was skin and bones due to the stress of studying combined with the examinations. She conducted herself well during the interim while waiting for her 'O' level results. The results were released sometime in February, and she managed to pleasantly surprise us all, including her own self. She had managed to pass the required five 'O' level subjects and had even afforded to throw in an A in one of the subjects. This was completely a pleasant surprise to all of us. However, I could not afford the tuition to keep her in a boarding school, so she had to be withdrawn from boarding school to come home and go to one of the Hartley local high schools. If this was not failing as a parent, I could not find any other word.

By 1998, Thelma was also in high school at St. John's, which was another boarding school and equally expensive. Thelma had managed to spend two years in boarding school by the skin of my teeth. The budget was becoming tighter, prices were soaring, and teacher's salaries remained stagnant. I remember one of the school terms, the school administrators sent her home to collect her tuition, and I did not have a single cent to spare. My father ended up helping me out. This was not how I had imagined educating my own children. My father had done his duty by me, and I was not happy asking for his financial assistance to educate my own children.

In as much as I valued my children's education the best money could buy, it was time I confronted reality. The second term, Thelma was again sent home to collect her tuition. Call it coincidence or whatever, that same day she arrived, somehow I had received a $100 US from Elvin. That amount was sufficient to pay for Thelma's tuition and take care of some of our bills at home. As a family, we were in real and extreme dire straits. That meant beginning of the year 2000; Thelma as well had to pull out of boarding school. She enrolled at the same local high school where Tiffany was a student. I, however, maintained a positive spirit and told them of my plans to migrate.

Elton had started high school as a day scholar at Thompson High in Spring Meadow in 1999. Thompson High is one of the elitist schools in Zimbabwe. I could by then afford to have my son continue to receive the best education money could buy. However, before long, I took a long look at our financial situation. The situation had taken 180 degrees turn around. Once more, my husband was not employed. We had a mortgage to cope with besides the children's education. My salary was not half as much as my husband earned. As such, financially, we were barely keeping our heads above water. We struggled to make ends meet.

Elton and I commuted together daily, Monday through Friday, between Hartley, our home, and Spring Meadow, my workplace and Elton's school. At times, my car would take us there; sometimes because of fuel costs, we found ourselves riding on the local buses or hitchhiking. The economic situation had a negative impact on us all. It would be years later that Elton would tell me how his grade seven teacher had unceasingly teased him because of our deteriorating economic situation. By the time Elton revealed this to me, we were in the United States. He was only sixteen years old and earning enough to pay five Zimbabwe teachers for a month with his two weeks' paycheck. We would then laugh about it, but inwardly, I was cursing that teacher and wished I had known. I would have confronted him for subjecting my son to such humility through no fault of his. I believe my son was the better person as he did not allow the teacher's jokes to tarnish his personality.

Throughout the year, we kept each other going. However, we had to face some truths home. By 2000, it became more and more apparent that I had to take drastic measures. Elton had to pull out of Thompson High School too, and we brought him home to attend St. Vincent High School, a local Catholic high school. I could no longer afford the bus fares back and forth Spring Meadow for both of us on a daily basis, let alone the lunch money he needed. I could no longer afford to keep him engaged in all the sporting activities that he wanted to participate in. As a parent, I looked myself in the eye and faced my worst fear that I was failing to fully provide and effectively for my own children. For the first time I was actually scared of failure, failure to educate my children.

Personally, it appeared as though I was throwing my children's education down the drain. Jonathan, due to his own background, never perceived education in the same light as I did and never afforded it the same priority as I did. He never gave me any proper feedback or ideas concerning the children's education. As such, most decisions were left to me, and I think I made the best decisions for them and us all at that particular time. I thought hard especially at night when all else was quiet, and I listened to my most inner voice and conscience.

While people were talking of the new millennium and the Y2K, I was worried on how I was going be able to support my children. I was financially tormented. No parent expects to provide the least for their children, and I found myself slowly sliding down the downward spiral into poverty. I had managed to send Elvin to the US. Part of the funds had come from the Old Mutual demutualization. Occasionally, Elvin would send us some much-needed cash and financial relief, but it would not take us far as we had so many obligations financially.

In my heart of hearts, I convinced myself that if Elvin could make it in the US; I could fare better than him. After all, Elvin had no proper educational qualifications, and my reasoning was I could go and utilize my degree in education while I pursued to improve on my educational credentials and keeping my children in school at the same time. I had no doubt whatsoever that I would make it. In my life, I had survived many hardships; and once again, I convinced myself leaving the country would ultimately put my family's life back on the right track.

As such, the dawn of the millennium, the year 2000, saw my elder sister Melody and me making plans to relocate to the USA. New Year's Eve December 1999, my sister was with us in Hartley. Plaxedes, my niece; Tim my nephew; Tiffany; Thelma; Teresa; my husband; my sister Melody; and I all ushered in the New Year and new millennium together. My sister and I had previously agreed we would spend the evening making drafts of our application letters. My sister might have taken it lightly, but I saw it as my only opportunity to making a breakthrough that I so much needed. As such, initially, my plans were that my sister and I would come together and support each other morally and financially in the USA.

Although we were living as a couple, my husband and I were no longer close. To the outside world, maybe we appeared as we were, but I had long divorced my heart of his love. I would sound him out about my plans, and he would not show any enthusiasm or commitment to any of my plans at all. It was only after one conversation with my friend who had made it to the US before me that I made up my mind to take my husband with me to the US. This was made out of completely selfish reasons to pursue my own dreams. I do not, for the life of me, ever regret using Jonathan like that at all. Up to this very day, I feel I had earned that much at least; I argued and convinced myself that through all the abuses he purposefully inflicted on me, I deserved something in return. I felt justified that at least I deserved one year or two out of his life of him working to provide us stability financially as I set toward achieving my personal goal. It was a cunning decision, of course, and I do not regret I used him like that up to this present day.

My friend had told me how difficult it would be to undergo my studies full-time and work to earn enough for our upkeep. Thus, due to her advice and influence, I made my decision. I justified my actions then by convincing myself that it was high time Jonathan paid for abusing me all my adult life. My siblings would not comprehend why I decided to bring my husband with me. They knew of the abuses; to them, my migration to the West would have provided the most opportune moment I desperately needed for a clear break in our relationship. Years later, my own daughters would also question why I had made that decision to bring their father instead of them. They too could not understand my reasoning as I thought they knew little about the abuses. They revealed to me that they thought my loyalties were to them first and foremost than to their abusive father. By the time they gave me the ninety degrees, they were fast becoming young adults, and it was becoming extremely more difficult for me to hide the infidelities from them especially when their father had continuously kept forcing his other illegitimate children on the family to take care of them.

I know you too might be condemning me for taking such a selfish standpoint, but we had five children together, and they still needed two parents to facilitate the finances needed for them to make it where their education was concerned. I was not going to give my husband an easy pass. I intended to hold Jonathan to a better standard as a parent even though I knew someday I would live to regret my actions. I know many children in the US have divorced and will divorce themselves from their parents; that would be the worst taboo for any Zimbabwean-born children culturally, mine included. Thus, I felt justified in my decision.

Traditionally and culturally, our children would never ever be allowed to divorce themselves from neither their father nor their mother. As such, I convinced myself my husband had to be there so that we could help each other educate our children. In as much as I know I have been educated in the West, that I have lived a Western life in a way; as such, I am expected to adapt the Western way of life. I might be that person, but I am not completely divorced from my African culture. I debated and convinced myself into bringing my husband with me into my new world. Again, I argued with myself that if he expected later to benefit from his children, and I knew he did, he had to be able to provide for them.

Theoretically, it made sense. I should have just left my husband in Zimbabwe but practically speaking, I would never be completely divorced from my culture and the values instilled in me all my upbringing. Whether my husband played an important role in my children's lives or not, he would always be part and parcel of their lives. Should hard times befall my husband, his children would be the first ones called upon to rally behind him financially. So there, I might have made selfish decisions, which I completely justified in my own way. I assumed he could not expect to have his cake and eat it! He had enjoyed that in the early years of our marriage, but by the year 2000, times had changed. He had to be held to a higher standard and expectation for once in his life to earn the support of his children eventually. Again, I made an executive decision. My decision caused a huge controversy with my siblings. They did not see the issue as I saw it. I did not blame them nor do I blame them now because they had been through thick and thin with me. They expected me to be strong enough to throw Jonathan to the curb than simply give him a free ride to a better life in the US.

Even today, as I write this, it is as though I have been proved right. Time and time again, my husband calls upon all our children to help him out financially. He does not call to develop a relationship with them but to ask for financial assistance all the time. Our children are no longer young kids; they are young adults capable of making their own decisions. They tell me of all the requests made by their father. At times, I find myself dying to tell my children things that would hurt them, but I try to hold myself. Jonathan is their father; all I ever wanted or still want is for him to be a better father to them. He now lives with another wife. He requests money that supports her in the process. I do not begrudge him the help he occasionally receives from the children, but he should know like other irresponsible fathers like him that first you have to take care of them before they can take care of you. I know he is their father and has a right to them taking care of him, but he should not demand and has no right to demand anything from them. And I know I too, have no right to demand anything from them.

Personally, I have occasionally asked my children for financial assistance; however, that is when I have been in serious dire straits. Most Zimbabwean parents still look at children as a form of investment;

that is not how it should be. Whereas I feel mothers, me included, have given of ourselves and energies into their welfare and their education, but I do not feel that entitles us to anything from them nor are they obligated to take care of us. It was our responsibility as their parents and should not compel them to do anything. At times, I feel he is now getting a free ride, and no parent should ever have to get a free ride from their children. Parents should be held accountable at all times.

Parenthood is a lifetime commitment. There has to be involvement on a daily basis. The saddest or happiest part of parenthood, depending on how you look at it, is that once you are a parent, you never stop being a parent. Whether they are grown up and working, your children will always look up to you for your approval, your love, your guidance, your support, your caring, your open communication, and your provision of the unconditional love they do not get from the outside world. To the deadbeat fathers, remember you have to take care of your children before they can take care of you. Yes, like in one good turn deserves another.

Back in 2000, my children's lives were at a high time low; their education was almost at next to nothing compared to what my father had provided me. If anything, those five children were five good reasons for me to migrate. I needed to give them a better life than what I had received growing up.

Chapter Twenty-Four

Where there is a will

In 1998, we had a golden sedan BMW as our family car. It was the one we were involved in the fatal accident with. As we did not have full insurance coverage on the car, we were not able to replace that beautiful car. Consequently, after I completed my studies at the UZ, I went back to Sir Robert Taylor Primary School in Spring Meadow to work, but then I did not have a car anymore. It would be nine months later at my graduation that Jonathan gave me a blue old Renault 6 as my graduation present. That at least made commuting to and fro school much easier. That was by far a downgrade from the car we had owned previously; hence the downgrade was the reason why one of Elton's teachers would make my son the brunt of his classroom jokes! Sometimes I would find people to ride with me, and some days it would be only Elton and me. Whenever I could find passengers, that meant I could afford to refuel for the next trip to school; if not then, we rode on the bus.

As alluded to earlier, prior to the mid-1990s, the economy in Zimbabwe was booming; after that, everything took a downward turn. The country's way of life, as we had become used to, started to deteriorate. I continued to work, but it became more and more apparent that is was becoming extremely difficult to make ends meet. In trying to address the issues, I decided to immigrate to the West and why on New Year's Eve 2000, my elder sister, Melody, and I spent the evening drafting application letters to send abroad. Personally, I made applications to Ohio State University, Michigan State University, Indiana State University, Iowa State University, and Pennsylvania State

University. Our resolutions for the year 2000 were that by the end of the year, we would be working and studying in the US. While I was making those resolutions, I had a strong feeling in my gut and my being that one of the universities would actually accept me. I started checking my mail daily a week after mailing, never losing faith that I would be accepted by one of the American universities.

In as much as I was making those resolutions, I was wondering how I would sponsor the trips abroad. One of the most difficult decisions to make was whom I would take with me—my children, or Jonathan. I, however, am a true believer in where there is a will there is a way. Without a single cent to call mine besides the monthly paychecks, my resolution to make it abroad before the end of the year remained as strong as the day the resolution germinated in my mind.

Though only one university responded by mid-January, I started the ball rolling with that university. Pennsylvania's State University registration assistants provided me with their office numbers, staff assistant names to speak with, their website to utilize resources that were readily available, and their e-mail addresses for easier and apt communication.

Little did they know that I did not have access to a computer, let alone access to the Internet? By then, I had only been in front of the computer for the classes I had taken as a student while at the Zimbabwe University in 1997. I knew access to the Internet would have speeded the process up for me, but I was as poor as a church mouse, and I could hardly afford a computer. As such, my younger sister, Diana, who worked in an office where she had access to all these, would immediately come to my rescue. Diana would be the one who communicated with the university administrators on my behalf as well as any international friends who had advice for my pending journey. Diana obviously became my lifesaver, and everything progressed well and in a timely manner with her assistance.

The first letter from Pennsylvania State University requested a page of my goal statement on policy, three letters of reference, my school transcript, and my bank statement to show that I would be able to sponsor myself. I also needed an affidavit from my sponsor if I could not sponsor myself. The first three—goal statement, references, and transcript—were not difficult to acquire, but the last one was the most difficult. That was the bank statement proving that I could finance myself, as I did not have such funds. Due to the fact that my decision was on the spur of the moment resolution, I did not have any savings I could depend on to tide me through this challenging adventure. To address that, I decided to approach my brother Louis and Diana's husband. My brother Louis was able to provide me with a bank statement and an affidavit on request for his financial support.

The other bank statement I received from my brother-in-law, my sister Diana's husband, took a while as he was an extremely busy man. I remember I was practically camped in their home for almost a week pursuing that bank statement and the affidavit. I had literally abandoned my duties as a teacher to pursue this new goal. I do not remember what lie I spoon fed my school principal then, but I know I was gone for a week. Ultimately, the week was not all in vain. My brother-in-law was totally supportive and graciously provided me with the desired statement and affidavit. I have yet to meet another brother-in-law who can be that supportive. Many times, I took full advantage of his position in his workplace and am grateful he had that position when I needed his help the most.

As soon as I had all the documents, they were all sent by FedEx to their destination. That fast-track delivery cost me an arm and a leg to return my documents, but it was well worth it. The wait in between would be excruciating. During those waiting periods, I leaned on my children to maintain a positive attitude and strength. I had known the transition was going to be extremely expensive while trying to make the transition as smooth as possible. My girls and I were nervous about everything, but we kept each other going. As usual I also drew strength from my family as well as encouragement.

Elvin by then (2000) was already in the States and affording to give us some much-needed financial assistance here and there, but it was not sufficient at all. As to Elton's attitude, it was hard to determine, maybe because he was still very young and tended to take things lightly. Jonathan basically pretended it had nothing to do with him. He was not gainfully employed then and had never shown any support for my personal endeavors. In this instance, I would occasionally hear from his friends that he was looking forward to the transition. Without financial contributions, maybe he felt he was not entitled to make any suggestions. I may never know as I did not ask him then or later.

As such, immediately after mailing those letters back by end of February, I had to start putting the finances together. I began by selling my old clothes. I put up some of my furniture for sale. I put up my pots and pans for sale. I would take several trips to Georgetown to sell bales of our old clothes. One of my close workmates even donated some of her old clothes to the fund, which was very touching to me personally. I definitely know I made some money, but it hardly accumulated. As soon as I had some cash, there would be some financial predicaments at home, and the money would be diverted to avert the emergencies. Those financial crises were multiple and seemed to be never ending.

I almost gave up the idea of going abroad because financially, it felt like it was a mammoth task; however, my elder sister, Melody kept encouraging me all the time. She helped me tremendously with my fledgling faith that had been tested too many times. One day, my sister Melody came up with an inspiration that I had to keep a real date with the Lord. The date was supposed to be a daily affair at the same time without fail. She gave me a handwritten prayer that I was supposed to repeat every day at the same time with a lit candle. Oh yes, I had my date with the Lord at seven o'clock every evening without fail. From early March until the day I boarded that plane on August 11, 2000, without fail, I kept our date. It became my ritual, and if I failed to be in my bedroom by that time, I would take some time out to repeat that prayer no matter where I was. My date with the Lord obviously helped me to actually believe and visualize the possibility that I was going to make it. I am not sure whether my sister never lived to regret that inspiration, as she ended up playing a major role in sponsoring my transition.

For a couple of years, my sister Melody, the one who had gave me the prayer, had been attempting to sell her home after her divorce. Each time she broached the subject with any of us (her siblings), we would all object and advise her against the thought. However, at the beginning of that year 2000, she mentioned it, and everyone was supportive of the idea, especially my brother Louis. Louis was the finances man. He had worked as a government auditor and CEO of several banks in Zimbabwe; as such, we considered him to be financially savvy. By end of January 2000, my elder sister sold her house. Our Brother Louis's advice was sought on how to invest her suddenly accumulated wealth as he was more knowledgeable regarding finances. She was advised to invest in cash deposits. The money was invested into some cash deposits that earned a good interest. Neither she nor I knew that would be my transitional fund. I am now happy that in the end, everything worked together for my journey, yet I am sad because my sister never got her home back. At times, I look back and wonder what I could have done differently. I console myself and say one day I will be instrumental for something good in her life.

In the meantime, letters continued back and forth between me and the Educational and Policy Studies Department at the Pennsylvania State University. By mid-May 2000, I had both names of my academic advisor and foreign student advisor. I was able to e-mail my academic advisor; we started getting acquainted before I even transitioned to the States. I knew when the semester would begin. I anxiously awaited the arrival of my I-20 so that I could visit the US embassy for our visas. By the end of July, I had all the necessary documentation needed for me to apply for a student visa, with Jonathan and my four children as my dependents.

The day I went for my visa application, I remember, was a Wednesday. I left my two girls, Tiffany and Thelma, in the park across from the US embassy in Zimbabwe, praying for the Lord's intervention. I could picture in my mind what they were saying. Probably asking the Lord to give me strength, the right words, and the confidence, and, on the opposite side of the counter, to provide a kind and sympathetic heart. My heart was pounding heavily as I left my daughters. I almost thought my heart had been transplanted into my mouth. I was almost hyperventilating, as I knew everything was dependent and hanging in the balance of our having the necessary visa, ultimately our travel documents.

When my turn came, I went confidently to the window. Outwardly, I might have appeared calm and collected; but inwardly, I knew I was a nervous wreck. I knew my future and my children's future depended on the outcome of my application that day. I handed over my two bank statements from my brother and my brother-in-law as well as their affidavits coupled with the I-20 from Pennsylvania University. I also handed over all my family's newly acquired passports. I stood there looking at the officer's face. I could not read anything from her facial expressions, but she went over my documents meticulously.

After the officer looked over my documents and was satisfied, all she needed was for me to hand over the application fee. I was applying for

Tiffany, Thelma, Elton, my husband, Teresa, and myself. Unfortunately, never having been through the process, I did not even know that the money was supposed to be paid up front. As it was almost lunchtime, I requested the officer that I bring my fees after lunch, as I needed to go to the bank, and she was agreeable.

I collected my girls from the park and apprised them of what had transpired at the embassy. We went to my Brother Louis's office, as I did not have sufficient funds even for our visa applications. That was how dire my financial situation was. I requested my brother to bail me out once again. Louis gave me enough to add on to the little amount that I had. That way, I had enough for our visa applications, and I paid for our visas. Inwardly, I was wondering about our airfares.

I know in my heart I was singing "I got Joy, Joy, Joy down in my heart." I was very cautious as I did not want to count my chickens before they hatched. In my inquiries, someone had told me that once the embassy had accepted the application fee, it was almost a guarantee that the application would be successful. I was being cautious as I did not want to be disappointed if I was not later approved. After lunch, I was once again at the embassy to present my application fee. I was told to report back after three days. That meant I had to be back the following Monday. The weekend was torturous. I was tense, as I anxiously awaited the outcome of my application(s).

Monday morning found me lined up at the embassy as anxious as ever before their doors were open to the public. I am not sure why, but Jonathan was there with me on that fateful day as well as all my children. As soon as I went to one counter, I was deliriously happy and sad at the same time. My gut had told me that everything had been too smooth. We had been granted our visas. Everyone was going to be my dependent except for Teresa. Teresa had turned twenty that May; as such, she was considered an adult to be under my visa. I was devastated.

In all my planning, I thought all my children were going to come away with me. I had not envisioned myself leaving behind any of my children. I was devastated. However, as her mother, I had to find the right words to tell her. I was able to console my daughter. I told her the Lord had something better in store for her. Later on, that turned out to be the best visa denial for her as the Lord had really mapped out a better destiny for Teresa than the rest of us. On the day, we were not as celebratory as we would have been because we were torn. That did not stop the plans. We had to proceed, and I felt somehow after my transition I would find a solution for my eldest daughter's plight.

The reality of my financial situation then hit me in the face. If I could not afford the visa application fees, how I could afford the fares for five people to fly was a real mystery to me. Nonetheless, I was resolute and optimistic that if it was meant to be, it was going to be. I put all my savings together, and I was able to raise funds sufficient for one person's airfare. I talked to family, and they all had one solution, and it was to approach my elder sister, the one who had provided me with the prayer. On approaching her for financial assistance, initially, my sister would not hear anything about me using her invested funds. She told me she wanted to earn enough interest so that she could put the down payment for a better home somewhere, which I completely understood.

Immediately, that source had closed in my face. I remained hopeful and optimistic. I raked my mind on how I could raise enough for us all. My husband was tight-lipped and would never give me any suggestions. A week went by before I could figure out how I was going to raise enough for the inevitable journey. Finally, one night, in the middle of one troubled sleep, an idea came to me. Once again, I approached my sister with a new idea the following morning. I told her I would borrow her money until November that year (that was August 2000). Our exchange rate back then was $1 US was equivalent to $45 Zimbabwe. So whatever she would lend me, I promised I would give her back US $3,000.00 The latest plan seemed to work the right magic, as immediately after telling her of my plan, she was willing to release her invested funds to enable my trip.

That was how I found myself early on the first Thursday in August of 2000 on Stanley Avenue in Harare going to my sister's bank to withdraw all of my sister's investment. In my heart, I was joyful as everything was shaping up well; however, I think I had celebrated too soon. Suddenly, my cell phone rang. It was my sister. She was telling me she had had a change of heart. I could not believe my ears. My world was spinning. I felt hot, and I started to sweat profusely on a windy August day. I could see the pursuit of my dreams crumbling to nothing. I sat down right there on the pavement, afraid I was going to faint in the middle of the street in Harare. Nothing had seemed so tangible; suddenly, it was so far away, I could not really fathom why she suddenly changed her mind. I could not think. I failed to function. I could not cry, but all I could see was my world crashing down around me. I knew I was not able to will my legs to carry me anywhere. I was feeling so weak; I remained seated for a while, trying hard not to pass out. I was wrestling with the idea of not admitting to myself that I had heard my sister correctly on the phone. I remained there on the edge of the pavement drained of any reasoning or energy to do anything. I could not will my mind to think of the next strategy. I was devastated.

After what seemed like eternity, my sister called back, and I realized it had only been a couple of minutes. I could not imagine what other disastrous news she had to deliver to me. Instead, she told me she once again had changed her mind and told me to wait for her until the following morning. She assured me she was coming to accompany me to the bank. She told me it we would be right for us if we did that together while I prepared for the trip. I could not believe my ears. This was another 180 degrees change of heart within minutes. I instantaneously broke down and started to cry. She promised me that this time she was not going to change her mind again.

I spent the night at my Brother Louis's home; it was another sleepless night. I was not sure whether my sister Melody was going to turn up after the previous day's incident. However, she lived up to her word and turned up early the following morning. I started to believe all she was telling me when my sister was there. We quickly conducted our business at the bank and were just being joyous in Harare like excited little girls. As I looked for people on the black market to sell my country currency to for the coveted USA currency, my sister remained supportive by my side right through the day.

That day I also purchased the flight tickets for two. Needless to say, my brother-in-law (yes, Diana's husband once again) had to play a lot of politics as the price could have been insurmountable. He told me later that he had literally put his neck on the line. By the time tickets were purchased, I did not have enough foreign currency; as such, my brother-in-law again, who worked for Zimbabwe Airways and my niece Doris pulled a lot of strings to make it happen. I knew that meant if the deal had fallen through, both had risked their jobs on my behalf. I am happy everything worked fine in the end; I would always remain forever grateful to him and my niece Doris for the roles in my realization of my life's journey. Above all, I would remain indebted to my sister Melody for making my dream become reality.

I reserved funds I thought would pay for accommodation, health insurance, food, and my tuition. All in all, I had less than US$5,000 for the trip, but that amount was a real fortune for me. This, however, did not deter my spirits. It seemed so easy to have that amount of money while still in Zimbabwe, but as soon as I was in America, I started wondering how I was ever going to repay my sister, let alone eke a living. The rent alone was going to take a $1,000 for the deposit and first month's rent. The fares for Jonathan and I had taken more than $800 US. My tuition was going to be more than $10,000 a semester for an out-of-state student. The situation on the ground was not what I had anticipated. Confronted with these realities, I clung to my faith as I had never done before. I prayed that the Lord's mercy would be poured on me somehow and be sufficient to carry me through the turbulent times.

After the purchase of tickets, I made it home to Hartley that night. Everyone was excited for us. I sat down with my children and explained that I was going to bring them over eventually, but for the time being, they would be living with their grandmother, their father's mother. On approaching my mother-in-law to broach the subject about her staying with the kids, she was completely agreeable. I did not anticipate any problems with her and the girls, at least not at the time. The girls remained in her care for eighteen months. It would be later that Tiffany would tell me the two of them used to butt heads a lot. Tiffany is the most outspoken of the girls, and on more than one occasion, her sisters took advantage of her personality. The other sisters put her in the line of fire with her grandmother, and that derailed their relationship. Despite the few mis-forgiving's, I am eternally grateful to their grandmother for taking care of my children when an adult's presence was really essential in their lives.

Let me hasten to say the repayment of my sister's money caused the first huge rift between my husband and me after we were in the States. A fight ensued between us exactly a year after we migrated. Despite having told him about the agreement between my sister and me, letting him in on the terms of the loan, my husband wanted me to renege on my word and promise to my sister. Having faced the hardships of working and living in America, he wanted me to repay my sister the exact dollar amount she had loaned me in Zimbabwe currency. I could not believe he even had the audacity to suggest that. Here was a man who had been my abuser most of my life and had never financially supported my personal ventures, yet he was suggesting I shortchange my own sister on our promise. He made one gross mistake. He underestimated the strength of the financial assistance I had received from my family repeatedly while he was engaged in his destructive behaviors early in our marriage. Had it not been for my siblings, my parents included, it would have been easy for my children and me to become destitute.

By the time, we had been in the USA for a year, the Zimbabwe currency had further deteriorated. There was no way I was going to give in to his pressure and repay my sister back the measly borrowed amount besides what we had agreed on. In my heart, it bothered me that I was not able to pay her back in a timely manner, let alone have it suggested that I pay her the little amount I had borrowed in Zimbabwe currency! I knew I owed my sister more than mere cash. If it had not been for her generosity, my life would not have turned out as it did, including my children's. No monetary value could ever be attached to her generosity, and my husband failed to see that. From then on, I knew I needed energies to bring our children and show the man where he belonged. It was high time I got rid of him. My husband had saved his purpose and his welcome in my life, only he was not in the know-how. Our roles in life had long been reversed, and he was the only one unaware of that role reversal. I knew then intellectually I was smarter than what I had given myself credit for.

Chapter Twenty-Five

The trip abroad and overcoming hurdles

The trip to the US had long been anticipated. I flew from Harare International Airport on August 11, 2000, with Jonathan by my side. This was my first trip by plane ever. Before leaving that night, my family gave us a farewell party. I remember one of my husband's brothers who came to bid us farewell, reminding us that we had to cling to each other as we were going to foreign lands. My brother-in-law also reminded us that some of the news from home would be good, and some would shock us, but all we had to do was to believe we would be reunited one day.

It still amazes me that the first shocking news we received was that my brother-in-law had passed away by February of 2001. My husband, in his farewell speech that evening, told everyone that he was never going to return to Zimbabwe. I could not believe he was saying that to our families. To me, Zimbabwe was home and as such would always hold pride of place in my heart. I knew no matter where I went in the world I would never forsake my country. Zimbabwe was in my blood, and I felt I could never abandon my land. It had shaped all that I was and who still is.

I instinctively knew I would go back because I loved my parents, my siblings, the extended families, and I loved my country. I was also leaving my best treasures in the country: my children. As such, I knew I would go back. Prior to this date, I had never been on an airplane. I had always hoped that one day I would board one but had never imagined how, why, where, and when that would be. I had at times imagined that my children would be the ones to fly me abroad as I always had harbored hidden ambitions to educate them abroad. In fact, I was glad everything had turned that way because in the back of mind, I pictured my parents visiting with us as well as my siblings. I am a strong believer of visions, for visualizing makes things become real. I kept that vision with me, and it helped take away some of the sadness as we continued to bid our relatives and loved ones farewell.

I know the decision to bring my husband with me was out of economic necessity more than love in our relationship and the influence of my friend than what everyone else believed. I knew I stood a better chance of making it with him and me both working than only the children and I. I left a huge piece of my heart in Zimbabwe that night, and I knew that. My mother was getting on and not enjoying the best of health. The last time I looked into my mother's eyes that night, bidding her farewell as I hugged her close to me, there was no happiness in her eyes for me, and somehow that made my heart sink. Looking back retrospectively, I think somehow in that moment we both realized that we would never see each other again in this world, but we were too scared to express our fears in words. I missed my mother from that moment in no way anyone would ever be able to understand.

My four children were another reason I was sad inwardly and why I would never say I would never go back. I did not know what fate had in store for me. I knew the responsibility depended on me to be able to fly them to join us within as short time as possible; only then I did not know the new world where I was going to start my life in and what was in store for me. With that in mind, it was not easy for me to say I would never go back to Zimbabwe. If I had known then how difficult life was going to be, I would have given it a second thought, but I do not think I would have thrown in the towel. I would have taken my time to work on strategies that would have made the transition much easier.

As I was flying above Africa and its interminable Sahara deserts, leaving all of Africa's troubles behind, it felt gorgeous and exhilarating. I could not believe I was leaving the never-ending political strife that surrounds almost every African nation. I could not imagine that I was leaving the epidemics that seem to erupt on a yearly basis in every corner of the continent. On the other hand, I felt like I was escaping the vicious cycles of poverty handed down from generation to generation.

I was tired of the dismantling of families due to industrialization and of women bringing up children on their own because men still cling to polygamy or have taken to the new trend of little houses[42] brought about again by industrialization. Inwardly, there was an ambivalence of emotions. I felt sad leaving yet somehow euphoric with happiness of liberation.

Ironically, for me, I was sitting beside the man who had caused me a lot of heartache. Fortunately, he had little knowledge of how much I now despised him as a spouse. No wonder I was really torn between excitement and sadness. I was excited to be on my way to the land of luxury, where dreams become reality, the land of opportunity, freedom, and liberty. Conflicting emotions were from the knowledge that I was leaving behind all that was familiar, all the people I loved, my parents, my siblings, and, most importantly, my children, and clinging to my abuser. I clung to him because I needed his physical strength and his labor to enable me to settle down in a foreign land. In that moment, I realized the true meaning of the saying "as cunning as a fox."

I was not nervous. I did not see much on that night flight, but I could not sleep all night long. The seats were uncomfortable. I had a lot to think about, and for once, I acknowledged to myself that I was fearful of the unknown. By morning, we landed at Gatwick Airport. To me it appeared enormous compared to the Harare International Airport. The numerous gates, the unending runways, the number of planes landing and taking off seemed all to have transplanted me to an alien planet. I had heard and seen on movies of the shopping malls within an airport, knew about the McDonald fast food outlet; but to actually set my eyes on one, it really was a new world to me, like my dreams coming true.

During the stopover, I had the privilege of meeting with my nephew whom I had not seen in more than two years. The two of them, my nephew and his wife, drove from Birmingham to meet with us. We spent a couple of hours catching up with each other's lives. Eventually, they had to leave, and I was sad to see them leave. The two of them had been extremely kind to me. My nephew's wife gave me some nice lipstick, and the two of them gifted us with a cash advance that I still appreciate. Needless to say, every little bit of cash would come in handy initially.

---

[42] Men who have other women whom they take care of outside of marriage are considered to be harboring little houses.

We flew from Gatwick into Newark, New Jersey. I loved everything about that flight. I was sitting by the window. I could actually see all the landmarks. Flying over the ocean was an exhilarating experience. It was heavenly. I loved every minute of it. Looking down into the deep blue waters below me that seemed ongoing made me wonder. I found us sometimes flying above the white clouds, which made me feel as though I was floating. I found myself singing the hymn "When peace like a river overcometh my soul." If anything had happened to me then, I knew all would have been well with my soul, except it would have been lonely without my children. The crossing made me wonder about the Creator and how He could have made everything so perfect. I questioned my own place in His creation. I also questioned why and how I had been made a part of this His wonderful creation and fitted in with his perfect plans. From then on, my faith in Him who created me became stronger.

We landed at our destination after four in the afternoon; that is in New Jersey. I had never seen so many people in an airport. They were all hustling and bustling as though their very lives depended on it. The yellow cabs from the movies were real, and on that first day, I rode in one. I thought they were only for movies and not for ordinary people like me to ride in. It was like a real dream come true. After we collected our luggage, a cab driver took us to a hotel to stay overnight. We had arrived too late to catch the Greyhound bus to Pennsylvania State University.

As a young child growing up, whenever I traveled to a new place, my grandmother used to tell me to eat the soil of the new place. Without fail that evening, as soon as I got off the cab, I looked for some dirt. I licked the tip of my pointing finger, touched the ground, and licked the soil off my index finger. Of what significance it was, I never questioned my grandmother, but that day it made sense that I tasted the soil of the USA. I remember wanting so much the need to taste the soil of the USA. Somehow I thought it would taste different from the Zimbabwe's soil, but that evening, I dictated no difference.

In our room, we ordered food and took a bath. By the time the food arrived, I was already dozing. I was amazed by the enormous helpings of food. Immediately, I thought of Zimbabwe Zimbabwean singer[43] who sang "Everything is big in America." My greatest wish then was

---

[43] He is one of the well-known song artists in Zimbabwe. His song, "Everything Is Big in America," could not have fully prepared me for how

hopefully the pay would be also as big. I know from all the excitement and jetlag, I slept like a baby that night. The following morning, we took another cab to take us to Penn Station to get on the Greyhound and be finally on our way to Pennsylvania State University.

The ride on the Greyhound was full of firsts. A first experience awaited me on the bus, the realization that it was fully equipped with the heating and air condition system. The bus had built-in toilets, which I quickly learned were referred to as restrooms or bathrooms. Needless to say, these would be the least of my culture shocks. The people had different accents. I could hardly understand as they spoke so fast, yet they accused me of having an accent. To me it was a matter of the pot calling the kettle black.

Some of the foods had different names from what I was used to, and it tasted so differently. I guess I needed to acquire a taste for the American foods. I had to relearn most of the things that I had just taken for granted. Despite some of the harsh exposure and lack of knowledge to certain things, I loved the scenery.

I enjoyed the beautiful rolling mountains. This was summer at its best. Every tree had an appealing shade of green; the grass obviously seemed greener than in Zimbabwe, considering it was end of winter when I left Zimbabwe. The vegetation in Zimbabwe was all brown and bleak. In comparison, everything here was a luscious green full of life and promise. I hoped against hope that my fortunes would definitely be changed. Everywhere I looked at, my spirits were uplifted, as I took in the vastness of the country and all it represents to the entire world.

The road networks were something out of this world. I found myself wondering whether I would ever be able to drive on them. Three, four, and at times five lanes of cars going in one direction were more than I was used to. Talk of speed; it appeared as though everyone was in a hurry to get somewhere. The highways were marked with all these exits, and I had no clue where they exited to. I wondered how they knew which exit to take and what would be waiting at the end of each exit. It was a whole lot of learning especially for someone of my age. That was a whole lot of culture shock.

---

vast the country is. At times, as outsiders, I think we imagine the States as our provinces, and nothing could be far wrong.

We had an hour's stopover in Harrisburg. By two thirty in the afternoon, we were finally on the bus that would eventually take us to our final destination. The Town of University College would be my home for the next seven years. After we arrived in University College, I had no clue where to go. Lucky enough, I had my friend's number. I called her. She was not home, but her daughter answered; and luckily, she knew who I was. A Good Samaritan gave us a ride to her place. University College was full of these Good Samaritans I learned to appreciate them as the longer I stayed there. I do not know what I had imagined in my head. The type of homes my friend and family were living in was the type students' use. As an adult, I had never pictured myself going back to living that way again like a conventional student.

However, there was no use crying over spilt milk. I was here, so I had to make the best of my situation. I realized looking for a place to live was going to be obviously my main priority. Seeing one of my friend's daughters and finally meeting her when she finally came home, I knew I would be working hard for my dream to become real. She did not take long in introducing me to the baptism by fire that I would be living as a graduate student. She told me how she was juggling two, three jobs at a time while studying full time. The lessons on how my situation had changed continued around five thirty that evening. She took me to a nursing home, to a client she was taking care of. I had never imagined that as one of the jobs I would be doing in order to complete my studies and a means to earn a living. I had always worked as a professional, and there was no way I was going to be reducing myself to be picking up menial jobs in order to advance myself, so I thought. Little did I know that was only the introduction; more was to come.

The sun was still up, and it was already eight thirty at night as we sat down to have dinner. I had never seen that in my world. Besides reading in novels of a stunning and beautiful sunset around nine at night, I had never thought I would ever witness such a beautiful sunset so late in the evening ever in my life. In my hemisphere, when the sun sets, it is nighttime, around six thirty at the latest. We watched a bit of TV, which did not make sense to me as there were so many channels, and I had been used to only two channels back home in Zimbabwe. I also had been used to watching lifetime movies, and I knew I would be making them my daily food as I enjoyed their romance stories. Little did I know that I would hardly ever have time for such luxuries!

The following morning, I joined fellow foreign students for our orientation. I met with my foreign student advisor; somehow we did not like each other right from the get-go. I met with one foreign student from Taiwan, and we immediately became good friends. The three orientation days went by very fast. In between, I was looking for an apartment. On Tuesday during lunch, I went to University College looking for a place where I could have lunch. I spotted my husband across the street, and seeing a familiar face among so many unfamiliar made my day. I was overjoyed to see him. That was how homesick I already was. We ended up having lunch together and exchanged notes on how the apartment hunting was going. We finally ended up signing a lease with a landlord for a two-bedroom basement apartment for less than $500 a month plus utilities. That Wednesday evening, we moved into our new apartment and were happy to be on our own. All the furniture was picked from the streets including our bed. Little did I know the struggle had just begun, and little did I know it was going to be a real struggle?

Earlier in the day, the first Wednesday, I went for a one-on-one meeting with my foreign student advisor. We barely saw eye to eye on all we discussed that day, and I can safely say we surely started on the wrong footing. Somehow while I was in her office, I forgot my purse, which I quickly learned was referred to as a pocketbook. However, I did not realize that until early evening when I needed some cash to buy food at the nearest grocery shop. When I realized I could not locate my pocketbook, I even made a trip to Booker Building even though it did not make sense, late as it was, but I was desperate. Booker Building doors were locked, so I spent a sleepless night wondering what would become of me as all our finances were in that pocketbook. Early morning, before the doors were open, I was waiting by the steps of the building.

At the reception desk, when I told them of my dilemma, they requested I describe everything in writing that was in my purse. I did and handed over the list when one of the associates finally appeared with my purse, and I had checked out everything. I realized that all my money was there; I broke down and cried hysterically. It was a cry of relief. The people in the office were all rather taken aback by my demonstration of emotion. Such things would never have happened in Zimbabwe. I had thought everything was gone. The moment I had forgotten my purse and cash in that office, had it been in Zimbabwe, would have been the time I would have kissed it goodbye. I could not believe my good fortune, and immediately, I knew that such good things could happen only in America. From there, we headed straight to the nearest bank. I only breathed a sigh of relief when the funds were safely deposited into a joint account with Omega Bank on the same street I lived on. For the second time in our married life I had a joint account with Jonathan. With my fingers crossed, I hoped that everything would go well with the second joint account.

This was almost three days after my arrival, and I had not been able to call home. My younger sister, Diana, frantically contacted my friend and told her back home they were all anxiously waiting the news of my arrival. I bought a $5 calling card. It barely gave me two minutes from a pay phone. At least she heard my voice, and I heard hers, and we wished each other well. Another problem prominent on my mind was my children. I had not spoken to them since I had landed. I got another calling card for five dollars, which I could hardly spare. I was barely able to ask all I needed, and hearing Tiffany's voice was real torture because I wanted to speak to them all. When the brief conversation was over, I asked my husband to pinch me so that I could tell I had not dreamed the whole conversation. It was surreal, and I had more questions than answers concerning their welfare. I literally cried myself to sleep, wishing my children were there, and I could cuddle them close to me while they went to sleep. That first week of my transition was the most difficult. On top of missing my children, I did not like the American food. To make matters worse, I was with a husband whom I no longer felt any passion for; furthermore, I was struggling to get a job and not sure when that would happen. I was taking classes and wondering what I was doing there as the classes made no sense to me; last but not least, I was worried how I would ever repay my sister all the money I had borrowed. These were real problems that made me feel more homesick.

I shared my disappointment of not talking with his siblings with my son Elvin. He bought me a $20 international calling card on the Internet. After two weeks of not hearing my children's voices and the card giving me two hours of air time, I felt like I had a piece of heaven. I was thrilled to have two hours on the phone with my children. I managed to speak to them all and their grandmother. It was honestly a bittersweet conversation. It was sweet in hearing their voices and bitter in having to say bye. It was also helpful in that I realized my children were still there, and we could stay connected by phone. One thing that still tortured me though was the fact that food here was affordable, and I could eat all I wanted, yet in my heart of hearts I knew my children were struggling. The need to provide for my children on limited resources made me take my next step, which I never thought I would ever do.

No matter what little pride I had as a professional woman, I threw caution to the wind and went to look for a job at the nursing home where my friend used to attend to a private patient. Though I had vowed never to reduce myself to that level, reality hit me in the face. I needed my children to have an easier life even though I was not there with them. I also realized there was no way we were going to be reunited as soon as possible if I did not pick up that other job. I could not see myself bringing them over on the measly salary I was making from one job. I swallowed my pride and went to the nursing home to care for the elderly.

I was still tortured in my mind; that was after I had one heart-wrenching dream[44] one night. I dreamt Thelma and I had been squeezing through a barbed wire fence into another country. As we were trying to squeeze through, I let go of Thelma's hold on me as I continued on my own. The dream was almost real, and it brought sadness to my heart when I woke up. To me, the implication was that I had abandoned my children to pursue the proverbial rainbow. All night after that dream, I wrestled with my mind what I had to do.

In the morning, I shared my dream with my husband. He told me if the separation was taking such a toll on me emotionally, maybe we needed to think of going back home. We still had about $1,500 in our account, and it could have afforded us return tickets to Zimbabwe. I thought of all I had given up, my clothes, my furniture, my job, my children's expectations, and to throw in the towel barely a year down the road. I realized I had to develop a tougher skin. I had to work harder to enable my children and me to be reunited.

I already had a job at the University Inn as a server for people attending conferences. I worked there twenty hours a week. The dream was what energized me to look for a second job at a nursing home where I worked thirty hours a week. I was also a full-time graduate student

---

[44] All my life I have always depended on my dreams to look into the future and predict how problems would be resolved or how plans would pan out. I am a strong believer in my dreams too.

studying for nine credits that fall. I worked hard, and my two major goals were to bring my children to me and accumulate as many credit courses as I could so as not to fall behind with my course work.

I had heard of the baptism by fire; this was a real baptism of fire like none I had experienced previously in my life. The hardships made me realize that it's true that when the going gets the tough, the tough get going, I did the same. I became tougher in order to conquer the going that was becoming tougher with each passing day. I had to set my priorities right in my mind. I knew I needed to diligently continue with my studies. There was no question of my juggling two jobs; I had to. On top of that, I tried to get along with a husband whom I felt nothing for except contempt. I was intelligent or smart enough not to let my disrespect for him show; as such, I nurtured dreams of being reunited with my children and constantly worried about my mother whose health I instinctively knew was failing while at the same time constantly worried how I would ever be able to sufficiently save to repay my elder sister.

Academically, I knew it was not a matter of my intelligence but time management and finances. I tried to work with both my academic and foreign student advisors to help me sort my financial issues. I hardly got what I needed from both. When my academic advisor, just before my first Christmas in the States, sent me an e-mail suggesting that maybe I needed to go back to Zimbabwe and re-plan my study in the USA, I immediately knew I had to rule him out. I decided to solve my financial problems alone without an academic advisor unless it became imperative that I needed one. As such, from December 2000 until March 2003, when I was now applying for a change in program, I worked without his services for more than two years. I only contacted him because I needed his references. To say he was surprised is to put it lightly. He was totally flabbergasted. He thought I had left and gone back to my roots in Zimbabwe; he was shocked that I had even completed my master's degree at all, considering the financial strain I had been under.

As for my foreign student advisor, it was another story. She had threatened to have my children's dependent visas revoked. Initially, I avoided her like the plague. Then three months after I arrived, I gathered enough courage to go and face her and literally take the proverbial bull by the horns, as the saying goes. I told her how hard I had worked to get my children's visas and how much I had invested in them to have the visas revoked just like that. I literally told her that there was no way I was going to let her do that and subject my children and me to a life of separation, one that we had not planned at all. I promised her that each time any of my children made it to the States, I would let her know. She seemed to soften a little to my plight. Our relationship was to take a turn shortly after.

Around Christmas, time there was the *War Cry* at the nursing home where I worked. A *War Cry* is a magazine internationally published by the Salvation Army. I had been trying to connect with the Salvation Army local officers without success. When I asked the director of the nursing home how they got it, she gave me a number to call, and I was connected with two Salvation Army officers. I celebrated my reconnection to the church in University College.

As the officers had not yet established a church in University College, we worshipped with a variety of churches in the local community. One Sunday, we went to another church, and whom should I see but my foreign student advisor! She acknowledged me from the podium as her advisee, and I really appreciated the recognition. I later related how strained my relationship with her was to my pastors, and we prayed about it. From then on, our relationship warmed up considerably, and the cold treatment seemed to thaw as the melting of snow from the mountaintop! Also, from then on, she would forward me e-mails of available resources. That change of heart in a way helped cement my faith and what faith can do.

The lessons I learned from interacting with both my advisors were that both parties (advisor and advisee) had to have mutual respect for the other. I also learned that student advisors are human beings and will never know the reality of their advisees' situations unless the advisees fully trust them. They cannot be found breaking rules and policies for one student in case they are accused of playing favoritism. I had never worked with an academic advisor before; as such, I had to educate myself on that relationship and its importance. From the beginning, as a rule, I learned to be a resilient and resourceful foreign student.

"Resilience" is an easy word to use, but most of us have never had to call upon their resilience because they have not been tested that much. According to the online dictionary, the word *resilience* either means "the power or ability to return to the original form, position, etc., after being bent, compressed, or stretched; elasticity." It also means "the ability to recover readily from illness, depression, adversity, or the like; buoyancy."

I found that I relied upon my resilience many times when challenged through all the trials and tribulations of my life's journey especially as an abused wife and a teacher, and now I was going to have to be resilient as a foreign graduate student. I believe a lot of resilience was involved in my marriage. Surviving my poor circumstances called for resilience and my having five children and never sure how I would educate and provide for them called on me to be a more resilient woman. To all the myriad of challenges I met in life, I believe I needed a certain degree of resilience for each one.

To a certain extent, I believe all of us have a certain level of resilience in enormous reserves, which we may never get to tap or utilize because we have never been called upon to rise to certain circumstances beyond our physical and emotional capabilities. Until that happens, we may continue underestimating our strengths and hence our resilience. However, resilience on the part of a foreign student is of utmost importance as some foreign students find it easier to give up than dig in and call upon their resilience. Many things challenge foreign students more than they would have anticipated when embarking on their journeys. First and foremost, the challenge of being in a foreign country, having neither friends nor family to support, shock of the change in culture, and possibly living under different weather conditions, and, most certainly and not particularly in all situations, being forced to live under or below circumstances than what they were used to. In such instances, foreign students are called upon to utilize their resilience rather than throw in the towel and give up.

I dug my fingers in, as all my life I had been used to and knew nothing else. I tried to adjust, and within eighteen months, all my children had joined us except for Teresa whose visa application kept being turned down by the US embassy in Zimbabwe. Nonetheless, she made it to another country. As it turned out, it was the best visa denial ever as she ended up getting a scholarship to attend the school of nursing, and she had it much easier in comparison.

I dug in in more ways than one. That first semester, I was also challenged to use computers for my first educational administration and budget classes. The American system of education was nothing compared to what I had been exposed to. I was not shy to ask for help from fellow students and my professors alike. I had always been the one who believed asking for help was not admitting ignorance rather a sign of confidence in others. That first semester, I learned to appreciate the difference, that if anything, asking for help exhibited strength of character and intelligence to recognize what one's shortcomings were.

I learned to work below my level of education and appreciate the difference the income could make despite how I got it as long I was making an honest living. I learned to appreciate what the funds could do than how I got the funds. In the process, we were able to pay off our mortgage in Zimbabwe. We paid off all the banks we owed lots of loans. We were able to bring our three children over to the States in less than two years and send another one to London, where she managed to study. We also managed to buy our son Elvin a car and a cheaper one for ourselves. In the meantime, I never missed any of my classes. For all the hardships we were living under, I believe we were very enterprising and very resourceful. We called upon the reserves of energy we never thought we had. If that was not resilience, then you have to demonstrate to me what true resilience really is.

Chapter Twenty-Six

Happy and sad times in terms of milestones

The first nine months of my life in the States were the longest and extremely difficult for me. This was the first time I had ever lived separately for so long and so far away from my children. My own relationship with my husband was not getting better. Besides having lived abroad, my husband had no clue as to what he needed to do in order to be employed. He would walk long distances to buy our groceries, trying to save on our limited finances, yet all he needed was a dollar. On numerous attempts to acquire the social security number (SSN), he would not know where to wait for the bus, where to transfer, and the like. He walked everywhere. Somehow it appeared he was completely lost in this transition to this culture. This was how I got the affirmation of the role reversal whereas initially I had just toyed with the idea.

One day, after he had walked for long in the rain, I had to shelve my commitments and take a bus ride with him. I had to show him that for only a dollar, he could make the trip, transfer halfway with the same amount, and not have to walk like he used to. This did not make it any easier for me as I had little time to spare. I used to go to bed around midnight and had to be up by four in morning in order to be at the inn most mornings by five. I was not getting enough sleep. I constantly worried about Jonathan like a child and almost regretted having brought him with me, at some point, but I knew I needed his services then more than ever.

Though my husband had a driver's license from Lucas, he needed one in the USA so that he could get his SSN. That proved to be a challenge as he could not pass his permit but finally got it after several attempts. He managed to secure a job as a second-shift dishwasher. He would work from four in the afternoon till midnight then put in four hours of overtime, which paid time and half of his hourly rate. The earliest he would be home would be four in the morning, in time to wake me up to take my shower and be on my way to the inn. I had never budgeted my hours while in Zimbabwe, but this transition made me realize how precious time in the Western world is. I used to hear that time and tide waited for no man, but those sayings had not made authentic significance in my life until then. His getting employed was the first milestone we needed to afford our rent and not be dependent on our son Elvin to bail us every month end.

Over Christmas time, Elvin was able to fly from Miami, Florida, and be with us for the holidays. He flew over with his friend, and they rented a car in Philadelphia. They stayed with us for slightly over a week. It was the best week I had spent ever since coming to the States. It also made my life easier for that week as they would drive me to work and pick me up at eleven after my shift. The distance I had been walking night and day for the last three months (in the snow), was only a ten-minute drive, yet I walked for more than an hour either way. Needless to say, I was really sad to see him leave. His stay had made it easier for me to go to work, and merely being reunited with him after more than a year was really awesome. In my heart of hearts, I knew if Elvin could make it, young as he was, I would also. This was my second milestone in settling in.

The next milestone would be in the paying off of the mortgage to our four-bedroom house in Hartley in Zimbabwe. Once the mortgage and the bank loans had been paid off, we planned on how we would bring the children to join us, our next milestone. Jonathan and I agreed that Elton would be the next one to join us. As the youngest child, we missed Elton the most. We worked hard, and we saved hard; and by mid-March, we had enough for his flight. That day I talked to my niece, and she assured me all Elton's flight reservations had been booked. The news made me the happiest mother in the world.

Elton was supposed to have arrived around one in the afternoon. We intended to start off at six in the morning. We overslept, and the phone woke us up around seven. It was the airline telling us that our son had not been booked on the earlier flight we thought he was going to arrive on. It was our lucky day, when we overslept, because if we had been at Newark and had missed him, we would have gone crazy. Finally, Elton's flight landed at 5:30 p.m. When I saw my son walk through the arrivals gate, I could not believe my good fortune. We clung to each other crying. It was St. Patrick's Day and the first time I learned about St. Patrick. I would always look upon St. Patrick's Day as my lucky day as I was reunited with my baby son on that day! Seeing him and holding my son made me realize that soon I could hold my girls in my arms if I worked hard enough to raise their fares. Reuniting with my youngest son was another huge milestone in my measurements of success in the United States. So I went on dreaming of the day the girls would make the ultimate journey.

I never gave up on the idea of us being together as a family. As a result, I applied for school places for my daughter Teresa, whose visa had been denied because she had aged out. I sent her the I-20 forms from the one of the SUNY Community Colleges, but her visa was denied again because she did not have a passing grade in math. To say I was devastated would be underestimating the hurt. I told her to appeal their decision, and once again, they denied her application. I was almost at the end of my tether when I thought maybe a different country would work for her. Plans were made for her to go to Britain. She would visit one cousin who was willing to host her for some time. We were able to purchase her return ticket with British Airways. During the holiday season, I picked up extra shifts at both my jobs as there were no classes. I worked as though my whole life and existence depended on me making enough for my children's trips. My husband too did the same. He worked equally hard. He also picked up extra shifts.

The girls all flew out of Zimbabwe the same week, but we were worried more about Teresa being deported back to Zimbabwe than Tiffany and Thelma coming to the States. Many people from Zimbabwe were being subjected to deportation from the United Kingdom, and visa requirements were being implemented as deterrents to more Zimbabwe nationals migrating to the United Kingdom as of early 2002. We booked her flight through British Airways to fly into Heathrow, which meant paying slightly more for her fare but ensuring that she would be subjected to less scrutiny. She made it to a cousin who had invited her without hiccups. We at least could breathe a sigh of relief and wait for the other two. Exactly two days later, we welcomed Tiffany and Thelma to the States. We may not have been all together, but I was happy my family was in the West. At least now they all stood a chance at having a better education than what I could have afforded them home. To my way of thinking, I had achieved three more milestones in their joining us.

Exactly eighteen months had gone by from the time my husband and I had left Zimbabwe for us to be reunited with our children. We were renting a two-bedroom basement apartment. Occasionally, my children would joke about living under a house, but they did not know how hard we were working even to put a roof over their heads. Tiffany was the first one to catch on to how much time we spent at work and commented that if I could juggle two jobs while going to school full-time, she could work three jobs. God bless her heart; she really helped in that transition as she was the only one not in school.

Immediately after their arrival, Tiffany was taught by her father how to drive. One afternoon in March, Tiffany came to pick me from the library where I was then working as a library assistant, and she was driving herself. I could not believe my eyes. When I saw her pull over to pick me up, I broke down and cried. In my heart, I was ecstatic; I could not believe my own daughter was navigating the streets and driving in America! We were making baby steps, but my children were starting to get acclimatized to the life abroad. At the same time as learning to drive, Tiffany was looking for jobs. She secured two. She had a day job with Burger King and night job with Wal-Mart as a stocker. These were milestones in our lives, and I was grateful.

I was happy to finally have my children. My studies were right on schedule. However, there was one thing I had not anticipated. February of 2002, I had managed to raise more than $3,000 so as to fly our daughters from home. By the time the girls came, all our savings were depleted. I was working crazy hours, at times forced to walk to work as we had one car. I had bought a car for almost $150 from a coworker at the nursing home in April of 2001. That same year, it failed to pass the State inspection. I bought another one for $300 so as to be able to go to work. This too would be a liability before too long as well, for it needed a lot of work done.

In November of the same year (2001), we bought Elvin an Altima for $800. Financially, we appeared as though we were working as a team for once. However, during my long hours at work, my husband was abusing our landline. He was calling friends in Zimbabwe, his girlfriend in South Africa, and anywhere else he took a fancy to. At one point, we had a phone bill of $600, and I told him we had to have it disconnected as I could not plow all my hard-earned cash into sweet nothings on the phone. Maybe that was the beginning of one of the major rifts in our relationship abroad, his assuming that he could abuse anything, and I would never be the wiser. It was also a welcome/unwelcome milestone in the relationship, depending on how I felt about our relationship on a daily basis.

When the girls came, we had lots of credit cards, we had rent to pay, our utilities took a chunk, and we needed to feed more people. Laundry fees were enormous, and our resources were still the same. Though my husband was now working as a full-time night audit for a holiday resort, he started feeling left out as my education kept on accelerating. Due to financing all the girls' flights, our savings were depleted, but my husband insisted on becoming an LCD driver. During the month of March, he went away for two weeks for his training and invested more than 2,000 dollars in that venture. Somehow the $2,000 he invested in the venture did not yield any results.

While he was away for his training, I decided to invest in a family car. On March 8, 2002, I took the family to Mifflinton in Pennsylvania to look for cars. I had received an invite to their President's Day car show. I had little intention of buying one, but after reviewing the cars there, I fell in love with a green Ford Taurus 1999 model with less than twenty thousand miles on it. The dealers were willing to let me trade in my 1993 Pontiac for $600 as deposit. Nothing could have prepared me for that deal; as a result, the deal was signed. We drove home in our brand-new car that afternoon.

I did not know about capitalism, but then the purchase of my car was the simplest and easiest introduction to capitalism that I ever experienced. I learned a lot from that first car purchase that I would never use anyone's money through credit cards ever again. I calculated how much I was going to be paying for the use of their money, and I felt revolted! However, the purchase was a huge milestone as we had never owned a better car. As such, I just set my mind to enjoy the car and not worry about the payments and the interest.

That whole winter of 2002, my gut had been nagging me, telling me I needed to go home that summer. The feeling was really strong to a point where it was almost tangible. Somehow my heart was telling me all was not well with my mother. I am not sure whether it was telepathy, but there was a sudden urgency and need within me to go home. I started to plan on a summer trip to be reunited with my family. I know I had both parents living then, but my feelings were really strong where my mother was concerned. But like the bible teaches us to say, we should never say on such a day or month I am planning on this and that, but we should all learn to say "God willing on this day or that day I will" Though I was busy making plans for the summer, God's plan was not for me to ever see my mother alive again.

On April 2, 2002, I was working a second shift at the nursing home when one of my supervisors told me my husband wanted to see me in the break room. When I saw my husband with Elton, I did not need them to tell me my mother had passed away. I saw something in his face that told he had the worst news he had ever delivered to me. I just crumpled on the floor in despair. I was inconsolable. I could not believe I would never see my mother again eyeball to eyeball in this world. For the first time, I cursed the evil illnesses of the world for taking my mother without giving me the last chance to bid her farewell. I just needed one more time with my mother, Doris, just to hear her utter one more word to me, her fourth-born child, but I knew it was never going to be.

That milestone in my life was the least welcome but somehow expected; for some time, my gut had been telling me something and nudging me to act. I had been planning to bring her to the US for the following summer after my own visit; as such, she was working on renewing her passport. Even though my resources were extremely limited, I instinctively knew I needed to be with my mother, Doris.

It was the worst time for me to receive the news. My time was all tied up in school and work. My financial resources had been completely depleted when I brought over the girls. My emotions were being torn in all directions, but I had to keep moving as breaking down was a luxury I could not afford then. I had to think straight and make hard decisions as I mourned the passing of my mother.

I did not have any funds to prepare for the inevitable journey for my mother's funeral. The last time I had spoken to my mother, she had told me she was preparing her traveling documents to come and visit me and the children. I had encouraged her, knowing that I had to work day and night to make that a reality; I was willing to sacrifice that much for my mother. As things turned out, there were no two ways; I was not going to attend my own mother's funeral. I reached out to friends that night to lend me money, and none had any to spare. I reached out to my pastors, but the church regulations did not allow them to lend money to church members. I called my sister Diana, and we cried more than we talked on the phone. I ended up telling her that if I did not call her back, they had to meet me at Harare Airport on Friday morning. That was only Tuesday our eastern time, and they were already into Wednesday, April 3. I somehow had this strong conviction that by hook or by crook, I would be able to make the trip. I could feel it in my bones that I was going to attend my mother's funeral, and I believed it that night.

During the night, one of my very good friends, Eileen, initially reached out to airlines for my flight reservations. She was really helpful and strong, and for that, I thank her forever. They were asking for some credit card information. Since all my credit cards were maxed out, I could not use them. I told the airlines I would be paying cash. Several did not like this form of conducting business, but one airline was agreeable. During the conversation, it was as though a light bulb had suddenly been switched on in my head. I found myself inquiring about compassionate fares. They stated that as long as on my return flight I would be able to show them the death certificate to prove I had traveled for a funeral, they had no problem with that. I knew then that my mother wanted me to be home for her funeral to bid her my last farewell.

In the morning, I prayed for direction, for my steps to be directed to the right people. I also asked for wisdom and the right words to use with the people I was going to approach for assistance before I left home. I reported first at the library. My female supervisor took only look in my face and knew what had happened. For weeks, I had been telling them about my ailing mother's health. She drew me into her arms. I told my supervisors what had transpired during the night. Up to this day, I am not sure whether they completely know the role they played in making that flight possible. They asked me whether I had enough for my trip, and I told them I did, yet I was lying between my teeth. I did not have even a $100 for the trip then. They told me they would collect whatever they could and that if I returned around ten o'clock that morning, they would have something waiting for me.

When I left the library, I went to the college of education dean's office. I had never met him before. I introduced myself and told him the reason for my early morning visit. I told him that I needed to borrow some money to attend my mother's funeral. The only two questions he asked me were how much I needed and whether I had reserved my flight. When I responded positively that I had made my reservations, he assured me all the questions he was going to ask me were for his own curiosity. I went ahead and told him that I needed to borrow $2,000; he did not flinch. He advised his secretary to cut a check of the requested amount in my name, and sure enough, I got the loan there and then in my name.

As the secretary was working on his request, he commented that I was a strong woman of faith, and he was going to do everything possible in order for me to attend my mother's funeral. He commented that most times many people would come into his office with such devastating news and not knowing what they needed to do. The fact that I had a flight number, time, and airport where I would be flying from enabled him to realize I was prepared to move mountains to attend my mother's funeral. I cried so hard in his office while he told me about his own aging mother whose health was deteriorating as well. It was the first time I had met with the dean of my college under such difficult circumstances. I appreciated his understanding, and I knew he was the best man for the job.

Every step I took in order to attend my mother's funeral was as though it was a revelation in its own. It was as though I was being merely directed where to go and what to say by this intense power, to the right place, to the right people, and with the right words. I left the dean's office with a check in hand and went to my head of department to let them know I was leaving to attend my mother's funeral in Zimbabwe. That semester, I had been taking nine credit courses. The first two professors told me all I had to do was present them with an extra paper each to make up for lost time. Only one professor was not agreeable. I was going to miss three weeks of his eight-hour sessions. According to him, it was too much time to lose for any course; as such, he recommended that I retake the class that summer, which I did.

I also needed letters of recommendation from my head of department as this was soon after September 11, 2001, and stringent travel measures were being implemented on immigrants. I also wanted to make sure I would not meet with any hardships on reentry. I went to the foreign student office to have my I-20 endorsed and updated for easier reentry. Where I usually waited for twenty to thirty minutes, it appeared as though I merely sailed through. I was in and out of that office within ten minutes. I knew I was chasing time because my flight was from New Jersey, a five-hour drive away from University College. Why I did not think of a nearer city or airport, I will never know. Probably it was because I had first landed in NJ. I probably thought that was the only airport in the East Coast that I could fly from. Talk of being ignorant!

After I left the foreign students' office, I went back to the library. What my colleagues and supervisors had done forever touches my heart. I found my two supervisors waiting for me. They had collected $600 as a contribution toward my travel expenses. This was more than generosity itself. I could not believe their good hearts. On top of that, they told me my contract with them would be renewed for another year to be a graduate assistant. It was as if my mother, though she was gone, continued to look out for me from beyond.

I felt as though from wherever my mother was, she had done all she could to make my trip back home as easy as possible. Three weeks prior, I had traded my old car for a better one, which made the trip to New Jersey much easier. Had I not purchased that car when I did, I would have been forced to rent a car, which would have been a strain on my finances and made my dire straits even worse than they were. From all the happenings of the night before and early morning, I knew my mother wanted me to go home for her funeral. As such, I can never claim any hurdles, but the path was completely cleared and made easy for me.

My husband, the kids, and my friend Eileen drove me to the airport in New Jersey. I made the journey on the Continental Airlines to the United Kingdom overnight. I have to honestly confess to getting drunk that night. I took two glasses of wine to help me sleep and rest my mind. I slept all night long as the previous night I had not slept a wink. When I landed in London, I was reunited with my eldest daughter, Teresa, after more than two years. She was accompanied by my nephew Admire. Teresa told me that though I was mourning the passing of my mother, she was happy to see me, her own mother. We hugged, and we cried in each other's arms with my eldest daughter and eldest nephew. We managed to spend the day together before I boarded my connecting flight that night homeward bound. Teresa and Admire took me to a lot of places during the day, but I have no idea what we did there. After six in the evening, we made our way back to Gatwick Airport.

It was another overnight flight into Harare. However, in that flight, I did not need to drink myself to a stupor, as I shared my seat with a fellow Zimbabwe woman who was being deported back to the country. She was heartbroken. All night long, we poured our hearts out to each other. She lamented the loss of precious resources that her aunt's daughter had been generous enough to give her. I mourned the loss of my precious, beautiful, caring, giving, kind, long-suffering mother. I think that night I was mourning due to the shock of the news as I believe I was not yet in total touch with my real emotions then until I landed at Harare airport where I found Diana waiting for me.

The reality of my mother's death hit me when I saw my sister and other relatives waiting. As we made the last leg of my journey, I could not help but hope against hope that my mother would be walking around like she used to when we were kids. Diana, had been accompanied to the airport with some family friends and relatives, honestly, today I do not remember who exactly. We cried in each other's arms, and from then on, I knew it was for real my mother was no more. As we were driving home, I worried about my attire. I had a pair of long pants (trousers as I was used to calling them). In the States, it was still cold that time of the year, and at home (as home is where the heart is, and despite all these years, I still refer to Zimbabwe as home), it was towards the end of summer. Though people were getting used to the idea of women wearing pants, it would have been one of the unseen and unforgivable and most taboo things for me to arrive for my own mother's funeral wearing pants! I asked my sister to stop the car so I could change into a skirt, but she stubbornly refused. She asked me who cared about my attire when all I wanted was to grieve for my late mother.

As soon as we got home, people were crowding around me. People were surrounding me in sympathy. Some I did not even recall their faces. I could not believe that all those people had gathered around for my own mother's death. I had never imagined that event coming so soon, but who knows when that final day is destined for any of us. Like I had feared, some elderly women started yelling to my sisters to give me a cloth (*chitenge*, Zambia, or whatever it was called) to wrap around my bottom.

Yes, despite all the hardships of my life in the US, I had gained a bit of weight. My bottom was bigger than it had ever been. Life in the States was much better compared to the one I had led at home. Whether my bottom was covered or in pants was not a big deal for me. I could not stop crying until some older women, my relatives, had opened that coffin for me to see my mother's body! I realized that her body was lifeless! My mother's face appeared as though she was sleeping. She was peaceful. Her face was the face that had shown me love unconditionally all my life. I could not stop crying as I could never again have that kind of love from my mother. I could not believe that this woman who had given me life as well as my eight brothers and sisters was gone forever.

This peaceful and quiet face was my loving mother. She had taught us many things, and most important of all was love for one another. She taught us how to respect our elders, she taught us how to give, she taught us how to be good Christians, and she taught us the very essence of human life. One important thing she taught us was never to hold on to abusive marriages because we thought we would never make it alone. At one time, she told me the abused women era had ended with their generation, as most women were dependent on their husbands for their economic welfare. Women of our era were working women, and as such, according to my mother, we could make it alone economically.

Many times my mother had consoled me when my husband had inflicted injuries on me. One thing she never told me was to stay with him for the sake of the kids. All the time she had told me to leave him. My only regret is she would never live long enough to see me abandon the abusive and traumatic marriage while I forged a way of life without him. She would have been the most proud mother of all because I did not give in to the abusive man and let him break my spirit and soul. She would have been most proud of that particularly than all the achievements I ever accomplished. So I say it to her right here and right now, *Amai*[45]

Amai!

---

[45] *Amai* is the Zimbabwean Shona word for "mother." People of my generation never called our mothers as mom or mommy like our children, but we used the respectful word that exudes love and respect. Amai!

I made it *Amai*
I survived my husband's abuse
And I am making it alone
As a survivor of his multiple domestic abuse
But I am never alone *Amai*

I made it *Amai*
I survived all the traumas
Meted on me over and over
As he pummeled my body and soul
Which he never could have control *Amai*

Thank you *Amai*
For letting me know that
I did not have to die first
Before the domestic violence could stop
For in leaving him it stopped *Amai*

It was your voice *Amai*
That kept telling me
I could always do better;
Even when you were gone,
Spiritually you were with me *Amai*

I did not disappoint you *Amai*
I kept your voice within me
And you continued to inspire me
Even from far beyond
I could hear your gentle voice *Amai*

You can rest in peace *Amai*
As I always listened to you as a child
I heard your voice as an adult
I finally left with my life
And I can live as my own adult *Amai*

I had to do that because I needed to pay homage to Doris, my loving mother. My mother's funeral service was conducted in church. The church was the one she had been a member of since the day my father married her as a young woman still in her teens. The church she loved so much and would never miss a Sunday service willingly. She was a member of the League of Mercy, she was in the rattle playing band, and she was an active member in every sense of the word. She never missed any women's league meeting; she attended all church congresses even when her health was failing. My mother's body lied in state in that church while the service was conducted. This was a first for me to have my own relative's body lie in state in church, as no one from my family had ever had their bodies lie in state in the church at my home school before.

I do not know how many people were in the church, but I could tell the church could not hold everyone, as some mourners were listening from outside. The service was beautiful. Many people gave witness on her good deeds and some that I had never imagined my mother doing for anyone. It was a total revelation to see the woman who carried me for nine months being witnessed to as such a wonderful person. It made us all feel proud she was our mother. After the service, all her children were the pallbearers of our mother's coffin from church into the vehicle, which would transport her home as our last sign of love and respect to our loving mother, Doris.

The burial was conducted at home. All I know is we all wanted to prolong that burial for as long as possible just to hold on to her longer. My mother's grave is directly in front of our main house. As soon as one steps out the front door of our main house, directly ahead is our loving mother's grave. The words inscribed on her tombstone are from Romans 6:16: "As we surely died with Christ we will also live with Him."

A few nights after the burial, we sat together as family, and my father revealed that he had never thought it was his wife we had buried that day. He confessed that he knew he had married a good woman but had known very little of the good deeds she did in her community. I remember that revelation also touched my eldest brother in a special way. He told me that from then on, he was going to give his life to Christ. I thought it was an empty promise, but a few months after our mother's death, my brother rededicated his life to Christ. Even though my mother's passing might have been one milestone that was least expected and least welcomed, the changes it brought impacted our lives individually and differently.

We consoled each other yet were comforted in the knowledge that we still had one living parent. We were no longer children but all adults, yet somehow we all needed our mother with us, especially then as though we were still young children to be told everything was going to be all right. Somehow her peaceful spirit calmed us down as we tried to move on without her. We all knew we would always carry her within our hearts forever.

I stayed home for the next two weeks. I could not remain home as I had classes that I had not completed. I also knew the debts that were waiting needed to be taken care of. On the day I left, all the women from the village descended on me. They would not let me bring back any clothes with me. I gladly shared the clothes, shoes, towels, sweaters, and whatever little things I had taken home with me such as deodorant, lotion, lip gloss, and all they could take. All I requested was they gave me an outfit that I could wear on my return trip.

This time out, there was no farewell party. I was leaving with a heavy heart. I knew the grieving would be worse on my own without the support of my siblings. I also looked forward to leaving because I had left the States before my own girls could be fully acclimatized to living abroad, so as a mother, I was anxious for their well-being. The milestone of losing my mother was nothing comparable to anything. I had lost two elder brothers and a younger sister, yet the pain of their loss was nothing compared to the loss of my mother. I grieved for a long time. I remember before leaving home how my elder sister Melody and I would welcome mourners home, and I could hardly accept that the role had been passed on to our generation. We were now being considered the elders just like our parents had been before us. Life is really a cycle, and if one misses any of the stages in the cycle, that is a great a pity and somehow a loss.

Chapter Twenty-Seven

My world turned upside down

When I came back from my mother's funeral, I again flew back to the US through London. This time I met with my eldest daughter, Teresa, who was accompanied by my other nephew Michael Jr. We had a lot to share. I had food from home such as peanut butter and green vegetables, and we shared news about the funeral. We also had a lot of catching up to do such as how their lives were in a foreign country. This time, Teresa did not break down and cry like she had on my way home. They both noticed my lack of luggage and asked why. When I explained how everyone had descended on me like vultures after my clothes before leaving, they understood. Michael Jr. managed to buy some deodorant for me at the airport. I thought that was sweet and very considerate of him. We found somewhere cozy to sit down and eat. Time went by so fast; I did not want to leave. I was enjoying my daughter and nephew as I knew it would be long before I saw them again.

When my flight was called for boarding, I could hardly tear myself away from my daughter. She[46] looked so young and innocent, and I did not have the heart to bid her farewell. I wanted to have her to myself forever. If I could have my own way, I would have brought her across the pond with me. She was and is still my eldest daughter. As such, she holds a special place in my heart that no one else holds. If ever there

---

[46]   If I had been a hen, I could have spread my wings and smuggled her into the plane without anyone being any wiser. Unfortunately, I could not hide a grown woman in my bare arms.

was a time I regretted my move to the USA, it was then due to the fact that I missed my daughter all the time. I was missing her then before I even boarded my plane. It might sound silly, but the feeling of loss was with me. I wished I could change the situation, but I could not. I consoled myself in the knowledge that she had other members of my family though they were not me.

I could not delay my boarding any longer. I had to leave in a hurry so that I would not be left stranded in London. In my haste, I dropped my passport on boarding the plane, but I did not realize it. The airline crew did not ask me for my passport. Fortunately or unfortunately, I enjoyed my trip without realizing that my passport was missing. I watched some movies most of the time, but I do not remember what I watched. I only became aware of the passport's loss just before landing. I could not believe it. I had crossed the Atlantic without my passport. I knew I was in for trouble in capital letters with immigration after we landed. I tried to remember what I could have done with it, but it was useless.

As soon as my plane landed, I knew I was going to have a hard time convincing the immigration officials that I had lost my passport. Consequently, I was taken from one office to the next. I was being handed from one officer to the next. I lost count of how many officers I met that day. I was interrogated again and again until I was physically and emotionally drained. I did not feel harassed, but the time and questions involved were just exhausting, especially the repetitive nature. The same things were repeated over and over. Periodically, I was left alone to wonder what my fate was going to be. I honestly know I completed mountains of paperwork, and I was not sure if it was of any good at all.

I was kept there for more than three hours after landing, and my family was not aware of my problems and neither were they sure what to do. However, the reference letters and my updated I-20 as well as my student identity card were the only official documents that I kept producing. Finally, someone must have felt sorry for me and let me go through. At the end, I felt as though I had been through the wringer of a drier after those long gruesome hours of interrogation. I was physically and mentally exhausted. I just needed to put my head on a pillow and go to sleep for a very long time.

Despite my personal heartache, I was happy to see my three children, and yes, their father too. As I was so exhausted, I slept all the way home. It felt good to be back with my children; even in my sorrow,

I had missed them. Nonetheless, for a weary body and soul, there is never rest until they are dead. The following day, I was back at work and that same evening back in the classroom attending my course work. I barely had time to grieve for my mother. I needed all my strength and energies to fend for my children and cope with the demands of my schoolwork. I managed to cope with my two jobs because I desperately needed the money. I had two papers to complete before the end of April. I did not have time to dwell on my exhausted body. I had to keep going or I would never be able to pull myself back up. Little did I know that the exhaustion was a way of my own body telling me to pay attention?

It was soon after coming back from my mother's funeral that I started to notice changes in my own health. My thighs would frequently have blue-black bruises that I could not explain where they were coming from. This was not the first time I had these bruises. While in Zimbabwe, I had approached my doctor, but he had just dismissed my concern. This time I decided to pay a visit to my family doctor. He gave me a blood test, but I did not request for an HIV/AIDS test. After two weeks, I went back to the doctor to obtain the results of my tests. He told me the results were troubling to him, but as he was no blood specialist, he recommended that I went to the hospital to see a blood specialist.

Before going to the blood specialist, I requested for an HIV/AIDS test. All the time I was pursuing these tests, my husband kept telling me that I was making a mountain out of a molehill. My rational was I knew my own body; as such, I did not listen to his negative advice. I have always been well tuned to my own body and its functions, and my gut feeling told me something was terribly wrong. On top of the bruises, I was always drained of energy; I was not motivated to do anything. I had to literally drag my body. As a result, I could not afford not to pay attention to what my own body was telling me. I knew I was not wrong to follow my gut.

I followed my doctor's advice and went to the blood specialist. He drew blood samples and told me to go back for the results in two weeks. I could hardly wait for the two weeks to come to an end since every fiber of my body was telling me something was terribly wrong with me. I felt tired all the time. I had no appetite to eat anything at all. My complexion had darkened a lot on my face; I started to see blemishes that I never had. I was struggling to basically make it through the day-to-day demands. I had to push through the daily burdens because I did not want to let my children know there was something terribly wrong with me. I did not want them to worry unnecessarily.

Before the two weeks were up, we moved to a bigger apartment. It was a three-bedroom apartment. Elton no longer had to sleep in the living room. Life was almost coming to normal except I was really worried about my health. When the two weeks were up, Tiffany and Elton drove me to the hospital to attain the blood test results. Because I had not requested specifically for an HIV/AIDS test, again, the specialist told me the results were worrisome and would be willing to conduct further tests. I told him that I had requested for an HIV/AIDS test from my family doctor. He called the doctor while I waited outside. After a couple of minutes he, gave me the phone and told me the nurse from the other office needed to speak to me.

Up to this day, I cannot believe it really happened.[47] The nurse asked whether it was Avis, and when I answered in the affirmative, she wanted to know whether I had requested an HIV/AIDS test, and again, I answered in the positive. What I heard next was enough to knock me off my feet and hang up the phone. I did not hear anything else besides the words that the results had come back positive. I was sweating; I was hyperventilating. I could not breathe; I wished the very floor would open up and just ingest me alive. What I had dreaded the most had come to pass. My worst fear of contracting HIV/AIDS had come to be real! I could not believe I had been told over the phone that my HIV/AIDS test results had been positive.

There was no counseling involved. There was no preparation for me to be receiving such devastating and traumatic news. For the nurse, it might have been something casual and ordinary like revealing any other normal tests that were not life threatening. I do not believe up to this day that she knows what she did to me. In the process, she doubled the traumatic experience by her lack of professionalism. My privacy had been compromised. I knew that much at least. I wondered how she could have known it was not someone else pretending to be me. The nurse had not asked me anything else to reassure herself that she was speaking to me.

---

[47] I feel my confidentiality was compromised. Some life shattering as the results of an HIV test should never have to be revealed over the phone.

My privacy was my least worry, and then it was how I was going to cope and survive the epidemic of HIV/AIDS! Whereas I had talked about it in the third person, I was now the one infected. I just wanted there and then to curl up and die without subjecting myself to the humiliation of living with HIV/AIDS as it was and still is a highly stigmatized disease.

I barely remember anything else except that the specialist was addressing me. He was telling me that my viral load was so low that I did not need to start treatment immediately. He told me my T-cells were the cause for concern if only I could live more carefully. To me, he sounded like a broken record repeating meaningless things that I could not comprehend. I knew nothing about T-cells and viral loads. Very little was making sense to me. I remember asking him to call my doctor again so I could speak with him before I went home. My family doctor told me he was about to leave and go home, but I demanded to see him before he left. He assured me he would be waiting to speak with me that evening before he left his office. I could not bring myself to face Tiffany and Elton. I was crying all the way to the doctor's office. I am not sure I told them there and then what the problem was, but I am pretty sure they guessed because I could not stop crying, and I would not answer their questions. They were young adults by then, so I think they consoled me as best as they could under the circumstances.

When I got to my doctor's office, I only had one question for him. I wanted to know whether he had ever worked with HIV/AIDS-positive people before. He told me he had not seen anyone in more than five years. That's all I needed to hear. If he had been current, there was no way his nurse would have told me the results of my tests over the phone like she did without any counseling involved. I had not paid him for the tests, and before I left his office that evening, I vowed to myself to look for another doctor. There was no way I was going to pay him for services poorly rendered; as a result, his bill contributed to the messing up of my credit score. I did not care how much my credit score would be messed; I would not pay that doctor another dime. I almost felt like I had to sue him, but I knew I needed to invest my energies in getting me better. At that moment, I also knew that I needed a doctor whose knowledge was current than stagnant.

That evening, I told my husband the results of my blood tests, and he laughed in my face and told me he was HIV free! That was like the hardest slap I had ever received from him in my face all my life.

I could not believe the denial of a lying and cheating man who had used and abused me at will for more than half my lifetime. He was further traumatizing me by his degree of denial. I felt such disgust for him and myself for putting up with him for so long. For the first time, I knew what it really feels like to be let down by someone you love. I loved my husband as a young girl. He had fathered my five children. I continuously forgave his infidelities because he was my children's father. As my husband, I thought he was supposed to protect me. The only gratitude he ever showed me was to infect me with a traumatic and life-threatening disease. Immediately I knew I deserved better. I bet then I heard my mother's voice telling me to leave him.

I did not sleep that night. I went over everything, what I could have done right in order to avoid this calamity. I could have used protection. I could have denied him his conjugal rights. I could have fought him all the time he forced himself on me. I knew I lost that battle most times. In the end, I concluded short of having become a nun there was nothing that I had not done to protect and educate my husband on the dangers of his continual contaminating of me and situating my life in jeopardy. As such, all the wouldas, couldas, and shouldas were all troubled water under the bridge. I needed to focus on the problem at hand. That problem at hand for me was my HIV/AIDS diagnosis.

Since its discovery, HIV/AIDS to me was a death sentence especially in developing countries. Zimbabwe had been in denial of the disease for a long time. Uganda had been the first African country to declare it a national disaster. I knew the barest minimum about HIV/AIDS. Though I had taught my students about HIV/AIDS, I had barely scratched the surface. It was only then I acknowledged to myself that I knew pretty much next to nothing about HIV/AIDS. I knew it had no cure. I knew it was spread sexually. I knew it affected poorer nations at much higher rates than developed nations. I knew black women were fast becoming the face of HIV and AIDS, and I knew that I had been vulnerable and was now the face of HIV/AIDS.

My vulnerability was due to the fact my husband changed women as he changed clothes, and he never used any protection. HIV/AIDS was initially identified as an illness for the men who had sex with men. I thought as a heterosexual woman, I was safe. I had not buried my head in the sand and pretended it would not happen to me, but my husband had let me down countless times by his continued infidelities. I had tried to educate Jonathan about it; obviously, my message fell on deaf ears. Under the new circumstances, I vowed to find a way to survive the illness and somehow outlive him. Outliving Jonathan became my priority initially.

I knew after my diagnosis that it was high time for me to educate myself more about HIV/AIDS. I wanted to know more on how I could help myself. I knew stress was not conducive to good recovery, but my life was filled with stress all the time. I worked two jobs. I was a full-time graduate student, and I had children who were dependent on me for their livelihood. If that was not stressful enough, tell me more. I needed to know about the numbers and what they meant in detail. I wanted to know what the normal number of T-Cells was. I wanted to know what the viral load would have to be before I could be deemed to be HIV/AIDS victim. That was another word I had to deal with being defined as a *victim*. I did not see myself as a victim.

I started to question whether I was a victim or not. Hold on, I told myself not to waste my time and my energy trying to understand whether I was a victim or not. That was secondary to the issues at hand. I found that I needed time to equip myself on how to deal with the illness for me. Though I felt I could make Jonathan understand my diagnosis, I felt I needed to be strong for myself before I could even think of assisting my husband or dealing with his macho man attitude. At that time, I knew I was not in denial, but he was and that made me angry. Jonathan's denial made it worse because he was totally ignorant. A lot was going on in my mind that night; no wonder the night seemed endless.

Though the specialist had told me my viral load was still low and I did not require any treatment, I knew my immune system had been dismally compromised. Up to until then I had enjoyed a healthy body constitution.[48] I knew it was time I called on my inner strength to be able to rebuild my health again. I was faced with many decisions to make in order to recover fully. Initially, I was crying a lot and could not think clearly. I knew my crying clouded my thinking through the problem, as eluded to prior. I had to advise myself to be strong if I needed to get better. Who says we do not engage in personal counseling? I know I did.

---

[48] Up until then, I had only been in hospital for childbirth, routine checkups, and my illness just before my firstborn. As such, I knew I enjoyed good health for someone in her mid-forties.

I had to decide whether to tell my siblings or not; I had to decide whether to tell my children or not. I had to decide whether to kill Jonathan or let him go. Regarding Jonathan, my initial reaction was to simply strangle him in his sleep, but I knew I would never be able to conduct that one. I resolved there and then that I had to get rid of the poor representation of men that had wasted my precious and valued life and had put my life in jeopardy in pursuant of his personal and selfish sexual gratifications.

Primarily, I called my younger sister, Brenda, and we discussed the issue. I told her about testing positive to HIV/AIDS, and she was devastated. I also needed her advice on whether I should open up to my children, and she advised me against. Next, I called my elder brother, Dr. Larry. I told him about the blood results without revealing everything. He responded by telling me that my T-cells could be low due to cancer and not to let my mind run away with me. While he was telling me that, in my mind, I could picture cancer as a more fatal illness than HIV/ AIDS, which was fast becoming more like a chronic illness than cancer. I found myself telling him that all I needed was to draw strength from him and not have him sugarcoat our discussion.

After all, he was the medical doctor, and I needed his honest opinion. When he realized that I did not need any sugarcoated discussion from him, he told me to confront my husband so that whatever the results were, we could shoulder that together. I revealed to my brother that my husband was not taking any responsibility, and I could tell my brother was at a loss for words. I assured him that I was grateful that whatever my health concerns were, I was lucky to be in America where advances in health issues were tremendous. After that, my brother was supportive. He also advised me against telling my own children. I am not sure what he based that decision on. Afterward, until my numbers improved, my brother would call me regularly. For such moral support from him, I am really appreciative.

After my first two siblings, I decided to tell Diana. She is my youngest sister but has always seemed wiser and worldlier beyond her years. Diana told me that I needed my children's support as I did not have anyone else with me besides them in the US. She came to the same decision as me; as such, I would end up asking her for more advice than any of my other siblings. She has been my staunchest supporter and most times, we think alike in matters that matter the most.

I do not remember when I told my elder sister, Melody. I think it must have been two years later when I went home for some much-needed vacation time. I am very close to my elder sister. Ways and means of communication must have prevented me from seeking her advice then. Somehow her cell phone reception at home was not as good as the other siblings. I almost wished then she had been able to come with me to the US, and I could have leaned on her for strength. My elder sister has continuously been a pillar of strength for me.

Deliberately, Louis and Levin were not told early on. I felt they would hear from the other siblings. I feel I did them an injustice, as they never learnt from my siblings but from me eventually. With the passage of time, unfortunately, in the end, I had to tell them both personally. They would both respond differently. Louis took it like everyday news; there was no reaction I could make from him. He did not have any questions for me. I think he took everything in stride like a man.

Levin, I told years later, but he assured me I would be all right, as I happened to be living in one of the most developed nations in the world. I was happy with his observation, as that was exactly how I felt personally. I was lucky my diagnosis came when I was in the States. I had access to the best doctors and best medication. From that perspective, I had a fighting chance to beat the disease and lead a more meaningful life. I felt that way too.

The only person I regret never having told initially is my niece Doris. She only got to know about my illness through an overheated and passionate conversation on the phone that had to do with Jonathan, of all the people! I hope in her heart she finds it appropriate to forgive me, as I did not intentionally overlook her. Doris was like a sister to us growing up. She was brought to live with our mother, Doris, her grandmother, when she was barely a year old. As such, Doris grew up with us. She is like another sibling to us all. I know she felt a little slighted by my oversight, but she should be happy I took her advice. I never quit on my dreams, but I had good reasons for quitting on my marriage.

I had already arrived at my decision even before sharing with Diana and all my siblings. I knew I wanted to share with all my children desperately. After all, if my health had to deteriorate any further, my children would be the ones to care for me. Essentially, I needed them to be more careful and able to assist me when that should ever be necessary. In the meantime, I became highly paranoid. I did not want them to use the same bathroom with me. I did not want them braiding my hair as usual in case I had some scratches and they touched my blood. I began to Clorox everything excessively. I started to look at the risks I was exposing them to every day, and I was not happy with myself. Though I knew the risks for them getting infected were minimal, I did not want to bear that burden of inflicting the illness on my children. I started leaving literature everywhere in the house, hoping they would find it and read. I knew I was almost going over the edge with worry.

One week after my diagnosis, I assembled my children to break the traumatic news to them. Once the opening conversation began with my children, I realized I was the one who was counseling them, telling them HIV/AIDS was not a death sentence that it was in Zimbabwe, merely a chronic illness that I had to learn to live with as there were proper medications. I told them the virus had no option but to be compatible with me as it needed my body to survive. I wanted them to draw strength from my strength in as much as I needed their strength.

I know we cried a lot in each other's arms, and my children did not ask a lot of questions, but I knew they would give me strength that I was going to desperately need in order to live to be a grandmother. In that moment, we agreed not to tell Teresa anything because she was far away and all alone. Later, I would just blurt it out to her over the phone because of something I had learned. I decided not to tell my husband what I was doing from then on because he was still in denial anyway and a complete deterrent to my recovery. I needed support instead of criticism, and it seemed that criticism was all I ever got from him. The more he criticized me, the more resolute I became to divorcing him and paving the way to making divorce a reality. I concluded that I did not need his negative energy around me if I was going to regain my physical strength and complete my studies successfully.

In the meantime, I knew I needed a close by nonprofit or charity organization that would assist me on this new journey. I needed someone to recommend me infectious disease doctors to work with. Financially, I was struggling, and I knew HIV/AIDS medications needed finances, and the medications did not come cheap. Though I had insurance, my copayment alone was highly prohibitive and would take quite a chunk out of my meager wages as a graduate student. Initially, I was frozen due to the great task of trying to figure out my next step regarding my health.

I focused on my illness; I kept praying for a solution and hoping my mind would open to what I needed to do. I have always been a strong woman of faith. One Sunday in August, after church and having prayed about my predicament, I was watching TV when they showed an 800 number to call for HIV/AIDS-related resources. I was able to take down the 800 number. It was like a very direct response to my personal prayer request earlier that day in church.

The following Monday morning, I called the number and was given a local number in my local town to call and an address in case I needed to go in to the office. I simply called to confirm the address and was told to come in whenever I felt like. They were just down the road from where my first apartment had been, and I must have passed that building hundreds of times but had never paid attention. The irony of it is how our eyes are blind and how they never open to certain issues until our own personal needs force them open. Mine were rudely forced open to many things I had never known existed in my community.

I must have visited that address three times before I could gather enough courage to go in. In trying to gather courage, I reminded myself of another saying in my language, *"makunguwo zvaakatya akafa mangani."*[49] I would get cold feet before opening the door, and my heart would be pounding in my chest. I now know what they mean when they say cowards die many times before their actual deaths. I had several scenarios of what would happen once I entered those doors. I knew I would never come out of that building the person I was before I entered. I knew I was definitely determined to have every possible resource I could access before I could ever reveal my status and that the AIDS Project (TAP) of University College was only the beginning.

Eventually, I gathered enough courage to walk through The Aids Project (TAP) doors. It was sheer determination to live that gave me courage to walk through those doors. However, as soon as I entered the doors, whom should I see there but one of my best friends. She had told me previously that she had started a new job as a case manager, but I had not associated the TAP with her new position. I almost chickened out. I

---

[49]   Msakunguwo zvaakatya akafa mangani . . . though crows are fearful birds, don't they continue to die . . . As such, I would not gain anything by not confronting my fears. I had to face my fears in order to save my life.

almost walked backward and fled. However, the director was right there next to me, reassuring me that it was a safe environment.

After being asked whether they could help me, I told the director that I did not want my friend to be included in our initial discussion, as I did not want her to know. She was excluded from our initial discussion. They were all very professional and totally understanding about my need for privacy. We discussed my health concerns without me revealing that my blood tests with my family doctor had already come back positive for HIV/AIDS. They counseled me as to what HIV/AIDS diagnosis entailed. They kept stressing on my privacy and confidentiality. I think that must have given me a sense of security. By the time I left TAP, they had conducted an HIV/AIDS test on me. (In case you are wondering, yes, I pretended I knew nothing so that I could tap into their resources). I knew financially and emotionally I could not cope on my own. I desperately needed their strength and support. My children by themselves would not be sufficient. I was to report back in two weeks. I went home; I came back after the two weeks.

I found a male caseworker/counselor from the coalition of the county waiting for me. He made me feel at ease by discussing my personal life. We also talked about his life, and he revealed to me that he had adopted two black children. He made sure I was completely comfortable and at ease with him. He wanted to know what word we use for saying grandmother in my language. I told him *Ambuya*; from that day onward, he addressed me as *Ambuya*. He gently broke the positive results of my blood work to me. Though I had known for some time, in my heart of hearts, I was hoping the second opinion would bring better results.

I cried a lot. I cried for my life that was perpetually changed. I cried for all the lives I had witnessed their passing without fully sympathizing. I cried for friends and relatives who had lost their dear ones. I cried for relatives and friends who were dealing with the epidemic while the world stood aloof and condemned them for bringing it upon themselves. I cried for my children as they were going to live with a forever-changed mother. I cried for my life as I knew it before and felt it was never going to be the same. All the time I was crying, Denis had his hand on my back.

He comforted me gently and with understanding. We discussed the way forward. He told me I was going to live to be an old *Ambuya*. Little did I know that Denis was struggling with a terminal illness himself?

Only his passing away that October really destroyed me and made me realize how giving and unselfish he was. I appreciated Denis for putting his pain aside and feeling my pain. Denis, in his own loving and caring way, provided me with more positive counseling than anyone had ever provided me in the short time we worked together. I accepted the fact that I was positive and that I needed to get treatment as soon as possible (ASAP) as my numbers were deteriorating really fast. I know now that I drew my initial inner strength and positive attitude toward the disease from Denis than anyone else I ever worked with.

Though initially I had said I would not like my friend to know about my diagnosis, I later realized we need our friends in good and in bad times. My friend had proved that she could be supportive especially during the time before my children came. She had helped me out financially and even had given me rides for grocery shopping and proofread some of my school assignments. I recalled my grandmother's saying of friendship and saying—in life we need two types of friends: all-season friends and seasonal friends. This one I decided qualified to be an all-season friend. As such, we went for lunch, and she assured me she would never let anyone know about my diagnosis. She proved to be my strongest ally and strongest resource besides my family. She also warned me against revealing my condition to everyone. I had to be very careful about whom I revealed my condition to.

During my testing, I had let many people know of my health concerns. Some of them were inquiring about the results. Their curiosity made me wonder whether it was out of genuine concern or out of their personal phobias. In the end, I offhandedly brushed off their queries and moved on with my life. I think that was one of my wisest decisions as I had underestimated the stigma and discrimination still attached to the disease. All thanks to my friend and her insights.

My friend arranged for me to meet with an infectious disease doctor. That doctor was a walking disaster area for me. He wanted me to have all my children tested for HIV/AIDS, and I would not agree with his phobias. I was learning fast that even doctors perpetuated the stigma attached to this illness. My youngest son was by then more than fifteen years old. He was in good health. Children who had been born positive were still failing to thrive beyond the age of five, and he could not justify why he wanted me to subject my children to the trauma of HIV/AIDS testing. I deemed that relationship was not at all a compatible one. I told my caseworker. She recommended another infectious disease doctor to me. I met him once, and we quickly hit it off.

My next doctor was not judgmental. He treated me like a human being. He had worked with HIV/AIDS patients from Africa. That alone allayed my fears. I knew he had dealt with different strains of HIV/AIDS. He was not stagnant in his knowledge. I believe for doctors to be able to deal with diseases, they have to be involved with similar cases; the different challenges make them investigate and find what works and what does not. I was comfortable from then on to have him as my primary care provider.

His only intrusive questions were how I had become positive and whether I was sexually active. Once I told him, I knew I had never been unfaithful in my twenty something years of marriage; hence, my husband had to be the source. I told him since August, I had been on self-imposed abstention. He then wanted to have my husband tested for HIV/AIDS, as that is a federal requirement. After I related about the struggle we were having, he had no option but to have a medical team sent to our home.

One of the persons sent was my Denis. As to how Jonathan reacted when the counselors visited him in our home, I have no idea as he never shared that with me. However, when the results came back, Jonathan shared with me his positive status but blatantly let me know that he was not going to take any medication at all. From that point, I knew, whether I was a victim or not, I could not waste my energies on Jonathan. It was his life and ultimately his responsibility; he could deal with it as he deemed suitable. I was not going to be his mother and persuade him otherwise.

My husband's numbers were still good compared to mine. His argument was that I had to have been infected before he was; thus, in his eyes I was the philanderer and not him. Initially, I would tell him I was not trying to lay blame on him but trying to get us back on a healthy track and being a healthy couple again. Scientifically, it has been proven that women's numbers deteriorate faster because of our biological composition. Women are also susceptible to more infections because of our larger surface areas in our private parts compared to men. Making that argument with my husband would not make sense. For him, things were either black or white. Explaining things scientifically would take me forever. As such, I did not bother my pretty head by explaining what

I knew my husband would never get due to his ignorance and complete denial. In my heart, I knew he had just signed his final marching orders.

I am a mother. I am a woman. I am a nurturer. I am a wife. I am a daughter. I am an aunt. All the women in me cried out and wanted to nurture my husband through this diagnosis, but the dynamics of our relationship had drastically changed. I had lost all patience and respect for him as a man the day he told me he was HIV free. I no longer cared what he did with his life. I no longer had love for him, but I needed him to be healthy for his children and his relatives. I wanted him to be healthy for his mother and his siblings, for I knew they depended on him for a lot in their lives.

When my husband accused me of cheating on him that was the final straw. I could not afford to be told that when I knew the truth and that he knew the truth even more than I did. I could no longer put up with his emotional abuse. I was so over him and whatever emotions I had for him. Despite that, biology supports that women are more liable to faster compromised immunity due to our biological composition and the monthly flow of the blood. I knew presenting that line of argument would most definitely fall on deaf ears; as such, I saved my breath and energy. I prayed to my living God. I prayed for a much-needed intervention or separation that would be immediate, and I got my answer almost immediately.

I am happy, though, to say the Lord continued to watch over me especially then when I needed more strength than just my own. The Lord found it suitable then to send Jonathan and his negative energies as far away from me as possible while I had time to concentrate on my health. It was sometime in late July that my husband had been fired from his hotel resort audit job. He resorted back to what he knew and was applying for UN jobs anywhere in the world. By mid-October, he was offered a position as a logistics officer in the Democratic Republic of Kantu (DRK).

On the night of October 29, 2002, I took my first pills. When my husband saw me take my medication, he again laughed in my face. I thanked God that he was leaving on November 8 of the same year so that I could concentrate on getting myself on the path to recovery. I did not need him rubbing salt into my fresh wounds, telling me I was accepting the disease as though it was a present that I could choose to accept or turn down as I deemed necessary. I also knew I had no responsibility or role in our being positive besides being a faithful loyal wife, yet all the blame was being laid at my feet. I knew I deserved better in the man who was my husband, the father of my children, and my presumed lover and protector. His posting by the United Nations to DRK could not have come at a better time, and it was a true blessing in disguise especially for me! It came at the right time when it was needed the most.

Before starting on my medication, my doctor gave me the relevant literature so that I could understand the side effects. I read every little detail, and the side effects scared the daylights out of me. I shared my fears with my friend from TAP. She took it upon herself to educate me on the need for me to start on my medication, considering my numbers were really low. She told me I needed to boost my immune system instantaneously. She kept nagging me until I took my first pill, and I would forever be grateful to her for the personal and professional care and support she gave me. I had kept those pills at home for more than two weeks before I gathered courage to swallow the first dose, which I did with my friend's coaxing.

I was initially prescribed Trizivar, Sustiva, and an antibiotic Bactrim for ninety days. The Sustiva I took once a day at night and the Trizivar twice a day, mornings and evenings. However, the antibiotics made me sick to my stomach; each time I took them, I would spend the night in the bathroom, emptying my bowels. It came to a point whereby I felt sick even to think of taking those pills. I discussed these issues with my doctor, and he agreed to reduce the dosage. Though the dosage was reduced, it did not help; as such, I abandoned the medication (antibiotic) altogether. However, I continued to take my other medications religiously whenever I remembered. I say when remembered because those initial days were extremely trying and complicated for me and proved more challenging than I had imagined.

My memory was becoming bad. I would forget whether I had taken my pills or not, then I would empty the pills from the containers and start counting each single pill. It was time consuming. I would forget my schoolwork and days I had classes and what papers were due. That complicated my course work. I would forget projects that I was working on at the library where I was a library assistant. It was a trying time with colleagues, as they would not know how to deal with me. At times, I would even forget where I was, whether I was in Zimbabwe or somewhere else. However, I never shared the last memory concern with anyone in case I scared them into thinking that I was totally losing my mind. This really became a scary issue to me. That was the time I realized that my decision to let my children know about my illness was the wisest decision I had ever made in those complicated times.

I alerted my children Thelma and Elton regarding my deteriorating memory where the taking of my medication was concerned, and they both chipped in. They both responsibly took it upon themselves to ask me whether I had taken my pill every morning and every night. My friend from TAP came up with a better solution. She gave me a pillbox that I would fill up every Sunday morning; that way, I would know whenever I missed a dosage. That's what true friendship is all about even doing such a simple thing as providing a pillbox to a friend can make all the difference. Not taking my pills was never intentional because I honestly needed to be healthy. Those days I was really scared inwardly of my health deteriorating further and I drew strength from my friend, my children, my family, as well as the health community in University College. My pharmacist, my doctor, and the staff members of TAP were really wonderful as well as a couple of HIV/AIDS-positive friends whom the case manager introduced to me. These people became my lifeline, and I cared less for what Jonathan was up to in the DRK. He could be as careless with his life, as I cared nothing for him anymore.

Three months after starting treatment, I went for a follow up, and both my doctor and I were thrilled. My viral load had become undetectable, and my T-cells had tripled in numbers. Though there was drastic improvement, I was still a very sick woman and far from being considered healthy. I became good at swallowing those pills so much that it almost became second nature for me to pop those suckers every day and every night, whenever a dosage was needed. I knew their significance to my recovery.

I knew my health depended on my medication, so I had to do everything possible to help myself. Each time I swallowed those pills, I felt stronger. Up to this very day, I feel strongly that mentally, it appeared as though I was telling the virus I would kick it to the curb! Honestly, right now, I feel that the day Jonathan moved out, I knew I would kick the virus, as I dictated how it survived in my body as the virus needs a host to survive. I was convinced the virus had no choice but to get along with me. I would be no good to the virus if I was dead. Each dosage I took to boost my immunity felt like I was kicking Jonathan where it hurt him the most. That anger kept me going.

I never shared my diagnosis with some of the closest friends, the ones I had in the US. I remember sharing with my dearest friend Samantha on the phone, telling her that what we had dreaded most of our married lives became a reality for me. I told her I had every reason to divorce Jonathan; otherwise, I would never be able to look at myself in the mirror again. We had supported each other through thick and thin in our marriages while in Falcon Gold Mines, and I knew I had her support no matter what. Samantha told me to do what was best for me.

Since getting pregnant with my first child, I had learned not to hold my head up high; however, when I was diagnosed as positive, I resolved that I was going to relearn how to hold my head up high. I claimed it then, and it made me feel really good that I needed to get real and face my fears without bowing down to those fears. I promised myself that Jonathan had paid me the ultimate prize and dues for all the pain, the suffering, and the traumas I had endured in our troubled, faithless, respect less, and loveless marriage. I felt I could finally let him go as he had paid for my studies unbeknown to him. He had worked his butt day and night; as such, I felt vengeance was mine. I had learned to fight smarter without any violence and pain inflicted on his body, soul, or mind. Thus in the end I felt I was the winner and he was the loser.

By migrating to the US, if it was not for my husband, I would never have been able to settle without his much-needed assistance. Revenge does not necessarily have to come in the form of inflicting emotional or physical pain on the one who hurt you. For me, revenge was in outwitting and outsmarting Jonathan and making him pay for my studies abroad. Yes, I was responsible for bringing the man to the USA, and I know Jonathan more than paid for the fares and everything in that he helped me realize my long-standing academic dream. He worked day and night to make sure my tuition was paid. He worked twelve-hour shifts, and most times he held two jobs. I would never thank my husband because I felt he owed me that much. I feel as though in the end, I had the final laugh for all the dehumanization of my being. I did not need to sink to his level and have an affair so as to administer justice for myself. I learned to fight cuter and smarter.

After Jonathan left for DRK, I continued leading a healthy lifestyle. I ate well, I slept well, I lessened my stress level, and it was not difficult to rebuild my health. I continued to thank and bless the good Lord for the mercies He has continuously and unconditionally bestowed on me annually. Today it is 2012. I have been living positively with HIV/AIDS for more than nine years now. I have opened up to a few organizations as well as trusted individuals about my status. However, I strongly believe there has to be a reason for me getting the disease. I was the most unlikely candidate for HIV/AIDS. I was not a gay white male; I never for once cheated on my husband. I was highly educated. I should have known how to protect myself, but I did not. I was a mature woman by the time I became positive. I never traded sex for financial benefits, yet here I am, HIV/AIDS positive.

If I was to point my finger at anyone who deserved to be infected, I could not but point at myself. I learned sex and intimacy is part of nature. There was nothing wrong in my loving and expressing my love for my husband. All people who become infected do not deserve it, but all illnesses befall on all kinds of people no matter how careful they lead their lives. I genuinely believe my infection had to be for a good reason. I truly believe that reason is to be revealed to me one day soon. Reminiscing over this I recalled what my youngest sister had told me in early 1993, that there was no need to lay blame on those infected. My sister was wiser beyond her age.

All I have always believed is everything happens for a reason. I believe the reason for my being HIV/AIDS positive is to educate, to teach, to train, to advocate, and to lobby for HIV/AIDS on behalf of battered, abused, traumatized, and displaced women no matter where they are in the world. It could not have happened to a better person with the capabilities and passions to take possession of such a cause. I believe this part of my life's journey had to be because of the person I am.

Henceforth, I embark on another phase of my life with fear of neither stigma nor discrimination because I know better. HIV/AIDS is a disease just like any other disease. I have known good people who have been diagnosed with cancer although there was no fault or carelessness on their part. Some who have succumbed to lung cancer, yet they never touched a single cigarette in their lives. Those people have used the adversity to their own advantage to touch many people's lives. I know Sally Mugabe died of renal failure. A renal unit was built in Zimbabwe, and up to this present day, it benefits many people than it benefitted her. Those who discriminate the HIV/AIDS affected and infected are the ignorant ones. As such, it needs strong infected abused and traumatized women to take control, educate, advocate, lobby, and stand up for what feels right. I do not apologize for being HIV/AIDS positive as I did not infect myself nor have I intentionally infected anybody.

Chapter Twenty-Eight

Dreams fulfilled and holding up my head

Despite all the unwelcome drama of my illness in 2002, I continued to work and study diligently; in May of 2003, I acquired my master's degree in Educational Administration. I think during that time I was just operating mostly on sheer strength of character and personal determination. I could not afford to fail; Financially, I was really struggling. My graduate assistantship could barely pay for my rent. I had four children without meaningful jobs, and I was shouldering the burden of their auto insurances. Besides the bills and utilities, I was barely keeping my head above water. I counseled myself and convinced my inner persona that where there is a will, there is always a way. I had never let any problem, big or small, get the better of me. As such, the financial problem was another hurdle where I had to draw on all my internal energy reserves to survive. I therefore continued to have two jobs and studying full-time while single-handedly supporting my children.

Somewhere from the crevices of my mind, I recalled that my grandmother had, on one occasion, told me once you sink your nails into anything; never bring them out without getting what you had delved in there to grab. I had embarked on this Western journey to acquire my doctorate, to improve my children's lives, to rise above feeling sorry for myself; as such, nothing was going to stand on the way to my success. I had given up my career and my life as I knew it in Zimbabwe. I could not afford to go home with nothing to show for my sacrifice. I could not let my children's education fall by the wayside. My nails had been sunk into this venture; as such, I had to bring something up. That something was success for my children and me. Failure was never an option no matter what the cost was; therefore, success for me was guaranteed.

By the end of 2002, Jonathan was living and working in the DRK. This was a very welcome separation on my part. I did not need him reminding me on a daily basis that I was acknowledging my illness as though it was a fly or some parasite that I could simply squat off. I continued to struggle financially, but I kept taking my classes faithfully. I had more determination, which bordered on stubbornness for never to ask him for financial assistance. I needed to be able to stand on my own two feet without his pittance. I did not need to give him reason to remain in my life.

My husband's banking accounts were in the USA. His contract paid him in American currency. Occasionally, he would request me to send him some cash; and honestly, if I did not have any money for my own, I obediently sent Jonathan his money. I felt I had done enough to educate Jonathan that our children were our primary responsibility. Their welfare, their education, and their well-being were our top priority. If my husband did not see the responsibility the way I did, I was ready to relinquish any expectations I had of him being a responsible father and husband. I was tired of beating a dead horse down. The time I relinquished any expectations from him also enabled me to financially stand on my two feet. I did not have to use him as my financial crutch.

I say this with no bitterness but strength of a person who has conquered most fears by herself. Relinquishing him from any financial obligations meant letting go of the tight grip I had on our farce of a marriage. He was no longer of any use to me. At times in the throes of my anger, I simply looked at him as an egg donor. Relegating him to that position allowed me in between the words time to forge ahead and put things into their better perspectives. I needed to prove to myself that I could carve a life for myself as an individual without my husband to prop me up. I no longer needed him. He had long outlived his welcome and, in the process, abused my life. He was welcome to do his womanizing elsewhere and with someone else! I was no longer going to be available for any uses, abuses, and favors rendered willingly or unwillingly provided. *Kaput,* I was done.

In December 2004, I sat my youngest children, Elton and Thelma, down. Elton had turned eighteen that year in November, and Thelma had just turned nineteen in July of that year. I revealed to them that I was going to start divorce proceedings with their father. Elton and Thelma then revealed to me how they had been harboring secrets of their father's infidelity to me. It so happened that our eldest daughter, Teresa, and her husband, who were in London, where their father was now living and working, happened to visit him, intending to give him their old computer. They had found their father cohabiting with his longtime mistress, the mother of his two children, the ones he had tried to force on me, several times in our marriage. For months, my children hid that from me.

My daughter had been devastated, and she shared with her siblings. They agreed among themselves not to let me in to the secret. However, during that time I noticed a lot of rage in Elton, I could not attribute the rage to anything I knew. I was relieved that day when Elton told me that was why he was angry. His siblings had been forcing Elton to keep that secret away from me. Elton, during our troubled marriage, had many times so innocently let me into some of his father's infidelities and secrets. To expect my son to keep this away from me was beyond Elton's loving and caring nature, especially toward his mother. I could tell Elton was relieved by letting me into their secret; a load had been definitely lifted from my younger son's innocent shoulders.

Right from the time my husband had left in 2002, my intention was to divorce him due to my final humiliation and trauma. I had not shared my intentions with my children and now truly believe I did them a major disservice. If they had known my intentions, they would not have had to deal with the burden of hiding their father's infidelity from me. I would have saved my children a lot of heartache. I was happy to share with them so that together we could start the healing process. It took me several weeks before I could collect my divorce papers, and Elton was pestering me until I had those divorce papers in my hands. I am happy; I waited until they were all adults. I needed my children's support to go ahead with the divorce without feeling as though I was alienating them from their father. I knew I had their support, as they were free to share their feelings openly with me as adults.

Divorce proceedings started in the spring of 2005. By then, my youngest son, Elton, was eighteen years old. I convinced myself that no one would ever accuse me of taking my children away from their father, thereby preventing them from cultivating a healthy relationship with him or him with them. After all, I was the outsider, and they were the same blood as their father. I was supposedly removing myself from the family dynamics and equation; I was truly hopeful that Jonathan would step up and teach his children to be better human beings befitting of any society or citizenry. From the initial step of divorce proceedings right to the end, my husband never acknowledged receipt of any divorce papers. By then, he was living and working in London after leaving DRK and Egypt.

In May 2005, I went home to Zimbabwe, passing through London. The reason for going home was to conduct research for my dissertation as well as spend some time with my father whose health was deteriorating fast. Jonathan never made the slightest attempt to come and meet me as I made the transit. I spent a few days with Teresa and her husband, and my husband never bothered to call. I was unbelievably disappointed and hurt. Even though we no longer loved each other, we basically were still legally married. Furthermore, I was living with and caring for his children in the States.

Despite our relationship falling apart, I thought at least he would have been interested in his children's welfare. I also had presents for his family from our children, which he would not even help transport to Zimbabwe. As I could not afford the freight fee, I left everything with my daughter. Deep down my heart, however, I knew that was the end of our relationship. If he could not afford to come and meet me, he had honestly moved on. As such, I moved ahead with the divorce proceedings that I had initiated in March of that year without one tiny little bit of guilt after I came back in August of the same year.

My time home was extremely difficult. Besides our mother's memorial service, our father was ill, and it was the first time to see my siblings after my own diagnosis. Our father was spending his time with my brother Louis in Harare. From the airport, we went to Louis's home. Our father was happy to see me and so was I. I was thrilled that at least I could spend these last days home, and we had those final moments together unlike with my mother. Regarding our mother, I did not witness her final days; the trip home for the funeral was the most difficult journey I had ever undertaken. For some time I had been concerned whether I would make the trip on time, as my father had been ill for a considerable number of months.

The evening of my arrival was a happy one and the last I remember that we spent together one more time as a family. The whole evening, our father was munching on chocolates that Plaxedes, my niece, Levin's firstborn, fed him and I had brought for everyone. Other siblings were not thrilled with me because our father was diabetic. Our father simply told us that he had no reason to hold on to life, as all his children were adults. However, it was sad to hear that from him, but he forced us to face the reality of his age and deteriorating health. That year, our father had turned ninety-four. At times, he would jokingly tell us we needed to add three or four more years, as he was sure he was older than ninety-four. No matter how old our loved ones are, we want them around us forever. Though I knew in my heart the possibility of his death, the dawn of the reality was another issue. Inwardly, I am happy that I had that last chance with Norman, my father.

A week after arriving home, we all assembled home at Destination for our mother's memorial service. It had been three years after she had passed away in April 2002. Many relatives gathered there especially elder ones who had been responsible for raising us. I enjoyed my aunts from my mother's side of the family. I had fun with my uncles, my mother's brothers. We always had a wonderful relationship. I took plenty of pictures during that weekend. It was apparent during that time that our father's health was going downhill fast. Our father was present, but most of the time, he was in bed. His legs were swollen. He was not eating well. For someone who used to have an early morning bathe in the river, he could not even stand having a bath at home.

All relatives tried to talk our father into going to the hospital, but he would not hear of it. After the memorial service, our father left with our brother and his family. A week would pass by, and I would take him some of his presents from my children. He smiled as he wore the watch my son Elvin had bought for him, and as for the rest of the presents, he did not show much interest. That evening, we tried to persuade him to eat, but he seemed to have lost his appetite. When we broached the subject of him going to hospital again, he gave us a day to have him admitted. That was one thing we all knew growing up, that our father could be very stubborn. Even as his health was failing, he remained equally stubborn.

On the day he had suggested we took him to hospital, my sister Melody, my brothers Louis and Marshall, and I took him to St. Patrick Hospital. It was July 5, 2005, and by evening, our father was admitted. All day long, he had continued to take himself to the bathroom as well as wait his turn for observation by the doctors without complaining. We went home feeling better that he was going to have medical attention. That day was similarly difficult on us as a family. Louis had been having health issues, and it became apparent on that day that Louis was really wasted. I look at the pictures I captured on that day at the hospital and wonder how Louis was able to spend the day with us as we attended our father's health. In those pictures it is apparent he needed help himself.

One thing that is still striking is our father's determination and strength of character. He was strong that day, and I never saw my father fail to get off the bed even after he was admitted. I was hopeful that he would get better. The following day, I left my sister's place where I was staying with Brenda. I arrived at the hospital slightly ahead of the rest of the family. My father had his plate of mashed potatoes. Father fed himself, and inwardly I was happy.

After eating, he took some cash out of his pocket and handed it over to me. I simply pocketed the cash without counting. Later, he asked how much he had handed me. When I reported that I had not bothered to count, he laughed at me. That was the last time I heard my father's laugh. One comment he made was he could not understand that educated as I was, I could not count money. Starting from that day, I do not pocket any cash without counting.

Later when the rest of the family came, our father kept asking which home he would be going to after he was discharged. As my siblings had always alternated taking care of our father, Norman, we literally thought he meant that. He also kept asking whether anyone had seen his daughter by the name of Brenda. Later, when Brenda, who had been on a business trip, arrived, he asked her the same question. Just as we had responded, Brenda also responded that we would take him to whichever home he wanted to go. We bid him farewell for the night. We all left hopeful. No one even wondered what bothered him about which home he would go. To me it would be a couple of days later that it would hit me.

Visiting time on Saturday, July 7, 2005, we arrived at the hospital. Something had definitely changed. Our father was struggling to breathe. He was gasping. His breath was coming as though he had some phlegm down his throat. We all wanted to do something to ease that breathing, but we all knew we could do nothing. One of our mother's nieces together with my Aunt Eileen's daughter fed him some yoghurt, and luckily, he ate it all. Personally, I was afraid he would choke on it. I could not look at him without the need to hold him to ease the pain.

At some point during that hour, I wanted to take a picture, but I did not want to have an image of my father in his dying moments. I had been taking pictures during that visit, but for that last one, I decided not to have an image. At the end of the visiting hour, we all wanted to stay with him, but the nurses would not let us. We left to go buy some cough mixture at a pharmacy. From there, we were literally killing time before the next visiting hour around 4:00 p.m. that day. During the interim, we managed to call our sister Diana. We told her of the inevitable. Diana reminded me of my dream that I had shared with her on my way home.

As I passed through London on my way home, I shared one of my most disturbing dreams with Diana. I was literally crying, telling her I was afraid my trip home was the end of our father's life. Sometime in March 2005, I had a disconcerting dream or vision. In the dream, I saw all my siblings, my niece Doris, and me crying by our father's deathbed. Somehow in the dream, I could not locate my youngest brother, Levin, and my eldest brother, Dr. Larry, with us in the hospital.

As the dream continued, I heard the nurse telling us that our father had passed away. In the dream, one of my sisters had commented that we had been there barely two hours earlier and asked why our father could not have waited for us to come back. The nurse had shown us our father's lifeless face as we cried by his bedside. We looked at him helplessly, and for the first time, an overwhelming feeling of being parentless overcame us all. We would not leave him. The sadness of that dream never left until the day my father passed away.

As we arrived for the evening visit, I had the feeling of déjà vu. Everything appeared as a rewind of the dream in March. Our two brothers who were absent in the dream, Levin and Dr. Larry, were not there. Levin was on a business trip to China, and our eldest brother was still in the west of Zimbabwe, where he had his own practice. After the nurse had shown us our father's face one more time, she took us into a private room. She had a hard time drawing us away from our father's side, just like in the dream. The only thing I prayed for that day was the ability to block away these disquieting dreams from me. The dreams were not welcome, and they were not fun. Who wants to know and foretell about their husband's affairs as well as the passing away of loved ones through vivid dreams? Call it being clairvoyant or whatever; for me it was becoming scary.

We gathered for our last parent's funeral in Howard at Destination, our rural home. Our hearts all went out to Diana, who could not make it. As for Levin, he managed to arrive on time. Our brother Dr. Larry arrived before the night was out on the day our father passed away. My father's children as well as his grandchildren all contributed toward his funeral. At my father's funeral, we realized he was survived by eleven living children (three had died before him), sixty-nine grandchildren, five great-grandchildren, and one great great-grandchild. That was Norman, the only son of Anna. Though he was late, his legacy lived on.

The funeral that our father received was another revelation of the influence he had in his community. It was nothing that the little abandoned boy brought up by his blind grandmother could have imagined for himself. It was a funeral fit for a king. Our beloved father died on July 7, 2007, and he was buried on July 9, 2007. Our caring and younger brother Louis was there grieving with us. Exactly two years later, on the same date, we lost him too. We always knew that Louis was close to our parents, but not so close that he chose his final day to be the same as our father's.

I stayed home until early August. As soon as the funeral was over, I conducted my research. I rode on buses to different schools in the town where my sister lived. Economically, it was a difficult time in Lucas. There was a shortage of almost everything—fuel, food, electricity. I was not even sure I could survive the hard times, but I did. My father's funeral had been the most difficult as we were ferrying his body home; we were forced to open his coffin to prove that we were actually going for a funeral, so that we could buy gas. I had never been subjected to such humiliating circumstances ever in Zimbabwe. That alone showed me the difficult times my relatives and friends were living under socially, politically, and economically.

Once again en-route, I passed through London. I spent three days with my younger sister Diana before she could go home for our father's memorial service. Diana was difficult to console. When I arrived from home, we mourned our father's passing in each other's arms. I had some home movies. We watched some, but it was still extremely difficult to accept that Norman was gone. However, I was happy to spend time with Diana. We managed to go to a few markets where she bought outfits for the three of them—Melody, Brenda, and herself—to wear on our father's memorial service day.

As soon as Diana left, my daughter and her husband, Marvelous, collected me. I spent a week with them before I made the final leg of my trip to the USA in mid-August. By then, Teresa was learning how to drive. She went for several driving lessons, and I had the privilege of watching her drive. On the evenings that she would be working late, her husband prepared meals for me. I was impressed by his domestication. I got to know my son-in-law as this was the only time I would spend with them after they had married. I found a side of him that was quiet but loving and caring. I was grateful that my daughter had found herself a good husband. After about nine days with them, it was time for me to go back to the States. I arrived home when the rest of the family were patiently waiting for their mother.

That period of my life was extremely painful. I no longer had my loving father in my life. I was in the process of divorcing the man whom I had loved but had abused and traumatized me most of my life. Both were issues that affected me, but I refused to focus on the sadness of it all. I looked forward to working on my dissertation and the ultimate goal of my doctorate. As for my divorce, I knew that spelt freedom and was equally important. I could not imagine that it had been almost twenty-eight years since I had married my husband. For more than half that time, I had made up my mind regarding divorce but somehow had continued to move the goalpost and hold on. However, this time, it felt right to be working on my divorce even though it was more than a decade too late.

My father had always encouraged me not to leave my husband. As such, the loss of my father enabled me to divorce my husband without any sense of guilt. If my father had lived, I am not sure I would have been courageous enough to hurt my father. Many times, my father had always told me that marriage had to be worked at. I had always told him that I was giving my marriage all my strength. I did not want to disappoint my father, so sometimes I followed his advice. By the time, I was in the States; I had grown tired of working on that sham of a marriage alone. I felt I could not afford any more energy to invest in it.

I am encouraged my father that never knew of neither my divorce nor of my terminal illness.

The divorce too would soon be over. What remained were only the hurtful memories and scars inflicted on my being and my mind. In my heart, I was also consumed by anger every single day and night. Initially, I was angry with all men who lied, cheated, and battered and, as a result, traumatized their wives. As time passed, I learned to differentiate other men's faults from my husband's misdemeanors. That gave me the energy to pursue that divorce while I was struggling with my dissertation. I think the main reason I never gave up on my studies was sheer determination to show my husband that I was stronger than he thought. He never responded to any correspondence I sent him as I pursued divorce. I felt it was very disrespectful and a nonchalant disregard of me as a person. Consequently, I focused on the reason why I needed the divorce and not his attitude.

My divorce hearing was set for January 3, 2006. The presiding judge in Bellum District Court in Pennsylvania pronounced the sweetest words I had waited for almost half my lifetime. The bonds of marriage that had bound me to my husband, my abuser, the father of my five children, for close two three decades, were finally dissolved. I was finally a free woman. I was free to go and come as I liked. I would not be answerable for my actions or lack of to him anymore. It felt excellent to be a single woman again, only I had a few regrets.

Though my children had requested to accompany me to the divorce hearings, I told them I had entered into the marriage alone; as such, I was going to leave the marriage by myself. The presiding judge could not believe that a marriage that had lasted as long as ours could simply be wiped off the slate just like that. He instructed his clerk of court during the procedure that he wanted to talk with me off the record. He quizzed me as to why my husband had not made an effort to respond. I could not answer that, as I could not fathom my husband's reasoning then. He even asked if I had made any efforts to serve him the papers in person, and I responded that I had and, in the process, accrued bills for long distance calls to him. Jonathan's simple advice to me had been to do what I deemed necessary. As such, to me, divorce at that point and time was beyond what I deemed necessary it was reasonable. I knew then it was the ultimate corridor to my happiness and personal redemption in the life I had led with my husband.

It appeared as though I walked into that courtroom a married woman, and ten minutes later, I walked out a free single woman ready to mingle; only I was not clean enough to mingle. Though I broke down after the hearing, it was not from sadness, but from joy, freedom, and wonderment of why I had kept myself in that bondage for so long. Finally, I was able to acknowledge to myself that Jonathan had never loved me. All I could do from then on was lift my head up and keep on walking. I kept on walking like the proud African woman that I am. I never apologize for anything; immediately, I knew stooping my head was not for me, as I never did anyone any wrong. I had to hold my head up high and look the world right into its eyes with no sign of shame but probably a couple of personal regrets

My first regret was to ask myself why I had not found a better father for my children. The second was why I had wasted the prime time of my life in a loveless marriage. The next regret was why I had let Jonathan beat me down for so long and lastly questioned why I had let him leave me feeling so dirty and unclean. As to the last regret, I felt dirty and unclean because of the illness that would be mine for the rest of my natural life. I felt I would never ever be a clean woman ever again, and Jonathan had caused that and ensured that I would never again be free to live my life the way I wanted and love as I wanted to love and be loved.

That was the worst emotion ever, the feeling of being dirty, contaminated, and not free to love again. I felt there was no way in hell I was ever going to forgive him. At that time, tangible anger and real hatred festered in my heart and my soul. For a long time, even after the divorce, the anger would obscure my thinking. It would be years down the road that I learned to forgive him because forgiving him, I surmised, was the only way I could move forward. I could not let Jonathan control my life forever as well as give him power over me for good. Only after forgiving Jonathan was I able to move forward with my life.

When I arrived home that day after my divorce hearing, I held my head up high for the first time. I did that after what felt like eternity of facades that were stressful to my being. I remember two friends brought me cards to celebrate my newfound freedom. I was thrilled no end that divorce was something that I could finally celebrate. I even had a glass of red wine to usher in the new beginnings. I thought I would grieve over the loss of a partner, but I did not grieve like that. I only felt happy privately. I was only sad because I felt forever contaminated. I felt as though I was spoiled goods, and no man would ever want me or love me. Undeniably, there was anger that festered for some time after the divorce before I could let it go. I wished he had been man enough to protect me as I had requested him many times. I wished at least he had the guts to apologize to me like a man; I never had that apology up to this day.

I had never been a vengeful woman, and I could never stop wondering why he behaved the way he did. Many times, I had warned my husband that his womanizing would be our downfall. I had pleaded with him to protect me, but he had continuously put stones in his ears. I had grown a lot from the young woman whom he had married until the time I started pestering him to protect me. I wish back then we had the female condom; maybe my safety would have been ensured. I feel if the female condom had been available, I would have been in control of my sexuality. The female condom would only be marketed in Zimbabwe as late as 1997. To make matters worse, the condom was very expensive even for me as a working person. Maybe if it had been readily available and affordable, then I would have protected myself. My husband had continuously told me that he would never use a condom and was immune to HIV/AIDS.

As a result, I think his lack of admitting and apologizing to me was born from his male stubbornness and chauvinism as well as ignorance that he was not immune to the disease. Let me tell you that disease does not discriminate at all. HIV/AIDS does not know race, religion, gender, sexual orientation, or sexual preferences. After my diagnosis, I felt I would never lie down and be intimate with him. I realized that especially after he accused me of cheating on him, yet he knew better than that. If I had lain down again with him, I would never have forgiven myself nor would have ever looked myself in the eye.

I decided self-pity would not reward me. I therefore realized I was in a race of the time of my life. Just as time and tide wait for no man, I continued with my studies diligently, illness or no illness, divorce or no divorce. I had to complete my studies. I defended my thesis in March of 2006, and in May of the same year, I celebrated my finest hour of success. For six years, I had worked diligently and tirelessly to obtain my third degree. I studied, I researched, I applied all that I knew into making it, hoping to grasp that illusive rainbow at the end of the rainy day, and yes, I did it. I did not let divorce obstruct me, I did not illness define me, I did not finances hinder me. I pursued what I had set out to do.

On that graduation day were the five people who supported me the most, my biggest fans, the ones who loved me unconditionally, and these were my five children. Luckily, Teresa had been able to travel for the occasion. For the first time in seven years, we were all together as a whole unit, mother and children. The coincidence is that it also happened to be mother's day weekend. What better mother's day present would I have wished for than my children and me together? They stood by me as I got my last and final degree. My ultimate success is as a mother, and what better way to usher in the new era than with my biggest fans?

My siblings, each in their own way, let me know that they were with me in spirit. My brother Louis called me that day, and he was the first person to ever address me as doctor. When my brother addressed me as such, I knew I had made it. I cried uncontrollably and with no shame in front of my advisors. By then, I knew my brother's health had deteriorated considerably. I lost my brother a year later in July of 2007. I could not afford to attend his funeral. My children were with me through the difficult time of the loss of my younger brother. I had not realized until then how much of a strong bond I had with the human beings that I had created.

On graduation day, when my name was finally called to go and receive my diploma, I could not believe that I, Avis, daughter of Norman and Doris, had actually done it. I so much wished that my parents were there with me. In my heart, I knew they were watching and smiling from above and were celebrating with me. I knew my other two siblings joined them in the celebration. I cried from the joy and unbelief that I had finally accomplished my dream. I did not need to prove to anyone but to myself that anyone can always challenge oneself to rise above personal circumstances. My dream had suddenly been turned into reality. It had been a long arduous and dramatic journey. The end was sweeter than everything I had ever tasted or achieved in my entire life.

Chapter Twenty-Nine

The anatomy of an abuser

Whereas I first took to the writing of this memoir to fill the void as I waited for the right job to come along, I now find it has also been the much-needed source of personal therapy. I had never opened up to the outside world about the physical abuses, emotional turmoil, and all the traumas endured yearly at the hands of the man I loved. Consequently, in trying to understand and heal, I have not only reexamined those times, but revisiting has also not been as painful as in the beginning. I even look at the scars my abuser inflicted on my body with all the electric cords that he used to beat me up with, and most of the scars have almost faded into nothingness. Outwardly, I seem to have recovered well, but sometimes I know I struggle emotionally. I know those emotional scars too will fade away as I have found my true passion that nurtures me with caring, understanding, giving, and thoughtfulness. I let myself go in my writing, and all the pain fades away. Furthermore, I have my children and now my two grandchildren, my deepest sources of strength.

Emotionally, Jonathan had affair after affair, and it took away my self-confidence as a woman but boosted my ego as a mother and a teacher. I doubted my sexuality and sensuality to please a man in any shape or form. At one point, I was even almost willing to consider what other women recommended about cheating on him. I never did because I knew people, or better still, my children would never know who the better parent was if I had sunk to his level. I am happy I never cheated on Jonathan, which is a part of my legacy to my sons, my daughters, and all my nephews and nieces.

I now know I remained a resolute confident African mother, as I was, confident in my capabilities even though Jonathan tried to reduce me to a level below my standard. I say below my standard because neither he nor all the women he had all his philandering with were better people than I was. I am happy I stood by my principles and values to maintain my virtue as a mother and a woman because now I can honestly hold my head up high and laugh in his face. His ambition to beat my spirit and soul down in order to break me completely failed. I am stronger mentally, spiritually, and emotionally. I feel I am a better person than Jonathan was or is now. I am going on with my life without wishing him back into my life as he always pleads with me whenever he has a chance to speak with me. I joyously tell him all the time that I will only get back with him only when pigs fly! I hope and pray pigs will never fly.

As for my diagnosis with HIV/AIDS, I am forever grateful to him. It has taught me one thing: to live in the moment and to love my life as it is. I no longer look back and curse Jonathan for inflicting this disease on me. Instead, I thank him and the related circumstances that caused the dissolution of our marriage; I have been blessed more than I ever thought possible. Initially, I thought no one would ever love me. I was wrong! I have been surrounded by a community of people who love me for me, people who have accepted me for the person that I am now. Had it not been for my positive status, I would never have met these wonderful, loving, caring, and supportive people.

In the meantime, something else unexpected happened. I have found love. Because of him, I now know what it feels like to be loved like a baby and a woman. I know what it feels to be loved unconditionally. I know what it is like to be someone's confidante; I thank Jonathan every day because I would have passed through this life without knowing what it feels like to have your man worship the very ground you walk on. I would never have known what it feels like to have a man worship my body as though I am a goddess. Love would have passed me by, but I am now living the time of my life free to love the man who supports me as a man should and ought to and not batter me.

I had never been to a movie house with Jonathan, neither had Jonathan ever sent me a bouquet of flowers, but I loved him with all his failings and all his shortcomings. Romance was never in his DNA, so I put up with the lack of not minding as long as he was in my life. Since meeting other men, I know it is an everyday occurrence, so what can a woman wish? In my marriage, it was all about him, and I did all I could to please him without any reciprocation of my love and affection but mounted abuses and infidelities in return.

At some point in our marriage, I was even reduced to unknowingly entertain his mistresses. I am happy now that in this relationship with me, it is all about Avis. Whether I get a new man or not, I need to be pampered! I need a man who attends to my every whim and need. I need a man who reads my mind before I can even tell him what I want. I want eventually to say I have been bestowed with years of loving even within the short time after we have been together. Consequently, I thank him, as the philandering representation of the male species that he was. If I failed to thank him that would be beyond my intelligence and beyond my own sane reasoning.

As such, I found myself, for the first time, composing and dedicating a poem to Jonathan, my abuser!

My Abuser's ways

All my life I wished for a man who loved me,
Life and love would have passed me,
I would never have known what it is like to be lover and
be loved,
Now I am no longer an observer, I am also a lover and
loved,

I had for the life of me wished for a man who could hold
my hands,
To tell me everything would be all right as long as we
clung together,
I never heard it from him because he had to hold many
hands,
As such, too many women's hands to be able to clung
together.

I longed for simple things such as to sit on the porch,
Him and I to watch the orange sunset,
However, I never had it with him,
Because he was, too busy pursuing other women as the
sunset.

I longed for a man, who wished to listen to simple music
with me,
And I never had that too, and you know why?
Because he was busy giving that to other women but me,
Busy in the clubs, And for me the club was out of bounds
and why?

I longed for a man, who would love my natural scents,
Moreover, to tell me it was sexy and sensual,
However, I never had that too, because he was busy as
usual,
With perfumes and baths taking away other women's
scents.

I am all-natural woman, who appreciates,
The love and desire of a man,
The man who appreciates an all-natural woman?
The one that I am, am I a crazy woman?

No I do not think that I am crazy,
Because I have found a man who desires me naturally,
The one who loves me but is not lazy,
To show me quality love unconditionally!

I have found a man, who challenges me intellectually,
Whereas I never sat down to discuss anything intellectually,
Because my ex never had time as he was too busy actually,
He was busy chasing flowers of the world that kept him away intellectually.

I had almost forgotten that I too in fact,
Am among the beautiful flowers, as a fact
And such count as a beautiful flower, that's a fact
He continuously ignored me too. Oh what an effect

I am challenged intellectually on a daily basis,
By the man in my life as my love oasis,
I can feel myself thriving,
No wonder I am surviving.

I have been a lifelong educator and learner,
How could he fail to see that learner?
That he had to challenge me intellectually,
And not beat me physically,
Something I cannot fathom up to this day, intellectually.

I drank from a swift flowing river,
All my life as a teacher, a learner, and a giver,
As I was never mentally a stagnant river,
Stagnant waters of the river cause malignant fever.

I could not continue to drink the stale waters of the
stagnant pond,
Of Jonathan's mind that believed in pounding a woman's
body,
Torturing her mind, and soul to possess her body,
To break her forgiving soul, and vibrant spirit so as to
own her body.

I am now drinking the fresh waters of the swift flowing
mind,
Peaceful man with all the nectar of a human mind,
And sweetness that comes with him and I bear in mind,
I am now in a peaceful world that cares and minds.

I say thank you, my ex, for mistreating me,
Otherwise, I would never have tasted these treats,
The softness and tender love of a real man for me,
The man who likes a real woman, like a man he treats.

I challenge my man intellectually,
And he promises me the same perpetually,
That is so refreshing,
To be drinking these waters refreshing.

I am happy my body longs for that soft touch,
The one my body expects of it night and day,
Than cringe from my man's touch,
For my body and soul are his night and day.

In my heart, I sincerely thank Jonathan for the opportunity after I divorced him. I want to include a part of one of his many letters, he now continuously sends via email. In a segment of such e-mail that I will share with, I thought I finally had my apology. I wanted to share with my reader so they can assess for themselves. This was copied verbatim and originated from an e-mail sent on April 16, 2010.

> *Avis,*
>
> *I now foresee a future in me that I cannot tell you now, but I am to tell about this anyway. I have lived a difficult life since we separated. I regret this having been so. I thought I was to be better in London and the relationship I was in, not knowing that this was a wrong move made. I messed up my life and can confess this to you and only you, so that you are aware of what I have gone through. I am glad the God almighty is answering my prayers, and with the advice from my Pastors at Church whom I told all about our life together back home in Zimbabwe. I showed them our photos with all the kids during the time. They have also heard about it from their daughter who is Teresa's neighbor there in London. I do not feel because of what I am soon to achieve. I have my children to keep me shine, and you are their mother, at least I do not wish you anything bad. I really miss the children so much but I earnestly commend you for the relationship with them to me, because you did not prevent them from me. They love me period.*
> *(Jonathan)*

As I read the e-mail that was meant for my eyes only, I felt hurt all over again. It appeared as though my spirit that had found peace was being robbed of the tranquility all over again. The document was full of self-pity from a man who had thought he had found a better relationship after me. The man did not even dare respond to my divorce proceedings; now he was regretting not having contested the divorce. I failed to comprehend his grounds for contesting. He had battered me, abused me, traumatized me, and finally abandoned me. He only thought of the hurt to me when his relationship was not what he expected.

He prophesied to have found religion, and not even once did he apologize. Did he even look deep down into his soul and thought I could honestly forgive him? I had loved him as a young woman of twenty-one years old. I continued to hope and pray for the next twenty-something years for a better husband. In all those years, he had fathered four children out of wedlock. He had beaten me multiple times, but in his newfound religion, he failed to give me one single word of apology.

I cannot deny he acknowledged his bad behavior during our years of marriage, but how could he not find it within his newly found faith and in his spirit to say he was sorry. I realized then that he did not know what he did not recognize. Once more, I had to be the better person and not respond to him in hurtful ways. All I could see was the anatomy of an abuser, always self-absorbed, selfish, egotistic, and almost narcissistic. He commended me on the beauty of our children and my role in their upbringing. I wish I could be able to say the same about him and his role as a father. If the children did not have a mother who taught them right from wrong, they would not have known how to do it.

I am no longer yours, Jonathan, to use and abuse. I have forgiven you, but I will never forget. I have put everything down in its proper perspective and healed myself. The uses, the abuses, the traumas, and the healing process, the beatings and the infidelities that were mine to bear for a long time are no longer as hurtful but a badge of honor that I wear proudly because I survived. These will remain forever etched on my mind, for that will be the legacy our children and our grandchildren will inherit. I sincerely wish I had a better story to tell them, but unfortunately, this was the story of my married life.

Chapter Thirty

Who am I?

After my third university graduation, I earned myself the title of doctor of philosophy (PhD). That was the ultimate title I had been working hard to achieve all my life. I was done with being Mrs. Jonathan, always someone's appendage. Before marriage, I was Avis, my father's daughter, and, after marriage, had given up my family name for someone else's. It does not make sense now, but then it was so prestigious to be someone else's wife and carry their name. I had five children with Jonathan; as such, after divorce, I felt I had lived more than half my life with his name, and I felt comfortable with the name Noel. I decided to remain with his last name for the sake of my children. Instead of a simple name, I had earned myself a deserving title that I was and am proud of being known by. That title is "doctor."

That was then early 2006, and it is now 2011. I came to the States at the age of forty-five, and I worked so hard to acquire the right educational credentials for me to become a doctor in education. I took on menial jobs so that I could afford my tuition in order not to jeopardize my immigration status with the United States Citizen and Immigration Services (USCIS). I worked below my profession in order to be able to put food on the table so that I would not starve my children. I never let down my focus on my educational goals because I believed so much in the turnaround of my circumstances after the completion of my academic studies.

Now that I have reached the end of my journey, it appears the economic climate is as cold as the weather is in fall in this northern hemisphere. Everything freezes with the coming of winter, and where my employment is concerned, I feel exactly like everything has been symbolically frozen like that. I try to reach out to one prospective employer after another, but all I get are these impersonal letters indicating that they have already hired someone who is better experienced for the job than I am. How am I going to get experienced and claim my own position into this field when I am not even afforded the opportunity to prove myself?

I sacrificed all I had in order to come and study and improve myself so that I could become highly viable. At one time, I believed this was the land of opportunity where dreams would become reality, where opportunity shines on everyone who works hard. How come my dreams seem to be obscuring into nothingness at every corner and every turn. Some of you might question why I do not start or initiate my own employment. I agree nothing would please me more than start my own organization. I would start an organization that would work with battered, traumatized, and immigrant women. Right now, I know if wishes were horses, all beggars would ride.

Maybe one day I will start that organization for women. I have to visualize it first. I know inwardly I am working toward the achievement of that goal. I have always set goals and each of them has been realized; as such, this one too will come to be, as I have proved that all my life. There are many abused, battered, traumatized, marginalized, and displaced women who need a voice. I am that voice as I have been through it all. War, domestic violence, issues with immigration, terminal illness, working two jobs, some of the struggles women deal with in their lives as they try to make an impact in this world. Who better represents these women than the one who has lived and experienced it all?

I know personally I have taken so many punches in life, and each time I have pulled myself up. I survived the physical and emotional abuses of a cheating and violent husband, I survived the trauma of living in a colonized country where people were caged like animals, and I survived the trauma of being diagnosed as being HIV/AIDS positive since 2002. HIV/AIDS is one of the most stigmatized and discriminated diseases. If one can survive that illness, what else can life throw at me that will make me crumble?

All of the above traumas and endurances demanded I pick myself and keep on walking. Pick myself up I did; as such, I see the unemployment phase as just another hurdle that calls upon my energy reserves to pick myself up and keep on walking. Like they say, the character of a strong man and, in my own case, of a strong woman is determined not by how many times life knocks them down, but by one's ability to rise up after each knock and to keep on walking. I am determined to pick myself up once more even from this too as I do not know anything else but how to survive. I know I am a survivor, and in every case, I have hustled my way back to where I was meant to be. I will not let this defeat me because I am going to survive. That is one reason I am not a victim. Victims usually do not survive, and I am surviving.

Nothing has been handed over to me on a silver platter. I do not take anything for granted, and I assume nothing is mine by right. Just like I fought for my parents' attention back then as a child growing up in colonial Zimbabwe, I have to fight in unique ways to break into the field that I love the most. Instead of moaning and feeling sorry for myself, I need to be visible out there so that I am not diminished and eventually rendered voiceless to once more become silenced and eventually give in to invisibility. I know I cannot do that because I have a voice and I have a platform.

I have a voice that some might consider accented; still it is my voice. I have a platform because I am the survivor of male battery, colonial turmoil, and the epidemics of HIV/AIDS while on the other hand an immigrant struggling in a foreign land. I will not let my voice die down just like that into oblivion. I will make it vibrant. It will be heard loudly across the seas and the mountains, the hills and the valleys, and its echoes should be heard worldwide. I can even hear it now. Listen, you too can hear my accented African voice vibrate.

Though I celebrated the immemorial milestone of my success in my studies now, years later in my new world, sometimes I feel like I had been forcibly hauled from my motherland's comfortable womb. I feel disjointed and disconnected to anything that had been familiar to me. I miss the long evenings of being cozy, sitting around the warm winter fires, roasting peanuts, corn, and salted pumpkin seeds as our snacks, while emptying bucketful's of water. I miss the closeness brought on by the need to listen to *Ambuya*'s stories and not sit in front of this TV that is so impersonal. The TV that does not talk back to me, which does not emanate human warmth, is not the best of company. I miss being with people; as such, I have to find my way back into working with people, young or old alike. I need voices around me. I need laughter even when people are hurting. They laugh. I grew up with voices. I worked with voices, and I heard voices with me all the time; and in my home, I had small voices in my home. I want to go back to familiar territory and firm ground of my career where I can talk and laugh with real people.

I am a natural storyteller. I told stories most of my life to my students and my children similarly. I miss the sounds of young children and particularly my children laughing happily in the sands and playing like children are supposed to do as they grow. The environment here is different. It is severe to growing children. In this environment, children are constantly monitored, never allowed to play outside as children should. They seem to be under lock and key all the time as the Western people fear for the numerous abductions and child abuses that seem to surround them and is a daily occurrence and constant reminder of how warped the human mind can be. Though children should be free and enjoy their youths and all the play children engage in, I feel the fear of abductions has paralyzed the parents of the West from letting children enjoy childhood as it is meant to be. That saddens my heart as I know my own offspring will be brought up in such closed environments. I long for the embrace of the village in the heart of Zimbabwe, where we played under the light of the moon and stars.

With such morbid and fearful images in my mind, I picture my own grandchildren and even my great-grandchildren and smile because somehow through this writing, they will know me physically and feel me intellectually. They will have the opportunity to know me as the person who gave life to their parents as well as the young girl who played *nhodo*, *pada*, and *chisveru*[50] at night in rural Howard without fear of abductions. I want them to experience my childhood as I experienced it.

I want them to know that we might have grown up in different worlds and different circumstances and eras, but as the indigenous people and my people say, "wisdom comes with age." Mine seemed to have come with age and exposure to other cultures. My wisdom was acquired through the teaching of my elders starting from when I was a

---

[50] Some of the childhood games I played in the early evening hours in my village, which included hopscotch and tag among many other childhood games. Unfortunately, not even my children know some of these games!

child in their arms. I have gained wisdom by interacting with people of different cultures, languages, religions, sexual orientations, and races.

The indigenous people of Zimbabwe have a popular saying "Kure kwemeso nzeve dzinonzwa," literally translated "distance is measured in eye duration, but ears will always hear." Though we might be far from each other, neither witnessing what you see every day but with your ears you will hear of what it was like, and your eyes you will see and read what I actually wrote with you mind. True, with ears, you can always hear and learn about things that are ancient and remote from you; yet eyes wait to see and witness everything just like the Bible's doubting Thomas, but no, not in today's world.

In today's world, there is contemporary technology. In this forever-shrinking global village, everybody can claim to have seen everything on TV, on the computer through the Internet, heard it on the radio, read about it on the multiple national and international magazines, or claim knowledge from one form of media or the most recent dot-coms. I, however, want to warn you that I have witnessed how these forms of media can be corrupted as well and be used to portray what the writer's or presenter's personal agenda is. Like all human beings, everything in life seems to be political and thus serves an individual agenda or self-interest.

Nothing is ever apolitical in the world we live in, for now I know better. I have learned to take everything with a grain of salt. Though I grew up in abject poverty, nothing was neither as poor nor as gut wrenching as some of the pictures of the African people that I have seen on various media. It appears most people who report from my continent and my motherland usually look for the worst images, and those are the images I have mostly seen exhibited. It is because they have personal or organizational agendas or policies they are promoting or trying to fund.

As such, it does not benefit them; to get the best, they have to appeal to people's hearts so that they can open their pockets and give to their causes. Honestly, I know these images; they neither fully represent me nor tell the complete story of my life truthfully. I do not deny that there is dismal poverty in my continent. I do not deny there is continuous strife. I do not deny there are diseases, but I would rather there be at least both positive and negative reports because to every coin, there are two sides, and so does every story. What I deplore is the fact that certain media ignore the good and concentrate just on the worst about the world that nourished and nurtured me to be a beautiful human being. Show me a world that does not have their dark side.

Oh my goodness, my world growing up was just an oyster shell full of pearls to be delicately opened out and be devoured by those eager to absorb knowledge in order to uplift their own circumstances. Like Michelle Obama said to the high school girls in the United Kingdom, "You are the diamonds in the rough." I am a living proof of what the diamonds in the rough look like and what they are capable of. I know there are many more where this diamond came from. Rather than feel sorry and take them for charitable cases, help us stand on our own feet.

There are many more diamonds in the rough like me with such positive stories; no pun intended. I lived a happy, fulfilling childhood. I had a good career. I was an honest wife. I thought I married for love but later realized I married the idea of being in love, for the man I married never really loved me. I endured the worst traumas of all such as war, domestic violence, and personal illness, but all those did not thrash me down. They all contributed to make me the stronger and prouder African woman that I am today. Best of all, despite the violence and adversity I lived through, I am the most proud and most successful as the mother to my five wonderful children. The world might see me differently, but in their eyes, I could do no wrong just as in my eyes they could never do any wrong. My children are an extension of my DNA. They are my extension.

However, as to everything else, you are entitled to formulate your own opinions and conclusions and classify me as you find necessary. HIV/AIDS positive or not, I am now holding my head up high like my grandmother Anna and my mother, Doris, taught me way back then when I was a child growing up in rural Howard in Zimbabwe. I apologize to no one, for I did no wrong to anybody. I walk on this earth as though I own it because right now, I do own the world. Anyway, for the time being, I own the world because I am still living and breathing, so I might as well walk with my head held up high and with a gait that dictates that I own the world. At least in my personal mind, I own my little corner of this world anyway.

Epilogue

In August 2002, after the HIV/AIDS diagnosis, I thought my life had come to an abrupt end. The HIV/AIDS diagnosis made me feel as though I no longer had anything to live for. My world came crashing down, and I had nothing to hold on to. Inwardly, I could never know my grandchildren, let alone see any of my children get married. My then ex-husband, Jonathan, was in total denial. All our married life, I thought he was my partner, my protector, my lover, but he turned out to be an abuser through and through. For more than twenty-five years, I had lived with his brutality mentally, physically, emotionally, and psychologically. Now I can say eight years after the divorce, I have survived.

Many times, I had been traumatized so much that I never thought I had any reason to live for. Jonathan was a big man; his physical brutalities left me hanging by a thread several times. However, as a mother, I convinced myself that I had five good reasons to keep on going. I also came from a large loving family, and no matter how hard the brutality was, I never wanted my abuser to kill me so that my family would have to endure the worst of my loss. For years, I pretended to Jonathan that I had succumbed to his brutality and given up on ever leaving him, but I was busy moving the goalposts to suit my own strategies.

He had beaten me physically, socially, emotionally, and the last trauma he inflicted on me was his total denial of my HIV/AIDS status. He added paraffin to a smoking fire by implying that I had cheated on him. His insinuation implied I was responsible for inflicting us with this disease. I could not believe my ears when he accused me of stepping out of our marriage and cheating on him. Jonathan had several children out of wedlock, and how dared he accuse me of such notoriety? I felt then that I did not need to be dragged in the mud of who was responsible for what. I decided in that moment to become my own destiny.

Initially, all I needed was for both of us to be back on the road to health. I even told my case manager at the TAP that I was not going to have a vengeful spirit and wish my husband ill health. After he threw his mud into my face, I realized Jonathan had long outlived his purpose. After all, I had made a promise to myself that I would divorce him when he least expected. I put my strength in getting myself better. I prayed that he could at least find a job, which would take him somewhere far away from me. I never wanted to see his face next to mine in bed ever again. My wish was granted, and he left the USA without suspecting that his leaving was the beginning of an end to an era.

I had loved this man with all the love a woman could give. I had never cheated on him. He had been the first man to take me to bed and teach me all the intimacy a woman could ever have with a man. In his philandering ways, he forgot my innocence. Jonathan clouded his mind and ended getting his mind mixed up, that his infidelities were mine to pay for. He accused me after all the years I endured his brutality; I continued to be a faithful wife. I had respected him as the father of my children, but he had never reciprocated my love and respect. I had all sorts of counseling with my relatives and even his relatives. It was clear to both sides of the family that I had continued to pull the weight of our marriage alone. Despite the counsel from both families, nothing had ever come to fruition. As such, by 2002, living so far away from everyone, the latest battle was now our battle to fight out alone. The stronger between the two of us was bound to win. I am happy I was not the loser because I was the one who decided to divorce him.

The day I decided to let him go, I felt light in my heart. I had continued to make excuses for him. This time I did not need any excuses. He had committed the ultimate, and no more forgiveness was warranted from me. I was bitter at the beginning, and forgiveness was far from my mind. However, forgiveness was another thing I had to struggle with for a long time. It took me years of harboring bitterness and anger inside of me. One night, I spent a sleepless night reflecting on our past-married years. I realized Jonathan had moved on without any regrets, and I needed to let him go.

Harboring anger and bitterness did not harm him in any way. I cleansed my spirit that night through tears. I remember that night crying for more than three hours in my lonely apartment. It was an intense and troubled soul-searching, and for the first time, I even thought of suicide. I realized then that I was at the lowest I had ever been as I had never thought I was capable of considering suicide. I was so gone mentally to the degree where I was gasping for breath. The gasping and my thoughts of suicide made me realize I had to do something ASAP.

I knew it was time to reach out to someone. I reached to my younger sister Diana but she was not home. I however found her husband and I had a heart-to-heart talk with him. We talked for an hour, and by the time I went back to sleep, I was no longer tortured mentally and psychologically. That day I was able to look at myself without hurting. My brother-in-law made me realize I would never get an apology from him because Jonathan had taken advantage of my loving heart. I knew I would never have an apology from Jonathan, so I needed to forgive him for his ignorance, his brutality, and ultimately his denial and accusations and, in the process, forgive myself and be able to heal.

I have continued to take my medications, and my health has improved. Now it had been ten years since my diagnosis. I was diagnosed in 2002. In 2003, I acquired my master's degree. In 2006, I graduated as a doctor of philosophy. In 2008, my first grandchild was born. I am now a grandmother of two. As my first counselor, Denis, had predicted at my diagnosis, sure enough, I would live to be a grandmother. I am now one. I look forward to having more grandchildren.

My children all have college degrees. Something we achieved working together. No one from their father's side of the family can boast of the same. I beat myself on the chest and tell myself I have really succeeded in life. I see my five children and their achievements, and whoever in my position would not be proud of such an achievement? I am surviving an illness that I now consider chronic than terminal because I survived longer than I thought at diagnosis.

I continue to be a positive influence in all the people I meet in life. I never question why I endured the abuses and traumas but accept them as part of my life's journey. Our journeys have been predestined, and we either enjoy or go into a corner to lick the wounds we have been dealt. I choose not to lick my wounds and extend my gratitude to Jonathan.

THANK YOU TO MY ABUSER

For all the times you struck me, you gave me strength.
For all the times you fathered a child outside our marriage,
you gave me my marching orders.

As for the denial of such, you gave me purpose.

IN AS MUCH AS I WOULD LOVE TO HATE YOU,
IT IS BENEATH ME.

Instead, I thank you for making me realize I could live my life
without you and realize I am a resilient woman of stature.
I am strong and better because now I know better.
Thanks to you I am now an educated abused woman!

Acknowledgment

Primarily, I want to thank my five children who have been my pillars of strength and inspiration for success all my life. I know without their unfailing support and unconditional love, I would not have made it this far. I see the five of them as the pinnacle of my success as they never stepped out of line; they have always respected me as their mother. No mother has been blessed with five wonderful children as I have been. I want to sincerely thank you for letting my responsibilities as your mother appear as an uncomplicated and effortless task. I take my hat off to you five, Elvin, Teresa, Tiffany, Thelma, and Elton, and encourage you to always support and love each other unconditionally.

I want to give special thanks to the health communities I met on this journey as a person living positively with HIV/AIDS. The unfailing support of the staff at TAP of University College, the pharmacist in University College the Apothecary, my first infectious disease physician, Dr. Michael Foltzer, my dentist in Pennsylvania, and last but not the least, the support group from the TAP in Pennsylvania. From each one of you, I knew I could count on you for your unwavering support. I also want to thank the Staff at Ches Penn Clinic in Chester, Pennsylvania, as well as Dr. Marina Sigidin. Even when I did not have insurance, you always found ways to work with me, enabling me to maintain good health. Last but not least, the nursing practitioners who celebrated my health milestones with me.

To many friends who read my manuscript and gave me feedback, I want to thank you sincerely. To Clara, Maureen, Mary Ann, Rosie, Kevin, and Bob, admittedly at times you all were brutal, but now we have a book we can all call our own. To Angele and your wonderful husband, Antoine, I say thank you for the unrelenting encouragement and for proofreading my manuscript. I benefitted a lot from your friendship and education in many ways. To my pastors for the prayers and though I never told you about my diagnosis, I am grateful for the strength I drew from you. I am thankful for the angel you gave me at my divorce, it means a lot in my life. I pray for you all. To you all, I say do not just extend your hands of friendship to a simple person like me, but all the persons you meet along your life's unique journeys.

My brothers Dr. Larry and Levin and sisters Melody (who unfortunately passed away February 2013 before I published my book), Brenda, and Diana, you were the strongest resources I ever depended and leaned on all my life. No matter where you all were and how difficult life would be, for each one of you, I knew I could count on your consistent and unquestioning support. Many times, we spent nights on the phone across the thousands of miles, and you never complained due to the sleepless nights. You supported me always. Thank you for helping me makes it when the going was difficult.

Special thanks also go to my brothers-in-law. It is difficult to marry one woman, and I know for you it appeared as though you were married to me as well. Many times I cried on your shoulders and in your homes because I needed someone to hear and advise me outside my own brothers. I believe at times you felt like I was an appendage to your marriage, yet you never complained about the extra burden. For that, you will always have my undying love, gratitude, and respect.

Strange as it may sound to some of you, I want to thank the most unlikely person, Jonathan. Even though in our marriage you beat me down, I have total respect for you as you are the father of our five children and grandfather to their children to come. For all the times you struck me, you gave me strength to go on. For the times you fathered a child outside our marriage, you gave me my marching orders; and for the last denial of the diagnosis, you gave me purpose. In as much as I would love to hate you, it is beneath me. I thank you for making me realize I could live my life without you and realize I am a resilient, proud African woman of stature.

The final person I want to thank is the person who now holds my heart and directs my every move (ME). The person may be a figment of my imagination, but that fomentation has helped me to remain resolute and focused. Though I had given up on loving myself you taught me that even I too in my condition could still love myself. Thank you, my dear heart, for teaching me to believe in unconditional love and for making me a better person than before.

Bibliography

Aidoo, A. A., *Changes: A Love Story*. New York: The Feminist Press, 1993.

Angelou, M. *A Letter to My Daughter*. New York: Random House, 2008.

Angelou, M. *Mother: A Cradle to Hold Me*. New York: Random House, 2006.

Behar, R. *The Vulnerable Observer: Anthropology That Breaks Your Heart*. Boston: Beacon Press, 1996.

Beyala, C. *Your Name Shall Be Tanga*. Johannesburg: Heinemann, 1988.

Cosby, B., & Poussaint, F. *Come on People: On the Path from Victims to Victors*. Beijing: Thomas Nelson, 2007.

Cvetkovich, A. *An Archive of Feelings; Trauma, Sexuality, and Lesbian Public Cultures*. Durham: DK University Press, 2003.

Dangarembga, T. *Nervous Conditions*. Seattle: Seal Press, 1988.

Djebar, A. *Fantasia: An Algerian Cavalcade*. Portsmouth: Heinemann, 1985.

Dougherty, S. *Hopes and Dreams: The Story of Barack Obama*. New York: Black Dog and Leventhal Publishers Inc., 2007.

Hailey, A. *Roots: The Saga of an American Family*. New York: Double Day and Company Inc., 1976.

High, J. R. *Spiritual Injuries, Assaults on the Soul: My Journey through Childhood and Family Trauma to Recovery*. Xlibris, 2009.

Issacman, C. *Clara's Story*. Philadelphia: The Jewish Publication Society, 1984.

Jacobson, N., & Guttmann, J. *When Men Batter Women: New Insights into Ending Abusive Relationships*. New York: Simon and Schuster, 1998.

Jakoubek, R. *Martin Luther King JR.: Civil Rights Leader*. Danbury: Grolier Incorporated, 1989.

Kennedy, E. M. *True Compass: A Memoir*. New York: Twelve, 2009.

Kirkwood, C. *Leaving Abusive Partners*. Thousand Oaks: Sage Publications, 1993.

Lakoff, G., & Johnson, M. *Metaphors We Live By*. Chicago: University of Chicago Press, 1980.

Mandela, N. *The Long Walk to Freedom: The Autobiography of Nelson Mandela.* Reed Business Information Inc., 1994.

Masundire, E. *Living Dreams.* Columbus: Lleemon Publishers, 2005.

Mead, M. *Coming of Age in Samoa.* New York: Quill, 1955.

Mernissi, F. *Dreams of Trespass: Tales of Harem Girlhood.* Cambridge: Perseus Books, 1994.

Meyer, J. *Battlefield of the Mind: Winning the Battle in Your Mind.* Cambridge: Warner Faith, 2000.

Meyer, J. *Beauty for Ashe: Receiving Emotional Healing.* Faith Words, 2003.

Ngcobo, L. *And They Didn't Die.* New York: The Feminist Press, 1999.

Obama, B. *The Audacity of Hope.* New York: Three Rivers Press, 2006.

Osborn, S. T. *Writing for Publication: A Complete Guide.* Bloomington, Minnesota: ACW Press, 1999.

Osteen, J. *The Best Life Now: 7 Steps to Living at Your Full Potential.* New York: Faith Words, 2004.

Pitt, A. J. *The Play of the Personal: Psychoanalytic Narratives of Feminist Education.* New York: Peter Lang, 2003.

Roper, G. G. *Balancing Your Emotions: For Women Who Want Consistency under Stress.* Wheaton: Harold Shaw Publishers, 1992.

Williams, H. *Great Speeches of Our Time.* London: Quercus Publishing Plc. 2008.

Forgiveness is the attribute of the strong and I consider myself strong that's why I forgive.

This book is based on true events which took place in Zimbabwe. The characters and locations of the story play significant roles in Author's life. However, to conceal the identities of these people, their names and the places have been altered to conceal their identity and protect their privacy.

Edwards Brothers Malloy
Oxnard, CA USA
May 12, 2014